# Campaign 2000

# Communication, Media, and Politics

Series Editor: Robert E. Denton Jr., Virginia Tech

This series features a broad range of work dealing with the role and function of communication in the realm of politics, broadly defined. Including general academic books, monographs, and texts for use in graduate and advanced undergraduate courses, the series will encompass humanistic, critical, historical, and empirical studies in political communication in the United States. Primary subject areas include campaigns and elections, media, and political institutions. *Communication, Media, and Politics* books will be of interest to students, teachers, and scholars of political communication from the disciplines of communication, rhetorical studies, political science, journalism, and political sociology.

## Titles in the Series

### Forthcoming

# Campaign 2000

## *A Functional Analysis of Presidential Campaign Discourse*

WILLIAM L. BENOIT
JOHN P. MCHALE
GLENN J. HANSEN
P. M. PIER
JOHN P. MCGUIRE

ROWMAN & LITTLEFIELD PUBLISHERS, INC.
*Lanham • Boulder • New York • Toronto • Oxford*

ROWMAN & LITTLEFIELD PUBLISHERS, INC.

Published in the United States of America
by Rowman & Littlefield Publishers, Inc.
A wholly owned subsidary of The Rowman & Littlefield Publishing Group, Inc.
4501 Forbes Boulevard, Suite 200, Lanham, Maryland 20706
www.rowmanlittlefield.com

PO Box 317
Oxford
OX2 9RU, UK

British Library Cataloguing in Publication Information Available

**Library of Congress Cataloging-in-Publication Data**

Campaign 2000: a functional analysis of presidential campaign discourse / William L.
    Benoit . . . [et al.].
        p. cm. – (Communication, media, and politics)
    Includes bibliographical references and index.
    ISBN 0-7425-2913-4 (cloth: alk. paper) – ISBN 0-7425-2914-2 (pbk.: alk. paper)
    1. Presidents—United States—Election—2000. 2. Presidential candidates—United
States—Language. 3. Political campaigns—United States—History—20th century.
4. United States—Politics and government—1993–2001. 5. Speeches, addresses, etc.,
American—History and criticism. 6. Communications in politics—United States—
History—20th century. 7. Mass media—Political aspects—United States—History—
20th century. 8. Rhetoric—Political aspects—United States—History—20th century.
9. English language—United States—Discourse analysis. 10. English language—
United States—Rhetoric. I. Benoit, William L. II. Series.

E889.C36 2003
324.973'0929—dc21                                        2003052443
Printed in the United States of America

# Contents

# Preface

We take up four topics here. First, we introduce our project. Then we sketch our functional approach to political campaign discourse (which is elaborated in chapter 1). Next, we describe the purpose and scope of our investigation. Finally, we argue that political campaign messages matter.

## Analysis of Campaign 2000

The most recent presidential campaign was an extremely interesting one. Al Gore was vice president in a time of impressive prosperity, with record surpluses projected for years. There was some unease abroad, but no obvious foreign policy crisis at the time (like the Iran hostage situation hanging over the White House in 1980). Gore's running mate, President Bill Clinton, had survived impeachment even though he lied (or, most charitably, intentionally misled) the American people about whether he had an affair with Monica Lewinsky. Although there were questions about Gore and fund-raising, one would have thought he faced clear sailing into his first term as president. Still, former Senator Bill Bradley announced in 1998 that he would contest the Democratic nomination.

It is clear that Bradley was fighting an uphill battle (given the advantages Gore enjoyed, mentioned above). Gore was not an exciting campaigner (something he acknowledged in his acceptance address), but Bradley seemed determined to provide a contrast that favored Gore. Bradley did raise interesting issues and forced Gore to address his base of support. Still, Gore managed to secure the Democratic nomination and did not seem to be too bloodied from the primary contest.

The Republican side of the presidential primary race involved a much more

diverse assemblage of candidates. First, it featured several retreads from 1996:
Lamar Alexander, Alan Keyes, and Steve Forbes. Dan Quayle, much maligned vice
president under George Bush, entered the contest for the 2000 nomination.
Elizabeth Dole, wife of the unsuccessful 1996 Republican presidential nominee,
Bob Dole, joined the party too. Gary Bauer and Orrin Hatch came later, but
participated for a time. Senator John McCain made the race interesting when he
won New Hampshire, but the front-runner (with more endorsements and money
than any other candidate, and possibly more of each than all combined) was
Governor George W. Bush. Pat Buchanan, who challenged President Bush for the
nomination when Bush sought reelection in 1992, and who ran in 1996, was
another Republican candidate. However, he switched political parties during 2000
and became the Reform Party nominee.

The Republican contest provided fireworks. Governor Bush assumed he had
the nomination locked up. Given his campaign war chest and the barrelful of
endorsements, he was the odds-on favorite to win. An indication of his presumption was the fact that Bush began the primary campaign by running toward the
middle as a "*compassionate* conservative." We don't want to suggest that
conservatives cannot be compassionate, but Bush abandoned this slogan after
McCain won New Hampshire and refused to go away quietly, rechristening himself
as a "reformer with results." Bush and McCain traded television spots in South
Carolina that accused each other of violating his pledge to run a positive campaign.
Once Bush managed to sew up the Republican nomination, he lurched back to the
center and became once again a "compassionate conservative." McCain champi-
oned an issue that we consider extremely important (campaign finance reform), but
he wasn't able to convince the majority of Republicans to join his crusade on this
question. The Republican primary race had exciting moments in 2000.

The fact that both major parties' primaries were contested made this campaign
different from the one held in 1996. President Bill Clinton could focus his primary
messages on Bob Dole. However, Bob Dole had to worry about Lamar Alexander,
Pat Buchanan, Steve Forbes, Phil Gramm, and others. This disparity gave Clinton
a clear advantage. In 2000, both party nominees, George W. Bush and Al Gore, had
to fight contested primaries.

The general campaign was fought in "battleground" states, in which either
nominee could win. Although Texas was considered safely in Bush's camp, Gore
had to struggle over his home state of Tennessee. On the other hand, Florida's
governor was Jed Bush, George W. Bush's brother. Nevertheless, Gore did better
than many predicted in the tracking polls.

Governor Bush led the public opinion polls until the Democratic Convention,
at which point Vice President Gore took the lead. However, Gore's performance
in the debates irritated some viewers and Bush exceeded the low expectations he
had cultivated. Questions about Gore's exaggerations (lies?) plagued him (and
Republican television spots fully exploited his statements) and Bush regained a
slight lead (his lead was within the margin of error in most polls, but more polls

showed Bush ahead than Gore). This race was too close to call right up to election day. Pundits predicted that Bush might win the popular vote while Gore would win the electoral vote. Ultimately, Gore won the popular vote by over half a million votes, but when the Supreme Court of the United States stopped the recounts in Florida, Bush won that state and the Electoral College (see chapter 16).

Buchanan never appeared to be a significant factor in the campaign. However, it was possible that Ralph Nader, Green Party nominee, might have drained away enough support from Gore in certain battleground states to allow Bush to win (he received over 95,000 votes in Florida, and Bush's margin during and after the recounts was never near that amount). An ad sponsored by the Republican Leadership Council featured video from a Nader speech attacking Al Gore. Unsurprisingly, it did not include any of the footage from the same speech attacking George Bush.

Furthermore, unlike recent elections (1996, 1992), there was no sitting incumbent candidate for president. Al Gore was the sitting vice president during this campaign, at times mentioning the Clinton/Gore record, but vice presidents just do not do as much—do not gain as much executive experience—as presidents. Even though Gore ran on the Clinton/Gore record, and even though George W. Bush attacked that record, it was not the same as Clinton running on the Clinton/Gore record in 1996, or as George Bush running on the Bush/Quayle record in 1992. In point of fact we think that Gore should have run harder on the record of the last eight years than he did. However, his attempts to distance himself from President Clinton's character travails may have led Gore to distance himself on policy grounds as well.

The Functional Theory of Political Campaign Discourse was applied to the 1996 presidential campaign (Benoit, Blaney, & Pier, 1998). The 2000 campaign merits similar scrutiny, given its two contested primaries (President Clinton was not challenged for the Democratic nomination in 1996) and the incredible closeness of the general election. Our goal is to analyze the functions and topics of a variety of message forms (e.g., speeches, television spots, debates) from the major candidates (we did not attempt to examine the myriad of third party candidates, for example). We wanted to study messages employed in all three phases of the campaign: primaries, conventions, and general election.

This study of campaign 2000 replicates portions of the study of the 1996 race (with analyses of primary and general TV spots, primary and general debates, and acceptance addresses). We wanted to make (at least some of) the results comparable across the two studies. On the other hand, we also wanted to make some different choices about the particular messages we studied. Unlike 1996, we were able to obtain enough 2000 primary radio ads to add that message form to our analysis. We decided to add two other message forms, television talk shows and candidate web pages, in this analysis (and we dropped radio addresses and free television time remarks, which were studied in 1996). The Republicans decided not to have a Keynote Speech in 2000, so we broadened this chapter to include other prominent speakers/speeches as well. Thus, our analysis of the 2000 presidential campaign will include both elements of continuity from 1996 and some elements of change in 2000.

## A Functional Approach to Political Campaign Discourse

Political campaign discourse possesses one encompassing goal: to win the election by convincing enough citizens to cast their votes for one candidate. We do acknowledge that some candidates may campaign to promote an issue (e.g., in our opinion, Ross Perot did the country a great service in the 1992 campaign by focusing attention on the national debt). However, modern presidential elections are always contested and force voters to choose between two leading (and some minor) candidates. Because voters must choose between competing candidates, campaign discourse is inherently comparative. When voters are lucky, they can choose the better of two excellent candidates. When they are not so fortunate, voters must choose the lesser of two evils. The fact that voters make an inherently comparative judgment means that each voter casts his or her ballot for the candidate who appears *preferable* on the factor or factors that are most important to that voter. Which criteria are most important in vote choice varies from person to person; however, each citizen votes for the candidate who seems to best satisfy the criteria that are most important to that voter.

This goal of appearing preferable leads political candidates to produce messages intended to make them appear *better* than their opponents. Political rhetors can have but three options available for convincing voters that they are the better choice: (1) they can acclaim (engage in self-praise of one's positive accomplishments or qualities), (2) they can attack (criticize other candidates for failures or negative qualities), and (3) they can defend (refute attacks). Each of these three message functions has the potential to foster the impression that one candidate is more desirable than opponents. In fact, these three kinds of utterances interact to function as an informal form of cost-benefit analysis. Acclaims reveal a candidate's benefits. Attacks reveal an opponent's costs. Defenses reject alleged costs. Together, these three campaign discourse functions help voters decide which candidate is preferable.

The Functional Theory of Political Campaign Discourse also holds that these utterances (acclaims, attacks, defenses) can occur on two topics: policy and character. Policy comments, sometimes referred to elsewhere as issues, address problems amenable to governmental action and governmental programs. Character remarks tell us more about the candidates themselves as individuals. We divide policy statements into those which address past deeds, future plans (means to an end), and general goals (ends). Character utterances are divided into those which discuss the personal qualities of the candidates (e.g., courage, honesty, compassion), the candidates' leadership ability (experience), and the candidates' ideals (values or principles).

## Purpose of the Study

This book applies the Functional Theory of Political Campaign Discourse to several different forms of campaign discourse in the 2000 presidential campaign: primary and general election television spots, primary and general radio spots, primary and general election debates, primary and general television talk show appearances, primary and general campaign web pages, and convention speeches.

To accomplish this purpose, we begin part I by describing the theory of the functions of political campaign discourse and some of the research produced by this theory (chapter 1). We then describe the method we will utilize to analyze the 2000 presidential campaign (chapter 2). Next, several chapters describe the results of our analysis of the 2000 presidential campaign, grouped into sections on the primaries (part II), the nominating conventions (part III), and the general election campaign (part IV). Finally we discuss the implications of our findings for the 2000 campaign and for political campaign communication generally (part V).

This investigation has multiple strengths. First, it analyzes several different kinds of messages (TV spots, radio spots, debates, television talk show appearances, campaign web pages, and speeches). Past research on presidential campaigns tends to focus primarily on television spots and debates, and principally on the general campaign. While we agree that these message forms merit scholarly attention, we believe other message forms deserve study as well. We would argue, for example, that although it has yet to reach its full potential, the Internet is on its way to becoming an important campaign tool. Furthermore, the candidates spent much more time in 2000 on television talk shows, a venue that disseminates their ideas to some viewers who might be less involved and therefore less informed by traditional media. Second, our analysis considers all three functions—acclaiming, attacking and defending. Other research has a tendency to slight defense. Furthermore, acclaims (positive messages) and attacks (negative messages) are usually studied only in television spots. We examine all three functions in every message form we study. Third, our study analyzes these messages on both policy and character grounds. Again, prior research on policy (issue) and character (image) is usually limited to studies of television spots. We also divide each topic into three subforms, as indicated above, to provide a more micro-analysis. While no single study could reasonably purport to provide a comprehensive analysis of anything as complex as a presidential election campaign, our investigation provides an extensive analysis of many of the key messages employed in Campaign 2000.

We have developed five specific research questions designed to guide our analysis of the messages in campaign 2000.

(1) How often do the major candidates employ each of the three functions

of political campaign messages (acclaiming, attacking, defending)?
(2) Do the candidates devote more utterances to addressing policy considerations (issues) or character concerns (image)?
(3) How many utterances are devoted to the three forms of policy utterances (past deeds, future plans, general goals) and the three forms of character remarks (personal qualities, leadership ability, and ideals)?
(4) In primary messages, do attacks target other members of the source's own party, the other party, or the establishment?
(5) Which candidates devoted more utterances to the issues of most importance to voters?

These first five questions will guide each of the analytical chapters.

We use the phrase "political campaign communication" to emphasize our focus. There are many forms of political discourse—like State of the Union addresses—that are not instances of *campaign* discourse; we purposefully exclude them from our analysis. The idea of the "permanent campaign" (Blumenthal, 1980) suggests that politicians never completely stop campaigning. This means that in a very real sense every message produced by a politician is a campaign message; acknowledging this fact of modern political life, we choose to focus our attention on messages that are explicitly devoted to seeking office. Similarly, there are other kinds of campaigns beyond political campaigns, such as commercial advertising campaigns or political movements. We also exclude those messages from the purview of this study (even though some of these campaigns are designed at least in part to influence the political process).

Thus, the 2000 presidential campaign merits scholarly attention for several reasons. First, we are working toward developing a multi-message longitudinal data base (e.g., we have analyzed primary and general TV spots back to 1952; acceptance addresses and keynote speeches back to 1960; general debates back to 1960; primary debates back to 1948). This campaign will provide another data point in our research program.

## Do Political Campaign Messages Matter?

Campaign messages can affect election outcomes. First, while it is clear that a portion of the electorate simply votes for their party's nominee, the power of political parties has diminished sharply since 1968 (Trent & Friedenberg, 2000). The White House has swung back and forth from Republican to Democrat five times in the ten campaigns from 1960–1996—and not because of huge vacillations in party affiliation during those years. In recent years fewer voters affiliate with the two major political parties: 38 percent of the electorate identified with neither the Republican nor the Democratic party; 34 percent are Democrats and 28 percent Republicans (Gallup, 1999). Party affiliation is undoubtedly an important factor in deciding presidential elections, but it is undeniable that party affiliation does not *determine* the outcome of presidential elections today. And, of course, because the primaries pit members of the same party (e.g., Gore against Bradley; Bush against McCain, Forbes, Keyes, Bauer, and Hatch), political party affiliation cannot determine the outcome of that phase of the election.

Second, we recognize that elections can be greatly influenced by voters' perceptions of the state of the economy and foreign affairs (although we would argue that candidates address these issues in their campaign messages). In 2000 we faced no all-encompassing foreign crisis (e.g., no Vietnam War, Iran hostage situation, or oil embargo) and the domestic economy was in good shape. However, recent research found that on the topics of energy and inflation (although not unemployment) *presidential speeches had considerably more impact* than televised news stories on public perceptions of the importance of an issue. Interestingly, the *actual figures* on unemployment and inflation had *no appreciable effect on public opinion* (Iyengar & Kinder, 1987). Although this study was not concerned with voting or campaign messages, it strongly suggests that voters' perceptions can be influenced more by what the candidates say about the economy than the economic figures themselves—or what the news media says about those figures (the "facts" do not speak for themselves).

Finally, we are accumulating research demonstrating that campaign messages do influence election outcomes. Some studies report significant correlations between money spent on television spots and election outcomes (Joslyn, 1981; Palda, 1973). For example, Wanat (1974) found that, for election winners, broadcast spending correlated highly (.56) with voting outcomes. McClure and Patterson (1974) reported that, in the 1972 campaign, "Exposure to political advertising was consistently related to voter belief change" (p. 16; see also Patterson & McClure, 1973). Mulder (1979) reported that exposure to ads in a Chicago mayoral campaign correlated significantly with attitudes (see also Atkin & Heald, 1976). Brians and Wattenberg (1996) found that "Recalling political ads is more significantly associated with knowledge of candidates' issue positions than is reading the newspaper or watching political news on television" (p. 185). Benoit and Wells (1996) summarized evidence that presidential debates can facilitate learning in viewers and can influence voting intention as well. So, research has shown that campaign messages can and do influence voting. Therefore, political campaign communication merits scholarly attention, and the 2000 presidential campaign in particular is worth studying.

## Summary

We develop a functional theory of political campaign communication, arguing that such discourse can be understood as acclaiming, attacking, and defending on topics of policy and character. We illustrate this theory through an examination of a variety of messages (debates, television ads, radio spots, speeches, TV talk shows) throughout the 2000 presidential primaries, the nominating conventions, and the general election. We limit our focus to the major contenders in the Democratic and Republican primaries and, in the general campaign, to the two major party candidates, Vice President Al Gore and Governor George W. Bush.

# Chapter 1

# Overview: The Functional Theory of Political Campaign Discourse

In this chapter we elucidate the Functional Theory of Political Campaign Discourse. Then we describe the several benefits of this approach to studying political campaign discourse. A functional analysis is especially apt for analysis of political campaign rhetoric because such discourse is clearly designed as a means to accomplishing an end: winning the election. Political campaign rhetoric is without question instrumental, or functional, in nature. In the case of presidential campaign discourse, the end in mind is occupancy of the most powerful elected office in the world. Of course, it is possible that some candidates may run to champion a point of view. For example, in 2000 it never appeared that Ralph Nader would come close to winning in any single state. However, for the viable candidates, the election is a means to gaining public office. This approach cannot answer every question about political campaign discourse, but it has several advantages that will be articulated below.

## Functional Theory of Political Campaign Discourse

The Functional Theory of Political Campaign Discourse is founded on several important assumptions. Five propositions provide the foundation for this theory. Each assumption will be addressed separately in this section.

1

## 1. Voting Is a Comparative Act

Voters face a fairly simple decision: For whom should I cast my vote? This decision is a choice between two (or more) competing candidates, and clearly entails a comparative judgment. We cannot expect any candidate to be ideal; on the other hand, no matter how much they vilify one another, no candidate is utterly and irretrievably evil. Nevertheless, in any contested election, each citizen who casts a vote is deciding which candidate appears preferable on whatever criteria are most salient to that citizen.

This proposition—that voting is a *choice between competing candidates*—is becoming increasingly important as political parties decline in influence (we would argue that the parties' most important influence is exerted via soft money and advertising). As Popkin noted, "Today, in an environment of diminishing party loyalty, campaigns and candidates exert a greater influence on voters than they did in the elections of 1940 and 1948" (1994, p. 12). In earlier contests, the party nominee was often selected at the convention. Levine notes that in the past "Presidential hopefuls generally did not even need to campaign in primaries, which were relatively few in number" (1995, p. 56). For example, as late as 1968, Hubert Humphrey was nominated despite the fact that he had not campaigned in any primary (Levine, 1995). Battles over who should be the parties' nominees were broadcast on national television. The Democratic National Convention in 1968 is a notorious example of a convention that may have dampened voters' spirits. To avoid contentious conventions and to decrease perceptions that party bosses instead of party members controlled the nomination (Kendall, 2000, p. 12), both parties expanded their reliance on primaries and caucuses for selecting their nominees. In 1968, there were only sixteen Republican and seventeen Democratic primaries (Crotty & Jackson, 1985). By 1996, there were Democratic primaries in thirty-seven states and Republican primaries in forty states (Davis, 1997).

The increased importance of political primaries has been a very important development in presidential campaigns, because one consequence is an increased importance of individual candidates (and their campaign consultants). While some voters still cast their votes for the candidate who represents his or her respective party, the individual candidates, and their apparent preferability to voters, are increasingly important determinants of election outcomes. Simple party loyalty is exerting less influence on voting decisions; the individual candidates and their messages are filling the void left by the diminishing role of party identification. For example, in 2000, Missouri voters elected a Democratic senator (Jean Carnahan, widow of Mel Carnahan) and a Democratic governor (Bob Holden), while giving the state's electoral votes to Republican presidential candidate George W. Bush. So, voters must choose between the competing candidates, and do not do so exclusively by party loyalty.

## 2. Candidates Must Distinguish Themselves from Opponents

The first assumption of the Functional Theory, that voting is a comparative act, leads directly to the second assumption: Candidates must distinguish themselves from each other. As a candidate, if you fail to articulate clear differences between yourself and your opponent, there is no reason for anyone to vote for you rather than for your opponent. In other words, if the candidates for a given office appear identical, voters have no reason to prefer one over another. This means that it is essential for candidates in contested races to develop distinctions between themselves and their opponents.

Of course, establishing clear distinctions between candidates can be difficult because in a very real sense the outcome of a general election campaign is determined by one group of voters: the undecided and independent. Today, neither the Republican Party nor the Democratic Party enjoys a majority of voters. The number of independent voters has increased from 22.6 percent in 1952 to 38.0 percent in 1992 (Weisberg & Kimball, 1993). Therefore, competing candidates in any given race often find themselves in the position of needing to obtain the votes of basically the *same group of voters*, and both candidates are often forced take fairly similar stands on the issues that matter to those voters. Often, this can lead candidates for a given public office to sound alike, adopting virtually indistinguishable stands on certain issues that are important to many voters. In the 1996 campaign, the *New York Times* joked that the campaign for president (Clinton versus Dole) would pit the "center against the middle" (Toner, 1996, p. 4.3). Therefore, political candidates often take similar stands on certain issues as a result of attempts to appeal to the same group of undecided voters. Still, if voters are to have any basis for choosing one candidate instead of another, the candidates must articulate some points of distinction.

Candidates have only two broad areas for setting themselves apart from their opponents: They can contrast their character and/or their policy stances. One candidate may attempt to portray himself or herself as a forceful leader. Another may try to create the impression that he or she is compassionate or honest. Policy can also be a means of appearing distinctive. In the 2000 campaign, for example, Bush advocated private school vouchers while Gore did not. On energy, Gore stressed conservation while Bush proposed to increase production. Bush favored across-the-board tax cuts whereas Gore touted targeted tax breaks. Political candidates do not need to differ on every point of comparison (in 2000, for example, everyone wanted to protect Social Security), but they must differ sufficiently to enable voters to choose one contender over the other. Clearly, the voters faced real choices in the 2000 presidential race.

Of course, which topics are most important to voters is a factor that varies by campaign. In the aftermath of Watergate, some voters felt betrayed, and character (especially honesty and integrity) seemed paramount. Foreign policy is more important when it seems to impact voters more directly (e.g., during the Mideast oil embargo or when the Vietnam War was being broadcast on television). Regardless of which issues appear most salient to voters, candidates must establish enough of a distinction between themselves to allow voters to choose among the contenders.

## 3. Political Campaign Messages Are Important Vehicles for Distinguishing between Candidates

Research makes it clear that voters cannot and should not depend on the news media to provide voters with information on which to base their voting decisions. Patterson and McClure (1976) concluded that in 1972 "during the short period of the general election campaign, presidential ads contain substantially more issue content than network newscasters" (p. 23). They also reported that viewers of television spots had higher levels of knowledge: "During the 1972 presidential campaign, people who were heavily exposed to political spots became more informed about the candidates' issue positions. . . . On every single issue emphasized in presidential commercials, persons with high exposure to television advertising showed a greater increase in knowledge than persons with low exposure" (pp. 116-117). After the 1984 election, Kern reported that "by a ratio of 4 to 1, Americans received the majority of their information about candidate positions on the issues from ads rather than the news" (1989, p. 47). Brians and Wattenberg (1996) analyzed 1992 NES data, revealing that issue learning is more likely to occur from seeing television spots than from watching television news or reading newspapers: "Recalling political ads is more significantly associated with knowledge of candidates' issue positions than is reading the newspaper or watching political news on television" (p. 185). Thus, voters obtain more issue-related information from campaign messages than from the national news media.

The importance of campaign messages in providing issue information is not limited to television spots. Lichter and Noyes (1995) found that, in the 1992 presidential campaign, "The candidates' own speeches actually discussed policy issues far more frequently and in considerably more detail than did either print or broadcast [news] reports" (p. xvii). They also reported that "voter knowledge does not increase from exposure to day-to-day TV coverage, and increases modestly with day-to-day newspaper reading. Voters do learn from TV coverage of live campaign events, such as convention speeches and debates" (p. 101). Therefore, political candidates' campaign discourse provides more information about issues than print or electronic news media.

There are several explanations for this finding. First, news reporting tends to concentrate on the "horse race" aspects of the campaign: Who is ahead in the polls? Who is running the campaign? Which states are being contested by the campaigns? Will the candidates attack one another? Who will be included in the presidential debates? The answers to these questions may be news, but they simply do not help voters decide which candidate should be elected president. As Patterson (1980) concluded, "In its coverage of a presidential campaign, the press concentrates on the strategic game played by the candidates in their pursuit of the presidency, thereby de-emphasizing the questions of national policy and leadership" (p. 21). In fact, he reported that "The election's substance . . . [in 1976] received only half as much coverage as was accorded the game" (p. 24). Substance may have played an even smaller role in 1980: From January through October of 1980, CBS and UPI devoted 65 percent of their coverage to the horse race, 26 percent to issues, and 10 percent to candidates (Robinson & Sheehan, 1983, p. 149). Presumably in an attempt to stimulate interest (and ratings or readership), the news media has a strong tendency to cover the campaign as a dramatic contest between competing candidates, with relatively little emphasis on the substance of the campaign.

A second reason why voters cannot rely on the news media for policy information is that campaign news is only one story among many. The network news, for example, is a half hour long, but subtracting commercials, stories on non-campaign topics, and horse-race coverage leaves little time to explain the candidates' opposing views on policy questions. Particularly in the latter phases of a campaign, political ads, presidential debates, and other message forms provide more issue information to viewers than the news media.

To make matters worse, there may be a trend toward less and less coverage. The length of a typical political news story decreased by about 20 percent (Hallin, 1992) and the number of political news stories dropped by 20 percent from 1968 to 1988 (Steele & Barnhurst, 1996). Lichter, Noyes, and Kaid (1999) found that this trend continued, as the average nightly news coverage of the campaign in 1996 was 12.3 minutes, down from 24.6 minutes in 1992. The network news is offering less and less coverage of the presidential campaign.

Furthermore, the news media have a tendency to offer short sound bites from candidates instead of thoughtful and extended consideration of issues. Hallin (1992) found that, in 1968, the average quotation from candidates in the news was forty-three seconds long. After twenty years, candidate quotations had shrunk to a mere nine seconds long. Lichter, Noyes, and Kaid (1999) found that this figure had dropped to 8.2 seconds in 1996. If the news relies on short sound bites from candidates, the candidates have no choice (if they wish to be heard on the news at all) but to offer sound bites to the news media.

During the same time period (1968-1988), journalists also spoke in shorter increments. However, reporters served as the sources of statements in political news stories almost twice as frequently in 1988 as in 1968: "Journalists inserted their voices more often, by an increment of .17 times per report per year" (Steele & Barnhurst, 1996, p. 191). Thus, the news presents fewer political stories, the stories are shorter, stories spend less time reporting the candidates's statements, and the stories feature journalists' commentary more frequently. Together, these factors mean that voters must look elsewhere for information contrasting presidential candidates: We just cannot rely on network news for comprehensive coverage of the candidates' issues positions.

This discussion is not intended as an indictment of the news media: We believe that it is not reasonable to expect the news media to excel at the task of informing the electorate about candidates' issue stands and their other qualities. The purpose of the news, by definition, is to report what is "new" to voters. As Patterson explains, "Policy problems lack the novelty that the journalist seeks. . . . The first time that a candidate takes a position on a key issue, the press is almost certain to report it. Further statements on the same issue become progressively less newsworthy, unless a new wrinkle is added" (1994, p. 61). In 2000, the first time Bush proposed private school vouchers or a plan for younger workers to invest Social Security funds in the stock market, that was news. However, later discussions were simply not as newsworthy as the initial announcement—even if they contained more specific details about his plans. Thus, we should not expect the news media to provide voters with information that distinguishes the candidates and helps them decide how to vote. At times the news media may convey useful information about the candidates; however, given the fact that this is not their purpose, we cannot rely on them to inform the electorate.

Candidates, voters, the news media, and scholars should all recognize and acknowledge this situation and the clear implication: Political campaign messages are the best places for voters to obtain information that distinguishes the candidates, information that can be used by voters to decide which candidate is preferable. We worry that these messages are biased and vague. However, Popkin (1994) explained that "Campaign communications . . . increased the accuracy of voter perception; misperceptions were far more likely on issues that were peripheral to the campaign." In fact, he concluded that "exposure to communication was the strongest single influence on accuracy of perceptions" (p. 39). Clearly, political campaign communication—TV spots, speeches, pamphlets, presidential debates, interviews, and the like—are important sources of information about the candidates, about their character and policy stands.

Of course, we do not assume that presidential candidates offer a thorough or unbiased discussion of every issue. Strategic ambiguity can be useful to political candidates. Some issues (like the specific details of proposals to save Social Security or fund Medicare) are so complex that discussion becomes unwieldy. Furthermore, it is in the candidates' best interests to present themselves in a favorable light and to portray their opponents in an unfavorable light. This can easily lead to omissions, inaccuracies, and misrepresentations of the issues. Nevertheless, voters must rely on candidates' campaign messages for much of the information they have about the candidates; it is a mistake to assume that the news media provides a comprehensive understanding of candidates' policy positions. Clearly, the messages from presidential candidates are important means of informing voters and helping them make their vote choice (see Benoit, Blaney, & Pier, 1998, for a critique of Lichtman, 1996).

## 4. Candidates Establish Preferability through Acclaiming, Attacking, and Defending

Of course, it is not enough simply for candidates to be distinctive in their messages, even on the issues that matter most to voters in that election year; a candidate must appear to be different from his or her opponents *in ways that will attract voters*. Popkin (1994) explains that "Somehow, candidates manage to get a large proportion of the citizenry sorted into opposing camps, each of which is convinced that the positions and interests of the other side add up to a less desirable package of benefits" (p. 8). For example, a statement like "I am the only candidate who wants to eliminate Medicare" would surely differentiate that candidate from his or her opponents, but it is not likely to help that person win votes.

This fundamental need for a candidate to appear preferable to voters means that all political campaign discourse has three potential functions. First, a candidate's message may acclaim, or engage in self-praise. This praise may focus either on policy stands or on character of the candidate. Emphasizing positive attributes or policies of one candidate tends to make that candidate appear preferable (for voters who value that attribute or policy) to his or her opponent(s). Therefore, one way to increase the likelihood that voters will perceive a candidate to be preferable is for that candidate to produce discourse that acclaims, or emphasizes his or her desirable points.

Second, a candidate's message can attack, or criticize the opponent. Again, attacks can focus on either the policies or the character of the opponent. Stressing an opponent's negative attributes or proposals tends to make that opponent appear less enticing (for voters who value that attribute or policy proposal). Thus, attacks can improve a candidate's net preferability by reducing his or her opponent's desirability.

Of course, a candidate may choose not to attack his or her opponent. It is well known that voters report their dislike of mud-slinging (Stewart, 1975). Accordingly, some politicians may not wish to appear to engage in character assassination. Notably, both McCain and Bush promised to run positive primary campaigns in 2000—and both ran television spots attacking the other for breaking that promise. However, a distaste for attacks does not necessarily mean attacking messages cannot persuade voters. Some political campaign attacks may hurt both sponsor and target, so the key question in deciding to use them may be who will suffer a net loss if a candidate attacks. Furthermore, some people believe that a sitting president ought not attack because that makes them appear less "presidential." Incumbency has its advantages, and challengers may need to attack more to overcome presumption (Trent & Friedenberg, 2000; Trent & Trent, 1995).

There is evidence that voters tend to consider policy attacks more acceptable than character attacks (Johnson-Cartee & Copeland, 1989), so some attacks might be more likely to backfire than others. Some research suggests that negative ads are no more powerful than positive ones (Lau, Sigelman, Heldman, & Babbitt, 1999).

Clearly, attacking is an option in a political campaign—even if some candidates choose not to use it—and it is capable of persuading voters that candidate is preferable.

Third, if one candidate is attacked by another—or perhaps we should say *when* one candidate is attacked by another—the target of such attack can defend himself or herself against that attack in a campaign message. Given the fact that an opponent's attacks can concern either policy (issues) or character (image), so too can a candidate's defense address either topic. A timely and apt defense has the potential to prevent further damage from an attack and it is possible that it could partially or completely restore a candidate's preferability (from damage caused by an attack).

It is quite possible that candidates will choose to forgo defenses when they are attacked. A response to an attack could appear to place the candidate on the defensive. It is possible that some candidates may not wish to "dignify" an opponent's accusations with a response. Engaging in defense has potential liabilities. First, assuming that attacks tend to occur on topics that favor one's opponent, responding to that attack takes a defending candidate "off-message," devoting precious message time to issues that are probably better for one's opponent. Second, the only way to respond to a particular attack is to identify it. Mentioning the attack, in preparation for refuting it, could inform or remind voters of the very weakness that the candidate is trying to combat. Thus, defenses may not be very common in campaign messages.

Of course, there are limitations on the power of campaign messages. Some voters may not accept a candidate's statements at face value. Candidates may not always address the most prominent concerns of voters, and that will inevitably diminish the impact of the message. Different voters may interpret a message in more than one way. Furthermore, we should not assume that a single message will make a voter choose the candidate presenting or sponsoring the message. However, we believe that the messages which each voter notices during the course of a campaign gradually shape his or her decision about how to vote.

Smith (1990) acknowledged the importance of two of these functions from the candidates' perspective when he explained that only in politics "do people pursue and defend jobs by publicly boasting and attacking others" (p. 107). Sabato (1981) made a similar point from the standpoint of voters' decision making when he explained that there are five possible ways of voting: "for or against either of the party nominees or not voting at all" (p. 324). Acclaiming provides the basis for voting for either candidate. Attacking (if not successfully defended against) provides the basis for voting against either candidate.

Similarly, scholars who investigate televised political advertising often distinguish between positive and negative spots (see, e.g., Devlin, 1989, 1993; Kaid & Davidson, 1986; Kaid & Johnston, 1991). Trent and Friedenberg (2000) explained that televised political ads perform three basic functions: extol the candidates' own virtues; condemn, attack, and question their opponents; and respond to attacks or innuendos. So, political scholars have recognized that political television spots acclaim and attack—and a few have even acknowledged the existence of defensive advertisements. However, this common distinction between positive and negative political advertisements is rarely applied to other forms of campaign discourse (outside of the framework of the Functional Theory of Political Campaign Discourse). Furthermore, only a few scholars acknowledge the presence of defense in political television spots.

A preliminary version of the Functional Theory was articulated in Benoit and Wells' study of the 1992 presidential debates. They concluded that "all three presidential candidates engaged in copious persuasive attack and defense during the course of the debates" (1996, p. 110). A limitation of this work is that its analysis did not conceptualize acclaiming as a distinct function, but folded it in with defense (specifically, as bolstering and corrective action). Still, it demonstrates the importance of these functions in political campaign discourse.

Thus, while writers do not always describe all three of these functions, political communication scholars in general acknowledge the importance of these goals of political campaign discourse. These functions have been studied in research on televised political advertisements (acclaiming and attacking) and in research on presidential debates (attacking and defending).

Politicians and their advisors also recognize the fundamental principle that campaign discourse performs multiple functions. For example, in 1972, H. R. Haldeman offered this advice on the reelection campaign to President Richard M. Nixon (quoted in Popkin et al. [1976] p. 794n): "Getting one of those 20 [percent] who is an undecided type to vote for you on the basis of your positive points is much less likely than getting them to vote against McGovern by scaring them to death about McGovern." Thus, Haldeman recognized that Nixon could seek votes by praising himself (stressing Nixon's positive points) or by attacking his opponent (frightening them about his opponent). Similarly, Vincent Breglio, who worked on Ronald Reagan's successful 1980 presidential campaign, explained that "It has become vital in campaigns today that you not only present all the reasons why people ought to vote for you, but you also have an obligation to present the reasons why they should not vote for the opponent" (1987, p. 34). So, political campaign advisors recognize that candidates can praise themselves and attack their opponents.

It is, therefore, appropriate to analyze political campaign discourse into utterances that *acclaim* the preferred candidate, *attack* the opponent(s), and *defend* the candidate from opponent's attacks. While these three political campaign communication functions do not occur with equal frequency, they are all options that candidates have available for use, and these three functions all occur to some extent in political campaign discourse. We believe that a complete understanding of political campaign communication must consider all three functions.

Scholarship on televised political advertising offers other lists of functions of political discourse. For example, Devlin (1986; 1987) discusses several functions of political ads.[1] However, we argue that our three functions are more basic than his list. One of the functions recognized by Devlin is raising money. Surely a candidate must praise his or her desirable qualities (and/or attack his or her opponent) in order to convince donors to contribute financially to his or her campaign. Furthermore, the money raised will often be used to produce acclaiming, attacking, or defending messages to get the candidate elected. Another function identified by Devlin is reinforcing supporters. Surely supporters are reinforced by discourse that stresses the candidate's desirable qualities (and, quite possibly, the undesirable qualities of the opponent). Gronbeck discusses several instrumental and consummatory functions of presidential campaigning (1978). Some of these ideas sound like uses and gratifications for the audience. Of course, it is important to know how auditors are likely to make use of the discourse produced by political candidates. However, those kinds of functions supplement, rather than compete with, our analysis of campaign functions. We explicitly privilege the viewpoint of the candidate's purposes in our analysis. Thus, we offer these activities—attacking, acclaiming, and defending—as the three fundamental functions of political campaign discourse.

## 5. A Candidate Must Win a Majority (or a Plurality) of the Votes Cast in an Election

This proposition may sound so simple that it is not worth mentioning. However, several key tenets of campaigning are implicit within this proposition. First, a candidate need not persuade everyone to vote for him or her. This turns out to be very important, because some policy positions will simultaneously attract some voters and repel others. That is, many issues are dichotomous. For instance, one of the distinctions between Bush and Gore in 2000 was that the former proposed across-the-board tax cuts while the latter recommended targeted tax cuts. Voters who cared about taxes would favor only one of these options. To embrace one policy position would make a candidate appear more desirable to one group of voters but less desirable to another group. It would be impossible to win the votes of every citizen on divisive issues like this one. However, the candidate does not have to receive all votes cast to win the election.

Second, only those citizens who actually cast votes matter. This means that a candidate need not win the votes of most citizens, but only of those who actually vote on election day. Ansolabehere and Iyengar (1995) argue that some candidates use negative television advertisements in order to depress voter turnout, hoping that those who might not vote are more likely to favor the candidate's opponent (but cf. Finkel & Geer, 1998). On the other hand, some candidates specifically attempted to encourage turnout. For example, in 1964 this television spot featured stormy weather and the announcer declared, "If it should rain on Nov. 3, please get wet. Go to the polls and vote for President Johnson. The stakes are too high for you to stay home" (Johnson, "Storm," 1964). At least seventeen of Johnson's television spots included the statement "The stakes are too high for you to stay home." Thus, it is possible to increase a candidate's likelihood of winning an election by increasing the turnout of voters who favor that candidate (or, although this seems antidemocratic and reprehensible, depress the turnout of voters who favor the opposing candidate).

Third, in a presidential election, a candidate only needs to persuade enough of those who are voting in enough states to win 270 electoral votes. This leads candidates to campaign more vigorously (e.g., spend more on airing political advertising; schedule more speeches and political rallies) in some states than others. The incredible story that unfolded in the weeks after the 2000 election underscored the importance of the electoral vote. Al Gore won the popular vote. Tuesday night Florida was "given" by the networks to Gore, taken back, given to Bush, taken back again. Then the recounts in Florida made the nation wait for the winner as the outcome of the election hinged on whether Florida's twenty-five electoral votes belonged to Bush or Gore. The U.S. Supreme Court (in a five to four vote) ultimately decide to halt recounts in Florida, giving the Electoral College majority to Bush. In 1960 Richard Nixon made the mistake of promising to campaign in every state, instead of just the ones where appearances were likely to help (he did not repeat this mistake when he ran again, and won, in 1968).

The idea that a candidate only needs to obtain the support of most of the voters is a very important proposition. As suggested, it is unreasonable to expect every eligible voter to prefer a single candidate. Given the fact that we enjoy a diverse electorate and an increasingly complex political environment, candidates must make choices that increase preferability among some voters while decreasing preferability among other groups of voters. Of course, at times candidates attempt to use strategic ambiguity to lessen this effect. However, as argued above, candidates must offer some distinctions or there is no reason to vote for one candidate over another. This means that audience analysis is essential to effective political campaigning (and the rise in the use of public opinion polls by the campaigns themselves attests to the importance of this notion).

Audience analysis helps candidates make two important decisions in their campaigns. First, presidential candidates must decide which states to contest. Kaid reports that "The 1992 campaign saw spot buys in selected markets reach new heights. The Clinton campaign particularly used this strategy on a national basis" (1994, p. 124). A candidate who uses national advertising buys spends money in states that he or she is almost certain to carry as well as in states he or she is virtually certain to lose. Bill Clinton used spot media buys to maximize his advertising in states that were close (Devlin, 1993). The 2000 general campaign was largely fought in these "battleground" states: Arkansas, Delaware (and Maryland), Florida, Georgia, Illinois, Iowa, Kentucky, Ohio, Oregon, Louisiana, Maine, Michigan, Missouri, Nevada, New Hampshire, New Mexico, North Carolina, Pennsylvania, Tennessee, Washington, West Virginia, and Wisconsin.

This makes for a much more efficient use of resources (candidate time and money).

Second, candidates must also decide which topics to emphasize in their messages—as well as which position to take on various issues. The candidate must persuade a majority of those who are voting that he or she is preferable on the *criteria that are most important to those voters*. The chase for electoral votes, a race "run" via audience analysis, also can influence which issues candidates decide to stress, and which to ignore (as well as what position they might take on the issues they do address).

These considerations suggest five specific strategies candidates can employ to try to maximize the probability of winning the election. First, a candidate can try to *increase the election day turnout of voters who prefer that candidate*. A decision that one candidate is preferable to another does not matter if that citizen fails to vote.

Second, a candidate can attempt to *win the support of undecided voters*. The number of independent voters has increased over time, as noted above, as the importance of parties has diminished. Much of a general election campaign does not concern committed partisans (who will almost certainly vote for their party's nominee) but focuses instead on the undecided voters. In 1996 we heard a great deal about the so-called "soccer moms," who allegedly held the key to the White House.

Third, a candidate can try to *entice those voters who lean toward his or her opponent to switch allegiance*, creating vote defectors from the other political party. Candidates may be unlikely to sway committed partisans, but there are vote defectors who cast their votes for the candidate of the other party (Nie, Verba, & Petrocik, 1999). Political candidates can try to steal away soft support from their opponents.

Fourth, a candidate can work to *firm up support from those who lean slightly his or her way*, keeping potential vote defectors from actually defecting to the opponent. Candidates are unlikely to lose the support of strong partisans, but some adherents are less firmly committed. The point here is to keep partisan supporters from defecting to the other party's candidate. Candidates can try to shore up their own soft supporters and prevent defections.

Finally, candidates may seek to *discourage voter turnout from those who support another candidate*. This strategy, as argued above, runs counter to democracy. In fact, we would argue that it is unethical. However, it is a possible option, and Ansolabehere and Iyengar (1995) have argued that some negative political advertisements are designed to do just this.

This analysis also explains why observers at times accuse candidates of "running to the right (or left) in primaries and then running to the center in the general campaign." The principal audience in these two phases of the presidential campaign is different. In order to obtain their party's nomination, a candidate must convince the majority of *his or her party members* that he or she is preferable to members of his or her own political party. For Republicans, this translates into emphasis of issues on the right of the political spectrum; for Democrats, it means a focus on issues on the left of the political spectrum. However, when the nominees reach the general campaign, the party's nominee can take for granted the votes of most committed party members. But in order to win this phase of the election, the candidate must appeal to *other groups of voters*—undecided, independent, and potential vote defectors–voters who may have disparate concerns from committed partisans. Candidates must therefore often discuss different issues and take positions that lie more in the middle of the political spectrum in the general campaign. In other words, the shift in target audience explains a concomitant shift in campaign discourse.

This analysis of political campaign strategies is not intended to suggest that every voter takes a rational approach to voting: gathering, weighing, and integrating as much information as possible to guarantee that they make the most rational decision possible. As Popkin (1994; see also Downs, 1957) argues most persuasively, many voters take information shortcuts. They do not seek out information about the candidates (or they wait until just before the election to do so). They base their voting decisions on the information that comes to them (oftentimes from television commercials and from acquaintances). Voters do not place the information they obtain about the candidates into mathematical formulas in order to calculate their votes.

Still, the principles we outlined should hold true generally, regardless of a given voter's degree of involvement in the election. Candidates disseminate information through various channels (television spots, debates, direct mail, radio spots, web pages, etc.) hoping to provide information to whichever voters happen to be paying attention to that medium at that point in time. Giving a voter information about a candidate's desirable qualities or issue stands has a tendency to increase that candidate's apparent preferability. Giving a voter information about an opposing candidate's undesirable qualities or issue stands tends to decrease the opponent's apparent preferability to some extent. Defending against an attack should help restore a candidate's apparent preferability. The effects of these three kinds of messages should have more impact on vote intention when they concern topics that are salient to a voter. Although the effect of individual messages may be small and depends upon how much attention voters accord them, and although some voters may have strong party preferences, the cumulative effect of such information over time may influence voters' decisions—especially undecided, independent, and potential vote defectors.

This analysis also explains why basic themes are, and should be, repeated throughout the campaign. For those voters who pay attention throughout the campaign, repetition serves to reinforce the candidate's message with those auditors. On the other hand, it puts out a relatively constant message so that voters who only pay sporadic attention to the campaign will sooner or later notice the campaign themes.

# Advantages of the Functional Approach

The Functional Theory offers several distinct advantages over other approaches to studying political campaign communication. We believe that televised political spots may be the most intensely studied forms of campaign discourse, so we will develop this claim initially by contrasting our method with previous research on political advertising. Our method begins where many analyses of televised political advertisements begin, by conceptualizing them as negative (attacking) and positive (acclaiming) messages. However, although they are not as common as attacks and acclaims, some political television spots defend, and our approach acknowledges the existence of defensive political spots. For example, a television spot for Nixon in 1960 began by explaining that, in this advertisement, "President Eisenhower answers the Kennedy-Johnson charges that America has accomplished nothing in the last eight years." It then featured Eisenhower, who declared that "My friends, never have Americans achieved so much in so short a time," clearly denying the accusation. We do not believe that a spot like this is adequately understood by describing it as negative (even though it rejects the opposition) or as positive (even though it touts past deeds). It takes an attack from an opponent and explicitly rejects that attack. Thus, by looking for defenses as well as attacks and acclaims, the Functional Approach provides a more comprehensive understanding of political campaign messages.

Second, many studies classify political spots as concerned with policy (issues) or character (image). Our analysis extends by analyzing both policy and character into finer subdivisions than does most current research (as we describe in chapter 2, we divide policy into past deeds, future plans, and general goals; we divide character into personal qualities, leadership qualities, and ideals). In our analysis of the 1996 presidential campaign, this finer grained analysis of policy utterances enabled us to argue that Bill Clinton's television spots were more comprehensive than Bob Dole's TV ads. Clinton addressed four potential ideas (actually, he addressed more than four ideas; we want to focus on these particular options) in his television commercials: He acclaimed *both* his past deeds and future plans, and Clinton's ads attacked *both* Bob Dole's past deeds and his future plans. In sharp contrast, Dole's ads acclaimed his own future plans (but rarely praised his past deeds), and Dole's spots attacked Bill Clinton's past deeds (but rarely criticized Clinton's future plans). An analysis that lumped all policy or issue ads together, without distinguishing between past deeds and future plans, could not have detected the places where Bob Dole could have acclaimed (his past deeds) but did not, or where he could have attacked (Clinton's future plans) but did not.

Third, because many television spots contain many different utterances, we do not classify entire ads as *either* positive (acclaiming) *or* negative (attacking) as is the case in most previous research. Some political ads are entirely positive or entirely negative, but many are mixed, and that mix is not always 50/50. We believe in fact that ads that contain a mixture of acclaims and attacks may be becoming more common over time. For example, Kaid and Tedesco (1999) use this 1996 advertisement from Bill Clinton to illustrate a negative spot:

*America's values. The President bans deadly assault weapons*; Dole/Gingrich vote no. *The President passes family leave*; Dole/Gingrich vote no. *The President stands firm: a balanced budget, protects Medicare, disabled children*; No again. Now Dole resigns, leaves gridlock he and Gingrich created. *The President's plan: balance the budget, protect Medicare, reform welfare. Do our duty to our parents, our children. America's values.* (p. 213; emphasis added).

In this excerpt, we italicized the acclaims and left the attacks in plain type. An analysis that classifies this spot as *either* positive *or* negative clearly provides an incomplete understanding of this spot. Accordingly, we analyze and classify *each utterance* in a given commercial, providing a more precise picture of *the degree to which* a political spot is positive, negative, or defensive. Note that a few analyses include a third option: positive, negative, and comparative (both positive and negative). However, we know that not every ad which combines acclaims and attacks divides them evenly (e.g., some have 25 percent or 10 percent acclaims and 75 percent or 90 percent attacks). Using three categories is a bit better than using two, but our approach of categorizing each remark as acclaiming, attacking, or defending is still superior.

Fourth, Benoit, Blaney, and Pier (1998) found that during the primaries, campaign messages which attack may have several different targets (for example, in 1996, Republican primary TV spots attacked other Republican candidates, the Washington establishment, and President Clinton). Similarly, in 2000, the Republican primary messages also attacked other Republicans, the establishment, and Al Gore. Surely it makes a difference whether, for example, John McCain's television advertisements attacked George W. Bush, Steve Forbes, or Al Gore. However, previous research tends to overlook this aspect of political campaign messages.

The Functional Approach combines analysis of function (acclaim, attack, defend) and topic (policy, character). Many studies of political spots examine one aspect or the other, but not both. Studies of other messages, like debates, tend not to examine topic. This means that the Functional Approach is more complete than other research on political campaign discourse.

Finally, we apply the Functional Approach to a variety of political campaign messages: televised political spots (primary and general), debates (primary and general), talk radio appearances (primary and general), web pages (primary and general), and nominating convention speeches. Most political campaign research focuses on television spots and debates (and predominantly on general campaign spots and debates) or on Keynote Speeches and Acceptance Addresses. We offer insight into a variety of message forms. It seems odd that the dimensions employed to study television spots (positive, negative; issue, image) rarely inform research on other message forms, like debates or Acceptance Addresses. We apply the same method to each message form we analyze, allowing for comparisons across media.

## Summary

We have discussed the five assumptions that provide the foundation for the Functional Theory of Political Campaign Discourse. We have identified the advantages of our approach to studying political campaign communication. The next two chapters explain our method and procedures in greater detail.

Thus, our approach to studying 2000 presidential campaign discourse is superior to previous approaches. We do not, and cannot, answer every possible question. However, the Functional Approach is a useful method for studying political campaign communication. Thus, we provide an analysis of the messages in Campaign 2000 that has great breadth (diverse message forms) and depth (detailed analyses of each message).

## Notes

1. Other scholars have addressed the functions of political campaigns at different levels of abstraction (e.g., Devlin, 1986, 1987; Gronbeck, 1978). For example, candidates need to raise money to finance their campaigns. Ultimately, though, a candidate obtains donations by convincing potential donors that he or she is preferable to other candidates. Of course, the reasons given to potential donors to convince them to contribute to a given candidate may not be identical to the reasons given to citizens to vote for that candidate. Nevertheless, we argue that the functions we identify are more basic than other lists of functions.

# Chapter 2

# Method and Procedures: Analyzing Functions and Topics

This chapter describes the method employed to analyze presidential campaign messages in the 2000 campaign. First, we discuss each of the three functions themselves: acclaiming, attacking, and defending. Then, we describe our approach to analyzing the content of political campaign messages: policy considerations and character of the candidates and parties. These two topics are illustrated through excerpts from political campaign discourse on each of the three functions. Third, we describe the procedures we employed for conducting our textual analysis. An example of acclaims and attacks on each form of policy and of character can be found at the end of this chapter.

## Analyzing the Functions of Political Campaign Discourse

In this section we describe our approach to analyzing discourse, identifying the functions and topics of political campaign discourse. Political campaign discourse is, of necessity, comparative: Each candidate strives to obtain enough votes to win by persuading voters that he (or she) is preferable to other candidates. There are only three ways to demonstrate one's preferability. First, one can *acclaim*, or engage in self-praise. The better a candidate for office appears, the more likely that candidate will receive a citizen's vote. For example, in this television spot, Gore offered these acclaims:

> Vietnam veteran. Father of four. Married 30 years. Al Gore will fight for families. Tax cuts for middle-class families, including a $10,000-a-year tax deduction for college tuition. Continue welfare reform with time limits, work requirements. Force deadbeat parents to take responsibility for their children. A crime victims' bill of rights to protect victims, not just criminals. Fight violence and pornography on the Internet, helping parents block out what children shouldn't see. Al Gore. He'll put his values to work for us. ("Veteran")

This advertisement does not mention his opponent; it focuses on providing positive qualities or policy positions adopted by Gore. This Bush television spot also focuses on extolling the Republican's good points:

> Today our children are forced to grow up too fast. Parents need tools to help protect them and nurture their families. We need filters for online content in schools and libraries. Family hours for TV programming. Character education in our schools. More effective drug prevention. Tough school safety so children learn discipline and love go hand in hand. And more flex-time for parents. I believe parents today need allies not adversaries to help raise moral, responsible children. ("Tools")

Again, this spot is entirely positive, focusing on Bush's favorable qualities or policy positions. Increasing positive perceptions of a candidate is one way to help increase preferability.

Second, a candidate can *attack* his or her opponents. To the extent an opponent appears less desirable, the attacking candidate gains in net preferability. In the last presidential debate, for example, Gore argued that "Under Governor Bush, Texas has sunk to be 50th out of 50 in the health insurance for their citizens." This utterance seems clearly designed to make Bush appear less desirable as a president. In the same debate, Bush charged that, if elected, Gore would dramatically increase governmental spending: "He proposed more than Walter Mondale and Michael Dukakis combined. This is a big spender—he is—and he ought to be proud of it. It's part of his record." Increasing federal spending is considered by many to be a bad idea, because they believe they will ultimately pay for that spending. Of course, candidates who attack must be careful to avoid backlash from voters against mudslinging (Merritt, 1984; Stewart, 1975), which would reduce the attacker's perceived preferability.

Third, when a candidate is attacked, he or she can *defend*, or refute the accusations. To the extent a candidate can defuse potential negatives through defenses, his or her net favorability should increase. At one point Gore declared that "I support a strong national patients' bill of rights. It is actually a disagreement between us." Bush rejected that attack, explaining that "Actually, Mr. Vice President, it's not true, I do support a national patients' bill of rights." This is a clear example of a defense. Similarly, Bush charged that Gore proposed a huge increase in federal spending: "Just add up all the numbers; it's three times bigger than what President Clinton proposed." Gore replied to the moderator, "That's in an ad, Jim, that was knocked down by the journalists who analyzed the ad and said it was misleading." This is another example of a defense that employs simple denial. A successful defense can restore a candidate's preferability after it has been damaged by an attack.

These three functions—acclaiming, attacking, and defending—allow voters to perform a simple form of cost-benefit analysis. Attacks *increase an opponent's apparent costs. Defenses can reduce a candidate's perceived costs.* Acclaims, then, can *increase a candidate's apparent benefits.* Any one of these strategies, or two or three employed together, have the potential to persuade voters that a candidate is preferable to his or her opponents. We do not assume that all voters constantly tally pros and cons, explicitly performing a cost-benefit analysis. However, the more acclaims of a particular candidate that are accepted by a voter, the higher that candidate's perceived preferability (and the more likely that citizen will vote for that candidate). The more attacks against a candidate that seem plausible to a voter (i.e., that are persuasively articulated and not effectively neutralized with defense), the lower the target's apparent preferability (and the less likely that person will vote for that candidate).

## Acclaims

Pamela Benoit developed the first analysis of acclaims, or self-praise, in the communication literature (1997; see also Schlenker, 1980). This kind of utterance functions to enhance the image of the speaker. Benoit, Blaney, and Pier (1998) found that in the 1996 presidential campaign, acclaims were the most common utterance in every campaign message form they analyzed. Acclaims comprised 54 percent of the statements in primary debates, 58 percent of the comments in primary television spots, and 66 percent of the remarks in primary talk radio appearances. At the conventions, 65 percent of keynote speech statements, 83 percent of the candidates' utterances in acceptance addresses, and 95 percent of the candidates' spouses' comments were acclaims. In the general campaign, acclaims accounted for 54 percent of television spot themes, 78 percent of the statements in radio addresses, 59 percent of the utterances in the debates, and 77 percent of free television time remarks. Unlike the other functions, there is no drawback to an acclaim, and in fact they are the most common function of campaign discourse. Individual candidates may at times violate this generalization (one of Dole's general message forms, television spots, had 55 percent attacks; one of Forbes primary message forms, debates, had 52 percent attacks), but the finding that acclaims are the most common function of presidential campaign discourse has few exceptions: Overall, 63 percent of all utterances analyzed from 1996 campaign messages were acclaims.

## Attacks

Several scholars have investigated persuasive attack (see, e.g., Benoit & Dorries, 1996; Benoit & Harthcock, 1999a; Felknor, 1992; Fisher, 1970; Ryan, 1982, 1988). Pfau and Kenski's *Attack Politics* (1990) presents a useful analysis of attacking messages, but they do not attempt to develop a list of strategies for generating persuasive attacks (they identify three very general options: attacking first, counterattacking, and prevention). Jamieson's *Dirty Politics* (1992) distinguishes between two approaches: identification (association) and apposition (contrast). However, this analysis tends to remain more general and, again, is not designed to articulate a set of strategies for developing or analyzing persuasive attack.

Johnson-Cartee and Copeland (1989) asked people to rate a list of topics for political attacks as fair or unfair. They arranged these options into two groups of topics called "Political Issues" (political record, stands on issues, criminal record, and voting record) and "Personal Characteristics" (personal life, marriage, family, religion, medical history, and sex life). At least 83 percent of respondents rated each political issue as a fair topic for an attack; and at least 64 percent considered the personal characteristics to be unacceptable topic for political attack. Therefore, it appears that there is general  agreement that policy attacks are more acceptable

Table 2.1. Functions of 1996 Presidential Campaign Messages

| Message Form | Acclaims | Attacks | Defenses |
|---|---|---|---|
| Primary Debates | 54% | 38% | 9% |
| Primary TV Spots | 58% | 40% | 2% |
| Primary Talk Radio | 66% | 28% | 6% |
| Keynotes | 65% | 35% | 0 |
| Acceptances | 83% | 16% | 0.5% |
| Spouses' Speeches | 95% | 5% | 0 |
| General TV Spots | 54% | 46% | 0.4% |
| General Radio Addresses | 78% | 22% | 1% |
| General Debates | 59% | 33% | 7% |
| Free TV Time | 77% | 23% | 0.2% |
| Total | 63% | 33% | 4% |

than personal attacks.

Turning again to Benoit, Blaney, and Pier's (1998) analysis of the 1996 presidential campaign, we find that attacks were generally the second most common function of campaign discourse. During the primary race, 38 percent of debate statements, 40 percent of television spot utterances, and 28 percent of talk radio comments were attacks. At the nominating convention, attacks constituted 35 percent of the keynotes, 16 percent of acceptances, and 5 percent of the spouses' speeches. During the general campaign, attacks were 46 percent of television spot remarks, 22 percent of radio addresses, 33 percent of debate statements, and 23 percent of free television time comments. While there were rare exceptions (noted above), attacks are generally the second most frequent function of presidential campaign discourse. Attacks have a drawback that does not inhere in acclaims: Many voters report that they dislike mudslinging (Merritt, 1984; Stewart, 1975). This may lead candidates to acclaim more than they attack. Nevertheless, 33 percent of the themes in these campaign messages were attacks.

## Defenses

Of the three functions of campaign discourse discussed here, the most research by far has examined persuasive defense, *apologia*, accounts, or image repair discourse. Benoit (1995a; see also 1997a, 2001) developed a typology of image repair strategies. This approach has been applied in studies of political, corporate, and other forms of image repair discourse (see also Benoit, 1995b, 1997b, 1998, 1999; Benoit & Anderson, 1996; Benoit & Brinson, 1994, 1999; Benoit & Czerwinski, 1997; Benoit, Gullifor, & Panici, 1991; Benoit & Hanczor, 1994; Benoit & McHale, 1999; Benoit & Nill, 1998a, 1998b; Blaney & Benoit, 1997, 2001; Blaney, Benoit, & Brazeal, 2002; Brinson & Benoit, 1996, 1999; or Kennedy & Benoit, 1997).

Jamieson (1992) describes ten responses to political attacks: counterattack (responding to one illegitimate attack with a like response), inoculation, forewarning of impending attack, reframing (providing an alternative and more favorable interpretation of the attacking message), taking umbrage (expressing outrage at the attack), using humor to reframe the attack, using credible sources to rebut the charges, using the press's credibility to rebut the charges, disassociation, and admitting mistakes and asking forgiveness. Like other inductively derived lists (see, e.g., Benoit, 1982), strategies appear at multiple levels of abstraction. For example, some strategies appear to relate to the *content* of the response (e.g., counterattack, inoculation, forewarning, reframing, disassociation, admission), others pertain to the *source of evidence* used in the response (credible sources, media credibility), and some seem to describe the *tone* of the response (taking umbrage, using humor). Gold (1978) and Trent and Friedenberg (2000) have also discussed political *apologia*.

Benoit, Blaney, and Pier (1998) also examined the frequency of defense in the 1996 presidential campaign. Defenses constituted 9 percent of debate comments, 2 percent of television spot utterances, and 6 percent of talk radio remarks. At the nominating conventions, no defenses occurred in either the keynote speeches or the spouses' speeches. Two of the utterances in Dole's acceptance were defenses (0.5 percent of total acceptance speech themes). In the general campaign, defenses accounted for 0.4 percent of televison spot statements, 1 percent of radio address comments, 7 percent of debate utterances, and 0.2 percent of free television time remarks. Thus, defenses occurred in most of these message forms, but were uniformly the least common function. There are three potential drawbacks to reliance on defenses. First, they can make the candidate appear to be on the defensive, reactive instead of proactive. Second, in order to refute an attack, the candidate must identify the accusation. This may remind or inform voters of a potential weakness. Third, a defense is more likely to occur on a topic that favors one's opponent. This means that a defense often takes a candidate "off-message," devoting precious message time to issues on which a candidate does not wish to dwell. Overall, defenses comprised only 4 percent of the utterances in these campaign messages.

## Topics of Political Campaign Discourse

The Functional Theory of Political Campaign Discourse divides message content into two topics: policy and character. These terms correspond to the more common distinction in the literature between issues and image. However, the word "issue" has two very different meanings. First, the term "issue" can refer to discourse that concerns policy questions (as we use it here). However, it can also have a second, broader referent, concerning any question on which disputants (including political candidates) can disagree. Because political candidates can, and do, disagree about character (e.g., how important is character in the campaign? what kind of character do the candidates possess?), that means that character or image can be considered an issue. Furthermore, it is possible to speak of the image a candidate projects on policy, or the issues. Thus, we prefer to use the word "policy" rather than "issues," and we prefer to write about "character" instead of "image."

It is important to recognize that image and issue, or policy and character, are inexorably intertwined (see, e.g., Friedenberg, 1994; Hinck, 1993; Leff & Mohrmann, 1974; Levine, 1995; Rosenthal, 1966; Rudd, 1986; Stuckey & Antczak, 1995; West, 1993). For example, Benoit and Wells (1996) argue that "candidates' images are intimately tied to their actions, the policies they embrace, and the stand they take (however vague) on the issues" (pp. 26-27). Devlin (1995) explains that "I make no distinction [between image and issue ads] because issue ads really do create image impressions on the part of the viewer, and image ads can convey substantive information" (p. 203). We believe that a "spillover" effect can occur in either direction. For example, a candidate who frequently emphasizes social policies (help for the poor, the elderly, and the disadvantaged) may create the impression that he or she is a caring and compassionate individual. Conversely, a candidate who frequently declares that he cares for people and understands their concerns and problems may be assumed to have a positive social agenda (see also Hacker, Zakahi, Giles, & McQuitty, 2000). Still, we believe that it is useful to classify campaign discourse by topic (policy, character) and that voters form impressions of both the candidates' policy positions and of their persona.

## Policy

Some discourse in political campaign messages addresses policy considerations. For example, this primary spot from Gore discussed the appropriate policy for financing education:

> I think it would be a big mistake to drain money away from our public schools with vouchers that give public money to private schools. Private schools are fine. But not with money that's already designated for the 90 percent of the American children who go to public schools. Now is the time when we ought to be really beefing up our public schools, making a very deep and firm commitment by the American people to really bring revolutionary progress to our schools. ("Vouchers")

This is a clear example of a campaign message that focuses on policy. Similarly, this primary spot from Bush focuses on policy: "As Governor he signed the two largest tax cuts in Texas history. He reduced the growth of state government spending to the lowest in forty years. He improved public schools by restoring local control, raising standards, and returning to basics. He cut welfare rolls in half, reduced junk lawsuits and cut juvenile crime 38%" ("Fresh Start"). This excerpt addresses several issues (tax cuts, government spending, schools, welfare, lawsuits, and crime), but it clearly concerns public policy. Policy utterances are divided into past deeds, future plans, and general goals.

Benoit, Blaney, and Pier (1998) analyzed the extent to which candidates discussed policy in the 1996 presidential campaign. All message forms but two discussed policy more than character. In the primary, policy was the topic of 58 percent of debate utterances, 48 percent of television spot remarks, and 57 percent of talk radio comments. During the nominating conventions, Keynotes (72 percent) and Acceptances (61 percent) devoted more themes to policy; the spouses' speeches, which might be expected to be largely biographical, discussed policy in only 33 percent of the statements. Every message form in the general campaign privileged policy: television spots:74 percent, radio addresses: 72 percent, debates: 72 percent, and free television time: 72 percent. Overall, 64 percent of the utterances in the campaign messages focused on policy. See Table 2.2.

Table 2.2. Topics of 1996 Presidential Campaign Messages

| Message Form | Policy | Character |
|---|---|---|
| Primary Debates | 58% | 42% |
| Primary TV Spots | 48% | 52% |
| Primary Talk Radio | 57% | 43% |
| Keynotes | 72% | 28% |
| Acceptances | 61% | 39% |
| Spouses' Speeches | 33% | 67% |
| General TV Spots | 74% | 26% |
| General Radio Addresses | 72% | 28% |
| General Debates | 72% | 28% |
| Free TV Time | 76% | 24% |
| Total | 64% | 36% |

## Character

Messages from candidates for elective office can also discuss their character. A primary spot from Bradley stressed his candor, a character trait: "Sometimes you'll agree with me. Sometimes you won't. But at least you'll know exactly where I stand" ("Different Campaign"). This advertisement for McCain stressed his character and courage: "John McCain. The character to do what's right and the courage to fight for it" ("Faces of Americans"). Neither of these excerpts addressed policy. Character remarks can discuss personal qualities, leadership ability, and ideals (Table 2.3 also provides examples of acclaims and attacks on the three forms of character).

As can be inferred from the discussion of policy, only two message forms devoted more time to character than policy. During the primary phase of the campaign, 42 percent of utterances in debates, 52 percent of comments in television spots, and 43 percent of remarks on talk radio concerned character. At the nominating conventions, 28 percent of keynote comments, 39 percent of acceptance statements, and 67 percent of the spouses' statements discussed character. In the general campaign, 26 percent of television spot themes, 28 percent of radio address comments, 28 percent of debate statements, and 24 percent of free television time remarks were about character. Overall, 36 percent of the candidates' (and their spouses') statements discussed character in 1996.

Thus, we divide the candidates' campaign utterances into policy considerations (issue) and candidate/party qualities (character or image). We subdivide policy discourse into that which concerns past deeds, future plans, and general goals. We subdivide qualities into personal qualities, leadership ability, and ideals (values, principles). This scheme has been applied to analyze political campaign discourse in several contexts: televised political spots, nominating convention keynote speeches, nominating convention acceptance addresses, and talk radio appearances.

Of course, other kinds of divisions are possible. One could, for example, divide policy discourse into domestic and foreign policy utterances (as seen later, we categorize policy utterances by issue; e.g., education, health care, taxes). Other research has delved into the question of what specific personality traits (e.g., honesty, compassion) are important in evaluating the character of a presidential candidate (see Trent & Friedenberg, 2000). Perhaps future research into the functions of political campaign discourse will extend our theory in these directions.

We have described our basic method, analyzing utterances into acclaims, attacks, and defenses. We also analyze whether the discourse concerns policy or character, and subdivide each topic into three components (past deeds, future plans, and goals on policy; leadership ability, personal qualities, and ideals on character). We reviewed past research on these functions and topics of presidential campaign discourse.

## Procedures for Analyzing Campaign 2000 Messages

We began by obtaining copies of a variety of forms of persuasive discourse from the 2000 presidential campaign. Whenever possible, we obtained both transcripts and videotapes of the messages we studied. From the primaries, we selected five sets of texts: television spots, radio spots, primary debates, television talk show appearances, and candidate webpages. From the party nominating conventions, we also chose three sets of texts: featured speeches (the Republicans decided not to identify a keynote speaker in 2000), acceptance addresses, and speeches by the candidates' spouses. From the general campaign, we again picked five sets of texts: television spots, radio spots, debates, television talk show appearances, and candidate webpages. In each application chapter we will discuss the details of the texts we analyzed and review other literature relevant to that message form.

As mentioned in the preface, we developed five specific research questions that guided our analysis of selected messages in the 2000 presidential campaign.

(1) How often do the major candidates employ each of the three functions of political campaign messages (acclaiming, attacking, defending)?
(2) Do the candidates devote more utterances to addressing policy or character?
(3) How many utterances are devoted to the three forms of policy utterances (past

deeds, future plans, general goals) and the three forms of character remarks (personal qualities, leadership ability, and ideals)?

(4) In primary messages, do attacks target other members of the source's own party, the other party, or the establishment?

(5) Which candidates devoted more utterances to the issues of most importance to voters?

In order to answer these questions, we established a six-step analytic procedure. First, we unitized the messages into themes, or utterances that address a coherent idea. Berelson (1952) explained that a theme is "an assertion about a subject" (p. 18). Holsti (1969) defined a theme as "a single assertion about some subject" (p. 116). Because naturally occurring discourse is enthymematic, themes vary in length from a phrase to several sentences. For example, consider this Gore primary television spot:

> <1> He's had the courage <2> to take on the big drug companies and fight for more affordable drugs. <3> Now Al Gore's leading the fight for a patients' bill of rights—to give control back to patients and doctors, not HMO bureaucrats. <4> He's proposed a realistic health care plan to cover America's children and <5> to put us on the road to universal coverage for everyone. <6> A new prescription drug benefit for seniors. The only candidate who <7> protects Medicare and <8> preserves Medicaid.

We unitized this message into eight themes, as indicated with numbers inside "<>" above.

The rule we followed was to break each part of a passage into a separate theme whenever we would have considered that part to be a theme if that part of the utterance had appeared alone. Because discourse is enthymematic, themes varied in length, but each theme addressed a coherent idea about the candidates (and/or their political parties).

Second, each theme was classified as an acclaim, attack, or defense according to these rules:

> *Acclaims* portray the candidate favorably.
> *Attacks* portray the opposing candidate or party unfavorably.
> *Defenses* repair the candidate's reputation (from attacks by the opposing party).

In the television spot unitized above, each statement is a potential reason to vote for Gore (positive trait or desirable policy proposal), rather than a criticism of an opponent, so they would be coded as acclaims. Other utterances were not analyzed. For example, at times campaign discourse describes events without attributing credit or blame to either candidate or party. Only utterances that acclaimed, attacked, or defended were analyzed in this research.

Third, during the primaries, the target of attacks was identified. In the general campaign, the potential targets are the (major) competing candidates: Gore attacked

Bush, Bush attacked Gore. However, in the primaries, candidates attacked one another (McCain attacked Bush, Bush attacked McCain) as well as the presumed nominee of the opposing party (McCain and Bush each attacked Gore). Candidates also at times attacked the Washington political establishment (Benoit, Blaney, & Pier, 1998, noted that candidates who had not held elective office were prone to attack the establishment).

Fourth, a judgment was made about whether the theme primarily concerned policy or character, according to these rules:

*Policy* themes concern governmental action (past, current, or future) and problems amenable to governmental action.
*Character* themes concern characteristics, traits, abilities, or attributes of the candidates.

Policy themes were further divided into utterances that concerned past deeds, future plans, and general goals. Character themes were further divided into utterances that addressed personal qualities, leadership ability, and ideals (see Table 2.3). In Gore's ad above (illustrating eight themes), the first theme addresses character (courage). The remaining themes all discuss policy (health care). None of these statements appears to reference accomplishments, so all are either future plans or general goals (e.g., "a patients' bill of rights" sounds more like a means to an end, or a future plan, whereas "protects Medicare and preserves Medicaid" sound more like ends or general goals).

Additionally, we located public opinion polls conducted during the primary, prior to the nominating conventions, and at the start of the general campaign. These questions asked respondents which issue was most important in their presidential vote choice. The data from these polls are summarized in Tables 2.4-2.6. This is an index of which issues are most important to voters (albeit not a perfect index: some issues may have changed in importance over time; the pollster may have omitted a topic that was important to voters). However, these poll data provide an indication of which issues were most important. The final step in our data analysis began with those themes identified in step four as concerned with policy (past deeds, future plans, and general goals). These utterances were classified into one of the issue areas from the relevant public opinion poll (and an additional possibility, "other"). Each of the policy utterances in the spot reprinted above addressed health.

Table 2.3. Examples of Acclaims and Attacks on Each Form of Policy and Character

## Policy

### Past Deeds

*Acclaim*    He cut welfare rolls in half . . . and cut juvenile crime 38% (Bush)

*Attack*    Five times [McCain] voted to use your taxes to pay for political campaigns (Bush)

### Future Plans

*Acclaim*    [I favor] Banning all Saturday night specials (Bradley)

*Attack*    Gore's targeted tax cuts leave out millions of people, over half of all taxpayers (Bush)

### General Goals

*Acclaim*    I will balance the budget every year. I will pay down the national debt . . . And I will cut taxes for middle-class families (Gore)

*Attack*    Governor Bush is proposing to open up our—some of our most precious environmental treasures like the Arctic National Wildlife Refuge to the big oil companies to go in and start producing oil there. I think that is the wrong choice (Gore)

## Character

### Personal Qualities

*Acclaim*    [Forbes] always gives a straight answer. He's a man of his word (Forbes)

*Attack*    Why does Al Gore say one thing when the truth is another? (Bush)

### Leadership Ability

*Acclaim*    Ready to lead: Al Gore (Gore)

*Attack*    Is he [Bush] ready to lead America? (Gore)

### Ideals

*Acclaim*    America is about expanding . . . human rights and dignity, . . . freedom of religion, . . . emancipation of slaves, from civil rights to equal opportunities for women (Bauer)

*Attack*    The Democrats trust big government only (Bush)

Excerpts from 2000 television spots.

Table 2.4. Issues Important to Voters, Primary Campaign (11/13-18/99)

| Democratic Voters | | Republican Voters | |
|---|---|---|---|
| Issue | Poll | Issue | Poll |
| Education | 23 | Education | 19 |
| Health Care | 19 | Taxes | 11 |
| Social Security | 13 | Morals/Family Values | 9 |
| Crime/Drugs | 12 | Social Security | 9 |
| Taxes | 5 | Crime/Drugs | 8 |
| Medicare/Prescription Drugs | 4 | Health Care | 8 |
| Foreign Affairs | 2 | Foreign Affairs | 7 |
| Morals/Family Values | 2 | Medicare/Prescription Drugs | 5 |

Enslow (1999).

We checked inter-coder reliability on a sample of texts from a variety of message forms: primary debate excerpts, primary television spots, primary radio spots, acceptance address excerpts, general debate excerpts, general television spots, and television talk show appearance excerpts. We calculated Cohen's *kappa* to control for agreement by chance. Inter-coder reliability for function ranged from .79 to 1.0; for target of attack in primary messages it varied from .96 to 1.0; for topic it ranged from .76 to .98; for forms of policy it varied from .91 to 1.0; for forms of character agreement ranged from .78 to 1.0; for issues it ranged from .86 to .97. Landis and Koch (1977) explain that values of *kappa* from 0.61 to 0.80 represent "substantial" agreement and values from 0.81 to 1.0 reflect "almost perfect" inter-coder reliability (p. 165). Thus, 88 percent of our *kappas* indicate "almost perfect" agreement and the remaining 12 percent indicate substantial agreement. These results give us confidence in the coding of these messages.

Table 2.5. Issues Important to Voters, Conventions (7/25-26/00)

| Issue | Poll |
|---|---|
| Economy | 12 |
| Education | 12 |
| Health Care | 9 |
| Social Security | 8 |
| Taxes | 6 |
| Guns | 6 |
| Abortion | 6 |
| National Defense | 5 |
| Medicare | 4 |
| Environment | 4 |
| Budget Surplus | 3 |
| Jobs | 3 |
| Foreign Affairs | 2 |

Gallup (2000).

Table 2.6. Issues Important to Voters, 2000 General Campaign

| Issue | Poll |
|---|---|
| Economy | 18 |
| Education | 16 |
| Health Care | 16 |
| Social Security | 11 |
| Taxes | 8 |
| National Defense | 8 |
| Environment | 3 |

NBC News/*Wall Street Journal* (2000).

We begin each analytical chapter by reproducing sample messages or excerpts from sample messages. While we created numerous tables of numerical data representing the results of our content analysis, we made a determined effort to keep our conclusions grounded firmly in the texts we analyzed by using frequent excerpts from the texts to illustrate our conclusions (copious use of illustrative excerpts also provides evidence for the appropriateness of our coding of the texts).

## Summary

Thus, this study applies the functional theory of political campaign discourse to a variety of texts—from primaries, conventions, and the general campaign—used in the 2000 presidential election. We analyze the functions of these messages into acclaims, attacks, and defenses. We divide utterances into policy and character, and subdivide each of these two areas into more specific categories. We analyzed the target of attacks in the primary campaign as well as the issues addressed in these messages. Inter-coder reliability was generally high, giving us confidence in the coding of texts. This should provide us with a variety of insights into one of the most exciting races for the highest elected office in the land.

# Chapter 3

# Primary Television Spots

People accuse me of offering big ideas that they say are risky. I say the real risk is not doing the things I've set out to do in this campaign. The real risk is doing nothing about gun control. The real risk is doing nothing about reducing child poverty. The real risk is ignoring the people who don't have health care, and those who are middle class and are having a difficult time paying for their health care. That's the real risk in America. If we can't afford to do these now, when will we ever be able to do them? If not now, when? If not us, who? (Bradley, "Leadership," 2000)

He's taken on the worst polluters in America and become a leading voice for clean air, clean water, and the environment. Al Gore. He fought efforts to cut Medicare and is the only candidate for President committed to protecting Medicare and preserving Medicaid. He's taken on the HMOs and big drug companies fighting for a Patients' Bill of Rights and more affordable prescription drugs. The experience to do the job. Al Gore. Fighting for us. (Gore, "Fighter," 2000)

There's a debate in New Hampshire on taxes critical to America. We can cut taxes for working families and protect Social security but it takes leadership. Washington politicians want to keep your money in Washington. Not me. I believe taxes are too high. The people of New Hampshire understand that you deserve your money back and that cutting taxes keeps the economy growing. You settle the debate: tax cuts or bigger government. (Bush, "Debate," 2000)

Announcer: This is George Bush's ad promising America he'd run a positive campaign.
Bush: I want to run a campaign that is hopeful and optimistic and very positive.

33

Announcer: This is George Bush shaking hands with John McCain, promising not to run a negative campaign. This is George Bush's new negative ad, attacking John McCain and distorting his position. Do we really want another politician in the White House American can't trust? (McCain, "Can't Trust," 2000)

Keyes: If we really want to see the change in the Social Security, if you really want to see the changes in the tax system that restore our control, if you really want to get back control of the schools so that parents can once again have the role they ought to have in the education of their children. We won't win any of these battles until we win the battle for the moral future of the country.
Announcer: On election day, vote your conscience. Vote Alan Keyes for a better America. (Keyes, "Moral Future," 2000)

Politicians shouldn't raid the Social Security Trust Fund. They shouldn't be stealing from it, plundering it. That belongs to the American people. You know, if you put a pot of honey in a forest, bears are going to come along and put their paws in it. If you put a pot of money in Washington, politicians are gonna come along and put their paws on it. And that's why we should phase in a new system where the bulk of your payroll tax, your Social Security tax, goes directing into your own retirement account. (Forbes, "Honey Pot," 2000)

The 2000 presidential campaign was a hotbed of television spot activity. Because both parties experienced contested nominations, the airwaves were filled with short messages eager to tell voters the pros (of the sponsoring candidate) and the cons (of their opponents). This chapter will review the literature on presidential primary television spots, present the results of our analysis of the 2000 versions of these messages, and discuss the implications of those findings.

## Literature Review

We begin by reviewing the literature on primary television advertising. We divide this work into two areas: the functions (acclaims, attacks, defenses; or positive and negative) and the topics (policy/issues, character/image) of these commercials.

### Functions of Primary Television Spots

One common topic in the literature is the function of primary television ads. Research prior to the development of the Functional Theory of Political Campaign Discourse ignored defenses, focusing only on negative and positive ads (Trent & Friedenberg, 2000, acknowledge the existence of defense ads, but they do not study them). Kaid and Ballotti (1991), who analyzed 1,089 primary advertisements, found that 18 percent of the ads from 1968 to 1988 were negative. West (1993), studying 262 primary spots and 135 general ads, reported that primary spots were more negative (55 percent) than general election ads (52 percent) between 1952 and 1992. Benoit (1999), who analyzed 765 primary and 828 general spots, found that primary spots were more positive than general spots: acclaims were 68 percent and 60 percent, attacks were 31 percent and 39 percent respectively (defenses were 1 percent of utterances in both phases of the campaign).

One difference in these studies is that most research uses the entire spot as the unit of analysis, which may be misleading. Kaid and Johnston (1991) explain that "Our method of dichotomizing the sample into positive and negative ads by determining a dominant focus on the candidate or his opponent is useful for analysis but may understate the amount of negative information about an opponent present even in a positive ad" (p. 62). Benoit's method uses themes as the unit of analysis, which permits a finer grained description of the content of spots. Estimates of the percentage of attacks in primary spots ranges from 31 percent (Benoit, 1999) to 18 percent (Kaid & Ballotti, 1991) to 55 percent (West, 1993). Our bias is obvious, but we prefer Benoit's use of themes, rather than entire spots, as the unit of analysis,[1] and Benoit's sample has clear advantages over that used by West.[2]

Some studies focused on television spots in particular primary campaigns. Payne, Marlier, and Baukus (1989) found that 11 percent of the 1988 primary ads were negative. Kaid (1994) found that about 17 percent of the Republican and Democratic primary ads in 1992 were negative. Kaid (1998) reported that 21 percent of the primary spots in 1996 were negative. Benoit, Blaney, and Pier (1998) found that 58 percent of the themes in 1996 primary ads were acclaims (positive), 40 percent were attacks, and 2 percent were defenses. While the percentages vary, as one might expect when considering different campaigns, this research suggests that primary ads do not consist predominantly of attacks (11 percent-40 percent). Benoit (1999) presents evidence that primary television spots have gradually become more negative over time. Our current study will provide data on the functions of the primary television spots in the 2000 campaign.

## Topics of Primary Television Spots

The ideas in presidential primary spots can also be categorized as addressing policy (issues) or character (image). Kaid and Ballotti (1991) analyzed 1089 presidential primary ads from 1968 to 1988, finding that 48 percent concerned issues and 32 percent images. West (1993) analyzed 150 presidential spots from 1972 to 1992, reporting that policy appeals were over twice as prominent in primaries (65 percent) than character (30 percent of ads; the remainder of the ads concerned the campaign and parties). Benoit's (1999) analysis of primary spots from 1952 to 1996 indicated that 52 percent concerned policy and 48 percent addressed character. He reported a trend, beginning in 1980, toward more emphasis of policy than character. He also subdivided each of these two topics (policy, character) into three subtopics. Of the policy themes, 40 percent concerned past deeds, 17 percent were (comparatively specific) future plans, and 43 percent were general goals. Character utterances consisted of 51 percent personal qualities, 29 percent leadership ability, and 20 percent ideals. Thus, candidates in primary campaign devote considerable time to discussing both policy (issues) and character (image).

Some studies focused on the television commercials in particular primary campaigns. Kaid (1994) found that the 1992 Republican and Democratic primaries stressed image more than issues: 59 percent of the television advertisements concerned image and 24 percent addressed issues. Kaid (1998) reported that 1996 primary spots were skewed to issues, 59 percent to 41 percent. Benoit, Blaney, and Pier (1998), however, found that 52 percent of the themes in 1996 Republican primary spots concerned character (image), while 48 percent concern issues. The discrepancy between their results and Kaid's could stem from either the difference in their procedures (coding entire spots, coding themes) or from the fact that Kaid seems to separate negative spots from image and issue spots. Still, these studies are unanimous in reporting that primary spots devote considerable attention to both policy (issues) and character (image), perhaps with the mix varying somewhat from campaign to campaign.

# Results

We located 145 primary spots: 63 Democratic and 82 Republican. We obtained

Table 3.1. Distribution of Primary Television Spots in the Sample

| | Number of Spots |
|---|---|
| Bradley | 36 |
| Gore | 27 |
| Democrat | 63 |
| Bauer | 4 |
| Bush | 35 |
| Forbes | 20 |
| Keyes | 5 |
| McCain | 18 |
| Republican | 82 |
| Total | 145 |

these ads from candidate websites, videotaped from C-SPAN, videotapes obtained from New Hampshire and Iowa, newspaper ad watches, and a tape purchased from Patrick Devlin. The distribution of spots among the candidates is described in Table 3.1. We will begin with the functions of these spots, then discuss target of attacks, then policy, forms of policy and character, and end with a consideration of the issues addressed in these messages.

## Functions of Primary Television Spots

These television spots devoted the overwhelming majority of their themes (86 percent) to acclaims. For example, Gore told voters that "We need to protect our oceans and beaches, and if elected president, I'll do that" ("Oceans"), declaring that he would work to protect the environment. Forbes acclaimed his policy on taxes, Social Security, and abortion: "I will eliminate the current tax code and institute the flat tax. I will preserve Social Security for older Americans and offer a new system for working Americans. I will not be apologetic about restoring respect for human life" ("United"). These three policy positions might appeal to many Republicans. These results are displayed in Table 3.2.

Attacks were much less common in these messages, accounting for 13 percent of the themes in these messages. Bush offered this attack on the establishment: "Washington politicians want to keep your money in Washington." This utterance takes for granted the Republican premise that the government spends too much of our money. Bradley attacked the establishment as beholden to special interests:

Table 3.2. Functions of 2000 Primary Television Spots

|            | Acclaims   | Attacks    | Defenses   |
|------------|-----------|------------|------------|
| Bradley    | 150 (84%) | 28 (16%)   | 1 (0.5%)   |
| Gore       | 172 (91%) | 16 (9%)    | 0          |
| Democrat   | 332 (88%) | 44 (12%)   | 1 (0.3%)   |
| Bauer      | 19 (86%)  | 3 (14%)    | 0          |
| Bush       | 224 (87%) | 30 (12%)   | 4 (1%)     |
| Forbes     | 109 (79%) | 29 (21%)   | 0          |
| Keyes      | 23 (85%)  | 4 (15%)    | 0          |
| McCain     | 121 (85%) | 19 (13%)   | 2 (1%)     |
| Republican | 496 (84%) | 85 (15%)   | 6 (1%)     |
| Total      | 828 (86%) | 129 (13%)  | 7 (1%)     |

"We have to liberate our government from the encrusted control of special interests" ("Liberate"). This is not a state of affairs that bodes well for America's citizens. Thus, these advertisements included a variety of attacks.

Defenses were relatively uncommon, comprising 1 percent of the themes in these television spots. For instance, Bush defended against two accusations in this passage: "One of my opponents says my tax cut for America is too big, too bold. Another has raised questions about my record. They're both wrong" ("Record"). This utterance is a clear example of simple denial. McCain also defended against attacks from Bush in this passage: "Mr. Bush's attacks are wrong: My plan cuts taxes, secures social security, pays down the debt. There is no tax increase" ("Bush Negative"). This is another example of simple denial. These passages illustrate the use of defense in these spots.

The Democratic spots were slightly more positive than Republican spots (88 percent to 85 percent), with correspondingly more Republican attacks (14 percent to 12 percent). However, a *chi-square* calculated on Republicans' versus Democrats' use of acclaims and attacks (there were too few defenses to include) was not significant ($\chi^2[df=1]=1.5$, *ns*).

Gore's spots were more positive than Bradley's (91 percent, 84 percent), whereas Bradley attacked more than Gore (16 percent, 9 percent). This difference was significant ($\chi^2[df=1]=4.5$, $p < .05$; again, defenses were excluded from the calculation). There were no significant differences in the distribution of acclaims and attacks among the Republican candidates ($\chi^2[df=4]=6.3$, *ns*). Forbes had the largest percentage of attacks at 21 percent but even he was not exceptionally negative in the 2000 campaign.

The current spots were significantly more positive than those from the 1996 primary television campaign ($\chi^2[df=1]=157.6$, $p < .001$). We also have data from one candidate who ran in the last two campaigns: In 1996 43 percent of Forbes' television spot utterances were attacks (Benoit, Blaney, & Pier, 1998) whereas in 2000 only 21 percent of the themes in Forbes's ads were attacks, so he had fewer than half as many attacks in the 2000 campaign as in 1996.

## Target of Attack in Primary Television Spots

The Democrats attacked Republicans twice as often as they attacked each other; on the other hand, Republicans devoted 44 percent of their attacks to each other and only 7 percent to Democrats (see Tables 3.3 and 3.4). Both parties directed a substantial portion of their attacks to the establishment (Democrats: 59 percent; Republicans: 49 percent). A *chi-square* reveals that the two parties differed significantly in target of attack ($\chi^2[df=2]=16.8$, $p < .001$).

For example, Gore criticized the private school vouchers endorsed by some Republicans: "I think it would be a big mistake to drain money away from our public schools with vouchers that give public money to private schools. Private

Table 3.3 Target of Attacks in 2000 Democratic Primary Television Spots

|  | Bradley | Gore | Republicans | SQ |
|---|---|---|---|---|
| Bradley | – | 5 | 0 | 23 |
| Gore | 1 | – | 12 | 3 |
|  | 1 (17%) | 5 (83%) |  |  |
| Total | 6 (14%) | | 12 (27%) | 26 (59%) |

schools are fine. But not with money that's already designated for the 90 percent of the American children who go to public schools" ("Vouchers"). This excerpt from a Forbes spot attacked a member of his own party: "George W. Bush *says* he wants a positive campaign. Then why are Bush's liberal supporters [Republican Leadership Council] running this negative ad attacking Steve Forbes?" ("Stop Attack Ads"). Gary Bauer managed to attack both Democrats and Republicans in this passage: "Sadly, President Clinton and even some of my Republican opponents have put foreign trade ahead of our national security" ("China Threat"). Another Forbes ad attacked the establishment here: "Current law has raised the age of eligibility for millions of Americans from 65 to 67" ("Broken Promises").

Not surprisingly, the two front-runners on the Republican side (Bush and McCain) were the recipients of most attacks by Republicans on Republicans, 57 percent and 43 percent respectively. There were far more attacks on themselves (twenty-one, sixteen) than on the Democrats (six) in these (Republican) spots. There were also a number of attacks on the status quo, which presumably included

Table 3.4. Target of Attacks in 2000 Republican Primary Television Spots

|  | Bauer | Bush | Forbes | Keyes | McCain | Dems | SQ |
|---|---|---|---|---|---|---|---|
| Bauer | – |  | 0 | 0 | 0 | 3 | 0 |
| Bush | 0 | – | 0 | 0 | 16 | 3 | 11 |
| Forbes | 0 | 10 | – | 0 | 0 | 0 | 19 |
| Keyes | 0 | 0 | 0 | – | 0 | 0 | 4 |
| McCain | 0 | 11 | 0 | 0 | – | 0 | 8 |
|  | 0 | 21 (57%) | 0 | 0 | 16 (43%) |  |  |
| Total |  | | 37 (44%) | | | 6 (7%) | 42 (49%) |

the Democrats. Not surprisingly, two outsiders (Forbes, who has never held elective office, and former Senator Bradley, who does not currently hold elective office) frequently attacked the establishment.

Gore devoted most of his attacks (75 percent) to the Republicans and completely refrained from attacking Bradley in these spots. Bradley, who trailed Gore, attacked Gore several times while not attacking the Republicans explicitly (although he also directed many of his attacks to the status quo, which could have included Gore). Bush leveled the most attacks at McCain, and McCain (closely followed by Forbes) was the Republican who attacked Bush most frequently. However, there were not enough instances of attack to calculate separate *chi-squares* on targets of attack in Democratic or Republican spots.

## Topics of Primary Television Spots

These television spots focused 56 percent of their comments on policy (see Table 3.5). For instance, Bush explained that "My top priorities will be to preserve Social Security and Medicare, and to strengthen education and our military" ("Top Priorities"). These comments clearly concern his policy agenda. Keyes listed several reasons to vote for him in this television advertisement: "If we really want to see the change in the Social Security, if you really want to see the changes in the tax system that restore our control, if you really want to get back control of the

3.5. Topics of 2000 Primary Television Spots

|  | Policy | Character |
| --- | --- | --- |
| Bradley | 107 (57%) | 81 (43%) |
| Gore | 123 (69%) | 55 (31%) |
| Democrat | 230 (63%) | 136 (37%) |
| Bauer | 13 (59%) | 9 (41%) |
| Bush | 164 (65%) | 90 (35%) |
| Forbes | 51 (37%) | 87 (63%) |
| Keyes | 23 (85%) | 4 (15%) |
| McCain | 52 (37%) | 88 (63%) |
| Republican | 303 (52%) | 278 (48%) |
| Total | 533 (56%) | 414 (44%) |

The Democrats in 2000 allocated more comments to policy than the Republicans ($\chi^2[df=1]=10.4, p < .01$).

schools so that parents can once again have the role they ought to have in the education of their children" ("Moral Future"). Keyes discussed three subjects in this excerpt that are all policy topics: Social Security, taxation, and education. Thus, these commercials spoke frequently about policy.

Character was also addressed in 44 percent of the utterances in these spots. Ordinary citizens described some of Steve Forbes's laudable personal qualities: "He's honest. He always gives a straight answer" ("Character"). Voters were told that "John McCain will bring back honor to the Oval Office" ("Duty, Honor, Country"), another acclaim that addressed character. McCain (63 percent) and Forbes (63 percent) were the only candidates who devoted more utterances to character than policy.

Gore's television advertisements focused more on policy than Bradley's commercials ($\chi^2[df=1]=5.8$, $p < .025$). There was a significant difference in the topics of the Republican advertisements as well ($\chi^2[df=4]=53.3$, $p < .001$). Inspection of Table 3.5 reveals that Bauer, Bush, and Keyes devoted more utterances to policy while Forbes and McCain stressed character. Finally, the ads in 2000 (56 percent) concentrated more on policy than primary ads from 1996 (48 percent; $\chi^2[df=1]=9.6$, $p < .01$).

## Forms of Policy and Character in Primary Television Spots

The proportion of comments devoted to the three forms of policy utterances in 2000 primary television spots were: past deeds: 21 percent; future plans: 17 percent; and general goals: 62 percent (see Table 3.6). For example, Bush acclaimed his past deeds as governor of Texas in this spot: "As Governor he signed the two largest tax cuts in Texas history. He reduced the growth of state govern-ment spending to the lowest in forty years" ("Fresh Start"). Gore boasted that he "cast the tie-breaking vote to keep guns away from criminals" ("Fight for Principle"), an example of a past deed on the issue of gun control. An example of an utterance addressing future plans can be found in a Bush spot: "If you're a family of four under my plan—making $50,000 a year in the state of New Hampshire you get a fifty percent tax cut" ("Real Time A"). This utterance discussed a means to an end or a specific proposal (a future plan) rather than a general goal. Similarly, Bradley had developed future plans to offer voters: "And that's why I've proposed training and placing 60,000 new teachers a year for the next 10 years" ("Education"). Bradley's acclaim is an example of a proposal concerning education policy. Gore outlined several general goals in this excerpt: "His cause is working families, affordable prescription drugs, improved health care for every American, a cleaner environment, education reform" ("Reporter"). Because he did not address the means of achieving these ends, this utterance represents a general goal rather than a future plan. McCain acclaims his general goals in this comment: "I'll begin to pay down the national debt so we don't

Table 3.6. Forms of Policy and Character in 2000 Primary Television Spots

| | Policy | | | | | | Character | | | | | |
| --- | --- | --- | --- | --- | --- | --- | --- | --- | --- | --- | --- | --- |
| | Past Deeds* | | Future Plans | | General Goals | | Personal Qualities | | Leadership | | Ideals | |
| Bradley | 12 | 13 | 22 | 0 | 52 | 6 | 48 | 10 | 7 | 1 | 5 | 0 |
| Gore | 16 | 5 | 13 | 6 | 92 | 1 | 34 | 3 | 12 | 1 | 5 | 0 |
| Dem | 28 | 18 | 35 | 6 | 144 | 7 | 82 | 13 | 19 | 2 | 10 | 0 |
| | 46 (19%) | | 41 (17%) | | 151 (63%) | | 95 (75%) | | 21 (17%) | | 10 (8%) | |
| Bauer | 3 | 2 | 2 | 0 | 5 | 1 | 1 | 0 | 0 | 0 | 8 | 0 |
| Bush | 31 | 7 | 25 | 6 | 89 | 6 | 32 | 10 | 15 | 0 | 32 | 1 |
| Forbes | 1 | 9 | 9 | 1 | 25 | 5 | 45 | 12 | 12 | 0 | 16 | 2 |
| Keyes | 0 | 1 | 0 | 0 | 10 | 0 | 0 | 0 | 0 | 0 | 13 | 3 |
| McCain | 3 | 7 | 3 | 3 | 36 | 0 | 54 | 9 | 14 | 0 | 11 | 0 |
| Repub | 38 | 26 | 39 | 10 | 165 | 12 | 132 | 31 | 41 | 0 | 80 | 6 |
| | 64 (22%) | | 49 (17%) | | 177 (61%) | | 163 (56%) | | 41 (14%) | | 86 (30%) | |
| | 66 | 44 | 74 | 16 | 309 | 19 | 214 | 44 | 60 | 2 | 90 | 6 |
| Total | 110 (21%) | | 90 (17%) | | 328 (62%) | | 258 (63%) | | 62 (15%) | | 96 (23%) | |

*Acclaims/attacks.

threaten the future of our children" ("Every Dime"). Again, this remark offered voters a desirable end without specifying a means of accomplishing that end. Thus, each of the three forms of policy occurred repeatedly in these commercials. There was no difference in the distribution of the forms of policy addressed in Republican and Democratic primary advertisements ($\chi^2[df=2]=0.6$, ns).

There was no significant difference between the allocation of policy comments by Bradley and Gore ($\chi^2[df=2]=5.6$, ns) or among the Republicans ($\chi^2[df=8]=9.2$, ns). However, the TV spots in our sample differ significantly from 1996 primary spots ($\chi^2[df=2]=118.6$, $p < .001$). The 2000 spots made greater use of past deeds (15 percent to 48 percent) but employed fewer general goals (51 percent to 23 percent) and fewer future plans (34 percent to 29 percent) in 2000 than in 1996.

Character remarks were distributed in this manner in these spots: personal qualities: 63 percent; leadership ability: 15 percent; ideals: 23 percent. For example, an endorsement from Congressman Sanford proclaimed that "John McCain has the character and courage to make us proud, again" ("Proud Again"), acclaiming his personal qualities. Jim Frush talked about Gore's character, based on his experience mountain-climbing with the vice president: "Strength of character, perseverance, grace under pressure—these are qualities you look for in a mountaineer—they're even better in a President" ("Frush"). Character, perseverance, and grace are desirable qualities. This spot for John McCain acclaimed his unique leadership qualifications: "There's only one man running for President who knows the military and understands the world. John McCain. As a navy pilot and POW he's seen the horrors of war. As a Senator, he's already one of the nation's leaders in knowing how to keep the peace" ("Commander"). Forbes had not served in elective office, but a spot for him argued that his business acumen would serve him well as *leader* of the free world: "With Steve as chief executive, *Forbes* has become the foremost business magazine in the world" ("Bio"). Ads for Bush touted his ideals, his "compassionate conservative vision." The conservative ideology might appeal to Republican voters (and compassion concerns his character). See Table 3.6.

Democratic spots devote a larger percentage of themes to personal qualities (75 percent, 56 percent), about the same percentage to leadership ability (17 percent, 14 percent), and a smaller percent of utterances to ideals than Republican spots (8 percent, 30 percent). A *chi-square* computed on forms of character and political party was significant ($\chi^2[df=2]=12.2, p < .01$).

There was no significant difference between the distribution of character comments by Bradley and Gore ($\chi^2[df=2]=3.9, ns$). On the other hand, there was a significant difference in the distribution of character comments by the Republican candidates ($\chi^2[df=8]=72.8, p < .001$). Inspection of the data in Table 3.6 reveals that two candidates devoted most of their utterances to ideals: Bauer and Keyes. McCain (72 percent), Forbes (66 percent), and Bush (47 percent) used personal qualities more than any other form of character utterance. Leadership ability was only addressed by Bush (17 percent), McCain (16 percent), and Forbes (14 percent). Analysis of forms of character in 1996 and 2000 spots reveals that the current spots differ significantly in their character emphasis from earlier spots ($\chi^2[df=2]=38.8, p < .001$). The percent of remarks allocated to personal qualities increased (43 percent to 63 percent), while the proportion of ideals decreased (44 percent to 23 percent). The frequency of leadership utterances remained about the same (13 percent, 15 percent).

## Issues Addressed in Primary Television Spots

Education was a frequent topic of discussion in these ads (see Tables 3.7 and 3.8). For example, Bush declared that:

We should make this solemn commitment: That every child will be educated. As President, I will give state and local school districts more authority and flexibility and encourage them to measure results for every child. I will challenge failure with charters and choice. And I will change Head Start to teach our youngest children phonics and reading. Every child must be educated, because there are no second rate children and no second rate dreams.

There is no mistaking the subject matter of this passage from Bush. Another topic, more frequent for the Republicans, was taxation. McCain illustrated this topic when he declared that "I'll target the large tax cuts to those who need it most, America's middle-class working families." The Republicans' spots also frequently discussed Social Security. Forbes addressed this topic in this television spot:

I propose removing all the taxes and penalties on Social Security benefits because you've already paid the tax during your working life. And for those about to go on the system, you keep the old system because they've made lifetime decisions based on those promises. But for younger people, we'll give you a choice. What I want to do is phase in a new system where most of your Social Security taxes will be deposited directly into your own private account. The money belongs to you. The government can't touch it.

Crime and drugs was neglected in comparison. Bush did acclaim this accomplishment: "cut juvenile crime 38 percent." Health care was a frequent topic for the Democrats. For instance, Gore explained that:

I think it's just unconscionable at a time when we have the strongest economy in history, we're the wealthiest nation on earth, to have millions and millions of

Table 3.7. Issues Addressed in Democratic 2000 Primary Television Spots

|  | Poll | Bradley | Gore |
|---|---|---|---|
| Education | 23 | 8 | 31 |
| Health Care | 19 | 47 | 32 |
| Soc. Security | 13 | 0 | 3 |
| Crime/Drugs | 12 | 10 | 9 |
| Taxes | 5 | 4 | 0 |
| Medicare | 4 | 5 | 17 |
| Foreign Affairs | 2 | 0 | 5 |
| Other | – | 33 | 26 |
| Spearman $\rho$ |  | .17, ns | .31, ns |

Table 3.8. Issues Addressed in Republican 2000 Primary Television Spots

|  | Poll | Bauer | Bush | Forbes | Keyes | McCain |
|---|---|---|---|---|---|---|
| Education | 19 | 1 | 58 | 3 | 3 | 1 |
| Taxes | 11 | 2 | 58 | 17 | 8 | 10 |
| Soc. Security | 9 | 1 | 13 | 18 | 1 | 9 |
| Crime/Drugs | 8 | 0 | 2 | 0 | 1 | 0 |
| Health Care | 8 | 0 | 4 | 3 | 0 | 0 |
| Foreign Affairs | 7 | 4 | 2 | 0 | 0 | 1 |
| Medicare | 5 | 0 | 1 | 0 | 0 | 0 |
| Other | – | 5 | 26 | 10 | 10 | 31 |
| Spearman $\rho$ |  | -.15, ns | .61, ns | .40, ns | .23, ns | .06, ns |

Enslow (1999)

> children who have no health care coverage at all. We ought to change that. And we ought to start by making a commitment to have affordable, high quality health care for every child in America before the end of the next president's term.

This goal clearly pertains to health care. Foreign affairs was another topic that was infrequently discussed in these primary spots. Gore also addressed this issue: "The Republican Senate has rejected the Nuclear Test Ban Treaty signed by 154 nations. This vote goes against the tide of history and the advice of former Chairmen of the Joint Chiefs of Staff from the Clinton, Bush, Reagan and Carter administrations. I believe in my heart this vote does not speak for the American people." Finally, Medicare was discussed by the Democrats in places. This excerpt from Bradley shows how this topic was addressed:

> Now, I served on the Senate Finance Committee for eighteen years, and I fought time and time again, and successfully protected Medicare from premium increases or from cuts. As president, I'd do the same. In fact, not only do I not cut back on Medicare, but we expand Medicare. What we do is provide a drug benefit that will allow senior citizens to have access to life-saving drugs.

So, these primary spot messages encompassed a variety of issue topics.

Table 3.7 reveals that Bradley devoted a large portion of his comments to one topic, health care. Gore devoted a larger portion of his utterances to the two top issues: education and healthcare. There was no significant correlation between the rank ordering of issue topics to voters and the frequency with which Bradley ($\rho = .17$) or Gore ($\rho = .31$) discussed these topics in their primary television spots.

Three of the Republican candidates discussed only four of the top seven Republican issues (Bauer, Keyes, McCain). Bauer (who had few spots and few policy utterances) devoted the most themes to foreign affairs, the sixth most important issue to Republican voters. Bush frequently discussed the two most important Republican issues: education and taxes. Forbes spent a considerable amount of time on the second and third most important Republican issues: taxes and Social Security. Keyes (another candidate with relative few spots and policy remarks) frequently addressed the top two issues. McCain, like Forbes, spent a fair amount of time on taxes and Social Security. None of the candidates had significant correlations.

## Implications

In many ways, the primary spots from the 2000 campaign resembled earlier primary spots. Acclaims outnumber attacks, which in turn are more common than defenses. This division is quite sensible. As noted earlier, voters say that they do not like mudslinging, so acclaims should outnumber attacks. At times candidates must defend, but there are several reasons to offer few defenses. First, defending against an attack takes them off message, forcing them to address issues that probably favor opponents. Second, the act of responding to an attack may make the candidate appear on the defensive, being reactive rather than proactive. Finally, one must identify the attack in order to defend against it. If some voters have not heard the attack, defending against it may ironically inform them of the candidate's (alleged) weakness. Thus, this division of functions—more acclaims than attacks and more attacks than defenses—is very reasonable.

The Democrats tended not to attack one another: More attacks were directed toward the status quo (59 percent) and the Republicans (27 percent) than to Bradley and Gore (14 percent). Research on general television spots indicates that the most attacks originate with those who trail throughout the campaign. Gore led throughout the primary, so he may have felt no need to devote many attacks to Bradley. Bradley was in a position to attack (he trailed during the primary), but chose not to. Perhaps this was because he wanted to run "A Different Campaign," as many of his ads declared.

The Republicans also attacked the establishment (49 percent) but aimed almost as many attacks at each other (44 percent). The Democrats were rarely targeted in these Republican spots (7 percent). Republican attacks were focused on their immediate opponents: Neither Bauer, nor Forbes, nor Hatch, nor Keyes, nor McCain could run against the Democratic nominee (presumably Gore at this point in the campaign) without first getting past Bush. Thus, Bush was the target of most attacks in these spots, and Bush repeatedly attacked his closest rival, McCain.

Nor surprisingly, those who were not a part of the political establishment (e.g., Forbes, Bradley) level more attacks against the status quo. Bush, too, portrayed himself as an outsider. For example, in the ad "Debate," Bush drew a sharp contrast: "Washington politicians want to keep your money in Washington. Not me." Those who were part of the Washington establishment were less eager to attack it, of course.

Turning to topic, the remarks are divided roughly equally between policy (56 percent) and character (44 percent), which nearly mirrors historical trends (52 percent policy, 48 percent character) in primary spots. Both policy and character are important bases for citizens to make voting decisions. Pomper (1975), for example, observed that in the general election many voters "change their partisan choice from one election to the next, and these changes are most closely related to their positions on the issues and their assessment of the abilities of the candidates" (p. 10). Of course, in primaries voters cannot use party affiliation to decide their vote, because the choice is between two or more candidates from the same party. This should mean that policy and character are even more important determinants of voting behavior in the primary than the general campaign. These candidates offer voters information about both topics in their primary television spots.

Finally, personal qualities were the most common form of character comment in early and current spots. For example, a Bradley ad declared that "Bill Bradley has the character to restore dignity" to the White House. McCain charged that Bush "twists the truth like Clinton" in his ads. Bush, on the other hand, promised to "restore pride in our Presidency" and voters were told that electing Forbes would "restore a sense of decency to the White House." Personal qualities accounted for 63 percent of the character utterances in 2000, above the level in 1996, 43 percent (Benoit, Blaney, & Pier, 1998). This could easily represent a reaction to questions concerning Clinton's character (despite Gore's frantic attempts to disassociate himself from Clinton).

However, there are other differences between early and current primary spots. Current advertisements have fewer attacks than earlier spots. As mentioned earlier, research has established that voters dislike mudslinging (Merritt, 1984; Stewart, 1975). These candidates may have been adapting to voter preferences by curtailing their attacks. In fact, one spot (sponsored by the Republican Leadership Council) explicitly criticized Forbes for being too negative in 1996:

> When Steve Forbes ran for President the first time, I kinda liked him. But then he spent all his money tearing down his opponents. He hurt the Republican Party. After the election, Forbes admitted he spent too much time discussing his opponents' record. But now I hear he's starting with the same negative ads again. That's just going to help the Democrats. Someone needs to tell Mr. Forbes, if you can't say anything nice, don't say anything at all.

Ironically, this spot provoked a counter-attack from Forbes which attacked Bush with guilt by association:

> George W. Bush *says* he wants a positive campaign. Then why are Bush's liberal

supporters running this negative ad attacking Steve Forbes? That's right, Bush supporters are using massive corporate contributions to run this negative ad to benefit George W. Bush. Even John McCain requested they stop, saying it appears you have violated federal election laws. If George W. Bush really opposes negative ads, should he tell his supporters to stop attacking Steve Forbes?

Similarly, Bush reacted harshly to attacks from McCain: "when John McCain compared me to Bill Clinton and said I was untrustworthy, that's over the line." Thus, television spots in the 2000 campaign reinforced voters' unfavorable attitudes toward attacks, and the frequency of attacks dropped sharply between 1996 and 2000.

Another difference in primary television spots is that future plans, general goals, personal qualities, and ideals became more common in 2000 than in earlier campaigns. We consider the increase in future plans to be a positive sign for campaigns: It means candidates are offering more specifics (and fewer vague promises). They are discussing means and not just ends. This means that voters have more information available about what the candidates propose to do if elected. We believe the drop in past deeds is in part due to Gore's reluctance to campaign on the Clinton/Gore record: Bush had over twice as many acclaims on past deeds as Gore.

We would not expect the topics addressed in candidates' television spots to perfectly mirror voter interests. Candidates need to pick a campaign theme that is well suited to each candidate's own background and philosophy and focus on that motif in the campaign. Still, presumably candidates would want to adapt their campaign messages to some extent to voter interests. Neither Democratic candidate's spots correlated with voter interests. The same was true of Bauer, McCain, and Forbes. Keyes' correlation was significant but, given the few spots (five) from him, this result does not seem to be particularly important. However, Bush, who won the nomination, did have a significant correlation (.96). Although we cannot establish causality on the basis of these data, it is interesting that he did a better job adapting his message content to match voter interests.

Thus, this study provides insight into one important campaign message form in the 2000 presidential primary campaign. It also adds to our longitudinal understanding of primary television spots. This analysis will also serve as a useful point of comparison for the general campaign, to compare the primary and general spots of the candidates who win their party's nomination.

# Notes

1. Another difference between these approaches is that Kaid divides spots into three categories—image, issue, and negative—as if negative ads concern neither image nor issue (Benoit, 1999, found that attacking utterances occur on both policy/issue and charac-

ter/image topics).

2. West chose to analyze spots mentioned in Jamieson's (1992) book (for 1952 to 1988) and broadcast on the *CBS Evening News* (for 1992). However, we doubt that Jamieson's purpose was to discuss random or typical television spots. Moreover, West's decision to include spots from 1992 because they were broadcast on the *CBS Evening News* may have been convenient, but it too is questionable because not all ads were nationally broadcast. In fact, West, Kern, Alger, and Goggin (1995) noted that in 1992 "Clinton targeted more expenditures on local markets in selected states. There were also important differences in ads aired in different cities" (p. 288). This means that ads which were broadcast nationally (on the *CBS Evening News*) did not reflect Clinton's (local market) advertising campaign (we believe that Bush and Perot also used some local ads buys in 1992). Thus, West's sample has important limitations and his results, while interesting, are not necessarily indicative of typical advertising.

# Chapter 4

# Primary Debates

Bradley: I could never appoint anybody to the Supreme Court that I thought might turn the clock back on civil rights. I think of affirmative action, I think of how overblown the criticism is, how true it is to just reach out and try to draw people in. It's the best of what America is. I mean, more people in this country lost their jobs in the 1982 recession because of bad economic mismanagement, than were helped by affirmative action since its inception. I look out there and I say, you know, I think that we've made progress. But I think now things are a little more subtle. It's not the school door being shut. It's not, you know, the overt prohibition of going into a hotel. What it is now, is you can't go to the bank and get a loan. You can't . . . the digital divide. You've got Medicaid; doctors won't accept Medicaid payments. There's a long way to go and until we get to that day, we still need affirmative actions.

Gore: I believe that we need vigorous enforcement of the civil rights laws. I believe that we need to understand and operate on the assumption that we should have prenatal care, high-quality child care, universal preschool, adequate child nutrition, raise the minimum wage a dollar an hour, expand the earned income tax credit, give access to higher education for every young person in this country, bring the crime rate down even further—much further—in our neighborhoods, and care for every single child in this country. Bring our people together with affirmative action, civil rights enforcement and with leadership to put civil rights right at the top of our national agenda. (Democratic Primary Debate, January 17, 2000, Des Moines, Iowa)

Keyes: I think it's critically important that we understand that if we want to be able to allocate our medical dollars to reflect the right kind of priorities, then we've got to take an approach that helps people to maximize the cost effectiveness of the medical care they receive. We shouldn't have government and other bureaucracies dictating to people who are trying to act responsibly. But instead, we need to empower them, through programs that voucherize the government system, that give people medical savings accounts, that allow greater choice on the part of individuals and families, allow them to make the decisions that can help us to keep the costs down. And by making better use of our medical dollars, we will then be able to allocate those dollars with priority to the things that families really can't handle for themselves. And that means giving top priority to the kind of long-term care that can have a catastrophic effect on the family budget. If we take the right approach, people will be armed to keep the costs down, and our medical dollars can be used more effectively to help people meet those needs, that they can't meet for themselves.

McCain: All of the proposals that my colleagues have mentioned are all good, including tax deductions for those who itemize, as well as those who don't— medical savings accounts, et cetera. But I want to talk about a special group of Americans that may not be able to do all these things, and that's our World War II veterans, our greatest generation. Thanks to Tom Brokaw's book, "The Greatest Generation," thanks to the movie "Saving Private Ryan," Americans are beginning to appreciate the service and sacrifice of these brave Americans who did make the world safe for democracy. They're leaving us at 30,000 a month. We promised them . . . we promised them . . . health care and benefits when we asked them to go out and serve and sacrifice. We're not doing that, my friends. They deserve the health care benefits that we promise them. And I . . . as I'm on this book tour for the book I wrote, and I see these World War II veterans, they deserve far better from they're getting. And this administration is AWOL on this issue.

Forbes: I think the key is putting patients in charge of health care resources again. There is no need for all of these third parties—HMOs, insurers, employers, gatekeepers, government bureaucracies that stand in the way. It's true: If you work for the federal government as a civilian, if you're a member of Congress, you have your choice of several hundred different health care plans. If it's good enough for Congress, it should be good enough for the elderly in America. So that way, if you need long-term care, you can choose a plan that does it. If you need prescriptive medicines, you can choose a plan that does it. And for those on Medicaid, you should be able to have vouchers and coupons and the like, so you make the choice, not where the government tells you to go. This issues also though brings up the life issue. We've talked about and I hope we will talk about the need for keep the pro-life plank in the platform, pro-life judges and pro-life running mates. It also brings up the issue of euthanasia and assisted suicide. We must fight both; they go hand-in-hand.

Bush: The danger in the health care debate is that America falls prey to the idea that the federal government should make all decisions for consumers and the federal government should make all decisions for the provider, that the federal government should ration care. The good news is none of us on this stage support that. The other two candidates running for the Democratic Party sound like they support that. The current issue, as far as the elderly is, there's an agency called HCFA. It's controlled by a 132,000-page document to determine how to allocate and ration Medicare dollars to the seniors. It is a plan that is inefficient. It is a plan that's antiquated. And what our government must do is empower our seniors to be able to make choices for themselves and support premiums for the poorest of seniors. In terms of long-term care for the baby boomers, I think we ought to encourage the purchase of long-term care insurance and allow deductibility of that insurance so that the new—younger generations are able to plan more aptly for when they retire and when they become more elderly. (Republican Primary Debate, January 15, 2001, Des Moines, IA)

The 2000 presidential primary campaign provided the American electorate with the opportunity to learn about and compare the candidates of both parties in several primary debates. During the course of the campaign the Democratic contenders participated in nine televised debates and Republicans had a total of thirteen debate opportunities. Both parties had contested primary elections and the Republican party had a large number of presidential hopefuls. Therefore, the primary debates became an important tool for the candidates to clarify their platforms for the American public. This chapter will review the literature on presidential primary debates, present the results of our analysis of the 2000 Democratic and Republican primary debates, and discuss the implications of those findings.

## Literature Review

Not only were the primary debates an important part of the 2000 election, they have historically been a part of the political landscape and are becoming increasingly central to the process (Hellweg, Pfau, & Brydon, 1992). The first primary debate, nationally broadcast on radio, dates back to 1948 in the contest between Stassen and Dewey (Best & Hubbard, 2000; Davis, 1997; Kendall, 2000). Since the advent of televised debates, primary debates have become an integral part of the presidential nominating process (Davis, 1997). Although some scholars argue the effects of watching debates are negligible (Jamieson & Birdsell, 1988; Swerdlow, 1984), Hellweg, Pfau, and Brydon (1992) argue that primary debates can be instrumental in developing voter perceptions about candidates. In fact, because voters have less information about primary candidates, primary debates may be more influential than general debates.

There is a relative dearth of research done on presidential primary debates. However, some studies indicate that those who watch primary debates learn more about a candidate's position, and thereby may impact voting decisions (Benoit & Stephenson, 2003; Benoit, McKinney, & Stephenson, 2002; Best & Hubbard, 2000; Lanoue & Schrott, 1989; Pfau, 1987; Yawn, Ellsworth, Beatty, & Kahn, 1998). In addition, several scholars have argued that debates have directly affected candidate success such as Jimmy Carter in 1976 (Martel, 1983), the primary debates held in Illinois, Pennsylvania, and New York in 1984 (Orren, 1985) and the Hart/Jackson debates of 1984 (Pfau, 1987). A few studies have taken a critical approach to analyzing the primary debates (Berquist, 1960; Blankenship, Fine, & Davis, 1983; Murphy, 1992; Ray, 1961; Stelzner, 1971) while others have looked at debate format (Kane, 1987; Pfau, 1984, 1988). However, none of these studies examined the functions of primary debates.

Hellweg and Phillips (1981) conducted a content analysis of the 1980 Houston Republican primary debate. By looking at turns in the debate they concluded that most candidate utterances discussed policy, that Bush attacked more than Reagan, and that both included evidence, emotional appeals, and historical references. Benoit, Blaney, and Pier (1998) examined three 1996 primary debates using the Functional Theory of Campaign Discourse. They found that acclaims were most frequent (54 percent) followed by attacks (38 percent) and defenses (9 percent). In addition, they found that policy (58 percent) was discussed more than character (42 percent). Although scholars have addressed the importance of the primary debates, the research on the nature of presidential debates has just begun to scratch the surface. Therefore, in this chapter we continue to contribute to a greater body of knowledge about the nature of the primary debate.

# Results

We analyzed all twenty-two debates from the 2000 presidential primary, nine Democratic debates and thirteen Republican debates. The transcripts were obtained from the CNN transcripts via Lexis-Nexis. First we will discuss the functions of these primary debates, then discuss target of attacks, followed by policy and character, forms of policy and character and finally we will discuss the issues addressed in these debates. Results from the Democratic primary debates will be discussed first, followed by the Republican primary debates, and finally, the results from the Democratic and Republican primary debates will be compared and contrasted.

## Functions of 2000 Primary Debates

The majority of the themes in the Democratic debates were acclaims (76 percent). For example, Gore acclaimed, "I will appoint justices to that court who understand and reflect in their decisions the philosophy that our Constitution is a living and breathing document" (January 17, Des Moines). In this passage Gore addresses how he will pick Supreme Court justices by acclaiming his method of selection. Bradley also provided us with an example of an acclaim in the December 17, 1999, debate in New Hampshire, "In my case, what I want to get done is increase the

Table 4.1. Functions of 2000 Primary Debates

|  | Acclaims | Attacks | Defenses |
|---|---|---|---|
| Bradley | 639 (74%) | 179 (21%) | 42 (5%) |
| Gore | 776 (78%) | 178 (18%) | 42 (4%) |
| Democrats | 1415 (76%) | 357 (19%) | 84 (5%) |
| Bauer | 266 (65%) | 143 (35%) | 1 (.25%) |
| Bush | 615 (82%) | 91 (12%) | 41 (6%) |
| Forbes | 392 (66%) | 200 (34%) | 3 (.5%) |
| Hatch | 326 (80%) | 77 (19%) | 3 (.7%) |
| Keyes | 447 (65%) | 231 (34%) | 8 (1%) |
| McCain | 560 (70%) | 219 (27%) | 19 (3%) |
| Republicans | 2606 (72%) | 961 (26%) | 75 (2%) |
| Total | 4021 (73%) | 1318 (24%) | 159 (3%) |

number of Americans with health care." In this excerpt Bradley clearly identified a policy goal that he thought was important to the electorate thereby presenting himself to the audience in a positive light. These results are displayed in Table 4.1.

Attack messages accounted for 21 percent of the themes in the Democratic primary debates. Bradley uttered the following attack against Gore, "Al said he's supported it for 20 years. Well, nothing's happened" (January 8, Des Moines). In this excerpt Bradley attacked Al Gore for not passing significant campaign finance reform legislation. Gore also engaged in attacking during the primary debates: "There are seven million disabled Americans who rely on Medicaid, many of them to get out of bed each morning—hold on one second. Half of the people with AIDS and two-thirds of all the seniors in nursing homes rely on Medicaid. He eliminates it, and he doesn't save a penny for Medicare" (December 19, 1999). This passage clearly criticizes Bradley's policy proposals. In another part of the debate Gore critiqued Bradley's approach to Medicare and Medicaid.

Although not frequent, defenses (5 percent) did occur in the Democratic primary debates. An example of defense was provided in the New Hampshire primary (January 5) by Gore: "Let me just say that independent analysis, including at the Emory School of Public Health, Marty Feldstein, have showed that we get just about the same amount of people." This statement was a response by Al Gore to an allegation made by Bradley that Gore's health plan only covered seven million people while Bradley's covered thirty million. In the same debate, Bradley responded to an attack by Gore when he stated, "Al is saying all the time about

$150 cap. That's not a cap. It's a weighted average. In some places it will be more, in some places it will be less." In this passage Bradley defended himself against an attack by Gore which criticized Bradley's health plan. There were no significant differences between Gore and Bradley and their use of acclaims, attacks, and defenses ($\chi^2[df=2]=3.3$, $ns$).

The messages in the Republican primary debates were mostly acclaims (72 percent). These results are displayed in Table 4.1. Forbes provided an example of an acclaim in the New Hampshire debate (October 28, 1999) when he stated, "As a father of five daughters, and my wife Sabina is here tonight, obviously I have a keen interest in clean water, a good environment, clean air." Here we see Forbes acclaiming his policies, or attitudes, concerning the environment (while mentioning that he is a family man). In the same debate Keyes offered an example of acclaiming as well when he stated, "The issue is the income tax itself. I am an abolitionist—shouldn't surprise you." Here Keyes boasted of his particular stance of the issue of income tax.

Attacks were also used in the Republican primary debates (26 percent). During the December 12 debate in New Hampshire Bush offered the following attack, "Those now in their 20s would not be eligible until they're 67 or 68. The author of that? Mr. Steve Forbes." In this statement, Bush attacked a earlier comment made by Forbes that outlined Forbes's plan for Social Security benefits. In the December 2, 1999, debate Bauer also provided an example of an attack when he said, "You know, the culture is more coarse now than it was four or eight years ago, the breakdown of values continues." Specifically, Bauer attacked the general democratic leadership and blamed them for the corruption of values which he argued was reflected in the current state of society.

Defenses were also present in the Republican primary debates (2 percent). For example, in the New Hampshire debate (January 26, 2000) McCain stated, "It is neither the intention nor the implication of the ad. The ad states clearly what I believe." This statement served as a response to an accusation that one of McCain's ads implied that the other candidates were not as qualified as he was to lead the country. Keyes defended himself in the December 6, 1999, debate when he declared, "And I have never suggested that I would use federal leverage to force state and local officials to adopt any particular approach to prayer in schools." This rebuttal was a response to an audience member who questioned Keyes' motivation for education reform.

There were significant differences between the Republican candidates and their use of acclaims, attacks, and defenses ($\chi^2[df=10]=191.2$, $p<.001$). Bauer, Forbes, Keyes, and McCain all acclaimed between 65 percent and 70 percent of their messages whereas Bush (82 percent) and Hatch (80 percent) tended to acclaim at a higher rate. Bauer (35 percent), Forbes (34 percent), and Keyes (34 percent) attacked at a higher rate than the other candidates. Differences between uses of defense strategies are also striking. While most of the candidates used defenses in fewer than 1 percent of their utterances, McCain defended slightly more at 3 percent and Bush engaged in defense messages 6 percent of the time.

Together Republicans and Democrats acclaimed (73 percent) more than they attacked (24 percent) and defended (3 percent). However, there were significant differences between Republicans and Democrats and their use of acclaims, attacks, and defenses ($\chi^2[df=2]=55.78, p<.001$). Although both Democrats (76 percent) and Republicans (72 percent) acclaimed more than they attacked, Republicans (26 percent) attacked more frequently than Democrats (19 percent). In addition, Democrats (5 percent) defended at a higher rate than Republicans (2 percent).

## Targets of Attack in 2000 Primary Debates

Together Bradley and Gore attacked members of their own party (85 percent) more than they attacked members of the Republican party (10 percent) or the status quo (5 percent) (see Table 4.2). For example, in the December 17, 1999, primary debate in New Hampshire, Bradley declared, "The main difference between our programs is that I do provide access to affordable quality health care for all Americans and his plan does not." In the January 5, 2000, New Hampshire debate Gore blasted Bradley with regard to health care: "If you look at the groups that are hurt when Medicaid is eliminated, and they're given instead a little $150 a month voucher for HMOs or healthcare." These passages attempted to highlight differences between the two candidates' health care plans via criticism, or attacking, each other. Republicans were targets of attacks in the Democratic primary debates as well. In the same New Hampshire debate Bradley provided an attack against the Republican party: "And so in this election, what I see this is, can we dream again, can the Democratic Party challenge people to advance together and win against a Republican Party that has a much narrower message?" Again, Bradley provides a contrast in which to couch his attack, this time between the ideals of the Democratic party and those of the Republican party. Gore also attacked his Republican

Table 4.2. Target of Attack in Democratic Primary Debates

| | Own Party (Democrats) | | | Republicans | Status Quo |
|---|---|---|---|---|---|
| | Bradley | Gore | Democrats | | |
| Bradley | – | 141 | 8 | 14 | 16 |
| Gore | 146 | – | 9 | 21 | 2 |
| | 146 | 141 | 17 | | |
| Total | 304 (85%) | | | 35 (10%) | 18 (5%) |

counterparts when he stated, "George Bush, all the Republican candidates, get rid of the entire surplus in the form of risky tax schemes" (December 17, 1999). Like Bradley, Gore attempted to provide a contrast between the candidates for the Republican and Democratic platforms when he accused the Republican candidates globally for their approach to tax cuts.

The status quo was also a target of attack in the Democratic primary debates. In the January 8, 2000, debate in Des Moines, Iowa, Bradley provided an example of an attack against the status quo, "You'd be in a meeting and you would have a big tax bill, hundreds of billions of dollars at stake. Cell phones, lobbyists, the whole room, line up outside. . . . Three days later, in the same room, there would be a discussion about child poverty. It would be virtually empty." Here Bradley attacked the status quo for a lack of integrity in prioritizing legislation. There were significant differences between Bradley and Gore and the targets of their attacks in these data ($\chi^2[df=2]=55.78, p <.001$). Bradley targeted the establishment more than Gore, whereas Gore attacked Republican candidates more than Bradley (see Table 4.2).

Somewhat less than half of the attacks made by Republican candidates were targeted to members of their own party (46 percent). A third of Republican attacks were directed toward Democrats (32 percent). Although not as frequent, the status quo (22 percent) was also the target of Republican attacks (see Table 4.3). Forbes provided an example of an attack targeted toward a fellow Republican in the January 26, 2000, in New Hampshire: "Under your leadership, spending has gone up 36 percent." In this excerpt Forbes criticized Governor Bush's spending habits in the state of Texas. By highlighting Bush's shortcomings as governor, Forbes had an opportunity to provide a contrast between the two candidates for the electorate. Bauer provided an example of a multitargeted attack when he said the following about the other Republican candidates: "Governor Bush and many others up here would give China Most Favored Nation status again. I will not. I will withdraw it the first week in office" (January 7, 2000). In this excerpt Bauer announced that other candidates would all take similar stances toward China and then he set up a direct contrast with his course of action in order to illustrate the undesirability of their plan of action.

Democrats were also targeted by Republicans. In the December 6, 2000, primary debate in Arizona, Forbes stated: "And it was the Republicans who stopped some of the destructive nonsense of the Clinton-Gore administration that enabled us to enjoy the prosperity we have today." The passage clearly criticizes the Democratic leadership of the previous eight years. Forbes attacked the Clinton-Gore administration again in the January 10, 2000, debate when he declared, "Unfortunately this administration I think put some pressure initially on the INS, and wanted this boy to become Bill Clinton's human sacrifice to Fidel Castro." Forbes clearly indicted the Clinton-Gore administration for their handling of the Elian Gonzalez. Again, type of attack provides a point of comparison between the two parties.

Table 4.3 Target of Attack in Republican Primary Debates

| | Own Party (Republicans) | | | | | | | Dem | SQ |
|---|---|---|---|---|---|---|---|---|---|
| | Bauer | Bush | Forbes | Hatch | Keyes | McCain | Rep | | |
| Bauer | – | 27 | 24 | 3 | 1 | 3 | 8 | 46 | 31 |
| Bush | 1 | – | 5 | 0 | 3 | 41 | 0 | 26 | 15 |
| Forbes | 0 | 62 | – | 1 | 1 | 2 | 2 | 72 | 60 |
| Hatch | 2 | 3 | 0 | – | 2 | 14 | 1 | 42 | 13 |
| Keyes | 6 | 53 | 8 | 4 | – | 64 | 0 | 49 | 47 |
| McCain | 0 | 79 | 0 | 2 | 14 | – | 10 | 66 | 48 |
| | 9 | 224 | 37 | 10 | 21 | 124 | 21 | | |
| Total | 446 (46%) | | | | | | | 301 (32%) | 214 (22%) |

Finally, attacks against the status quo were present such as the one by John McCain in the December 2, 2000, primary debate in New Hampshire: "When I see the Congress of the United States spend $6 billion on unnecessary, wasteful pork barrel spending, and we have 12,000 enlisted families, brave men and women, on food stamps, yeah, I get angry." Here McCain, although a Washington politician, separates himself from the "typical" politician, or status quo, by attacking Congressional legislation. Other Republicans attacked the status quo as well such as the following offered by Forbes, "I don't want to play by Washington's rules; I want to do it for the American people" (December 2, 1999). In this statement Forbes clearly attacked those who are part of the Washington insider group, or status quo, and attempted to offer the electorate something other than "business as usual."

Because McCain and Bush were considered the front-runners in the Republican primary it is not surprising that they would be the most frequent targets of other Republican candidates. Bush received 23 percent of the total number of attacks and 50 percent of the attacks made on Republican candidates whereas McCain was the recipient of 13 percent of the total number of attacks and 28 percent of the attacks made on Republican candidates.

There are significant differences between Democrats and Republicans and the targets of their attacks ($\chi^2[df=2]=164.3$, $p < .001$). Democrats attacked their own party (85 percent) to a far greater extent than did the Republicans (46 percent). Republicans attacked the status quo (22 percent) and Democrats (32 percent) at a greater rate than the Democrats attacked the status quo (5 percent) and Republicans (10 percent).

## Topics of 2000 Primary Debates

The majority of the messages in Democratic primary debates focused on policy (72 percent) (see Table 4.4). For example, in the January 17, 2000, debate in Des Moines, Bradley acclaimed, "That means 400,000 more slots for Head Start, getting kids ready to learn." In this excerpt Bradley responds to a question about his future plans for education in the United States. Here he clearly articulates a specific plan for the future. Gore also discussed policy when he stated, "I helped to pass the toughest new gun control measure in a generation" (January 5, 2000). In this excerpt Gore praised legislation he enacted in the past. Presumably, if he was effective in the past he will create equally desirable policies in the future.

Messages concerning character (28 percent) were also present in the Democratic primary debates. In the January 17, 2000, debate Gore offered an example of a message focusing on character, "We've got work to do, and I want to lead this country toward a future that is bright and hopeful for all our people." This statement illuminates Gore's character by discussing his leadership ability. Bradley also provided an example of character when he stated, "It was a very special place to grow up. I learned a lot of values there: courage, discipline, respect, responsibility, resilience. I carry them with me" (January 8, 2000). This passage was created to make the electorate aware that Bradley possessed values that could be considered desirable in a national leader.

There were significant differences between Gore and Bradley and their

Table 4.4. Topics of 2000 Primary Debates

|  | Policy | Character |
|---|---|---|
| Bradley | 557 (68%) | 261 (32%) |
| Gore | 725 (76%) | 229 (24%) |
| Democrats | 1282 (72%) | 490 (28%) |
| Bauer | 293 (72%) | 116 (28%) |
| Bush | 487 (69%) | 219 (31%) |
| Forbes | 451 (76%) | 141 (24%) |
| Hatch | 265 (66%) | 138 (34%) |
| Keyes | 330 (49%) | 348 (51%) |
| McCain | 520 (67%) | 259 (33%) |
| Republicans | 2346 (66%) | 1221 (34%) |
| Total | 3628 (68%) | 1711 (32%) |

discussion of policy and character in the Democratic primary debates ($\chi^2[df=1]=13.7$, $p < .001$). Although both candidates discussed policy more than character, Gore was less likely to discuss character (24 percent) than Bradley (32 percent).

Republicans focused 66 percent of their messages in the primary debates on policy (see Table 4.4). For example, in the December 13, 1999, Des Moines debate Bush stated, "But I also know we need to have laws that keep guns out of the hands of people who shouldn't have them. I mean, that's why I'm for instant background checks." This statement illustrates an acclaim of policy. Clearly Bush indicated that when elected president he intended to introduce legislation that requires a background check for those purchasing firearms. Hatch also provided an example of policy when he said, "We have currently a moratorium on taxation on the Internet, and I happen to agree with that. I really don't want the Internet to be taxed" (December 2, 1990). Although he did not articulate specific policy, Hatch's statement implied that he did have a certain preferences for Internet taxation.

Character (34 percent) was also discussed in the Republican primary debates. In the December 13, 1999, debate McCain declared, "I can inspire a generation to commit themselves to causes greater than their self interests. I am prepared to be president of the United States." In this statement McCain praised his character, specifically his leadership ability. Bauer discussed character when he attacked Bush, "Governor Bush, we've been in about four debates now. And I have to say that I'm getting more and more worried whether you're serious about defending conservative values" (January 6, 2000). In the preceding statement Bauer clearly called Bush's ideals, values, and commitment to the party into question.

There were significant differences among the Republican candidates and their discussion of policy and character. All but one candidate, Alan Keyes, discussed policy more than character. Keyes mentioned policy (49 percent) and character (51 percent) almost equally. From the beginning of the debates Keyes made it clear that he was in the race to discuss the issue of abortion and to promote morals and values. In light of this declaration, plus the fact that Keyes was an ambassador but never held an elected office, it is reasonable to expect that he would concentrate on character considerations rather than discuss multiple policy issues. Forbes (24 percent) was the least likely to discuss character. Because Forbes was the only candidate who had never served in a political position, elected or otherwise, it would be necessary for him to highlight any past policy actions or plans for the future that might convince voters that he is fit to serve as a policy maker.

There were significant differences between Democrats and Republicans and their discussion of policy and character ($\chi^2[df=1]=23.5$, $p < .001$). While both Democrats (72 percent) and Republicans (66 percent) discussed policy more than character, Republicans (34 percent) were more likely to discuss character than Democrats (28 percent). During the primaries voters learn about the personalities and leadership qualities of the candidates as well as their stand on policy. However, when there are several candidates vying for the nomination, as was the case for the

Republicans, it may take longer for the American electorate to get to know who the candidates are and the differences between them. Therefore, it is not surprising that the Republican candidates spent more time than the Democrats focusing on character.

## Forms of Policy and Character in 2000 Primary Debates

The three forms of policy were discussed as follows: pasts deeds 30 percent; future plans 23 percent; and general goals 47 percent (see Table 4.5). Gore provided us with an example of past deeds when he attacked Bradley in the January 26, 2000, debate in New Hampshire, "Now on public school vouchers—private school vouchers, Senator Bradley voted every time it came up in the Senate, for private school vouchers." In this passage Gore criticized a policy action made by Bradley in the past, in this case a vote on school vouchers in the Senate. Bradley also discussed past deeds in the debate, "I defended Medicare for 18 years. It was through my efforts that we prevented premiums from going up on a number of occasions" (December 17, 1999). Clearly Bradley praised his past efforts with regard to Medicare. By showing previous conviction to Medicare Bradley indicated to the voters that he did have a prior, positive experience with important public policy.

Bradley praised his future plans for education in the January 26, 2000, debate when he stated, "In addition, I propose college scholarships for 10,000 kids at $7,500 each if they would agree to teach in urban schools." This excerpt clearly outlined a specific plan of action that Bradley would take in the future if elected. Future plans were also a form of policy mentioned by Al Gore: "That means rigorous peer review of current teachers and making it easier within due process to fire the ones that are not doing the job" (December 19, 1999). In this statement Gore outlined a feature of future policy aimed at improving education.

General goals were also discussed by Bradley in the January 26, 2000, debate: "I think it's critical that we help community colleges, because that is the place where most kids begin the process of higher education." In this statement Bradley indicated policy changes he would make in the future. However, these policies are described as general goals and not a specific action. Gore provided an example of general goals when he said, "I believe very strongly in protecting the environment, and I know we can do it in a way that protects our way of life and standard of living" (January 5, 2000). There were no significant differences between Bradley and Gore and the three forms of policy utterances ($\chi^2[df=2]=2.5$, ns).

Gore and Bradley focused on forms of character as follows: personal qualities 53 percent; leadership ability 22 percent; ideals 25 percent. The January 5, 2000, debate in Des Moines provided an example of personal qualities when Bradley attacked Gore when he said, "The one that was most particularly offensive to me was when he said in his campaign that I was going to hurt African Americans,

Table 4.5. Forms of Policy and Character in 2000 Primary Debates

| | Policy | | | | | | Character | | | | | |
| | Past Deeds | | Future Plans | | General Goals | | Personal Qualities | | Leader-ship | | Ideals | |
|---|---|---|---|---|---|---|---|---|---|---|---|---|
| Bradley | 75 | 81 | 99 | 23 | 267 | 12 | 87 | 56 | 44 | 4 | 67 | 3 |
| Gore | 176 | 43 | 99 | 76 | 311 | 20 | 78 | 37 | 60 | 2 | 52 | 0 |
| Dem | 251 | 124 | 198 | 99 | 578 | 32 | 165 | 93 | 104 | 6 | 119 | 3 |
| | 375 (30%) | | 297 (23%) | | 601 (47%) | | 258 (53%) | | 110 (22%) | | 122 (25%) | |
| Bauer | 9 | 51 | 47 | 30 | 134 | 22 | 15 | 36 | 5 | 0 | 56 | 4 |
| Bush | 90 | 26 | 74 | 19 | 263 | 15 | 54 | 29 | 70 | 1 | 64 | 1 |
| Forbes | 6 | 121 | 78 | 17 | 218 | 11 | 18 | 42 | 15 | 6 | 57 | 3 |
| Hatch | 70 | 32 | 22 | 11 | 121 | 9 | 37 | 20 | 32 | 2 | 44 | 3 |
| Keyes | 6 | 66 | 51 | 22 | 153 | 32 | 34 | 102 | 9 | 0 | 194 | 9 |
| McCain | 49 | 81 | 72 | 29 | 274 | 15 | 63 | 85 | 38 | 7 | 64 | 2 |
| Rep | 230 | 377 | 344 | 128 | 1163 | 104 | 221 | 314 | 169 | 16 | 479 | 22 |
| | 607 (26%) | | 472 (20%) | | 1267 (54%) | | 535 (44%) | | 185 (15%) | | 501 (41%) | |
| Total | 982 (27%) | | 769 (21%) | | 1868 (52%) | | 793 (46%) | | 295 (17%) | | 623 (36%) | |

Latinos with the health care that program that I have offered." In this excerpt Bradley argued that Gore behaved in a manner that was deceptive when he discussed Bradley's health care proposal thereby casting aspersions on Gore's personal character. In the same debate Gore defended himself against this attack when he stated, "I didn't say any of the things that you heard." Here he is trying to reclaim his "good name" when he denies, or disputes, Bradley's attack against him.

Leadership ability was frequently discussed in the Democratic primary debates such as the example Gore offered when praising when he stated, "They deserve somebody who's willing to fight for them, not just theorize about them" (January 28, 2000). In this passage Gore indicated that the "somebody" is him. He intimated he has the leadership abilities it takes to see plans and policies to fruition. Bradley also praised his leadership ability, "I have always had advisers at the highest level who were African American, who were Latino, who were Asian Americans. And I did that because I thought that made me a better leader" (January 17, 2000). This statement showed how Bradley discussed his approach to leadership in the past to demonstrate to the electorate that he is fit to lead in the future—specifically, his fitness for the highest office in the land.

Finally, ideals were discussed by the Democratic candidates. For example, when responding to a question about campaign finance reform Bradley stated, "The rich in this country should be able to buy as many vacations and homes and cars as they want, but they shouldn't be able to buy our democracy" (January 28, 2000). In this statement Bradley clearly asserts that he believes in democracy as the ultimate American ideal. Another example of ideals was provided by Gore, "I strongly support the separation of church and state" (December 17, 1999). In this excerpt Gore clearly identified a core belief in his value system. There were no significant differences between Bradley and Gore and forms of character mentioned in the primary debates ($\chi^2[df=2]=5.4$, ns).

General goals (54 percent) were the most common form of policy mentioned in the Republican primary debates followed by past deeds (26 percent) and future plans (20 percent) (see Table 4.5). When discussing his plans for world trade in the South Carolina debate held on January 7, 2000, Bush provided an example of discussing general goals, "I would be a free-trading president, a president that will work tirelessly to open up markets for agricultural products all over the world." This message by Bush demonstrated that he has general plans for agricultural trade but he does not outline any specific policy in this statement. McCain also offered an example of general goals in the October 28, 1999, debate in New Hampshire, "We need to improve foster care dramatically in America." Like Bush's statement, no specific policy is outlined; rather, a general commitment to the problem of foster care is expressed.

Past deeds were also frequently discussed in the Republican primary debates. In the South Carolina debate Bush discussed some of his past deeds, "I have cut taxes. I've reformed welfare. And I have insisted upon educational excellence for every child." In this brief passage Bush acclaimed three past deeds as governor of Texas. In the December 12, 1999, debate Hatch offered an example of past deeds as well, "Also, passed the Hatch-Lieberman bill to reduce capital gains rates from 28 percent down to 20 percent. I've actually done it. I've been there." While engaged in an overall discussion of tax reforms, Hatch attempted to set himself apart from the rest of the pack when he mentioned his past success with tax cuts.

Although not as frequent as past deeds and general goals, future plans were discussed in the Republican primary debates. For example, when discussing tax plans Bush declared, "Under the plan that you laid out, Mr. Senator, here in South Carolina, they will receive a $200 tax cut. Under the plan that I propose and will get though the United States Congress, they receive $1,852.00 tax cut" (January 7, 2000). In this excerpt, Bush attacked Senator McCain's future plans for cutting taxes while praising his own. While discussing future tax policies in the December 13, 1999, debate Keyes stated his commitment to "abolish the income tax, fund the federal government with tariffs, duties, and excise taxes so the people of this country get back control of every dollar that they earn." Here Keyes pledged he will take very specific policy actions should he be elected.

There were significant differences between the Republican candidates and the focus of their policy messages ($\chi^2[df=10]=44.1$, $p <.001$). All of the Republican candidates discusses general goals more than any other form of policy. However, Bauer and Hatch were the only two candidates more likely to discuss future plans rather than past deeds. Because Bauer and Hatch could be considered "dark horses" in this particular primary, it is feasible that they focused on future plans rather than past deeds in order to differentiate themselves from the front-runners.

Personal qualities (44 percent) and ideals (41 percent) were somewhat equally utilized by the Republican candidates whereas leadership ability (15 percent) was less frequently mentioned (see Table 4.5). In the Michigan debate Forbes attacked Bush's personal qualities when he stated, "Pledges should not be lightly made, and a pledge is a promise, and a promise made should be a promise kept, and a pledge should not be used as a trinket to win the election." In this passage Forbes attacked Bush's character by pointing out that Bush pledged to cut taxes in his bid for the Texas gubernatorial seat and then broke his promise once in office. Forbes suggested that Bush will promise anything to win an election, including a promise to cut taxes if elected president. Ideals were also the focus of many messages in the Michigan debate. During a discussion of racial profiling Bush said, "I intend to say each individual counts. Each individual matters. The American dream belongs to each individual who's willing to work hard to achieve it." This excerpt exemplifies the use of ideals in the primary debates. When asked to discuss his plans to combat racial profiling, Bush also spoke of the values, or ideals, that he accepts (in this case, the ideal of equal treatment under the law). Although not as frequently mentioned, leadership ability was also a form of character used in the Republican primary debates. In the Michigan debate Bush outlined his leadership qualifications to the audience, "I am the one on the stage who has had executive experience when it comes to government. I know how to set agendas; I know how to bring people together to achieve the agenda." Clearly, Bush was making an argument that he is the most qualified to serve as the next president.

There were significant differences between the Republican candidates in the focus of their character messages. While the majority of the candidates closely matched the overall averages for the forms of character used, three candidates stand out in their deviation from the norm. Bush was more likely than the other candidates to discuss leadership abilities. This finding is understandable because he was the governor of Texas at the time of the primary. Many executive duties of the governor are similar to the executive duties of the president. For example, both must maintain a budget and work with legislators. Therefore, it is reasonable to expect a candidate like Bush to draw those parallels between the offices and highlight his leadership experience. Keyes also differed from other Republican candidates in the forms of character used in his message. Fifty-eight percent of Keyes' character utterances concerned ideals. This finding is not surprising because Keyes declared early on in the primary campaign that he was concerned with issues of morality and family values. Finally, McCain was more likely than the other candidates to discuss personal qualities. Early on in the campaign McCain achieved name recognition for his service in Vietnam and the time he spent as a prisoner of war. It makes sense that McCain would capitalize on character since it strikes a chord with the audience.

There were significant differences between Democrats and Republicans and the forms of policy used in the primary debates ($\chi^2[df=2]=15.3, p<.001$). Although both parties mentioned general goals most frequently, Republicans were more likely to focus on general goals than Democrats. There were also significant differences between Democrats and Republicans and the forms of character mentioned in the primary debates ($\chi^2[df=2]=41.7, p<.001$). Republicans focused on personal qualities (44 percent) and ideals (41 percent) somewhat equally and less frequently on leadership ability (15 percent) whereas Democrats focused more heavily on personal qualities (53 percent) and fairly equally on leadership ability (22 percent) and ideals (25 percent).

## Issues Addressed in 2000 Primary Debates

The results, as shown in Table 4.6, show that Bradley focused most of his policy messages on the topics of health care and education. For example Bradley praised his general attitudes about health care when he said, "We're going to help the middle-class Americans, in addition to covering people who don't have any health insurance." Here it is clear that he was addressing future health care policy (December 19, 1999). He also discussed the issue of education in the same debate when he stated, "I've proposed a specific program for early child care. I proposed

Table 4.6. Issues Addressed in 2000 Democratic Primary Debates

|  | Poll | Bradley* | Gore |
|---|---|---|---|
| Education | 23 | 84 (2) | 109 (2) |
| Health Care | 19 | 105 (1) | 198 (1) |
| Social Security | 13 | 15 (6) | 19 (5) |
| Crime/Drugs | 12 | 8 (7) | 9 (7) |
| Taxes | 5 | 25 (5) | 16 (6) |
| Medicare/Prescription Drugs | 4 | 28 (4) | 56 (3) |
| Foreign Affairs | 2 | 37 (3) | 38 (4) |
| Other | – | 255 | 280 |
| Spearman ρ |  | -.14, *ns* | -.07, *ns* |

*Frequency (rank)  Enslow (1999)

Table 4.7. Issues Addressed in 2000 Republican Primary Debates

| | Poll | Bauer* | Bush | Forbes | Hatch | Keyes | McCain |
|---|---|---|---|---|---|---|---|
| Education | 19 | 25 (4) | 72 (2) | 55 (3) | 19 (3) | 32 (4) | 67 (2) |
| Taxes | 11 | 50 (2) | 114 (1) | 112 (1) | 44 (1) | 69 (1) | 74 (1) |
| Social Security | 9 | 16 (5) | 22 (4) | 30 (5) | 3 (7) | 4 (5) | 27 (5) |
| Crime/Drugs | 8 | 6 (6) | 1 (7) | 10 (6) | 13 (5) | 0 | 4 (7) |
| Health Care | 8 | 32 (3) | 12 (6) | 47 (4) | 10 (2) | 35 (3) | 28 (4) |
| Foreign Affairs | 7 | 60 (1) | 52 (3) | 60 (2) | 18 (4) | 42 (2) | 46 (3) |
| Medicare/ Prescription Drugs | 5 | 0 | 8 (5) | 5 (7) | 5 (6) | 0 | 8 (6) |
| Other | – | 104 | 206 | 132 | 123 | 148 | 266 |
| Spearman ρ | | -.18, *ns* | .10, *ns* | .00, *ns* | -.01, *ns* | -.14, *ns* | .06, *ns* |

*Frequency (rank)   Enslow (1999)

doubling the number of people in Head Start." Here Bradley mentioned specific legislation with regard to the issue of education. When ignoring the category of "other" we see that 35 percent of Bradley's utterances are about health care and 28 percent focus on education. The majority of Gore's remarks also centered around healthcare (44 percent) and education (24 percent). An example of Gore discussing healthcare can be found in the December 17, 1999, debate: "I'm in favor of universal health care and I want to start by having universal health care available for every child immediately to reach the goal within the next four years." In the same debate he mentioned the issue of education: "We're going to devote the resources necessary to dramatically improve our public schools." Clearly the issue of education is central to this praise of Gore's general policy plans. Both of the Democratic candidates devoted their remarks to the two issues ranked as most important by the electorate. We used Spearman's ρ to determine the strength of the relationship between the number of themes devoted to each policy topic and the importance of that policy topic to the Democratic electorate. Neither Bradley's nor Gore's ρ was significant.

As reported in Table 4.7, all of the candidates, with the exception of Bauer, discussed taxes most frequently in their debate messages. For example, Forbes stated, "You know either a flat tax or a national sales tax would be much better than what we have today" (December 6, 1999). The electorate ranked education and taxes as the two most important topics. Bush and McCain were the only two candidates whose most frequently mentioned topics were education and taxes. McCain provided an example of an education issue when he stated, "I want to reform the education system (December 13, 1999). We used Spearman's ρ to determine the strength of the relationship between the number of utterances devoted to each policy topic and the importance of that policy topic to the Republican voters. None of the $\rho$'s were significant.

# Implications

The 2000 primary debates are similar to previous primary debates. Benoit, Blaney, and Pier (1998) found that in the 1996 primary debates acclaims were the most frequently used function, followed by attacks and defenses were rarely used. Benoit et al. (in press) studied twenty-five debates from ten primary elections and found again that acclaims dominated the functions and that attacks were somewhat common but defenses were rare. The results from the 2000 primary debates support previous findings. Acclaims were used in 73 percent of the utterances, attacks 24 percent, and defenses 3 percent.

These results are readily explicable. Attacks are less common than acclaims for several reasons. Voters report that they do not like mudslinging (Merritt, 1984; Stewart, 1975), which may moderate the frequency of attacks. Second, because the primaries provide the first opportunity for candidates to present themselves to the public, a positive image is paramount. Attack messages so early in the campaign cycle may disillusion voters or draw their attention away from viewing the debates. Third, attacks may be less frequent in primary campaigns because the candidate who secures the nomination (in this case, Bush for the Republicans and Gore for the Democrats) will not want to attack so much that other candidates will not provide support in the fall (or that the other candidates' supporters are alienated). Furthermore, there should be fewer policy differences between the various contenders in the primary (because all competitors belong to the same party), which should provide fewer opportunities for attack.

There are several reasons for defenses to be so rare. First, defenses can take a candidate "off message," forcing a candidate to spend time on issues that may favor opponents. Second, one must identify an attack to defend against it, and such identification could remind or inform the audience of potential weaknesses. Finally, defenses are inherently reactive rather than proactive. Still, candidates occasionally do issue defenses.

In the 2000 primary debates, candidates of both parties attacked members of their own party more than any other group. This is consistent with previous research done by Benoit, Blaney, and Pier (1998) and Benoit et al. (in press). It is necessary for primary candidates to distinguish themselves from their opponents (other party members) so voters would have a reason to prefer you over other Republicans (or other Democrats). Also consistent with earlier research we see the front runner in the Republican (Bush) primary was attacked more frequently. Every Republican had to "get past" Bush, the front-runner, so everyone had a strategic reason to attack him. In contrast, those candidates ahead of, say, Bauer or Hatch, had little to gain from attacking them.

We found a difference between the parties in their targets of attack in the 2000 primary. Democrats overwhelmingly attacked each other (85 percent) and the Republicans, while still attacking each other 46 percent of the time, focused their attacks on the status quo (22 percent) and the Democrats (32 percent). Because the Republicans are the challenging party they may feel that attacks on the Democrats serve to bolster their position among Republican voters. In addition, by attacking the incumbent party the Republicans can create unity within their party. Regardless of the outcome of the primary the true opponent of the Republican nominee is the Democratic nominee. Again, this finding supports earlier research conducted on the 1996 primary debates.

The topics discussed in the 2000 primary debates were also consistent with findings from previous research. Policy (68 percent) was discussed a majority of the time while discussions of character (32 percent) were less frequent. Benoit et al. (in press) argued that public opinion poll data from 1976 to 2000 indicated that more voters consider policy to be a more important determinant of their vote for president than character. In addition, the majority of the questions posed by the moderators in the debates focus on policy matters. Therefore, it is understandable that candidates would spend more time discussing policy than character in these debates.

Consistent with previous research (e.g., Benoit, Blaney, & Pier, 1998), the candidates in the 2000 primaries acclaimed general goals with a great deal of frequency. It is easier to discuss ends (goals) than means (future plans) in acclaims, and, at the same time, it is more difficult for opponents to attack goals than specific proposals. Also consistent with earlier findings, personal qualities and ideals were discussed more than leadership abilities. Because many of the candidates are unknown to the electorate, candidates must introduce themselves to the audience. Before the voter can be convinced on leadership ability they must be convinced that a candidate is fit in character and morality. Thus, an emphasis on personal qualities and ideals in the primary.

Gore used past deeds more than Bradley. There are several possible explanations for this difference. First, as the incumbent candidate Gore has a clear policy record which he can acclaim during the debates. Even though Senator Bradley can claim a record in the Senate, Gore served in a vice presidential role which allows him to make direct comparisons between past and future policy actions in the executive office. A second explanation for Gore's relative reluctance to discuss character also lies in the fact that he enjoys an incumbency position because he served as the vice president. In order to acclaim his accomplishments during the previous eight years he must associate himself with President Clinton. Although it would be advantageous to praise past policy triumphs, a negative association with Clinton with regard to character could be detrimental to Gore.

Less than half (42 percent) of the issues addressed in the 2000 primaries concerned the topics that were the most important issues to voters. No statistically significant relationships were found between topics thought important by voters and the topics discussed by candidates. This may be due in part to the fact that candidates respond to questions in debates (and the questions may not reflect what matters most to voters). Hansen and Benoit (2001) report data that show a positive relationship between the candidates' utterances and debate questions. However, they also show that candidates can have different emphases in their comments than the topics of the questions. Hence, while they do operate under a constraint (questions), candidates could do a better job discussing the topics that are most important to voters.

This examination of the 2000 primary debates provides us with useful insight into an integral part of the campaign process. In addition, it adds to the longitudinal body of research being conducted on primary debates. In combination with other message forms from the 2000 election, it can give us insight into the "big picture" of campaign 2000.

# Chapter 5

# Primary Web Pages

Today, 13.5 million American children (18.9% or almost one in five) live in poverty. The percentage of minority children who live below the poverty line is even higher: 34.4% for Hispanics and 36.7% for African Americans. Bill Bradley's goal is to eliminate child poverty as we know it. He will commit to lifting 3 million children out of poverty in his first term, and at least an additional 4 million children in his second term. (Bradley, 2000 Internet site)

Declaring that he has "just begun to fight for American seniors," Al Gore today told senior citizens at a retirement community here that he will work to make prescription drugs more affordable and fight to protect Medicare, Medicaid, and Social Security. Gore's record and agenda differ markedly from Senator Bill Bradley's on these issues, which are critical to senior citizens. (Gore, 2000 Internet site)

Governor Bush believes the state's role in education should be limited to setting measurable goals and then holding school districts accountable for achieving those goals. Today, Texas has four clear goals: excellence in math, science, English, and social studies. Texas has put fewer bureaucratic burdens on schools, but still holds them accountable to achieve these goals. (Bush, 2000 Internet site)

As President, I will . . . Strengthen the family . . . Oppose the political agenda of the organized "gay rights" movement, including same-sex marriage and "special rights" legislation. Permit voluntary prayer in schools. Protect religious freedoms and pass federal legislation to permit state facilities to post the Ten Commandments. (Bauer, 2000 Internet site)

I will immediately reverse the Clinton-Gore tax hikes upon my election. I'm looking forward to announcing my tax plan later this year, but I'm pleased to say it will begin with a repeal of federal death taxes on family farms and businesses left to children and grandchildren, and immediate deductibility of health insurance premiums for the self-employed. (Dole, 2000 Internet site)

John McCain supports making health care insurance purchased by the self-employed 100% tax deductible and allowing tax deductibility for long-term care. He supports managed care reforms that will improve the quality of care without massive increases in insurance premiums that cause people to lose their coverage, or imposing unfair costs on small businesses struggling to provide adequate health coverage to their employees. (McCain, 2000 Internet site)

If the Declaration of Independence states our creed, there can be no right to abortion, since it means denying the most fundamental right of all, to human offspring in the womb. The Declaration states plainly that we are all created equal, endowed by our creator with our human rights. But if human beings can decide who is human and who is not, the doctrine of God-given rights is utterly corrupted. Abortion is the unjust taking of a human life and a breach of the fundamental principals of our public moral creed. (Keyes, 2000 Internet site)

With the Steve Forbes' Flat Tax, you would pay a low rate of just 17% after generous personal exemptions for individuals and families. Twenty million low-income Americans would be taken off the tax rolls altogether. The average family of four would pay no federal income tax on their first $36,000—a tax cut of over $1,600. Also, there would be no marriage tax penalty, no "death tax," and no federal taxes on savings, pensions or capital gains—and you could fill out your taxes on a simple postcard. (Forbes, 2000 Internet site)

## Literature Review

Several authors have addressed the content of candidates' presidential primary Internet sites. First, Margolis, Resnick, and Tu (1997) were somewhat pessimistic about Internet political campaigning after their analysis of the 1996 primary Internet sites. They concluded that the Internet will be used more to perpetuate consumerism than to spur political action and that big business and the major parties (Democrats and Republicans) have dominated politics on the Internet. In their analysis of the 1996 primary, Klinenberg and Perrin (2000) suggested that candidates did not fully utilize the interactive features of the Internet. Instead, they reported that candidates used the new medium to transmit traditional media messages (e.g., video, graphics, voting records, speeches). Next, Schneider (2000) reported that all major party candidates in the 2000 primary had an Internet site that featured issue positions, biographical information, fund raising, volunteer recruitment, speeches, press releases, and event promotion. Schneider (2000) also reported that the candidates tended not to respond to campaign events and developments in a timely fashion. In addition, Benoit and Benoit (2000) studied candidate websites in the 2000 presidential primary and discussed the advantages and disadvantages of candidate Internet sites for candidates and voters. They also developed criteria for evaluating candidate Internet sites and reported that candidates varied considerably in the effectiveness of their Internet site. Finally, Hansen and Benoit (2001) analyzed candidate Internet sites in the 2000 primary using computer content analysis and found that two of eight candidates had a significant relationship with the issues addressed on their Internet site and the issues most important on the public agenda.

In addition, several studies have examined audience reaction to candidate Internet sites. Hansen (2000b) reported that viewing presidential primary candidate Internet sites (Bradley, Gore, Bush, and Dole) changed certain perceptions that viewers have about the candidates but did not alter levels of trust or support for the candidate. Next, in their experimental study of candidate Internet sites in the 2000 presidential primary Ahem, Stromer-Galley, and Neuman (2000) reported that levels of interactivity increased liking for the candidate and perceived learning about the candidate. Finally, Stromer-Galley, Foot, Schneider, and Larsen (2001) conducted focus groups during the New Hampshire primary and found that citizens responded positively to the following Internet site characteristics: (1) breath and depth of content and comparisons with other candidates; (2) simplicity of navigation; (3) unambiguous privacy statement, transparency of source, and control over the level of exposure to information; (4) ability to interact with the campaign; and (5) a web design that is entertaining. As indicated, several studies have addressed audience reactions toward candidate Internet sites.

Research in the area of campaign Internet sites has also examined other national (nonpresidential) and state offices. Several studies have examined the content of candidate Internet sites for U.S. Senate and House campaigns (e.g., Davis, 1999; Dulio, Goff, & Thurber, 1999; Klotz, 1997, 1998; Klotz & Broome, 1998; Sadow & James, 1999). Likewise, one study (Benoit, 2000) examined the Internet sites for various state elections using the Functional Theory of Political Campaign Discourse. To date no study has utilized the Functional Theory to examine presidential campaign Internet sites.

# Results

In this section, we will first provide information regarding the sample of Internet sites analyzed. Secondly, we discuss the functions of primary web pages and the targets of candidates' attacks. Finally, the topics, forms of policy and character, and issues addressed will be presented.

We analyzed the official candidate Internet sites for two contenders in the Democratic primary (Bill Bradley and Al Gore) and six contenders in the Republican primary (Gary Bauer, George W. Bush, Elizabeth Dole, Steven Forbes, Alan Keyes, and John McCain). The candidates' Internet sites were analyzed based on their content on February 9, 2000. February 9 was chosen because it was early in the primary schedule (about one week after the New Hampshire primary) and most of the candidates were still competing for their parties' nomination.[1] For each candidate we analyzed the "homepage" of their Internet site, the biography section, and their issues section (we analyzed text but not video or audio). The "homepage" was included because it is the page most visitors to the site will view and also the most often updated page on the Internet site (Hansen, 2000a). The biography and issues sections of the candidates' Internet site were analyzed because these are two areas where the candidates provide important information about themselves, their candidacy, and their position on various issues.

## Functions of Primary Web Pages

The candidate web pages focused predominantly on acclaiming (95 percent). For example, Bradley told viewers of his Internet site: "The primary goal of the Bradley Second-Chance Homes would be to reduce additional teen pregnancies by providing disadvantaged young mothers a supportive and nurturing environment during their pregnancy and their baby's first year." Bradley had the goal of reducing teen pregnancies, which could appeal to many Democrats. Likewise, in the following excerpt, Bush stated his position on campaign finance reform: Bush "supports banning 'soft money' contributions from labor unions and corporations because members/shareholders have no say in how those contributions are given." This utterance acclaimed Bush's proposal for campaign finance reform that may be appealing to viewers of his Internet site. The results for the functions of primary web pages are displayed in Table 5.1.

Attacks were much less common throughout the candidates' Internet sites: Only 5 percent of all themes analyzed were devoted to attacking. Gore presented this attack: "Al Gore also believes that the Republican tax scheme currently being considered by Congress squanders our best chance in a generation to tackle our long-term challenges and bring this nation completely out of debt." This utterance took aim at the Republicans' tax scheme for not applying the budget surplus towards debt reduction. Keyes leveled this attack on his Internet site: "It is now clear that some American politicians have been so corrupted by internationalism that they will not resist the temptation to erect the United Nations into a supra-national entity that undermines our sovereignty." Keyes clearly attacked the position of some regarding the authority of the United Nations. From these excerpts, it is obvious that the candidates did utilize attacking strategies on their Internet sites.

Defenses were virtually nonexistent on the candidate Internet sites. With the exception of McCain, no candidate utilized defenses. In this statement, McCain denied that he opposed better compensation for the armed services, explaining that he voted against the bill because of unclear wording: "Senator McCain voted against the bill because he felt it was a poorly written bill, not because he did not want the men and women of the Armed Services to receive better benefits and higher pay raises." McCain obviously defended his past voting record in this

Table 5.1. Functions of 2000 Primary Web Pages

|  | Acclaims | Attacks | Defenses |
|---|---|---|---|
| Bradley | 455 (97%) | 14 (3%) | 0 |
| Gore | 1165 (99%) | 9 (1%) | 0 |
| Democrats | 1620 (99%) | 23 (0.5%) | 0 |
| Bauer | 182 (90%) | 21 (10%) | 0 |
| Bush | 564 (98%) | 11 (2%) | 0 |
| Dole | 154 (91%) | 15 (9%) | 0 |
| Forbes | 313 (90%) | 35 (10%) | 0 |
| Keyes | 117 (74%) | 42 (26%) | 0 |
| McCain | 643 (92%) | 53 (8%) | 4 (0.5%) |
| Republicans | 1973 (92%) | 177 (8%) | 4 (0.2%) |
| Total | 3593 (95%) | 200 (5%) | 4 (0.1%) |

utterance. This illustrates a candidate's use of defense, which again was quite rare in these candidate Internet sites.

The Democrat' Internet sites were more positive than the Republicans' (99 percent to 92 percent), with more Republican than Democratic attacks (8 percent to .5 percent). The *chi-square* calculated on Democrats' versus Republicans' use of acclaims and attacks (there were too few defenses to include) was significant ($\chi^2$ [$df$=1]=87.0, $p < .001$).

A comparison between Bradley (97 percent) and Gore (99 percent) indicated that Gore acclaimed more than Bradley did, whereas Bradley attacked more than Gore (3 percent to 1 percent). This difference was significant ($\chi^2$[$df$=1]=11.9, $p < .001$). A comparison of the six Republican candidates also revealed a significant difference between the candidates' acclaims and attacks ($\chi^2$[$df$=5]=103.2, $p < .001$). Bush and McCain were the most positive (98 percent and 92 percent acclaims respectively) with Keyes, Bauer, and Forbes the most negative (26 percent attacks for Keyes and 10 percent for Bauer and Forbes).

## Target of Attack in Primary Web Pages

Examination of Table 5.2 indicates that Bradley and Gore attacked each other (41 percent) more than they attacked the Republicans (23 percent) or the status quo (36 percent). The Republicans (see Table 5.3), in contrast, devoted the majority of their attacks toward the status quo (55 percent) followed by attacks directed towards Democrats (39 percent) and only rarely to each other (5 percent). A *chi-square*

Table 5.2. Target of Attacks in 2000 Democratic Primary Web Pages

|  | Bradley | Gore | Republicans | SQ |
|---|---|---|---|---|
| Bradley | – | 8 | 0 | 5 |
| Gore | 1 | – | 5 | 3 |
| Total | 1 (11%) | 8 (89%) | | |
| | 9 (41%) | | 5 (23%) | 8 (36%) |

reveals that the two parties did differ significantly in the target of their attacks ($\chi^2[df=2]=29.7, p < .001$).

For example, Forbes attacked the establishment in this quotation for its performance on "protecting" our borders: "Despite vast new resources at its disposal, the Federal government continues to do a dismal job of protecting our borders and protecting Americans from felons who enter the U.S. illegally." In the next utterance, Bauer attacked the Democrats for their lack of a proposal to change Social Security: "If we do nothing, as the Democrats propose, Social Security will go broke sometime early in the next century." This example is from Gore's homepage and was the "headline" for a story regarding a trip that Gore made to Detroit: "Gore details plans to make collage more affordable. Bradley offers no proposals to help families save for collage." This headline both acclaimed Gore's education plan and attacked Bradley for the lack of an education proposal.

## Topics of Primary Web Pages

These Internet sites focused 79 percent of remarks on policy (see Table 5.4). For

Table 5.3. Target of Attacks in 2000 Republican Primary Web Pages

|  | Bauer | Bush | Dole | Forbes | Keyes | McCain | Repub | Dem | SQ |
|---|---|---|---|---|---|---|---|---|---|
| Bauer | – | 0 | 0 | 0 | 0 | 0 | 2 | 9 | 10 |
| Bush | 0 | – | 0 | 0 | 0 | 2 | 0 | 3 | 6 |
| Dole | 0 | 0 | – | 0 | 0 | 0 | 0 | 14 | 1 |
| Forbes | 0 | 0 | 0 | – | 0 | 0 | 0 | 4 | 31 |
| Keyes | 0 | 0 | 0 | 0 | – | 0 | 5 | 6 | 30 |
| McCain | 0 | 0 | 0 | 0 | 0 | – | 0 | 33 | 11 |
| | 0 | 0 | 0 | 0 | 0 | 2 (22%) | 7 (78%) | | |
| Total | | | | 9 (5%) | | | | 69 (39%) | 95 (55%) |

Table 5.4. Topics of 2000 Primary Web Pages

|  | Policy | Character |
|---|---|---|
| Bradley | 374 (80%) | 95 (20%) |
| Gore | 1133 (97%) | 41 (3%) |
| Democrats | 1507 (90%) | 136 (10%) |
| Bauer | 137 (67%) | 66 (33%) |
| Bush | 531 (92%) | 45 (8%) |
| Dole | 101 (60%) | 68 (40%) |
| Forbes | 143 (41%) | 205 (59%) |
| Keyes | 69 (43%) | 90 (57%) |
| McCain | 505 (72%) | 195 (28%) |
| Republicans | 1486 (69%) | 669 (31%) |
| Total | 2992 (79%) | 805 (21%) |

example, Bradley proposed a policy for gun control: "His plan includes the only complete registration and licensing proposal, the best means of ensuring that handguns remain in responsible hands." Similarly, Dole advocated Internet filters: he "proposed to cut federal funds for Internet connections unless libraries throughout the country use filtering devices to ensure that taxpayer dollars would not be used to provide children with access to pornography." This policy utterance addressed Dole's plan for limiting children's access to pornography. Finally, this quotation from Forbes's Internet site is a clear attack on the Clinton-Gore budget policy: "If the Clinton-Gore administration wants to spend more and break the caps, let them explain to the American people why." These above three examples illustrate policy themes utilized by the candidates on their Internet sites.

Character was addressed in 21 percent of the themes analyzed on candidate Internet sites (see Table 5.4). The following excerpt from Keyes's Internet site is an example of a character utterance: "I do not believe that means that all peoples of faith should become socialists. God wants us to care about the souls of our fellow men." This portrayed Keyes as a caring individual. Likewise, McCain suggested his character traits of "service" and "devotion" to America in the following: "At the age of 17, young John followed his father's and grandfather's footsteps to the U.S. Naval Academy at Annapolis. There he began a remarkable lifetime of service—and devotion—to America."

Both the Democrats and Republicans focused more on policy than character. However, Democrats allocated significantly more of their Internet sites' themes to policy and less to character whereas the Republicans focused significantly more on character and less on policy ($\chi^2$ [$df$=1]=289.3, $p < .001$). The Democrats discussed policy 90 percent of the time whereas the Republicans discussed policy only 69 percent of the time. In other words, the Republicans devoted 21 percent of their utterances to character and the Democrats mentioned character in only 10 percent of their utterances. Further examination of Table 5.4 indicates that Gore (97 percent) focused more on policy than Bradley (80 percent) ($\chi^2[df=1]=124.0$, $p < .001$). There were also significant differences in the topics of the Republican Internet sites ($\chi^2[df=5]=330.2$, $p < .001$). Forbes and Keyes were the only Republican candidates to devote more than half of their Internet site themes to character versus policy (59 percent and 57 percent respectively). The remaining candidates focused more on policy (Bauer: 67 percent, Bush: 92 percent, Dole: 60 percent, and McCain: 72 percent).

## Forms of Policy and Character in Primary Web Pages

The proportions of statements devoted to each of the forms of policy are: past deeds 27 percent, future plans 36 percent, and general goals 37 percent (see Table 5.5). For example, Bush acclaimed a past deed (his creation of the Science and

Table 5.5. Forms of Policy and Character in 2000 Primary Web Pages

| | Policy | | | | | | Character | | | | | |
|---|---|---|---|---|---|---|---|---|---|---|---|---|
| | Past Deeds* | | Future Plans | | General Goals | | Personal Qualities | | Leadership | | Ideals | |
| Bradley | 46 | 6 | 204 | 6 | 112 | 0 | 41 | 0 | 32 | 2 | 20 | 0 |
| Gore | 333 | 6 | 609 | 2 | 182 | 1 | 11 | 0 | 11 | 0 | 19 | 0 |
| | 379 | 12 | 813 | 8 | 294 | 1 | 52 | 0 | 43 | 2 | 39 | 0 |
| Dem | 391 (26%) | | 821 (54%) | | 295 (20%) | | 52 (38%) | | 45 (33%) | | 39 (29%) | |
| Bauer | 8 | 2 | 31 | 0 | 83 | 13 | 6 | 0 | 5 | 0 | 49 | 6 |
| Bush | 76 | 7 | 132 | 0 | 315 | 0 | 11 | 2 | 2 | 1 | 28 | 1 |
| Dole | 16 | 12 | 23 | 0 | 50 | 0 | 20 | 0 | 36 | 3 | 9 | 0 |
| Forbes | 2 | 19 | 20 | 0 | 96 | 6 | 18 | 0 | 18 | 1 | 159 | 9 |
| Keyes | 0 | 24 | 9 | 1 | 33 | 2 | 14 | 1 | 13 | 0 | 48 | 14 |
| McCain | 204 | 44 | 52 | 0 | 198 | 3 | 28 | 2 | 20 | 0 | 141 | 4 |
| | 309 | 108 | 267 | 1 | 775 | 24 | 97 | 5 | 94 | 5 | 434 | 34 |
| Repub | 417 (38%) | | 268 (18%) | | 799 (53%) | | 102 (15%) | | 99 (15%) | | 468 (70%) | |
| | 688 | 120 | 1080 | 9 | 1069 | 25 | 149 | 5 | 137 | 7 | 473 | 34 |
| Total | 808 (27%) | | 1089 (36%) | | 1094 (37%) | | 154 (19%) | | 144 (18%) | | 507 (63%) | |

*acclaims/attacks

Technology Council) in the following quotation: "In 1996, Governor Bush created the Science and Technology Council to devise a strategic plan to ensure Texas remains at the forefront in high tech job growth." Likewise, Gore acclaimed his past record in the area of fighting crime in this statement: "As Vice President, he has helped lead the way to record reductions in crime over the past six years, with more police on the streets, more crime prevention programs then before, new measures to keep guns out of the hands of criminals and tougher penalties for violent criminals." In contrast, this statement from Bradley's Internet site exemplified a future plan utterance: "First, to attract new teachers, the program would offer up to 4 years of loan forgiveness for 50,000 students each year—up to $5,000 per year for 4 years—for a commitment to teach in an elementary or secondary school of high need." In this utterance, Bradley presented his future plan (a means) for attracting new teachers. In this quotation, McCain discussed his future plan for ensuring tax cuts do not increase the national debt: "I would fully pay for family tax relief by cutting billions of dollars of pork barrel spending and special interest tax loopholes, such as sugar and ethanol subsidies, and using nearly one-quarter of the non-social security budget surplus." Inclusion of specific cuts means that this is a future plan. This excerpt from Bauer's Internet site exemplified general goals, which are more about ends than means: "The worldwide deflation has taken a mounting toll on American agriculture. As president, I will fight to open the door to new export and trade markets on every continent." This statement is clearly a goal that Bauer has for American agriculture. This statement from Dole also exemplified a general goal: Dole "called for investing in a strong national defense, restoring basic readiness and making the development of a missile defense system a top priority." In this statement, Dole established her goals for national security.

A *chi-square* indicates the difference between the Democrats and Republicans was significant for the three forms of policy ($\chi^2$ [$df$=2]=513.7, $p < .001$). The Republicans focused more on past deeds than the Democrats (38 percent to 26 percent). In addition, the Democrats focused more on future plans than Republicans (54 percent to 18 percent). Finally, the Republicans focused on general goals more than did the Democrats (53 percent to 20 percent).

Bradley and Gore differed significantly in their allocation of policy comments ($\chi^2$ [$df$=2]=55.4, $p < .001$). Gore focused more on past deeds (30 percent to 20 percent) and general goals (16 percent to 10 percent) than Bradley did whereas Bradley emphasized his future plans (70 percent to 54 percent) more than Gore. The Republican candidates also differed significantly in their policy comments ($\chi^2$ [$df$=10]=213.4, $p < .001$). McCain and Keyes discussed their past deeds more than the other four Republican candidates (50 percent and 35 percent respectively). Bush discussed future plans more than the other candidates (25 percent) with Bauer and Dole having the second largest portion (10 percent each). Finally, for general goals Forbes and Bauer had the greatest percentage (71 percent and 70 percent respectively).

Character utterances were stressed (63 percent) more than personal qualities (19 percent) or leadership ability (18 percent). For example, Bauer acclaimed his personal quality of plain speaking: "Bauer made it clear if he does run, people will know where he stands." Similarly, Bradley's Internet site noted that: "Bill was a self-described 'workhorse' in the Senate." In this quotation, Bradley acclaimed the personal quality of hard work. This statement from McCain is an example of a character utterance that concerns leadership: "John McCain is a man more tested and better prepared than anyone to lead America into the $21^{st}$ century." As indicated in this quotation, McCain feels he is better prepared than others to lead the nation. This statement from Forbes is an additional example of acclaiming leadership ability: "Steve Forbes is a successful chief executive and international business leader." The final form of character utterance is ideals. This excerpt is an example of a Bush utterance on ideals: Bush "set the goal that all children should be welcomed in life and protected by law." Bush's pro-life position in this statement is driven by his values and therefore is an ideal. Finally, Dole provides another example of ideals in this quotation: "I believe in and will fight for the constitutional right of the people to own and use firearms for sport, hunting, or protection." This quotation is a clear statement of Dole's values in the area of gun control.

Democratic webpages addressed personal qualities more than the Republicans' (38 percent to 15 percent). In addition, the Democrats addressed leadership in a greater proportion than the Republicans (33 percent to 15 percent). However, the Republicans had far more utterances that were coded as ideals when compared to the Democrats (70 percent to 29 percent). A *chi-square* computed on forms of character and political party was significant ($\chi^2$ [$df$=2]=82.9, $p < .001$).

There was also a significant difference between the distribution of character statements by Bradley and Gore ($\chi^2$[$df$=2]=9.1, $p < .025$). Examination of Table 5.5 reveals that Bradley emphasized personal qualities more than Gore (43 percent to 27 percent). Bradley also emphasized leadership more than Gore (36 percent to 27 percent). Although Gore focused more on ideals than Bradley (46 percent to 20 percent). The Republicans also differed significantly in the distribution of character statements ($\chi^2$[$df$=10]=154.3, $p < .001$). Bush (29 percent) and Dole (29 percent) focused the most on personal qualities. Dole also focused more on leadership than the other Republican contenders did (57 percent). Forbes (82 percent) and Bauer (83 percent) addressed ideals more than the other Republicans did.

## Issues Addressed in Primary Web Pages

Inspection of Table 5.6 indicates that Bradley devoted the majority of his policy statement to the issue of health care (excluding the "other" category). For example, Bradley had this comment about health care on his Internet site: "Bill Bradley's health care proposal is designed to revitalize America's approach to improving the health of its people." Health care was the second most important issue among Democrats. Gore, on the other hand, devoted the majority of his policy statements to the issue of education (again, excluding the "other" category) which was also the most important issue among Democratic voters. Gore included this comment about

Table 5.6. Issues Addressed in 2000 Democratic Primary Web Pages

| Issue | Poll | Bradley* | Gore |
|---|---|---|---|
| Education | 23 | 67 (3) | 261 (2) |
| Health Care | 16 | 103 (2) | 102 (4) |
| Social Security | 13 | 4 (6) | 8 (7) |
| Crime/Drugs | 12 | 0 (7) | 121 (3) |
| Taxes/Tax Cuts | 5 | 6 (5) | 26 (6) |
| Medicare/Prescription Drugs | 4 | 0 (7) | 6 (8) |
| Foreign Affairs | 2 | 21 (4) | 34 (5) |
| Other | – | 173 (1) | 575 (1) |
| Spearman ρ | | -.02, *ns* | .05, *ns* |

*Frequency (rank)  Enslow (1999)

education on his Internet site: "States and school districts that turn around failing schools should receive performance bonuses recognizing their achievements and rewarding their hard work." The Spearman ρs computed on the rank of issues most important to Democrats and how frequently the Democratic candidates referred to these issues were not significant.

The issues addressed in the Republican candidate Internet sites are displayed in Table 5.7. With the exception of the "other" category, Bush addressed the issue that was the most important to Republican voters (education) the most. Bush said this about education on his Internet site: "Texas school districts are allowed more

Table 5.7. Issues Addressed in 2000 Republican Primary Web Pages

| Issue | Poll | Bauer* | Bush | Dole | Forbes | Keyes | McCain |
|---|---|---|---|---|---|---|---|
| Education | 19 | 6 (6) | 115 (2) | 9 (4) | 9 (5) | 5 (2) | 67 (3) |
| Taxes/Tax Cuts | 11 | 8 (4) | 32 (4) | 11 (3) | 29 (2) | 5 (2) | 101 (2) |
| Social Security | 9 | 17 (3) | 10 (6) | 5 (6) | 15 (3) | 3 (6) | 48 (4) |
| Crime/Drugs | 8 | 8 (4) | 0 (8) | 27 (2) | 14 (4) | 0 (7) | 10 (7) |
| Health Care | 8 | 7 (7) | 18 (5) | 0 (7) | 7 (6) | 4 (4) | 40 (6) |
| Foreign Affairs | 7 | 25 (2) | 114 (3) | 7 (5) | 0 (7) | 4 (4) | 46 (5) |
| Medicare/Prescrip-tion Drugs | 5 | 2 (8) | 6 (7) | 0 (7) | 0 (7) | 0 (7) | 1 (8) |
| Other | – | 66 (1) | 235 (1) | 42 (1) | 69 (1) | 48 (1) | 192 (1) |
| Spearman ρ | | -.33, *ns* | -.01, *ns* | -.12, *ns* | .16, *ns* | .12, *ns* | .23, *ns* |

*Frequency (rank)  Enslow (1999)

flexibility than ever before to seek out creative alternative [sic] for at-risk or special needs students. No longer limited to public sector solutions, districts can contract for services with private entities and organization [sic] to serve most effectively the needs of all Texas children." McCain addressed taxes/tax cuts and education second and third most when compared to the other Republican issues of importance (excluding "other"). For example, McCain made these comments about taxes/tax cuts on his Internet site: "I would fully pay for family tax relief by cutting billions of dollars of pork barrel spending and special interest tax loopholes, such as sugar and ethanol subsidies, and using nearly one-quarter of the non-Social Security budget surplus." In addition, McCain said this about education: "Education reform is not an option, it's a must if our country is to remain strong, and our children are to be prepared for a future worthy of their potential." The Spearman $\rho$ did not reach significance for any of the Republican candidates.

# Implications

The candidate Internet sites in many ways resemble other campaign message forms (e.g., TV spots, radio spots, and debates) in that acclaims outnumber attacks, which in turn are more common than defenses. This distribution of utterances seems reasonable because voters do not like mudslinging, so acclaims should outnumber attacks. At times candidates must use a strategy of defense but there are several drawbacks to using defenses. First, when defending against an attack the candidate is taken off message and forced to address a topic that may be more favorable to the opponent. Second, when engaging in defense the candidate could be perceived as reactive versus proactive. Finally, the candidate must identify the attack in order to defend against it. If voters have not heard of the attack, defending against it may inform them of the candidate's alleged weakness.

Even though as indicated above acclaims should outnumber attacks, which in turn should be greater than defenses, we would argue that these candidates went too far in their high percentage of acclaims (95 percent) and low percentage of attacks (5 percent) or defenses (0.1 percent). While voters dislike mudslinging it is also true that voters need comparative information from the candidates on their Internet sites (Stromer-Galley et al., 2001).[2] With web pages candidates can please those who dislike mudslinging and provide comparative information. First, it should be noted that placing additional information on campaign Internet sites does not significantly increase the overall expense of design or maintenance (Benoit & Benoit, 2000). Next, candidates could have made comparative information available and simply placed hyperlinks to that information. If visitors to the candidate's Internet site do not want this comparative information, it is easy for them to ignore the hyperlink and read only what they are interested in reading. If candidates had done this, their Internet sites would be more appealing to those who are interested in comparing candidates and their policy positions. Finally, this strategy of using hyperlinks to make comparative information available to viewers could also apply to defenses (as noted above the candidates devoted only a small portion of their web page discourse to defending themselves and their positions).

For target of attack several findings are worthy of mention. First, Bradley attacked Gore more than Gore attacked Bradley. This result is not surprising given that Bradley trailed Gore throughout the primary. In fact, this finding is consistent with previous research in that Benoit (1999) found that the most attacks in TV spots were from candidates who trailed throughout the campaign. In other words, Bradley simply employed the same strategy on his Internet sites as he and others have done with their TV spots. Likewise, given that Gore never trailed Bradley, Gore attacked the Republicans more on his Internet site. As for the Republicans, they only devoted 5 percent of their attacks towards each other and the majority of their attacks towards the status quo or the Democrats. Therefore, Republican strategy was one of attacking the previous eight years of Democratic rule rather than attacking each other.

One question concerns why the Republican candidates did not attack Bush more given that he led in the polls throughout the primaries.[3] One possible explanation is that the candidates were not able to target their Internet site messages like other media formats. For example, radio listeners' demographics tend to be homogeneous and cater to a narrow segment of the population (Vivian, 1999). Given this, candidates can target a particular radio station (that caters to a homogeneous population) in a particular primary state (with issues important to that state or location). Likewise, particularly in the primary, candidates are not producing TV spots for national distribution. On their Internet sites, candidates needed to cater their message to the population of citizens with Internet access given that they have no controls over who the viewing audience will be. In other words, the candidates who trailed Bush may not have attacked him because they where unsure who the audience to the attack would be.

The topic of candidate Internet sites varied widely between the parties and the candidates. The Democrats addressed policy 21 percent more than did the Republicans and, of course, this means that the Republicans focused on character 21 percent more than the Democrats did. Of all of the candidates, Forbes (41 percent) and Keyes (43 percent) addressed policy the least and character the most and Gore (97 percent) and Bush (92 percent) addressed policy the most and character the least. The fact that the Republicans as a group and Forbes and Keyes individually addressed policy the least is not surprising given that four of the six Republican candidates have not held an elected office and therefore their depth of policy proposals may be limited when compared to the candidates who have held elected office. In addition, the finding that Gore and Bush addressed policy the most is consistent with research on other message forms in that, in the aggregate, winners discuss policy more than character (Benoit, 2000). Given this, we think it was a mistake for Forbes and Keyes to devote such a large percentage of their utterances to character versus policy.

Bauer (7 percent) and Forbes (15 percent) focused least on past deeds and McCain (50 percent) focused the most on his past deeds. This is also understandable given that Bauer and Forbes has never held a publicly elected office and McCain had been in a public office since 1982. In other words, McCain simply has more experience in public office, which gives him more past deeds to discuss than Bauer or Forbes. For the other forms of policy, Bradley provided viewers with the highest percentage of future plans (70 percent) and McCain provided the lowest percentage (10 percent). For general goals, Forbes (71 percent) and Bauer (70 percent) had the highest percent with Bradley having the lowest at only 10 percent. Bradley's use of specific plans for reform my have been intended to, indirectly, show Gore's weakness. This proposal for change works as an implicit attack (there would be no need for future plans if there were no problems). In addition, it may have been a mistake for Forbes and Bauer to rely so heavily on vague general goals.

The forms of character were distributed somewhat evenly for the Democrats (personal qualities: 38 percent, leadership: 33 percent, and ideals: 29 percent) while the Republicans devoted 70 percent of their character themes to ideals and only 15 percent to each personal qualities and leadership. Why is it that the Republicans focused disproportionately on ideals when compared to the Democrats? One explanation is that the Republicans as a group were trying to take the moral high ground to contrast with Clinton/Gore. Bauer (83 percent) and Forbes (82 percent) had the largest percentage of their utterances focused on ideals and Dole (13 percent) had the least.

One final implication for these results concerns the issues addressed in the primary web pages as Hansen and Benoit (2001) indicate: "If a set of policy issues is important to the American public, it seems reasonable for the candidates to address those issues most often. In addition, it would seem irresponsible or counterproductive for a candidate to ignore or to give little attention to the policy issues that are important to the voters" (p. 2092). They go on to argue that this holds true for most campaign message forms (TV spots, radio spots, and debates) with the exception of candidate Internet sites. They indicate that candidate websites are different from other media forms in how they address important issues, given that candidates have the ability to place virtually unlimited amounts of material on their Internet site. In other words, there is no need for candidates to be selective in what material is placed on their Internet site; they only need good navigational tools. Having said this, the fact that there were no significant relationships between the public agenda and the candidate's Internet site is not troubling.

In conclusion, this chapter has provided an in-depth understanding of primary web pages and is important given the lack of scholarship in this area. This chapter will serve as a point of reference for making comparisons with the candidate Internet sites in the general election.

## Notes

1. Bradley withdrew from the election in March of 2000, Bauer left the race after the New Hampshire primary on February 1, Dole dropped out of the presidential race in October of 1999, Forbes's withdrawal was during the week of February 12, and McCain withdrew from the race in March of 2000.

2. The assumption here is that if candidates provide comparative information the information will be attacks against opponent.

3. In national polls of registered Republicans Bush led throughout the primary (see Gallup News Service, 2000).

# Chapter 6

# Primary Radio Spots

Woman: You know, after 17 years in Washington, Senator John McCain has become an expert at saying one thing but doing another.
Man: Like what?
Woman: Well, McCain went to Saginaw and denounced special interests, but then held a Washington fund raiser and accepted contributions from special interests with legislation before his committee.
Man: Oh, brother. (Bush, "Michigan-McCain")

McCain: This is Senator John McCain. I'm running for President to give you your government back and take the big special interest money out of politics for good. But some power brokers fear our conservative reforms. They're using every old political trick they can to fool you about me. But you know the truth. (McCain, "Michigan Appeal")

Harkin: This is Tom Harkin, and as many of you know, I'm strongly supporting Al Gore, and I wanna tell you why. Al Gore is a man of real character and strong family values. He's been a fighter for working families and he's put forth a clear national agenda to improve health care and education and keeping our economy strong. But there's another reason I support Al Gore. It's his record of helping Iowa. Time after time, I've been able to call on Al Gore to help us. Time after time, Al Gore has come through for Iowa. (Gore, "Harkin Testimonial")

At one time in the United States, radio was the dominant medium by which presidential candidates communicated with voters. As early as 1924, candidates were using the radio to deliver political speeches, with their messages reaching more potential voters than ever before. Between the Democrats and Republicans, $160,000 was spent on radio broadcasts that election year (Chester, 1969). Radio continued enjoying a dominant place in the presidential elections until the 1960s, when the growth of television in the United States provided candidates a way of reaching a large, general audience.

In a presidential primary contest, radio still offers advantages to candidates compared to television advertising. First, radio advertising is less expensive than television advertising. This is critical when one considers the cost of staging a state-by-state campaign. Davis (1997) noted that, by the end of the twentieth century, candidates had to raise $20 million dollars by the start of a presidential election year in order to be a serious contender for their party's nomination. For campaigns without substantial financial backing, radio provides a cost-effective manner of communicating with voters. Even candidates with a large war chest can benefit from using radio, stretching out dollars over the course of a campaign that extend for several months. Radio's more affordable advertising rates also allow candidate messages to be aired with greater frequency, allowing potential voters to be exposed more often to a campaign message (Hutchens, 1999). Second, with its multitude of program formats, radio is capable of delivering specific audience demographic groups to advertisers. In a presidential primary campaign, candidates are seeking to connect with specific groups of voters. Campaigns can buy advertising time on radio stations which attract these desired demographic groups and, thus, reach those potential voters (Fletcher, 1999; Hutchens, 1999). Third, a candidate's radio spots can be produced more quickly than television spots. As presidential primary contests can turn on the news events of a single day, the ability to quickly produce and air a candidate's radio commercial in a timely fashion can influence the outcome of the election. Fourth, radio messages can be localized. In many local and regional elections, such as state or congressional contests, radio becomes an important medium for reaching voters (Whillock, 1991). Although presidential primaries and caucuses will eventually lead to one national winner, these events are staged either one state at a time (Iowa, New Hampshire) or on a regional basis (Super Tuesday, with numerous states across the country holding elections on the same day). Thus, presidential primaries can take on the feel of a state or regional election. In races where candidates are speaking to a specific audience, the message can be personalized mentioning the state's or a particular city's name or using politicians or other citizens popular in that state.

We believe the medium of radio played a significant role in the 2000 presidential primaries, as candidates introduced themselves to voters, stated policy positions, and providing a vehicle for vigorously attacking opponents for their party's nomination.

## Comparing Radio and Television

Radio and television are distinct media in that radio only requires a message receiver to process information by listening; in contrast, television requires the message receiver to pay attention to process information through listening and viewing (Bucholz & Smith, 1991). This difference in processing messages has been examined in research efforts comparing the effectiveness of radio messages and television messages. Klein (1981) looked at the ability to recall advertising messages seen in radio, television, and print. While subjects had better recall of the print and radio spots immediately after viewing them, a post-test taken two weeks later revealed subjects retained more information from the television advertisement than either the radio or print ads. Bucholz and Smith (1991) reported that consumer involvement was a key element for retaining information. Subjects seeing television advertisements generally reported the same level of message processing, regardless of whether test subjects had low or high involvement with the content of the ad. For radio, involvement with ad content correlated positively with levels of processing the message. When subject involvement was high, message processing approached the same level as television. When subject involvement was low, the ability to process messages declined. Although not conclusive, this suggests that radio advertising may be effective in the short term (important in a compact presidential primary schedule) and for undecided voters who might be expected to have high involvement.

Researchers have also examined the effectiveness of politicians on radio versus television, although the studies have concentrated on broadcast speeches rather than spots. Pool (1959) examined the impact on voters in the 1952 campaign and found Eisenhower was perceived as being a more effective communicator on television whereas Stevenson was better on the radio. Cohen (1978) argued that in a controlled environment, subjects who were potential voters found some candidates to be more effective on television commercials, whereas others sound better on the radio. But Cohen could not explain why candidates had fared better on one medium than another.

One of the most famous comparisons of candidates' performance on radio versus television in American politics occurred in 1960, when John F. Kennedy debated Richard Nixon. Sindlinger and Company, a Pennsylvania research agency, reported people listening to the first Kennedy-Nixon debate on the radio thought Nixon had won, while those watching on television declared Kennedy as the winner. This prompted Rubin (1967) to argue that radio forced voters to concentrate on words and ideas, while television forced voters to concentrate on images. It should be noted that the Sindlinger research, as well as other studies on the first Kennedy-Nixon debate, has been called into question because of problems with the data used (Vancil & Pendell, 1987, among others). Kraus (1996), however, in analyzing the various arguments, supports the belief that people listening to the debate on radio believed Nixon had won the debate while people watching television thought Kennedy had won. The conflicting and controversial research into the impact of radio and television messages suggests additional research into the effects of radio would be useful. Still, no research denies the efficiency of radio advertising.

There has been relatively little research into the content of radio spots. What research has been conducted on the content of presidential radio spots focuses on general election contests (see chapter 14 for a discussion of this research). This brief literature review suggests there are no content analytic studies of primary radio spots in a presidential election. Providing a functional analysis of authentic radio spots from the 2000 presidential primaries allows us to see how candidates utilize the medium in delivering their campaign messages. The functional approach also allows us to make a comparison between radio and television spots used during the 2000 primaries.

## 2000 Primary Radio Spots

We obtained a total of sixty-eight radio spots, forty-nine from the five Republican candidates and nineteen from the two Democratic candidates. Spots were obtained from over-the-air stations, state radio networks, radio stations broadcasting over the Internet, and from candidate web sites. Among Republicans, we studied twenty spots from Forbes, thirteen from McCain, eleven from Bush, four from Keyes, and one from Bauer. Among Democrats, we studied fifteen by Gore and four by Bradley. The distribution of these spots among candidates is described in Table 6.1. The limited number of spots on the Democratic side can be attributed in part to having only two major candidates in the race.

Of the spots that we examined, sixty-two were a full minute long, five were a half-minute long, and one was a quarter-minute in length. This is in contrast with 2000 primary television spots we studied: Most primary television spots were a half-minute in length. As previously suggested, radio is a less expensive medium than television. This may allow candidates to purchase more time for these longer commercials to communicate with voters.

Table 6.1. Length of 2000 Primary Radio Spots in Sample

|  | 15 | 30 | 60 | Total |
|---|---|---|---|---|
| Gore | 0 | 1 | 14 | 15 |
| Bradley | 0 | 0 | 4 | 4 |
| Democrat | 0 | 1 | 18 | 19 |
| Bauer | 0 | 0 | 1 | 1 |
| Bush | 0 | 0 | 11 | 11 |
| Forbes | 1 | 4 | 15 | 20 |
| Keyes | 0 | 0 | 4 | 4 |
| McCain | 0 | 0 | 13 | 13 |
| Republican | 0 | 4 | 44 | 49 |
| Total | 1 | 5 | 62 | 68 |

## Functions of 2000 Primary Radio Spots

Primary radio spots were mostly positive, with 75 percent of all utterances consisting of acclaims (these data are displayed in Table 6.2). For Democrats, the percentage was even higher (87 percent). In "New Hampshire Endorsements," Bradley emphasized his desire to change government: "Bradley truly wants to change business as usual and the status quo. Bradley's candidacy and message are good for New Hampshire and America. He deserves to be heard in more states." This is an acclaim because Bradley is promoting his ability to reform government. In a Gore spot called "Monday," New Hampshire Governor Jean Shaheen told her home-state voters "I know Al Gore. I trust him. I know he's the best for New Hampshire. He's a fighter, standing up for our jobs, our environment, our families, and for a women's right to choose." In this case, Governor Shaheen touted the vice-president's work on issues critical to Democratic voters: jobs, the environment, and abortion rights.

Republicans also had a high percentage of acclaims in their utterances (70 percent). Forbes had the greatest number of acclaims among GOP candidates. In "Daughters," Moria Forbes told radio listeners "I think my father's been a wonderful role model for my four sisters and I." Forbes used his family to identify himself with family values, an issue identified in polls as important to Republican voters. Many of McCain's spots in the primaries also acclaimed his character, such as one featuring Congressional Medal of Honor winner Bud Day:

> Christmas service of 1971 was centered around scripture that John had gotten from the first Bible that we had been able to get from the Vietnamese, and it was wonderful to have the written word of God. John composed an extremely

Table 6.2. Functions of 2000 Primary Radio Spots

|  | Acclaims | Attacks | Defenses |
|---|---|---|---|
| Gore | 28 | 16 | 0 |
| Bradley | 173 | 14 | 0 |
| Democrat | 201 (87%) | 30 (13%) | 0 |
| Bauer | 6 | 8 | 0 |
| Bush | 105 | 46 | 0 |
| Forbes | 164 | 68 | 0 |
| Keyes | 22 | 15 | 0 |
| McCain | 140 | 36 | 0 |
| Republican | 437 (72%) | 173 (28%) | 0 |
| Total | 638 (76%) | 203 (24%) | 0 |

compelling sermon that night about the importance of Christmas. Everyone sat just glued to their seats. I think it was certainly a shot to everyone's morale to hear those Christian words in that very un-Christian place.

This utterance acclaimed McCain's character, and specifically, his religious faith. In the process, McCain introduced himself to Republican primary voters who may not have know about his background.

Attacks accounted for 25 percent of all utterances in primary radio spots. Attacks in Democratic spots accounted for only 12 percent of all utterances. Bradley used attacks in "Economic Disparity," highlighting problems facing middle-class families: "If you are a hard working middle class family that has a wife working and a husband working, sometimes two jobs, that means that you are just a couple of paychecks away from having serious economic problems, of losing your health insurance, of not being able to send your child to college." In this attack, Bradley argued that despite good economic times under the Clinton-Gore administration, many in the middle class were still facing tough economic prospects.

Republican spots used attacks with greater frequency (30 percent) than the Democratic spots we examined. In "Honey 30," Forbes states, "You know, if you put a pot of honey in a forest, bears are gonna come along and put their paws in it. You put a pot of money in Washington, politicians are gonna come along and put their paws on it. They can't help it." Forbes used this utterance as an attack on politicians' spending habits.

Defenses accounted for less than 1 percent of all utterances in primary radio spots we coded. All of the defenses found in Democratic spots (1 percent) were utilized by Gore. When Bradley attacked Gore on his past failure to strongly support abortion rights, Gore ran a spot ("Trailing in the Polls") which attempted to refute Bradley's claims: "Here are the facts. Al Gore is pro-choice." This is an example of defense by simple denial by Gore, countering the claims made by the Bradley spot. We found no defenses among the utterances in Republican primary radio spots. We found a significant difference in the use of acclaim, attack, and defense utterances found in Democratic spots, which featured a higher percentage of acclaims, versus Republican spots, which included a higher percentage of attacks ($\chi^2[df=2]=34.5, p < .001$). A significant difference was also found in the use of acclaim, attack, and defense utterances between Democrats Bradley and Gore ($\chi^2[df=2]=22.8, p < .001$). While Gore's primary radio spots had a higher frequency of acclaim than Bradley (91 percent for Gore versus 67 percent for Bradley), Bradley had the higher percentage of attacks (33 percent versus 7 percent for Gore). We also found a significant difference in the use of acclaims and attacks among the five Republican candidates ($\chi^2[df=4]=16.5, p < .01$). McCain had the highest percentage of acclaims in his primary radio spots (80 percent), followed by Forbes (71 percent) and Bush (65 percent). Bauer had the highest percent of attacks (57 percent), but it should be noted only one Bauer campaign spot was obtained for our sample. Keyes had the next highest percentage of attacks (41 percent), followed by Bush (35 percent) and Forbes (29 percent).

Table 6.3. Target of Democratic Attacks in 2000 Primary Radio Spots

|  | Bradley | Gore | Republicans | SQ |
|---|---|---|---|---|
| Bradley | – | 11 | 0 | 5 |
| Gore | 10 | – | 5 | 0 |
|  | 10 (50%) | 10 (50%) |  |  |
| Total | 20 (67%) |  | 5 (33%) | 5 (33%) |

## Target of Attack in Primary Radio Spots

Democrats attacked each other with more frequency (67 percent) than they attacked either the status quo (18 percent) or Republicans (15 percent). Bradley made Gore the target in 64 percent of his attacks while the status quo was targeted in the other 36 percent of his attacks. Bradley did not attack Republicans in any of his spots. Gore targeted Bradley in 69 percent of his attack utterances and Republicans in the other 31 percent. Gore made no attacks on the status quo in any of his primary radio spots (these data are reported in Table 6.3).

Republican candidates made their primary opponents the target of 62 percent of all attack utterances in primary radio spots. This compares with 23 percent of attack utterances targeting the status quo and 15 percent targeting the Democrats (see Table 6.4). Bush had the highest percentage of attacks on his fellow candidates (94 percent). Bush targeted McCain in particular, making the Arizona senator the subject of 85 percent of his attack utterances. An example of this can be found in

Table 6.4. Target of Republican Attacks in Primary Radio Spots

|  | Bauer | Bush | Forbes | Keyes | McCain | Repub | Dem | SQ |
|---|---|---|---|---|---|---|---|---|
| Bauer | – | 0 | 0 | 0 | 0 | 1 | 7 | 0 |
| Bush | 0 | – | 0 | 0 | 41 | 5 | 8 | 2 |
| Forbes | 0 | 21 | – | 0 | 0 | 4 | 15 | 28 |
| Keyes | 0 | 0 | 0 | – | 5 | 0 | 4 | 8 |
| McCain | 0 | 20 | 0 | 0 | – | 6 | 5 | 5 |
|  | 0 | 41 (40%) | 0 | 0 | 46 (45%) | 16 (16%) |  |  |
| Total |  |  | 103 (56%) |  |  |  | 43 (23%) | 39 (21%) |

"Breast Cancer,"which ran after Bush's loss to McCain in the New Hampshire primary. In this spot, a breast cancer survivor attacked McCain's record on funding women's health programs: "Like many, I had thought of supporting John McCain in next week's presidential primary. So I looked into his record. What I discovered was shocking. John McCain opposes many projects dedicated to women's health issues." Bush made the status quo the subject of only 4 percent of his attack utterances while Democrats accounted for the remaining 2 percent.

McCain made his Republican opponents the target of 78 percent of his attack utterances and Bush was the specific target in 61 percent of those utterances. In "Rocker," McCain ran a spot in New York state that compared Bush with Atlanta Braves pitcher John Rocker, who had made inflammatory statements about gays and minorities living in New York City: "The Sierra Club said it best. Quote, praising George Bush on clean air is like thanking John Rocker for contributions to civil rights." McCain targeted the status quo in 14 percent of his attack utterances while Democrats were targeted on the fewest occasions (9 percent).

Forbes made his Republican opponents and the status quo the primary targets of his attack utterances (40 percent each). When attacking members of his own party, most of those targeted Bush (34 percent). In "Education," Forbes went on Iowa radio to attack Bush on his education record in Texas: "George W. Bush likes to say that when it comes to education, no child will be left behind. Well, then, how does he explain that since has been Governor of Texas, the SAT score for Texas school children has dropped from the 40th worst in the nation to 46th worst in the nation." One example of Forbes attacking the status quo is found in "Honey," when he attacked politicians in Washington for the way they handle Social Security: "Politicians shouldn't raid the Social Security trust fund. They shouldn't be stealing from it, plundering it. That belongs to the American people." Instead of blaming any specific party in this case, Forbes blamed the mindset of Washington politicians, making the case to elect someone like himself, who has never held elected office. The other 20 percent of attack utterances from Forbes targeted the Democrats. While some attacks were directed at the Clinton-Gore record, Forbes also went after Gore on the issue of abortion: "I support restrictions. I support parental consent. Al Gore doesn't. I would stop using taxpayer funds for abortion. Al Gore won't. And I oppose partial birth abortions. Al Gore doesn't." In that passage, Forbes was both acclaiming his views on abortion and attacking Gore, the anticipated Democratic nominee, trying to convince Republicans concerned with this issue that he represents their views.

Keyes made the status quo the most frequent target of his attack utterances (53 percent). In "Michigan," Keyes attacked the manner in which the national government is financed: "We've worked to build a nation to prosperity with principles. So why have the American people surrendered control over their hard-earned dollars in the form of an income tax?" Thirty-three percent of the attack utterances by Keyes were focused on his own party, all targeting McCain: "Here I contrast myself with Senator McCain. If he's so interested in America's military, why does he follow the Clinton policy when it comes to gays in the military" ("Michigan"). Keyes targeted Democrats in only 13 percent of his spots. In the only spot from Bauer that was analyzed we found 88 percent of the attacks targeted Democrats with the other 12 percent targeting his own party.

When comparing targets of attacks between Democrats and Republicans, no significant difference was found ($\chi^2[df=2]=.33$, *ns*). Due to our small *n*, we were unable to use *chi-square* to determine if there was a significant difference in the targets of attack utterances among candidates in their own party.

## Topics of Primary Radio Spots

The character of the presidential contenders in the 2000 election was a theme that resonated in primary radio spots. We found that 58 percent of all utterances in these spots concerned character whereas 42 percent dealt with policy. See Table 6.5.

Among the Democratic candidates, 53 percent of all utterances dealt with policy. Gore had the higher percentage of policy utterances (55 percent) among the two candidates. In "Going Strong," Gore cited a litany of policy pledges to Democratic voters: "Keep the budget balanced. Pay down the nation's debt. Use the surplus wisely to fix health care, to invest in our schools, to protect Medicare, to save Social Security." Bradley focused on policy in only 45 percent of his utterances: "Bill Bradley has a health care plan for insuring all children" ("The News").

Character was discussed in 47 percent of all Democratic utterances found in primary radio spots. Bradley was the Democratic candidate who made the most use of character (55 percent). In "The News," Bradley's vision and understanding of how the government should operate were extolled in a newspaper editorial: Table "Bradley . . . understands how things get done in government." This one passage

6.5. Topics of 2000 Primary Radio Spots

|  | Policy | Character |
|---|---|---|
| Gore | 19 | 25 |
| Bradley | 104 | 83 |
| Democrat | 123 (53%) | 108 (47%) |
| Bauer | 13 | 1 |
| Bush | 65 | 86 |
| Forbes | 94 | 138 |
| Keyes | 14 | 23 |
| McCain | 44 | 132 |
| Republican | 230 (38%) | 380 (62%) |
| Total | 353 (42%) | 488 (58%) |

emphasized the leadership skills that Bradley accumulated while serving as a member of the U.S. Senate. Gore discussed character in only 45 percent of his utterances. A number of character utterances found in Gore radio spots stressed that the vice-president is "fighting for us," the voters. An example of this is found in "Super Tuesday," where Gore spoke directly to voters: "If you entrust me with the Presidency, I will fight for you." An announcer who reiterated this message followed Gore: "Al Gore. Fighting for us." This refrain was found consistently in Gore's radio spots and other campaign discourse during the 2000 election year.

Policy accounted for 37 percent of all Republican utterances in their primary radio spots. Bauer had the highest percentage of policy utterances among Republican candidates (93 percent). In "Bauer-Iowa," he warned of threats against the United States posed by other nations and broadly outlined: "As President, I'll end business as usual with China and, if necessary, re-open our military bases in Panama to protect our interests." Forbes also discussed policy in 42 percent of his themes. Bush discussed policy in 40 percent of all utterances while Keyes discussed policy in 38 percent of his comments. McCain made least use of policy utterances among Republicans (25 percent).

Character was addressed in 63 percent of all Republican utterances found in the primary radio spots we examined. McCain made the most frequent use of character utterances (75 percent). As stated before, the Arizona senator used many of his early radio spots to tell personal stories to introduce himself to voters. "Cindy," a spot recorded by Senator McCain's wife, described the adoption of their daughter Bridget:

> I was working in Bangladesh. We were a medical team, and we made the decision to go see Mother Theresa's orphanage. And I came to know Bridget. I was getting ready to leave and the nuns said, "Could you please to take her, she needs medical help." So I made the decision without ever calling John to bring her back. And I realized on the plane that I simply couldn't give this child up. I showed up in Phoenix and John just leaned over to me and kind of quietly whispered, "Where is she going to go?" And I said, "Well, I thought maybe she'd go to our house." And, he said, "Well, I had a feeling that might be the case. She's welcome in our    ' home." And that was all we said.

This testimonial from McCain's wife should resonate with potential voters on several levels, including McCain's belief in family, his generosity in opening his home to a child he had never met, and respecting the wishes of his spouse, a point which could appeal to female voters.

Keyes favored character utterances in the primary radio spots we examined from his campaign (62 percent). In "Michigan-2," Keyes discussed the importance of values in the campaign: "We must address the moral crisis of this country's life as our top priority in every area of our life. To restore our self-discipline and our claim to liberty." This was an appeal that Keyes tried to make time and again with the so-called religious right of the Republican party.

Bush discussed character frequently (60 percent) in the radio spots we analyzed. Many of Bush's spots sought to contrast him with the image Republicans held of President Clinton. In "Iowa-Leadership." an announcer proclaimed "Elect a proven leader who will restore dignity and honor to the Oval Office." The passage also tried to call attention to Bush's experience as governor of Texas. Forbes also utilized character utterances most frequently (58 percent). An example in which Forbes emphasized his character was "Montage," in which a collection of speakers made short statements such as "He's honest" and "He's a leader."

We found a significant difference in the use of policy and character utterances between Democratic and Republican candidates in primary radio spots ($\chi^2[df=1]=17$, $p < .001$). While Democrats emphasized policy utterances (53 percent of all utterances compared to 37 percent for the Republicans), Republicans focused on character (63 percent versus 47 percent for the Democrats). A significant difference was also found in topics of Republican primary radio spots ($\chi^2[df=4]=32.2$, $p < .001$). McCain used character utterances most often (75 percent) followed by Keyes (62 percent) and Bush (60 percent). Bauer discussed character (7 percent) least often among the Republican candidates. No difference was found between the two Democratic candidates' use of policy and character utterances ($\chi^2[df=1]=1.4$, $ns$).

## Forms of Policy and Character in 2000 Primary Radio Spots

In our examination of 2000 primary radio spots, we found candidates used the medium to stress general goals when discussing policy and personal qualities when discussing character (see Table 6.6). Sixty-seven percent of all policy utterances in primary radio spots dealt with a candidate's general goals, while only 23 percent touched on past deeds and 10 percent on future plans. Fifty-three percent of all character utterances stressed personal qualities of a candidate, 36 percent percent focused on ideals, and 11 percent discussed leadership. These data are reported in Table 6.6.

Among the Democratic policy utterances, 78 percent focused on general goals, with Gore making more frequent use of them than Bradley (85 percent versus 42 percent). In "Rare," Senator Ted Kennedy endorsed Gore and discussed what Gore would do to improve education: "Al Gore has proposed the biggest national commitment to education since the GI bill's smaller class sizes, modernized schools, help families save for college." This utterance is a general goal as it discussed what Gore would accomplish to aid education if elected. Bradley also used general goals to discuss education priorities: "Bradley wants to spend heavily on education beginning early on in a child's life and continuing through adulthood" ("The News"). In this case, Bradley gave the assurance that he will make education a spending priority.

Twenty percent of the Democratic candidate utterances concerned past deeds, with Bradley making greater use of them than Gore (47 percent versus 15 percent). Bradley used past deeds to attack the record of Gore: "As a conservative Congressman from Tennessee, Al Gore voted against a woman's right to choose

Table 6.6. Forms of Policy and Character in 2000 Primary Radio Spots

| | Policy | | | | | | Character | | | | | |
| | Past Deeds* | | Future Plans | | General Goals | | Personal Qualities | | Leader-ship | | Ideals | |
|---|---|---|---|---|---|---|---|---|---|---|---|---|
| Bradley | 0 | 9 | 2 | 0 | 7 | 1 | 6 | 6 | 6 | 0 | 8 | 0 |
| Gore | 16 | 0 | 0 | 0 | 84 | 4 | 43 | 10 | 14 | 0 | 19 | 1 |
| Dem | 16 | 9 | 2 | 0 | 91 | 5 | 49 | 16 | 20 | 0 | 27 | 1 |
| | 25 (20%) | | 2 (2%) | | 96 (78%) | | 65 (57%) | | 20 (18%) | | 28 (25%) | |
| Bauer | 0 | 5 | 2 | 0 | 3 | 3 | 0 | 0 | 0 | 0 | 1 | 0 |
| Bush | 26 | 0 | 1 | 6 | 19 | 13 | 15 | 16 | 14 | 2 | 30 | 9 |
| Forbes | 0 | 6 | 15 | 1 | 48 | 24 | 57 | 14 | 7 | 4 | 38 | 19 |
| Keyes | 0 | 6 | 1 | 0 | 2 | 5 | 2 | 0 | 1 | 0 | 16 | 4 |
| McCain | 11 | 4 | 0 | 0 | 25 | 4 | 70 | 26 | 74 | 0 | 27 | 2 |
| Repub | 37 | 21 | 19 | 7 | 97 | 49 | 144 | 56 | 29 | 6 | 112 | 34 |
| | 58 (25%) | | 28 (8%) | | 242 (69%) | | 200 (53%) | | 49 (11%) | | 146 (38%) | |
| Total | 53 | 30 | 21 | 7 | 188 | 54 | 193 | 72 | 49 | 6 | 139 | 35 |
| | 83 (23%) | | 28 (8%) | | 242 (69%) | | 265 (54%) | | 55 (11%) | | 174 (35%) | |

*acclaims/attacks

84 percent of the time" ("Super Tuesday"). The ad "A Leader" talked about one of Gore's past deeds as vice president: "Al Gore stood up to the Republicans and fought to make sure Carol Mosley-Braun got her appointment as Ambassador." The spot was targeted to African-American voters, as Braun was the first female African-American senator in U.S. history.

These Democratic radio spots made use of future plans in only 2 percent of all policy utterances. Only 11 percent of Bradley's policy utterances were future plans, such as a demand to register all handguns. Gore made no use of future plans in any of his policy utterances.

Nearly two-thirds of Republican comments dealt with general goals (61 percent). Forbes made the most use of general goals (71 percent) in his primary radio spots. In "Code-3," Forbes appealed to voters frustrated by the current tax system: "That's why I proposed a simple flat tax: throw out the current code and have something in that looks like it was designed by a normal human being." Forbes acclaimed a general goal because he offered no specifics on how the flat tax would be implemented. McCain also made frequent use of general goals (66 percent): "As President, I'll reform education with school choice, re-build the military, and use the budget surplus to fix Social Security, lower taxes, and finally start paying down our debt" ("McCain-Michigan"). This utterance allowed McCain to cover the priorities he would have as president. Keyes stated general goals in 50 percent of his policy utterances, compared with 46 percent for Bush and Bauer.

Past deeds accounted for 25 percent of all Republican policy utterances. Keyes (43 percent) used past deeds with the greatest frequency among his party's presidential candidates. In "Keyes-Michigan," the candidate faults McCain: "John McCain supports Bill Clinton's 'Don't ask, don't tell' policy that allows homosexuals to serve in the military." Keyes was attacking McCain's support of a policy implemented by a president from the opposing party. Bush made frequent use of past deeds (41 percent), but as a means of boosting his own candidacy. In "McCain-Michigan," an announcer summarized Bush's record as governor in Texas: "Governor George Bush. He's cut taxes, reformed welfare, and improved schools." In summarizing these past deeds, Bush tried to show Republican voters that he has succeeded in addressing concerns of Republican voters. McCain discussed past deeds in 34 percent of his policy utterances: "The McCain bill protected 3.5-million acres of wilderness. Protected the Grand Canyon National Park from various forms of pollution. And John McCain wrote the law to foster responsible solutions to environmental problem" ("Rocker"). By citing his work as a senator, McCain attempted to draw a comparison between his record and that of his opponents regarding the environment. Forbes had the lowest percentage of past deeds among his policy utterances (6 percent). An example is found in "Parade": "The politicians in Washington are raiding the Social Security trust fund." This use of a past deed by Forbes attacked the status quo in the federal government.

Future plans represented only 14 percent of all policy utterances among the Republican primary radio spots we examined. Forbes had the highest percentage of future plans among his policy utterances (23 percent). In "Iowa-Taxes," an announcer stated "Only one leading candidates plans to abolish the marriage tax penalty, abolish capitol gains taxes, and immediately abolish death taxes. Only one leading candidate will permanently ban all new Internet sales taxes, repeal the Clinton-Gore tax increase, and the Bush tax increase of 1990." In this utterance, Forbes was citing specific actions that he would take to reform the tax codes. Bauer's spot (15 percent) stated specific plans for dealing with the threat posed by China, such as "He'll revoke China's most favored nation trading status." Again, Bauer specified a proposal to persuade voters to support his candidacy. Bush used future plans in 13 percent of his policy statements: "The McCain plan would eliminate the right of donors to receive a full deduction on some gifts to charity" ("Charity"). In this utterance, Bush attacked a future plan of McCain regarding tax cuts. Keyes relied on future plans in 7 percent of his policy utterances while McCain offered no future plans among his policy utterances.

A significant difference was found between Democratic and Republican candidates in the form of their policy utterances ($\chi^2[df=2]=17.1$, $p < .001$).

Democrats had a higher percentage of general goal utterances than the Republicans (78 percent versus 61 percent), while the GOP made more frequent use of utterances concerning past deeds (25 percent to 20 percent for Democrats) and future plans (14 percent to 2 percent for Democrats). Due to our overall small $n$, we were unable to use *chi-square* to determine if there was a significant difference in the form of policy utterances among candidates in their own party.

In examining forms of character utterances in 2000 Democratic primary radio spots, the candidates' personal qualities were most often addressed (57 percent). Gore emphasized personal qualities (62 percent) in his primary radio spots. In spots like "Turnout," an announcer highlighted Gore's willingness to fight for others: "We need a President who will fight to protect Medicare and Social Security. In my opinion, that's Al Gore." In other spots, Gore used utterances to attack personal qualities of his opponent: "Bill Bradley promised to run a positive campaign. But now, trailing in the polls, he's running attack ads" ("Trailing"). Negative campaigning on the part of an opponent is considered to be an attack on the personal qualities of that candidate. In the radio spots we examined from Bradley, personal qualities were discussed in 37 percent of his character utterances: "He might prove to have the backbone and ability of a Harry Truman" ("Country"). This utterance, pulled from a newspaper editorial supporting Bradley, highlighted Bradley's courage and ability while comparing him with former President Truman, a Democratic icon.

Ideals accounted for 26 percent of Democratic character utterances. Bradley (37 percent) called for common sense in how the government operates: "You should be fixing your roof when the sun is shining. The sun is shining now" ("Economic Disparity"). In this case, the ideal stressed by Bradley is that the country must invest in programs that will have long-term benefits. Twenty-three percent of Gore's character utterances dealt with ideals. In "Why I Switched," a surrogate for the Gore campaign discussing the issue of abortion claimed the real enemy in this election are "The Republican candidates who don't trust women to make responsible reproductive choices." Gore called attention to his own belief that women have the right to choose whether to have an abortion.

Leadership ability was the subject of 17 percent of Democratic character utterances found in the primary radio spots we examined. Leadership ability was discussed in 25 percent of Bradley's character utterances. When discussing Bradley's view that all handguns should be registered, an announcer said, "Few other candidates would be so bold." Bradley implied that he, and not Gore, will take the leadership role on a controversial issue like registering handguns. Gore discussed leadership ability in 15 percent of his character utterances: "See what positive leadership has meant and can mean for America" ("Trailing"). Gore called attention in this utterance to his role in the two Clinton administrations and that he has the necessary leadership skills to serve in the White House.

In Republican primary radio spots, we again found personal qualities were the most frequently used form of character utterance (52 percent). McCain made the most use of character utterances mentioning personal qualities (73 percent). Testimonials like "Gamboa," delivered by a Naval Academy classmate of McCain, dealt with nothing but the Arizona senator's personal qualities:

> John and I decided to take noon meal in the mess hall and found ourselves sitting with a first classmate. As the steward started serving the table, the first classman was very demeaning and arrogant. The Filipino steward appeared flustered. I looked over at John and I could tell he was getting angry. John said to the first classman, "Mister, why don't you pick on someone your own size?" And I about choked on my food when he said that.

In telling a story about McCain standing up for someone he didn't know, the spot portrayed McCain as being someone who would be willing to do the same thing as president. Forbes discussed personal qualities in campaign in 51 percent of his character utterances. An interesting example of how Forbes used personal qualities to acclaim himself and attack an opponent occurred in "Fight Back": "The extremist National Abortion League is running an ad attacking me and George Bush. I don't know about Governor Bush, but I'm ready to fight back." While proclaiming himself as a fighter for the anti-abortion movement, Forbes cast doubt on Bush's willingness to stand up on abortion, an issue critical to some Republican voters. Bush discusses personal qualities in 36 percent. In "Tax Cuts," an announcer noted Bush was "Earning support for his campaign for President the New Hampshire way: one voter at a time." Bush was highlighting his ability to relate to voters of New Hampshire through personal contact, something New Hampshire voters have come to insist upon from primary candidates who come to their state. Keyes only addressed personal qualities in 9 percent of his character utterances while Bauer made no mention of personal qualities in any of his character utterances.

Ideals represent 38 percent of all character utterances found in the Republican primary radio spots we examined. Keyes expressed the highest percentage of ideals among his character utterances (87 percent). In "Keyes-Michigan," Keyes stated, "On Tuesday, February 22, vote for the one who understands that the strength of our military depends on the moral integrity of our troops." Keyes stressed the idea that the strength of the United States defense extends beyond funding to the idea of morality. Bush had the next highest percentage of utterances dealing with ideals (45 percent). In "The Spotlight is on us," Bush reached out to Latino voters before the Iowa caucus: "So, once again, the spotlight is on Iowa. And for the first time, it's shining on the Latino community. We're voters too, and George W. Bush believes that all Iowans should help elect a President." Bush advanced one of his primary themes: inclusion of all groups in Republican politics. Forbes also had a high percentage of ideals among his character utterances (41 percent) An example of how Forbes expressed his ideals is found in "Compare": "I believe that America today can experience a new birth of freedom, but we have to make it happen." Forbes expressed his belief in the ideal that the American people are willing to make needed changes in government. Twenty-two percent of McCain's character utterances concerned ideals while Bauer used no character utterances dealing with ideals.

Leadership ability constituted only 9 percent of Republican character utterances. Bush stressed leadership ability more than any other Republican (19 percent): "Only one candidate has a record of proven leadership: George W. Bush" ("Bush-Iowa"). Bush tried in this utterance to show a clear difference between his record of leading a state versus his opponents. Forbes mentioned leadership ability in only 8 percent of his character utterances: "And he'll lead by giving it to you straight" ("Forbes-Iowa"). Forbes attempted to contrast himself not only with other Republican candidates, but also with Clinton. McCain discussed leadership ability in 5 percent of his character utterances. In "Decision," a series of actors mention personal qualities they find appealing about McCain, concluding that those were "Qualities I expect to find in a leader." McCain, as noted earlier, emphasized personal qualities in his character utterances. He equated these personal qualities as necessary for an individual to lead the country. In examining the available primary radio spots from Keyes and Bauer, we found each candidate had only one character utterance dealing with leadership ability.

A significant difference was also found between Democrats and Republicans in use of forms of character utterances ($\chi^2[df=2]=7.8$, $p < .025$). Democratic candidates focused on personal qualities and leadership ability while Republicans emphasized ideals. Due to our overall small $n$, we were unable to use *chi-square* to determine if there was a significant difference in the form of character utterances among candidates in their own party.

## Issues Addressed in Primary Radio Spots

Education was deemed as the top issue before the 2000 primary season in a poll of Democratic voters. Health care was rated second and Social Security was third. The next three issues mentioned by voters in this poll were taxes and tax cuts, Medicare and prescription drugs, and foreign affairs (see Table 6.7). We found, however, that Bradley and Gore most often discussed issues other than those not mentioned in the Democratic poll: 50 percent of all policy utterances were on other topics. These other issues included subjects like the environment, gun control, and abortion. Gore used 47 percent of his policy utterances to address issues other than those discussed in the Democratic poll while Bradley discussed other issues in 63 percent of his policy utterances.

We found that health care (rated second in the Democratic poll) was the issue discussed most frequently in Democratic primary radio spots (24 percent). Health care was the most frequently mentioned issue for Gore (25 percent): "On health care, Al Gore proposes a step-by-step plan to get to universal access for all Americans. The Gore plan starts with health care for all children and coverage of millions of Americans" ("Trailing"). Gore was setting general goals for improving health care, such as providing universal coverage for Americans. Bradley mentioned health care in 21 percent of his policy utterances: "Bill Bradley has a health care plan for insuring all children" ("The News"). Education, which was the top issue in the Democratic poll, was discussed in 16 percent of the Democrats'

Table 6.7. Issues Addressed in 2000 Democratic 2000 Radio Spots

|  | Poll | Bradley* | Gore |
|---|---|---|---|
| Education | 23 | 3 (3) | 16 (3) |
| Health Care | 19 | 4 (2) | 25 (2) |
| Social Security | 13 | 0 (4) | 4 (5) |
| Crime/Drugs | 12 | 0 (4) | 0 (6) |
| Taxes/Tax Cuts | 5 | 0 (4) | 0 (6) |
| Medicare/Prescription Drugs | 4 | 0 (4) | 8 (4) |
| Foreign Affairs | 2 | 0 (4) | 0 (6) |
| Others | – | 12 (1) | 47 (1) |
| Spearman ρ |  | .08, *ns* | .10, *ns* |

*Frequency (rank)   Enslow (1999)

policy utterances found in primary radio spots we examined. For Bradley, education constituted 16 percent of his policy utterances: "Bradley wants to spend heavily on education beginning early on in a child's life and continuing through adulthood" ("The News"). Gore also discussed education as an issue in 16 percent of his policy utterances. An example is found in "The Times," when Gore suggests using the budget surplus "to invest in our schools." Medicare and prescription drugs were discussed in 7 percent of the policy utterances while Social Security was discussed in only 3 percent of the policy utterances. The issues of taxes (and tax cuts) as well as crime/drugs and foreign affairs were discussed by neither Democratic candidate in their primary radio spots.

Republican voters surveyed before the 2000 presidential primary season ranked education as their top concern, followed by taxes and tax cuts. Social Security was ranked third among issues, followed by crime and drugs, health care, foreign affairs, and Medicare-prescription drugs. As with the Democrats, issues that were not mentioned in the Republican poll were discussed most often by GOP candidates (38 percent). For instance, half of all McCain's policy utterances dealt with issues other than those mentioned in the poll of Republicans such as rebuilding the military. Issues other than those brought up in the Republican poll also accounted for 33 percent of the policy utterances for Forbes and 28 percent of Bush's policy utterances (see Table 6.8).

Despite the importance placed on education by Republican voters, the issue was discussed in only 10 percent of the GOP policy utterances in radio spots we analyzed. Bush was the Republican candidate who gave education the most attention, as the issue was mentioned in 21 percent of his policy utterances. In spots like "Education," Bush gave a laundry list of education reforms he helped enact in

Table 6.8. Issues Addressed in 2000 Republican Primary Radio Spots

|  | Poll | Bauer* | Bush | Forbes | Keyes | McCain |
|---|---|---|---|---|---|---|
| Education | 19 | 0 (3) | 13 (2) | 5 (4) | 2 (3) | 2 (5) |
| Taxes/Tax/Cuts | 11 | 0 (3) | 22 (1) | 26 (3) | 4 (2) | 8 (2) |
| Social Security | 9 | 0 (3) | 2 (5) | 29 (2) | 0 (4) | 6 (3) |
| Crime/Drugs | 8 | 0 (3) | 0 (6) | 0 (6) | 0 (4) | 0 (6) |
| Health Care | 8 | 0 (3) | 7 (4) | 4 (5) | 0 (4) | 6 (3) |
| Foreign Affairs | 7 | 6 (2) | 0 (6) | 0 (6) | 0 (4) | 0 (6) |
| Medicare/Prescrip-tion Drugs | 5 | 0 (3) | 0 (6) | 0 (6) | 0 (4) | 0 (6) |
| Others | – | 7 (1) | 17 (3) | 12 (1) | 8 (1) | 22 (1) |
| Spearman $\rho$ |  | -.66, *ns* | .36, *ns* | .17, *ns* | .08, *ns* | .09, *ns* |

*Frequency (rank)  Enslow (1999)

Texas: "For Governor George W. Bush, education reform is his top priority. He's reformed education by insisting on local control, accountability, and high standards." In contrast to Bush, education was brought up in only 5 percent of policy utterances in radio spots for Forbes and only 4 percent for McCain.

Taxes and tax cuts, ranked second among issues concerning Republican primary voters, were mentioned most often in policy utterances in Republican primary radio spots we examined (26 percent). It was the issue that Bush discussed most often (36 percent): "I have fought for and signed the two largest tax cuts in the history of the state of Texas" ("Tax Cuts"). Bush, citing his record in Texas, is establishing that he has always had an interest in seeing taxes lowered. Forbes also made taxes and tax cuts (27 percent) a prominent part of his campaign.

Social Security, which was the third highest rated concern in the Republican poll, received the third highest number of mentions among all GOP candidates (16 percent). Forbes (30 percent) discussed Social Security more frequently than any other Republican candidate, as in this spot called "Bear": "That's why we should phase in a new system, with the bulk of your payroll tax, your Social Security tax; especially if you're a younger person—goes directly into your retirement account." Forbes not only stated general goals for Social Security reform, but reiterated his push for new ideas in Washington. Health care was mentioned as an issue in only 8 percent of the Republican primary radio spots we examined while foreign affairs accounted for only 3 percent of the issues raised in policy utterances. Two of the issues listed in the survey of Republican voters (crime and drugs, Medicare and prescription drugs), were not discussed by any of the GOP candidates in their primary radio spots.

We used Spearman's $\rho$ to determine the strength of the relationship between the number of utterances devoted to each policy topic and the importance to Democratic or Republican voters. There were no significant correlations between the issues discussed by these candidates and the importance of these issues to the public.

## Implications

Through our functional analyses of 2000 primary radio spots, we found candidates used acclaims more frequently (75 percent) than attacks (25 percent). As primaries involve candidates appealing to voters in their own party, it would make sense to be positive rather than attack fellow party members running against you, thereby damaging your image with the rank and file. Defenses were used in less than 1 percent of all utterances coded in primary radio spots we examined. Benoit, Blaney, and Pier (1998) suggest the reluctance of candidates to spend their own campaign funds to refute claims of opponents may be one reason why so few defenses appear in radio spots, as well as other forms of paid media.

We found a significant difference between Democrats Bradley and Gore in the functions of their radio spots. Gore's spots used acclaims more frequently than Bradley, while Bradley utilized attacks more frequently than Gore. As Benoit (1999) has noted, it is common for a candidate leading in the polls (in this case, Gore) to use more acclaims while a candidate that is trailing (Bradley) will tend to have more attacks. We also found a significant difference in the use of acclaims and attacks among Republicans. McCain, Forbes, and Bush all relied heavily on acclaims in their radio spots compared with Keyes and Bauer. One reason for this heavy emphasis on acclaims is that Republican candidates often drew comparisons with Clinton. Acclaiming one's character in comparison with the negative image of Clinton was a common ploy in Republican radio spots we examined.

When we examined targets of attack in 2000 primary radio spots, we found Republicans targeting each other 62 percent of the time. Democrats in 2000 primary radio spots also had a high percentage of attacks (67 percent) on opponents in their own party. The finding is reasonable because candidates must overcome fellow party members who seek the same prize. Thus, it is these competitors that are the primary targets for attacks.

When we examined topics in 2000 radio primary spots, we found the majority of all utterances dealt with character (58 percent) rather than policy (42 percent). Although this finding runs counter to past research, we can suggest that the circumstances of the 2000 election, with personal integrity as a key issue, were distinctive. This seemed to be especially true in the Republican primary of 2000, as candidates declared the goal of restoring integrity and decency to the White House after the various scandals that plagued the second Clinton administration. The greater reliance on character utterances in this particular primary season represents a logical outcome.

Republican spots particularly relied on character utterances in their message content (63 percent). Democratic radio spots in 2000 were about even (53 percent policy utterances to 47 percent character). Thus, the first implication that we suggest from this study is that the circumstances of the 2000 election contributed to the increased emphasis on character, especially on the part of Republicans. Trust and integrity are considered important factors when voters are making their selection of a presidential candidate (Benoit, 1999). Republicans made these themes central to many of their primary radio spots.

When we examined forms of policy utterances in 2000 primary radio spots, we found two-thirds of these utterances concerned general goals (67 percent), more than past deeds (23 percent) or future plans (10 percent). While general goals have been the most common type of policy utterance used in past primary campaign spots we have examined, the 2000 primary placed a far greater emphasis on discussing general goals. We suggest part of the reason can be found in the heavy reliance on general goals in Gore's radio spots. Eighty-five percent of Gore's policy utterances dealt with general goals, compared to 15 percent past deeds. It would be expected that Gore, running as the incumbent party candidate, would want to stress past deeds of the Clinton-Gore administrations. Instead, it appears Gore used these radio spots to create a rationale for his own candidacy, stressing policy issues he would address as president. In examining character utterances, our analyses of primary radio spots found personal qualities were discussed 53 percent of the time. Ideals were discussed in 36 percent of utterances and leadership ability was addressed in 11 percent of utterances. The emphasis on ideals also appears to stem from the circumstances of the 2000 election. In an election year where Republican candidates sought to contrast themselves with President Clinton, it would be expected that utterances about ideals such as values would be more numerous.

When we examined the issues discussed in primary radio spots, we failed to find any significant positive correlation between what the candidates were discussing and the issues reported as important to primary voters. It could be that presidential candidates are simply guilty of poor judgment for failing to address issues that generate national concern. The nature of presidential primary campaigns can influence the types of issues discussed by candidates. Presidential primary campaigns are fought out on a state by state basis. Thus, while a candidate may have core issues they address throughout the country (health care for Bradley and Gore, taxes and tax cuts for Bush, Social Security for Forbes), candidates must also discuss issues unique to a particular state or region of the country. In Gore's radio spots, for example, an issue of importance to potential caucus participants in Iowa (agriculture) is not mentioned in any of the other spots we examined. Likewise, in New York City, an issue important to African-Americans (racial profiling by the police) living there was discussed in radio spots, but the same issue was never addressed in Iowa. As a result, many issues that are not considered national issues still make their way into spots run by candidates. It should be noted that Bush, the eventual Republican nominee, addressed the two top issues among Republican voters (education, taxes/tax cuts) in the majority of his policy utterances in primary radio spots (57 percent) while McCain, his top rival, discussed the same issues in only 23 percent of his policy utterances. If we had poll data from individual states (e.g., Iowa, New Hampshire, South Carolina) and a sufficient number of spots for each state, we may have found significant relationships between issues concerning potential voters and radio spot topics.

Another implication that could be made from this research, although not as a result of our functional analysis, is that 2000 presidential primary radio spots served the purposes generally associated for using radio advertising in elections. First, it was suggested candidates would use campaign spots on the radio. All of the candidates who were in the presidential primaries as of January 1, 2000, used radio advertising to promote their campaigns. Candidates ran longer commercials on radio than on television, taking advantage of the more affordable advertising rates on radio. Second, candidates targeted radio spots to specific audiences. With its multitude of program formats, radio lends itself to delivering specific audiences to advertisers or, as in this case, campaigns. There were numerous examples of radio spots targeted to specific audiences found in 2000 presidential primary radio spots that were analyzed. Gore, for instance, discussed agriculture issues like farm credit and federal crop insurance in Iowa radio spots, but not in any other state. In New York, Gore targeted spots on stations with formats that attract African-American listeners, touting issues like school building improvements and calling for an end to racial profiling. Third, we found numerous examples of 2000 presidential primary radio spots that were localized either through the use of surrogates familiar to voters in those states or by making reference to specific states or cities in the spots. In Iowa, Gore had Senator Tom Harkin speak to his fellow Iowans about supporting the vice president in the caucuses. Bush employed Iowa's other senator, Charles Grassley, for the same purpose. Spots that Bush ran attacking McCain in Michigan named specific communities (Grand Rapids, Royal Oak) as a way of localizing the spot to capture listener attention. A fourth benefit of using radio advertising in elections, quick turnaround for messages in the campaign, cannot be quantified, except to note that the tone of spots tended to change based on the developments in the primaries. For instance, spots run by the Bush campaign in Iowa emphasized acclaim utterances. But after a defeat in New Hampshire to McCain, spots aired by the Bush campaign in places like South Carolina and Michigan contained considerably more attacks against McCain. These factors support our argument that radio played a significant role in the 2000 presidential primaries, as candidates utilized the medium to get their messages out to voters.

While we have no past research on primary radio spots to draw comparisons to, Benoit (1999) does provide trends from research done on primary television spots dating back to 1952. As discussed earlier in this chapter, radio and television are distinct media in that radio only requires a message receiver to process information through listening while television viewers must process information through both listening and viewing. The message, however, is the common component, or as in the case of presidential primary elections, the political spot. We argue, therefore, that using long-term trends produced by functional analyses of political spots is useful for identifying potential trends in this initial study of primary radio spots (in some cases, data is only available going back to 1996).

Our functional analyses found 2000 primary radio spots are generally consistent with historical trends involving the use of acclaims, attacks, and defenses. Benoit has found a majority of all utterances in primary television spots through 1996 were acclaims (68 percent) as opposed to attacks (31 percent). In the 2000 primary radio spots we examined, that ratio was 75 percent acclaim to 25 percent attack. Defense utterances accounted for only 1 percent of all utterances in 2000 primary radio spots, matching the trend for using defense utterances in primary television spots since 1952 (1 percent).

When we examine the targets of attacks in primary radio spots, we find some similarity with 1996 primary television spots. In that election, Republicans targeted those in their own party most often for attacks (70 percent). The same held true for Republican candidates (62 percent) in the 2000 radio spots we examined. Democrats also had a high percentage of attacks (67 percent) on opponents in their own party during in primary radio spots (no Democratic data was available from 1996, as Clinton ran unopposed as an incumbent).

Our results of 2000 primary radio spots on the use of policy and character utterances ran counter to Benoit's past research on presidential primary spots. Primary television spots studied between 1952 and 1996 show candidates emphasized policy over character utterances (52 percent versus 48 percent). In 2000 radio spots, 58 percent dealt with character, to only 42 percent policy. Republicans in 2000 radio spots dealt extensively with character (63 percent) over policy (37 percent) while Democrats were similar to long-term trends (53 percent policy to 47 percent character). Again, the 2000 campaign may be unique because Republicans were responding to Clinton's personal scandals.

Forms of policy and character utterances in 2000 primary radio spots followed historical trends established in past research of primary television spots. In 2000 primary radio spots, general goals (67 percent) are mentioned with greater frequency among policy utterances than past deeds (23 percent) or future plans (10 percent). When looking at trends in primary television spots, we find general goals (43 percent) are discussed slightly more than past deeds (40 percent) and future plans (17 percent). When discussing character, 2000 primary radio spots put an emphasis on personal qualities (53 percent) compared to ideals (36 percent) and leadership (11 percent). While the long-term trend in primary television spots suggests personal qualities are discussed more frequently (51 percent), leadership ability (29 percent) has been discussed more often than ideals (20 percent).

# Chapter 7

# Primary Television Talk Show Appearances

I'm very excited to take this message of continued prosperity with an approach that is going to build on the all-time record that was just broken yesterday, with the strongest economic expansion in history. (Gore, *Meet the Press*, 2000)

I am the reform candidate in this [primary] race. And I think Washington state is open to that. I think the rest of the country is yearning to have someone come to Washington, like a clear mountain stream, and clean out the corruption that's there and change the way things are done, and that's what my candidacy offers. It offers a candidacy that's actually truer to Democratic principles than the vice president's. (Bradley, *Face the Nation*, 2000)

Let me also say to you that a lot of United States Senators are asking the same question. Republican Senators saying, "Which one of these two, Senator McCain or Governor Bush, should—should we endorse? Who should we help, based upon their leadership skills?" And, by far, the overwhelming majority of United States Senators, who are Republicans, are supporting me. (Bush, *Face the Nation*, 2000)

What the Bush campaign is doing is exactly what Forbes did to Dole, this pick—selecting one particular vote on a particular issue and then distorting someone's record. Look, not only have I supported breast cancer research, but I don't know any congressmen or senator that hasn't, to tell you the truth. So this kind of negative attacks is—just shows that Bush wants to win in the worst way. (McCain, *Meet the Press*, 2000)

Previous literature has failed to recognize the importance of appearances of presidential candidates on television talk shows. Proliferation of cable television technology has increased the visibility of talk shows as a forum for candidate publicity. Unfortunately, this unique discourse has been afforded scant academic attention. In this chapter we critically evaluate the appearances of the presidential candidates on television talk shows. We review the pertinent literature, and then evaluate the functions, topics, targets, and issues addressed in this discourse. We conclude that on television talk shows candidates discuss character more than most other discourse forms.

During the 2000 primary elections, the major candidates frequented the talk show circuit. Appearances by politicians on news talk shows are not new. Politicians have used the news talk shows like CBS's *Face the Nation* and NBC's *Meet the Press* as venues for campaign discourse since their onset. John Kennedy once appeared on *Person to Person*, hosted by Edward R. Murrow (Moore, 2000). Ross Perot received much free air time through his appearances on *Larry King Live* in 1992 and 1996. Television talk show programs have been arenas of political discourse for several decades, at least in the form of the material for the humorous slings and arrows from our late night pseudo-friends.

## Literature Review

Various aspects of television talk shows have been explored by a number of scholars. Several studies have focused on general aspects of television talk show programs. The appeal of talk show television programs has been explored (Armstrong & Rubin, 1989; McKenzie, 2000; Surlin, 1986). Radio talk shows have also been the focus of previous research (Andreasen, 1985; Benoit, Blaney, & Pier, 1998; Bierig & Dimmick, 1979; Tramer & Jeffres, 1983; Turow, 1974). Specific television talk shows have been the subject of critical analyses (Borgers, 1962; Cloud, 1996; Haag, 1992/1993; Hammerback, 1974; Schaefer & Avery, 1993; Tolson, 2001).

The appearance of politicians on European television talk shows has been the focus of some research (Bock, 1982; Fibiger, 1981; Hoffman, 1982; Holly et al., 1986; Lang & Lang, 1961, 1968, & 1984; Schutz, 1995; Weiss, 1976). However, this previous research has not systematically studied this phenomenon in the American context, during a presidential campaign, or systematically examined the composition of personality discussion.

Several scholars have studied the influence of presidential candidate appearances on television talk shows. Just, Crigler, and Buhr (1999) studied the tone and emphasis of the appearances of the presidential candidates on television talks shows in the 1992 presidential race. The results, according to the authors, indicated that these programs contained much information about the policy positions and character of the candidates. The authors also found that talk show programs offer more opportunity for the candidates to speak for themselves than television news programs. The authors concluded that television talk shows offered much substance, the voice of the candidates, and low cynicism. Pfau, Cho, and Chong (2001) explored the impact of various forms of presidential campaigns on audiences' perceptions of the candidates and the political system as a whole during the 2000 presidential elections. The results of this study indicated that non-traditional campaign discourse forms, including television entertainment talk shows and television talk shows, exerted much influence on perceptions of the candidates. Pfau and Eveland (1996) studied the influence on voting intentions of the presidential candidates' television talk show appearances during the 1996 election. Path analysis revealed that candidate appearances on these programs have an indirect influence on voter intentions. Pfau and Eveland revealed that non-traditional news media (television talk shows) were more influential in the early stages of the race than in the latter, and that their influence may be less than that of tradition television news programs. They found that the influence of these non-traditional news sources was stronger for Clinton than for Bush or Perot. Nevertheless, this research does suggest that television talk shows can influence voters. When an election is close, the authors contended, nontraditional television news media could influence the outcome of an election.

While scholars have studied general aspects of television talk show programs, study of specific programs, use of talk shows by European politicians, and the impact of candidate discourse of television talk show programs, the existing literature does not analyze the functions of the rhetoric of U.S. presidential nominees on talk shows. These include general study of television talk show programs, study of specific programs, use of talk shows by European politicians, and the impact of candidate discourse of television talk show programs. Unfortunately, virtually no academic attention has been afforded television talk shows as a venue for U.S. presidential candidates during the primary campaign.

# Results

We obtained transcripts of nineteen television talk shows broadcast during the 2000 primary season from Lexis-Nexis. Six of these programs featured interviews with the Democratic candidates, Al Gore and Bill Bradley. We included appearances from both candidates on *Larry King Live* (CNN), *Meet the Press* (NBC), and *Face the Nation* (CBS). Thirteen appearances by Republican candidates on these three programs were also included in this study (see Appendix 7.1). Bush, McCain, and Bauer appeared on all three programs. Steve Forbes did not appear on *Larry King Live*. Orrin Hatch, who entered the race late and whose candidacy did not last long, was featured only on *Larry King Live*. Alan Keyes appeared only on *Meet the Press*.

## Functions of Primary Talk Show Appearances

The candidates devoted most of their talk show themes (72 percent) to acclaiming. For instance, in his discourse on *Larry King Live*, Gore offered praise of his position on gun control when discussing shooting deaths in Ft. Worth, Texas: "What we are talking about here are the kinds of weapons that are used by criminals in this—used in this tragedy, the weapons that get into the wrong hands that—we've got to do something about." Such goals as gun control would likely appeal to many Democratic voters. In another excerpt, on *Face the Nation*, Bush acclaimed: "Good people can disagree on this issue [abortion], and they do. I'm the kind of Republican who says I recognize that. That's not going to change my opinion or my view on the issue. But I do welcome people of other voices into the Republican Party. I know I'm a uniter, not a divider." Here Bush acclaimed his ability to bring Republicans together. These results are displayed in Table 7.1.

The candidates attacked far less than they acclaimed, as attacks accounted for only 17 percent of their utterances. In one example, McCain attacked Bush's personal qualities on *Meet the Press*: "It's the low road that the Bush campaign began in South Carolina with some of the most scurrilous phone calls and advertisements in history." McCain insinuated that the Bush camp was using unethical practices. In an example from the other party, on *Face the Nation*, Gore charged, "Bill Bradley voted for Reaganomics, he voted for all those budget cuts." This was an attack on Bradley's support of Reagan's budgets. This might cast

Table 7.1. Functions of 2000 Primary Talk Show Appearances

|  | Acclaims | Attacks | Defenses |
| --- | --- | --- | --- |
| Bradley | 134 (81%) | 26 (16%) | 4 (3%) |
| Gore | 123 (79%) | 21 (14%) | 11 (7%) |
| Democratic | 257 (81%) | 47 (15%) | 15 (4%) |
| Bauer | 41 (59%) | 26 (38%) | 2 (3%) |
| Bush | 339 (74%) | 39 (8%) | 82 (18%) |
| Forbes | 79 (68%) | 26 (23%) | 10 (9%) |
| Hatch | 60 (78%) | 17 (22%) | 0 |
| Keyes | 16 (89%) | 2 (11%) | 0 |
| McCain | 104 (56%) | 54 (28%) | 29 (16%) |
| Republican | 639 (69%) | 164 (18%) | 123 (13%) |
| Total | 896 (72%) | 211 (17%) | 144 (12%) |

Bradley in an unfavorable light for Democratic primary voters.

Overall, defenses accounted for 12 percent of the talk show discourse of the Democratic and Republican candidates. For instance, on *Face the Nation*, Gore defended himself against the charge that he could not be elected: "Obviously, I disagree with his assessment." In this instance, Gore enacted a simple denial of the charge. On *Larry King Live*, Bush defended himself against charges that he was religiously intolerant after he said that Christ was the political philosopher who has had the most influence on him: "I wasn't saying I'm a Christian, and therefore, you're not worthy." In this utterance, Bush defended himself, denying he was too religiously conservative. These examples illustrate the range of acclaims, attacks, and defenses enacted by the candidates on television talk shows during the primary.

There were differences between the campaign discourse of the Republican and Democratic candidates when they appeared on television talk shows during the primary. The functions employed in Republican and Democratic talk show interviews were significantly different ($\chi^2[df=2]=27$, $p < .001$). Democratic candidates acclaimed more (81 percent) than the Republicans (69 percent). The Republicans attacked somewhat more (18 percent to 15 percent) and defended much more (13 percent to 4 percent) than the Democrats.

The functions of the discourse of Gore and Bradley on television talk shows were similar. A *chi-square* calculated on the use of acclaims, attacks, and defenses enacted by Gore and Bradley revealed no significant difference in the distribution of functions ($\chi^2[df=2] = 4.01$, On the other hand there were differences in the distribution of functions in the Republican discourse on television talk shows during the 2000 primary ($\chi^2[df=10]=90.7, p < .001$). These differences were evident in several areas. Bush defended most frequently (18 percent of utterances), more than any other candidate. McCain attacked more than the other candidates (28 percent), whereas Bush devoted fewer of his utterances to attacks (8 percent) than the other Republicans (the average percentage of attacks for the Republicans was 18 percent).

## Target of Attack

The Democratic primary candidates attacked each other (51 percent) more than they attacked Republicans (36 percent), or the status quo (13 percent). See Table 7.2. Republicans also attacked each other (73 percent) more than they attacked the Democrats (15 percent) or the status quo (12 percent), as evident in Table 7.3. A *chi-square* revealed that the two parties differed significantly in target of attacks ($\chi^2[df=2]=11.2, p < .01$). Specifically, Republicans attacked one another even more than Democrats; Democrats attacked the opposing party more than did Republicans.

For example, on *Face the Nation*, Gore attacked Bradley: "As I mentioned, he [Bradley] voted for Reaganomics." Here, Gore criticized Bradley's support of a

Table 7.2. Target of Attacks in 2000 Democratic Primary Talk Show Appearances

|  | Bradley | Gore | Republicans | SQ |
|---|---|---|---|---|
| Bradley | – | 18 | 5 | 3 |
| Gore | 6 | – | 12 | 3 |
| Total | 6 | 18 |  |  |
|  | 24 (51%) |  | 17(36%) | 6 (13%) |

Republican policy initiative. The candidates also attacked members of the opposing party. For example, on *Larry King Live*, Bush chastised the Clinton/Gore administration for its reaction to unrest in Seattle surrounding the November 1999 meeting of the WTO: "I thought the president blinked. I thought the president walked in as a free trader, heard the labor unions scream, is worried about the political career of his compatriot, Vice President Gore, and blinked." Bush criticized the political motivations of Clinton's trade policy, attributing a policy shift to Clinton's concern for Gore's political future. Finally, the candidates also attacked the status quo. For instance, Bradley blamed the political status quo for campaign corruption when, on *Meet the Press*, he said, "I think this country wants a different kind of politics, a politics based on belief and conviction. They're tired of 1,000 attacks, 1,000 promises. Politics in America has not produced what our potential is as a country." Here Bradley chastised politicians in general: He took exception to the *modus operandi* of most politicians rather than singling out a single candidate or even a single party for criticism.

Table 7.3. Target of Attacks in 2000 Republican Talk Show Appearances

|  | Bauer | Bush | Forbes | Hatch | Keyes | McCain | Dem | SQ |
|---|---|---|---|---|---|---|---|---|
| Bauer | – | 17 | 3 | 0 | 0 | 0 | 6 | 0 |
| Bush | 0 | – | 0 | 0 | 0 | 22 | 14 | 3 |
| Forbes | 0 | 20 | – | 0 | 0 | 1 | 0 | 5 |
| Hatch | 0 | 8 | 0 | – | 0 | 5 | 1 | 3 |
| Keyes | 0 | 0 | 0 | 0 | – | 0 | 0 | 2 |
| McCain | 0 | 43 | 0 | 0 | 0 | – | 4 | 7 |
|  | 0 | 88 (75%) | 3 (2%) | 0 | 0 | 28 (23%) |  |  |
| Total |  |  | 119 (73%) |  |  |  | 24 (15%) | 20 (12%) |

Bradley attacked Gore three times as often as Gore attacked Bradley. Gore also attacked Republicans twice as much as Bradley did. There were significant differences in the targets of attacks of the Democratic candidates ($\chi^2[df=2]=8.4$, $p < .025$). Differences also occurred in the distribution of the targets of the Republican candidates' attacks ($\chi^2[df=10]=40.9$, $p < .001$). The most evident difference in distribution was that Bush attacked the Democrats more than the other Republican candidates.

## Topics of Primary Talk Show Appearances

These candidates devoted 35 percent of their utterances to policy on television talk shows in the 2000 campaign (see Table 7.4). For example, Bush discussed his tax policy:

> I've put out a tax plan that I want people to look at. It's a tax plan that not only cuts the taxes and lowers the marginal rates, but it says something most Republican candidates have never said, "I understand that there are people, what I call, on the outskirts of poverty, who are working hard to get in the middle class, who pay high marginal rates on additional dollars earned, and that's not fair."

This statement obviously acclaimed Bush's policy on the tax issue. On *Meet the Press*, Bradley acclaimed his policy position on gun control: "I don't know how

Table 7.4. Topics of 2000 Primary Talk Show Appearances

|  | Policy | Character |
|---|---|---|
| Bradley | 72 (45%) | 88 (55%) |
| Gore | 64 (44%) | 80 (56%) |
| Democrats | 136 (45%) | 168 (55%) |
| Bauer | 17 (25%) | 50 (75%) |
| Bush | 132 (35%) | 246 (65%) |
| Forbes | 56 (49%) | 59 (51%) |
| Hatch | 15 (19%) | 62 (81%) |
| Keyes | 1 (6%) | 17 (94%) |
| McCain | 33 (21%) | 125 (79%) |
| Republicans | 254 (31%) | 559 (69%) |
| Total | 390 (35%) | 727 (65%) |

anybody in America can look at what's happening in the streets of this country in terms of guns and say we should not have common sense gun control. And I'm the only candidate that's laid out a program where you get registration and licensing of all handguns." In this statement, Bradley praised his policy preference on gun control, with which many Democratic primary voters likely would agree. Thus, the candidates did discuss policy on television talk shows.

Character was discussed in 65 percent of the utterances featured on television talk shows during the primary. For instance, Gore acclaimed his character when, on *Larry King Live*, he said: "Well there are people of many different faith traditions in our country, who fall back on their faith in times of tragedy and challenge. And one article of my faith is that we are not given to know the reasons for all the things that can happen in this world." In this acclaim of his character, Gore portrayed himself as a man of faith. He also appears to recognize and appreciate a variety of religious traditions. In another instance, Gary Bauer displayed the kind of person he is when, on *Larry King Live*, he said, "But I know what they [the people] don't like, though, is dissembling. I don't think they want us to try to fine-tune words or play words games with them. And I think every candidate would have good advice if we just spoke directly to the American people." In this example, Bauer advertised his personal quality of honesty.

There was a significant difference in the distribution of topics in the Democratic and Republican talk show discourse ($\chi^2[df=1]=17.7$, $p < .001$). The Democrats discussed policy 45 percent of the time, whereas the Republicans addressed policy in only 31 percent of their utterances. Conversely, the Democrats discussed character 55 percent of the time and Republicans talked about character in 65 percent of their utterances.

The distribution of policy and character utterances of Gore and Bradley were similar. A *chi-square* calculated on the talk show appearances of the two Democratic candidates revealed that there was no significant difference in the distributions of topics in their discourse ($\chi^2[df=1]=.009$, *ns*). Statistical analysis revealed, however, that there was a significant difference in the distribution of topics in the discourse of the Republican candidates ($\chi^2[df=5]=29.7$, $p < .001$). While all of the Republican candidates focused on character more than policy, there were differences in their emphasis of character utterances. Keyes referred to character 94 percent of the time, while Forbes only discussed character 51 percent of the time. Likewise, Bush addressed character 65 percent of the time.

## Forms of Policy and Character in Primary Television Talk Show Appearances

The proportion of comments devoted to the three forms of policy utterances are: past deeds, 15 percent; future plans, 10 percent; and general goals, 75 percent (see Table 7.5). Texas Governor Bush touted his past deeds in that state. On *Meet the*

Table 7.5. Forms of Policy and Character in Primary Talk Show Appearances

| | Policy | | | Character | | |
| | Past Deeds | Future Plans | General Goals | Personal Qualities | Leader-ship | Ideals |
|---|---|---|---|---|---|---|
| Bradley | 0 8 | 4 0 | 55 5 | 59 10 | 6 0 | 10 3 |
| Gore | 13 7 | 4 0 | 33 7 | 56 7 | 3 0 | 14 0 |
| Dem | 13 15 | 8 0 | 88 12 | 115 17 | 9 0 | 24 3 |
| | 28 (20%) | 8 (6%) | 10 (74%) | 132 (79%) | 9 (5%) | 27 (16%) |
| Bauer | 0 0 | 0 1 | 9 7 | 27 16 | 1 1 | 4 1 |
| Bush | 12 5 | 20 1 | 86 8 | 159 21 | 21 1 | 41 3 |
| Forbes | 0 6 | 5 2 | 36 7 | 29 9 | 0 0 | 19 2 |
| Hatch | 3 2 | 0 0 | 7 3 | 34 10 | 9 1 | 7 1 |
| Keyes | 0 0 | 0 0 | 1 0 | 11 0 | 0 0 | 4 2 |
| McCain | 2 1 | 3 0 | 22 4 | 52 45 | 5 0 | 20 4 |
| Rep | 17 14 | 28 4 | 161 29 | 312 101 | 36 3 | 95 13 |
| | 31 | 32 | 190 | 413 | 39 | 108 |
| Total | 30 29 | 36 4 | 249 41 | 427 118 | 45 3 | 119 26 |
| | 59 (15%) | 40 (10%) | 290 (75%) | 545 (75%) | 48 (7%) | 135 (18%) |

*Press*, when discussing his record in Texas, Bush stated, "Given the chance to reform education, I've reformed education." In this example, Bush pointed to specific action successfully initiated in the past. On *Meet the Press*, Bradley attacked the Clinton administration for past deeds in U.S. relations with Russia:

> And in the last eight years you've seen the Russian GDP drop 50 percent. They have sustained a depression greater than the United States in the 1930s. And we, in the best of circumstances, are considered irrelevant to that. And in the worst of circumstances, we're considered the cause of that. And all of this could have been averted if we had a clearer idea of what we wanted to do in Russia.

This attack on the past deeds of the Clinton administration took the Democrats to task for an unclear policy towards the Russians. The candidates also discussed future plans. For instance, Gore discussed his future health care policy plan on *Larry King Live*: "Look at the patient's bill of rights. I think these decisions on health care ought to be taken out of the hands of these HMO bureaucrats, who don't have a license to practice medicine and who don't have a right to play God. I think these decisions ought to be in the hands of doctors and medical professionals." The Republican candidates sometimes became specific and addressed their future plans, such as McCain did on the Social Security issue on *Face the Nation*: "I want to put the surplus in—62 percent of it into Social Security." In this example, McCain outlined particular characteristics of his future policy plans. Forbes provided an example of a general goal when he acclaimed his position on the tax issue: "We can't have more of the same old stuff. We need a genuine tax cut and we start by simplifying the code." Here Forbes acclaimed a policy goal of tax code revision. On *Larry King Live*, Bradley acclaimed his general goals on the drug problem: "I think the idea is to reduce demand, and not that we can't do something about supply, but the ultimate answer rests on demand." In sum, each of the forms of policy statements was evident in candidate talk show discourse.

The policy remarks of the Democratic candidates contained more discussion of general goals (74 percent) rather than past deeds (20 percent) or future plans (6 percent). These results are also displayed in Table 7.5. Most of the Republican policy statements were in the form of general goals (75 percent), while future plans (13 percent) and past deeds (12 percent) were less common. There was a difference between the forms of policy addressed in Republican and Democratic appearances on television talk shows ($\chi^2[df=2]=8.02$, $p < .025$). This difference between the candidates of the two parties was a result of their differences of emphasis on past deeds, future plans, and general goals.

A *chi-square* reveals a significant difference in the distribution of forms of policy utterances by the two Democratic candidates ($\chi^2[df=2]=8.7$, $p < .025$). Bradley acclaimed his past deeds (11 percent) less frequently than Gore (31 percent), but emphasized his general goals (83 percent) more than Gore (63 percent). However, there was no significant difference in the distribution of the forms of policy statements made by the Republican candidates on television talk shows ($\chi^2[df=10]=13.5$, *ns*).

The distribution of character utterances on these talk shows was personal qualities, 75 percent; leadership ability, 7 percent; ideals, 18 percent. For example, McCain discussed his personal qualities on *Face the Nation*: "I'm going to keep on with the positive message that people want to hear. We're having a great time. And I cannot tell you how exuberant I am about this whole campaign." In this excerpt, McCain acclaimed the character of his campaign, which reflects his personal qualities (positive, exuberant). Likewise, Bradley criticized Gore's behavior during the campaign: "I think he [Gore] has distorted the record considerably. He said a number of things untrue about his own record and mine, and I think that—I had hoped that we could get to an election where people would be choosing between two politicians they esteem, as opposed to one they can barely tolerate." This attack on Gore's alleged distortions was an attempt by Bradley to make Gore look lacking in honesty, a personal quality. In an example of an acclaim of leadership abilities, Orrin Hatch proclaimed his ability to lead on *Larry King Live*: "If you look at some of the most important legislation in the past 23 years, I've reached out and we've been able to bring together Democrats and Republicans to pass it." In an example of ideals, Alan Keyes articulated his fundamental principle: "We shouldn't cut deals on issues like slavery and civil rights, because at the end of the day, as a people, we're defined by one simple premise: All men are created equal and endowed by their creator with unalienable rights." Here, Keyes extolled an ideal that he repeated throughout the campaign: Because there is a God, people should be treated fairly. This ideal could appeal to Republican primary voters who share Keyes's conservative ideology, particularly religious conservatives. These data are also reported in Table 7.5.

The Democrats uttered about the same percentage of personal quality themes (79 percent, 74 percent), leadership ability themes (5 percent, 7 percent), and ideal themes (16 percent, 19 percent) as the Republicans. Not surprisingly, no significant difference occurred in this distribution between the candidates of the two parties ($\chi^2[df=2]=1.6$, *ns*).

When the Democratic candidates discussed character, the distribution of the utterances was similar. There was no significant difference in the distribution of the forms of character utterances in Gore and Bradley's talk show discourse ($\chi^2[df=2]=.93$, *ns*). However, a differences was found in the distribution of the forms of character utterances from Republican candidates ($\chi^2[df=10]=32.8$, $p <$ .001). Discussion of personal qualities ranged from 64 percent (Forbes) to 86 percent (Bauer), leadership ability ranged from none (Forbes and Keyes) to 16 percent (Hatch), and ideals ranged from 10 percent (Bauer) to 36 percent (Forbes).

## Issues Addressed in Primary Television Talk Show Appearances

Education was a frequently discussed during the talk show appearances of the primary candidates (see Tables 7.6 and 7.7). For instance, Bush pledged, "I want to make sure every child is educated." Health care was a topic frequently discussed by the Democrats. For instance, Gore declared on *Meet the Press* (repeating an observation he made on *Larry King Live*): "I think these decisions on health care ought to be taken out of the hands of these HMO bureaucrats, who don't have a license to practice medicine and don't have a right to play God. I think decisions ought to be in the hands of doctors and medical professionals." Gore's acclaim of the health care issue would appeal to a wide variety of Democratic primary voters. A topic that the Republicans frequently addressed was taxes. While on *Face the Nation*, Gary Bauer indicted the tax and Social Security plans offered by Forbes: "I want to go after Mr. Forbes on his tax plan. Talk about special interests. He would let big corporations pay zero, while the average guy, between income tax and Social Security, would pay 25 percent." Here Bauer differentiated himself on both the tax issue and the Social Security issue from his fellow Republican. In another example, Orin Hatch talked about both Social Security and Medicare: "I

Table 7.6. Issues Addressed in 2000 Democratic Primary Talk Show Appearances

|  | Poll | Bradley* | Gore |
|---|---|---|---|
| Education | 23 | 5 (5) | 10 (3) |
| Health Care | 19 | 12 (4) | 8 (4) |
| Social Security | 13 | 0 | 1 (7) |
| Crime/Drugs | 12 | 13 (3) | 12 (2) |
| Taxes | 5 | 0 | 2 (6) |
| Medicare | 4 | 5 (5) | 4 (5) |
| Foreign Affairs | 2 | 14 (2) | 0 |
| Other | – | 23 (1) | 27 (1) |
| Spearman $\rho$ |  | -.52, *ns* | .05, *ns* |

*Frequency (rank)   Enslow (1999)

think we've got to have a president with the courage to solve the Social Security crisis in this country and to solve the Medicare crisis." While Medicare was not a prevalent topic, some candidates, such as Hatch, did mention it. Crime was a prevalent issue in the appearances of the candidates. For instance, Gore addressed the issue of crime through pledges of gun control. On *Larry King Live* Gore said, "And I think that the vast majority of the American people believe that enough is

Table 7.7. Issues Addressed in 2000 Republican Primary Talk Show Appearances

|  | Poll | Bauer* | Bush | Forbes | Hatch | Keyes | McCain |
|---|---|---|---|---|---|---|---|
| Education | 19 | 0 | 8 (4) | 7 (2) | 0 | 0 | 1 (4) |
| Taxes | 11 | 1 (3) | 19 (2) | 16 (1) | 5 (1) | 0 | 1 (4) |
| Soc. Security | 9 | 0 | 4 (5) | 6 (3) | 1(2) | 0 | 5 (2) |
| Crime/Drugs | 8 | 2 (2) | 10 (3) | 0 | 1 (2) | 0 | 2 (3) |
| Health Care | 8 | 0 | 2 (6) | 5(4) | 0 | 0 | 2 (3) |
| Foreign Affairs | 7 | 6 (1) | 47 (1) | 5 (4) | 0 | 0 | 7 (1) |
| Medicare | 5 | 0 | 1 (7) | 1 (5) | 1 (2) | 0 | 0 |

| Other | – | 8 | 41 | 16 | 6 | 1 | 15 |
|---|---|---|---|---|---|---|---|
| Spearman $\rho$ | | -.50, *ns* | -.13, *ns* | .26, *ns* | -.29, *ns* | -.58, *ns* | -.41, *ns* |

*Frequency (rank)    Enslow (1999)

enough, and among the changes that we ought to make is a new approach to trying to outlaw guns like these assault weapons." The Democratic candidates consistently discussed gun control as a viable means for decreasing violent crime. The candidates also addressed foreign affairs. On *Larry King Live*, Bradley explained his foreign policy position towards Cuba: "I've seen the [Castro] regime and what it's done to people's lives, and I support the embargo." Obviously, this stance on foreign affairs would appeal to voters who opposed opening relations with Cuba. The messages enacted by the candidates on television talk shows covered many issues.

Bradley most often discussed foreign affairs, which was only noted as important by 2 percent of poll respondents. 29 percent of Bradley's issue statements dealt with foreign affairs, if "other" is disregarded. Gore discussed the issue of crime more than any other (32 percent), often in the form of statements about gun control, discussed education in 27 percent of his issue statements, and health care 21 percent of the time he was addressing particular issues. Gore's issue statements were more diverse than Bradley's (Bradley did not discuss Social Security or taxes on these programs), and Gore discussed the issues that were important to voters more than Bradley.

Of the Republican candidates, only Bush, Forbes and McCain discussed the issue that was most important to voters: education. Bush discussed foreign affairs more than the other candidates (52 percent), despite the fact that only 7 percent of Republican poll respondents felt that the issue was important. Keyes discussed none of the issues noted as important by Republican voters. The tax issue was discussed by all of the candidates except Keyes. The issue was the second most frequently mentioned by Republican voters and it ranked high among the issues discussed by the candidates: it was the third most frequently addressed issue by Bauer, second by Bush, first by Forbes, first by Hatch, and fourth by McCain.

Our analysis revealed that Gore and Bradley discussed a range of specific issues on television talk shows. Spearman's $\rho$ established the strength of the relationship between the number of utterances devoted to each policy topic and the importance of that policy topic to voters. Neither correlation of the Democratic candidates with voters' issue rankings was significant. Similarly, none of the correlations for Republican candidates were significant.

## Implications

As with other campaign discourse venues, acclaims outnumbered attacks on television talk show appearances, which outnumbered defenses. Voters do not like negative campaigning; thus, the candidates would likely want to minimize their reliance attacks. Defending can take candidates off-message, make them appear defensive, and force the candidate to reiterate attacks before defending against them. So this distribution of functions is readily understandable.

Bradley attacked Gore three times as often as Gore attacked Bradley. Gore also attacked Republicans twice as much as Bradley did. This is easily explained by the fact that Bradley was approaching his campaign as an outsider, and Gore would obviously attack his own party less as a sitting vice president. As the front-runner, Gore would not need to attack Bradley as much as Bradley would be inclined to attack Gore. The Republican candidates often attacked each other (73 percent) when they attacked. The high percentage of attacks on their own party reinforces the idea that, in the primary, the candidates' principle opponents are other members of their own party rather than the candidates from the other party, as is the case in the general election. Differences were evident in the functions of the Republican utterances on talk shows during the primary. Bush defended himself more than any other candidate, likely because he was the target of most of the Republican attacks (74 percent of the attacks enacted by the other candidates were against Bush). Bush devoted more utterances to defending also as a result of his position as front-runner, an established politician, and a sitting governor of the state of Texas.

The data on target of attacks reveals that Bush attacked the Democrats more than the other Republican candidates attacked the Democrats. As the front-runner, Bush would feel less need to attack the other Republicans, and with the knowledge that he would likely be running against Gore, Bush would want to begin his race against Gore as soon as possible. This is also likely a result of the inner-party posturing that unfolds during a presidential primary: The front runner knows he or she will have to run against the Democrats, and also does not want to upset the supporters of other Republican candidates, because those supporters might be converted. Another difference is found in the large proportion of attacks enacted by the lesser known candidates, Hatch, Forbes, Bauer, and Keyes. McCain also attacked Bush in many instances whereas Bush devoted fewer of his utterances to attacks than McCain. The significant difference revealed by *chi-square* analysis results from the dynamics between the front-runner and challengers.

Topics of character (65 percent) were more frequent in the discourse of the candidates on television talk shows than policy (35 percent). This prominence of character talk is consistent with the nature of the television talk show genre. Talk shows are a personal medium, as identified in previous studies (Haag, 1992/1993). The candidates' target audiences when they appear on these talk shows are likely more concerned with the personalities of the candidates rather than their policies. Accordingly, the candidates would want to emphasize their character to these audiences: The candidates seek to portray an impression of high character value.

General goals (75 percent) were the most common forms of policy utterances, followed by past deeds (15 percent) and future plans (10 percent). The audience for talk shows is probably less interested in policy details than general policy direction, as opposed to audiences for traditional news programs. Results indicated that there was a difference in the distribution of forms of policy utterances between the Republicans and the Democrats. The main areas of difference were past deeds (Democrats, 20 percent; Republicans, 12 percent) and future plans (Democrats 6 percent; Republicans 13 percent). This is likely the result of the Democratic candidate's lengthy tenures in office, especially Gore, while the Republicans, especially Forbes, Bauer, and Keyes, could acclaim fewer past deeds in national politics. There were also differences in the distribution of the forms of the Democratic policy utterances. Bradley acclaimed his past deeds (11 percent) less frequently than Gore (31 percent). As a vice president, Gore would likely have more past deeds to acclaim than Senator Bradley. This was a notable difference in the distribution of forms of Democratic policy statements.

Personal qualities (75 percent) were the most often evoked character forms, while ideals accounted for 18 percent and leadership abilities accounted for 7 percent of character utterances. Personal qualities are particularly frequent in the talk show venue. Again, the candidates likely see these appearances as a way that voters can get to know the candidates as people rather than just as possible policy makers. This is true even in news-oriented talk shows. The candidates often took the opportunity on television talk shows to sell themselves as good people by emphasizing personal qualities and general goals. There was also difference in the distribution of the forms of character utterances enacted by the Republican candidates. There were differences in the amount the candidates used each of these forms. These differences were likely the result of idiosyncrasies of the candidates' personalities and campaign styles. It is also possible that the message distribution deemed most appropriate by pollsters and handlers is disregarded in the dynamic, semi-spontaneous interplay between host and guests on talk shows.

None of the candidates (except Forbes) consistently address the issues that were most important to voters in the order reflected in polling data. This may be the result of the extemporaneous nature of television talk shows: There is a general plan for the segment, but a good host will adapt to substantive discussion that probably will make for lively and interesting intercourse. Also, the issues that are most important to the hosts may not be the most important issues to the public or the candidates (and their handlers), and since the host controls the direction and flow of the program segment, the issues which interest them the most may be more salient throughout an interview. Future research on campaign discourse on television talks shows should more closely examine the content of the questions and comments of program hosts.

Candidates appear to have adopted their discourse to the particular features of the television talk show genre. Rather than simply rehearse their prepared statements crafted by poll driven handlers, the candidates extolled their admirable character and positive personalities when appearing on television talk show programs in the 2000 primary campaign.

## Appendix 7.1: Selected Texts

## Democrats

### Al Gore

*Meet the Press* (NBC), February 2, 2000
*Face the Nation* (CBS), October 3, 1999
*Larry King Live* (CNN), September 16, 1999

### Bill Bradley

*Face the Nation* (CBS), February 27, 2000
*Meet the Press* (NBC), March 5, 2000
*Larry King Live* (CNN), September 28, 1999

## Republicans

### George W. Bush

*Larry King Live* (CNN), December 16, 1999
*Meet the Press* (NBC), February 13, 2000
*Face the Nation* (CBS), January 23, 2000

### John McCain

*Face the Nation* (CBS), February 13, 2000
*Larry King Live* (CNN), October 21, 1999
*Meet the Press* (NBC), March 5, 2000

### Gary Bauer

*Meet the Press* (NBC), August 15, 1999
*Larry King Live* (CNN), August 20, 1999
*Face the Nation* (CBS), October 10, 1999

### Steve Forbes

*Meet the Press* (NBC), January 23, 2000
*Face the Nation* (CBS), October 24, 1999

## Orrin Hatch

*Larry King Live* (CNN), July 1, 1999

## Alan Keyes

*Meet the Press* (NBC), August 22, 1999

# Chapter 8

# Featured Speakers

> In this election, they will speak endlessly of risk; we will speak of progress. They will make accusations; we will make proposals. They will feed fear and we will appeal to hope. They will offer more lectures and legalisms and carefully worded denials; we offer another way, a better way, and a stiff dose of truth. (Cheney)

> Two weeks ago, our Republican friends actually tried to walk and talk a lot like us. Did you notice? Yeah. But let's be honest about this, we may be near Hollywood tonight, but not since Tom Hanks won an Oscar has there been that much acting in Philadelphia. (Lieberman)

Political conventions were at one time an important force on the political scene, as the party's candidates for president and vice president were chosen at these quadrennial events. Today, a political convention's primary function is to serve as a coronation for the nominee selected during the primary and caucus season. Organizers of political conventions are now in the business of what Edelman (1988) calls "spectacle construction," where events are contrived and publicized for a specific purpose. The political conventions in the late twentieth century have become spectacles designed to reach television audiences, with elaborate staging and special effects to create stirring visual images (e.g., the colorful balloon drops and explosions of confetti above the triumphant nominee) to help tell their story. Even the cochair of the Republican convention, Andrew Card, suggested the 2000 event was "a mini-series that has to be told over four nights" (Marks, 2000). Convention organizers now look at the scheduling of these events as any television programmer would: Determining how to attract and then keep the attention of the audience at home.

The changing role of political conventions and the influence of television over such events became more salient in 2000. The Republican convention went as far as eliminating the traditional role of a keynote speaker. The party instead presented what it described as theme nights, where the speakers on a particular evening concentrated on a particular issue. On the first night of the 2000 Republican convention, for example, the theme was "Opportunity with a Purpose: Leave No Child Behind." Other theme nights discussed the economy and national security (Marks, 2000). Democrats chose to continue the practice of having a keynote speaker, tabbing Tennessee Congressman Harold Ford to serve that traditional role. Ford's role in the 2000 convention was overshadowed, however, as prominent Democratic stalwarts such as Massachusetts Senator Ted Kennedy, New York senate candidate Hillary Rodham Clinton, and President William Jefferson Clinton received the coveted prime-time television spots.

Past research on political conventions has examined the role of keynote speakers. Since 2000 marked a change in that tradition, this chapter will examine what we will refer to as featured speeches from the Democratic convention in Los Angeles and the Republican convention in Philadelphia. In addition to the Democratic keynote address by Congressman Ford, we analyzed the address of Colin Powell to the Republican convention. Although Andrew Card referred to George W. Bush's speech as the *de facto* keynote address of the 2000 GOP convention (Marks, 2000), we suggest that Powell's speech is a better candidate for this designation. Benoit, Blaney, and Pier (1998) suggest a keynote speech is meant to be a highlight of the proceedings, helping set a tone for the rest of the convention. Powell, a popular national figure, spoke on the issue of education, one of the cornerstone issues of the Bush campaign. We also analyzed the speeches given by the vice presidential nominees, Democratic Senator Joseph Lieberman of Connecticut and Republican Richard Cheney of Wyoming. In recent general elections, greater attention has been focused on the vice presidential candidates, particularly through nationally televised debates between the number-two candidates. Vice presidential nominees can serve as a surrogate for the person with whom they share the ticket (Trent & Friedenberg, 2000). It would be useful, therefore, to study the speeches of these political figures through a functional analysis.

## Literature Review

The role of keynote addresses at political conventions has been examined in past research into political communication (see Benoit, Blaney, & Pier for a more detailed listing of this research). Miles (1960) suggested that keynoters have generally been expected to acclaim their own party and ridicule their opponents in these convention speeches. Benoit and Gustainis (1986) found that keynote speakers at the 1980 conventions employed this tack of acclaiming their own candidate and party while attacking the opposing candidate and his party. DeRosa and Bystrom (1999), while focusing on the gender style of speech used in 1996, found that in convention speeches (including the keynote addresses), men were more likely than women to employ attacks on the opposing party or their presidential candidate.

Benoit, Blaney, and Pier (2000) conducted the most extensive study of Democratic and Republican keynote addresses using a functional analysis. They found keynote speakers from 1960 to 1996 frequently used acclaims (51 percent) and attacks (48 percent) but defenses were seldom found in such addresses (1 percent). Utterances dealing with policy (56 percent) were emphasized over those dealing with character (44 percent). A closer examination of policy utterances found that past deeds (74 percent) were discussed more than future plans (21 percent) or general goals (5 percent). When they examined the character utterances, ideals (66 percent) were discussed more than personal qualities (17 percent) and leadership ability (16 percent). The authors also considered trends involving which party currently held the White House. Their study found that keynote speakers from the challenging party would make greater use of attacks while the speakers for the incumbent party would make greater use of acclaims in their keynote addresses.

Benoit, Blaney, and Pier (1998) provided a more detailed analysis of the 1996 convention keynote addresses by Democrat Evan Bayh and Republican Susan Molinari. In examining these texts, the authors found the 1996 keynote speakers used a greater percentage of acclaims in their speeches (65 percent) than found in the historical trend (51 percent). The speakers also placed a greater emphasis on discussing policy utterances (72 percent versus 28 percent character) than found historically in such speeches (56 percent versus 44 percent character). Both chose to emphasize past deeds in their policy utterances and ideals in their character utterances, consistent with past trends. The analysis of the 1996 speeches also upheld the long-term finding that the keynote speaker for the challenging party uses more attacks than the keynote speaker for the incumbent party. In 1996, Molinari, speaking for the challenging party, used more attacks (46 percent for Molinari versus 23 percent for Bayh) while Bayh, who spoke for the incumbent party, used more acclaims (77 percent for Bayh versus 54 percent for Molinari).

This brief literature review reveals that patterns have emerged in past discourse. Speakers who deliver keynote addresses will employ both acclaims and attacks, but few defenses. Policy was discussed with greater frequency than character in the keynote speeches, with past deeds being the most frequent type of policy utterances and ideals being cited most often among character utterances. Past research also shows that a keynoter of the party out of office is more likely to employ attacks (and fewer acclaims) than the incumbent party keynoter. Although the 2000 conventions are unique in that the Republican party failed to designate a keynote speaker, it is still useful to analyze featured speeches from the two nominating conventions and contrast them to speeches at prior conventions.

# Results

We will discuss first the functions of these speeches. Then we report the results of the analysis of topics. Next we take up the forms of policy and character in these speeches. Finally, we report our results of the analysis of issue topics in these campaign messages.

## Functions of 2000 Featured Convention Speeches

We found featured 2000 Democratic and Republican convention speeches to be mostly positive, with 78 percent of all utterances consisting of acclaims (these data are displayed in Table 8.1). Democratic speeches also featured a high number of acclaims (77 percent). Ford, the acknowledged keynote speaker for the Democratic convention, used acclaims in 77 percent of his utterances. Ford, for example, cited Al Gore's commitment to campaign finance reform: "More than 20 years ago, Al Gore called for serious campaign finance reform." Ford, in his keynote role, acclaimed Gore's commitment to achieving reforms. Lieberman (who used 78 percent acclaims) declared "We Democrats will expand the prosperity." In this case, Lieberman acclaimed the objective of Democrats to continue improving the economy.

Republicans also used acclaims in 78 percent of all utterances in their featured convention speeches. Powell had a very high percentage of acclaims in his speech at 91 percent: "Governor Bush now offers the leadership that he has demonstrated in Texas to the nation." This particular acclaim reminds people that George Bush had experience as a government leader. Acclaims accounted for nearly two-thirds of all utterances (64 percent) coded in Cheney's speech to the Republican convention. An example of an acclaim used by Cheney was found in his discussion of the Social Security system: "George W. Bush and I, with a united Congress, will

Table 8.1. Functions of 2000 Featured Convention Speeches

|  | Acclaims | Attacks | Defenses |
|---|---|---|---|
| Ford | 37 | 11 | 0 |
| Lieberman | 62 | 17 | 1 |
| Democrats | 99 (77%) | 28 (22%) | 1 (1%) |
| Cheney | 47 | 26 | 0 |
| Powell | 68 | 7 | 0 |
| Republicans | 115 (78%) | 33 (22%) | 0 |
| Total | 214 (78%) | 61 (22%) | 1 (0.4%) |

save Social Security." This utterance acclaimed Bush's desire to bolster the Social Security system in coming years.

Attacks accounted for only 22 percent of all utterances in featured convention speeches. We also found Democratic and Republican featured convention speeches had the same percentage of attacks (22 percent). Ford (with 23 percent attacks) took on Republican economic proposals in his speech: "But some in the other party would have us go back. Back to a past where prosperity touches only the well-off and well-connected." This is classified as an attack as Ford accused Republicans of supporting economic policies that favored the rich. Lieberman (22 percent) used attacks to undermine Republican promises about education: "You know, sometimes it seems to me like their idea of school modernization means buying a new calendar for every school building." In this case, Lieberman belittled Republican promises to provide more money to education.

When we examined Republican featured speeches, we found Cheney used far more attack utterances (36 percent) than Powell (9 percent). Cheney used attacks to undermine claims of achievement by the Clinton-Gore administration in education: "Clinton and Gore have done nothing to help children oppressed by bureaucracy, monopoly, and mediocrity." In this case, Cheney attacked the past administration for failing to reform the education system. Powell also attacked on education. After stating a series of Republican proposals to reform education, Powell exclaimed, "What are they afraid of?" We classify this as an attack on Democrats, as Powell implied that education reform was blocked by Democratic opposition.

Defenses accounted for less than 1 percent of all utterances we coded in featured convention speeches. The only defense found in the Democratic speeches we examined was employed by Lieberman, concerning the military: "Two weeks ago, our opponent claimed that America has a hollow military. I must tell you that, that made me angry. America, America, you know better than that. Our fighting men and women are the best trained, best equipped, most powerful fighting force in the history of the world." This is an example of defense by simple denial by Lieberman. We found no defenses among the utterances in featured Republican convention speeches.

When comparing the use of attacks and acclaims between Democrats and Republicans in featured speeches, no significant difference was found ($\chi^2[df=1]=0$, $ns$). We found a significant difference in the use of acclaims and attacks in the featured Republican speeches given by Powell and Cheney ($\chi^2[df=1]=14.8$, $p <$ .001). While Powell had a higher percentage of acclaims (91 percent versus 64 percent for Cheney), Cheney had a higher percentage of attacks in his speech to the convention (36 percent versus 9 percent for Powell). We also found no significant difference in the use of acclaims and attacks in the speeches given by Democrats Ford and Lieberman ($\chi^2[df=1]=.3$, $ns$).

## Topics of Featured Convention Speeches

The four featured convention speeches we examined discussed character with greater frequency than policy. We found that character was discussed in 55 percent of all utterances found in these speeches, whereas policy accounted for 45 percent of all utterances (see Table 8.2).

Democratic speakers discussed policy in 53 percent of all utterances. Ford (52 percent) discussed Gore's record in Congress: "He held some of the first hearings investigating global warming and its affects on our environment, our health, and our economy." This utterance demonstrates Gore's past record in dealing with national environmental policy. Lieberman (53 percent) made reference to environmental policies in attacking Bush: "I'm sad to say that in Texas the quality of the air and water is some of the worst in America." Lieberman called attention to Bush's alleged failures in environmental policies while Governor of Texas.

Character was discussed in 47 percent of all utterances in the featured Democratic speeches. Ford (48 percent) outlined one of the broad themes of party's ticket: "Al Gore and Joe Lieberman believe the future is for everyone." In this utterance, Ford highlighted the desire to help all American citizens, regardless of their economic or racial class. Lieberman (47 percent) praised his running mate: "I can tell you that Al Gore is a man of family and a man of faith." In this case, Lieberman acclaimed Gore's character in two ways: Gore's personal quality in his role as a father and Gore's faith, which we code as an ideal.

Among featured Republican convention speeches examined here, character was much more frequently discussed (62 percent). Cheney, in particular, stressed character in his speech to the 2000 convention in Philadelphia (67 percent). Some of Cheney's character utterances were used to criticize Gore's campaign tactics: "This is what Bill Bradley was up against, and others before him: 'The Gore campaign,' Senator Bradley said, 'is a thousand promises, a thousand attacks.'"

Table 8.2. Topics of 2000 Featured Convention Speeches

|  | Policy | Character |
| --- | --- | --- |
| Ford | 25 | 23 |
| Lieberman | 42 | 37 |
| Democrats | 67 (53%) | 60 (47%) |
| Cheney | 24 | 49 |
| Powell | 32 | 43 |
| Republicans | 56 (38%) | 92 (62%) |
| Total | 123 (45%) | 152 (55%) |

Cheney attacked Gore's character in this utterance, citing the Democrat's willingness to use negative advertising against his opponents.

Powell also emphasized character in his speech to the Republican convention (55 percent). An example occurred when Powell praised Bush for seeking to help improve the performance of school children from minority groups: "Some call it compassionate conservatism. To me, it's just caring about people." Powell acclaimed Bush's personal qualities; in this case, the Texas governor's concern for all people.

Only 38 percent of all utterances in featured Republican convention speeches dealt with policy. Powell had the higher percentage of policy utterances (45 percent) among the featured speeches we examined. When discussing Bush's record on education in Texas, Powell said "He [Bush] increased state funding by $8 billion." In this particular utterance, Powell cited a past deed by Bush to increase education funding. Cheney (33 percent) used policy as a way to attack the Clinton-Gore administration: "For eight years, Clinton and Gore have talked about Social Security reform; never acting, never once offering a serious plan to save the system." In this case, Cheney discussed the administration's failure to act on the future of the Social Security system.

We found a significant difference in the use of policy and character utterances between the featured Democratic and Republican convention speeches ($\chi^2[df=1]=6.2$, $p < .025$). While Democrats emphasized policy utterances (53 percent of all utterances compared to 38 percent for the Republicans), Republicans focused on character (62 percent versus 47 percent for the Democrats). No significant difference was found however in the use of policy versus character utterances in either the Republican featured speeches ($\chi^2[df=1]=1.5$, $ns$) or the Democratic speeches ($\chi^2[df=1]=0$, $ns$).

## Forms of Policy and Character in 2000 Featured Convention Speeches

In our examination of featured convention speeches, we found candidates stressed general goals when discussing policy and ideals when discussing character (see Table 8.3). Policy utterances in the featured convention speeches we examined discussed general goals (53 percent) more than past deeds (44 percent) and future plans (3 percent). Among all character utterances, ideals were discussed more than leadership ability and personal qualities (44 percent ideals versus 28 percent for both leadership ability and personal qualities).

General goals accounted for nearly three-quarters of all policy utterances used in the Democratic featured speeches (72 percent). Ford (80 percent) spoke of one of the broad goals for the next Democratic administration: "Imagine a debt-free economy." Ford expressed the general goal of having the federal government continue operating in the black. Lieberman (67 percent) referred to budget surpluses achieved during the Clinton-Gore administration in suggesting a series

Table 8.3. Forms of Policy and Character in 2000 Featured Convention Speeches

| | Policy | | | | | | Character | | | | |
| | Past Deeds* | | Future Plans | | Goals | | Personal Qualities | | Leader-ship | | Ideals | |
|---|---|---|---|---|---|---|---|---|---|---|---|---|
| Ford | 4 | 0 | 1 | 0 | 14 | 6 | 2 | 1 | 7 | 0 | 9 | 4 |
| Lieberman | 5 | 6 | 2 | 1 | 22 | 6 | 14 | 0 | 8 | 0 | 12 | 4 |
| | 9 | 6 | 3 | 1 | 36 | 12 | 16 | 1 | 15 | 0 | 21 | 8 |
| Dem | 15 (22%) | | 4 (6%) | | 38 (72%) | | 17 (28%) | | 15 (25%) | | 19 (47%) | |
| Cheney | 8 | 8 | 0 | 0 | 7 | 1 | 16 | 6 | 8 | 10 | 10 | 2 |
| Powell | 19 | 4 | 0 | 0 | 8 | 1 | 5 | 0 | 11 | 0 | 27 | 2 |
| | 27 | 12 | 0 | 0 | 15 | 2 | 21 | 6 | 19 | 10 | 37 | 4 |
| Repub | 39 (70%) | | 0 | | 17 (30%) | | 27 (28%) | | 29 (30%) | | 41 (42%) | |
| Total | 36 | 18 | 3 | 1 | 51 | 14 | 37 | 7 | 34 | 10 | 58 | 12 |
| | 54 (44%) | | 4 (3%) | | 65 (53%) | | 44 (28%) | | 44 (28%) | | 70 (44%) | |

*acclaims/attacks

of general goals for a Gore administration: "preserve the future of Social Security and Medicare, to pay off our national debt, to cut the taxes of middle class families." These utterances state goals for a Gore-Lieberman administration on several key issues for voters.

Twenty-two percent of the featured Democratic speeches concerned past deeds, with Lieberman making greater use of this type of utterance than Ford (26 percent versus 16 percent). One way that Lieberman made use of past deed utterances was in attacking Bush on his record in Texas: "You know, Texas led the nation in the percentage of residents who did not have [health care] insurance." In this utterance, Lieberman faulted Governor Bush for not addressing the affordability of health care insurance. Ford cited the economic progress made under the Clinton-Gore administrations: "8 years and 22 million jobs later, the future is something to be excited about again." This utterance discussed gains made in creating jobs over the eight years Democrats were in the White House.

Future plans in the featured Democratic speeches we examined accounted for only 6 percent of all policy utterances. Lieberman described one of the campaign goals for health care: "And I will tell you tonight, that Al Gore and I are the only candidates in this race who will extend access to health care coverage to every single child in America." This is regarded as a future plan because it states a specific proposal. Ford noted a future plan for Gore regarding campaign reform: "Al Gore is ready to sign a campaign reform bill his first day in office." This utterance again specifies a specific action Gore will take if elected.

When we examined the Republican featured convention speeches, we found past deeds were emphasized heavily by both Powell and Cheney. Many of the past deed utterances by both Republicans dealt with Bush's experience as governor in Texas. Powell spoke about Bush's record on education: "The number of students in Texas passing all parts of the standardized tests since 1994, when Governor Bush came into office, the number has increased by 51 percent." Powell cited improved student performance on required state tests while Bush was governor. Cheney spoke about Bush's economic record in Texas: "Not only is the budget in balance, its running a surplus of more than a billion dollars." In this utterance, Cheney called attention to Bush's budget record during his tenure as governor.

General goals represent 30 percent of the Republican policy utterances found in the speeches by Cheney and Powell. Cheney discussed the goal of tax relief in his convention speech: "We can reform the tax code so that families can keep more of what they earn." This utterance is simply a declaration that tax relief is one of the objectives of a Bush-Cheney administration. Powell made repeated use of general goals, nearly all when discussing education: "Let's experiment prudently with school voucher programs to see if they help." This was one of a number of goals that Powell cited regarding education reforms supported by Republicans.

Noticeably absent in the speeches given by Cheney and Powell was the discussion of future plans. In our examination of these two speeches, we found neither Republican expressed a specific plan that would be carried out by a Bush-Cheney administration.

A significant difference was found between Democratic and Republican featured speakers regarding the form of policy utterances they used ($\chi^2[df=2]=28.7$, $p < .001$). Democrats made greater use of general goals (72 percent) while Republicans spoke more about past deeds (70 percent) in these featured speeches. We found no significant difference, however, between the featured Democratic speeches on forms of policy utterances ($\chi^2[df=2]=1.4$, $ns$). Due to the overall $N$, we were unable to use a *chi-square* calculation to determine if there was a significant difference in the form of policy utterances among the featured Republican convention speeches.

In examining forms of character utterances in featured Democratic convention speeches from 2000, we found that ideals were discussed most frequently (47 percent). Ford was found to use more ideals in his speech: "If you want a future that belongs to everyone, then join with us to make Al Gore and Joe Lieberman the next President and Vice President of the United States." Ford is expressing the ideal of inclusion of all Americans under a new Democratic administration. The majority of Lieberman's character utterances also dealt with ideals. An example occurred when Lieberman praised Gore for his time in the military as well as in government: "He believes in service to America." In this utterance, Lieberman is citing Gore's belief in serving his fellow citizens.

Personal qualities were discussed in 28 percent of character utterances found in the featured Democratic speeches we examined. When Lieberman said "Al Gore is a man of courage," he acclaimed a personal quality Gore would bring to the job of president. Ford discussed personal qualities when he argued America needed a president "with the intellect to understand the complexities we face." This utterance by Ford was to call attention to the public perception that Gore was more intelligent than Bush.

Leadership ability was discussed in 25 percent of all character utterances in the speeches given by Ford and Lieberman at the Democratic convention. For example, Ford described Gore as "A leader with experience," acclaiming the leadership ability he displayed while serving in Congress as well as vice president. Lieberman discussed Gore's readiness to become president: "He meets the challenges that lie ahead." This utterance acclaimed Gore's leadership ability to guide the country in coming years.

We found that featured Republican speeches discussed ideals most frequently among character utterances (42 percent). An example of this occurred when Powell described how Bush would govern if elected: "Good for America—that must be the measure for all that we do. I believe that's the measure that Governor Bush will use to guide his actions as President." Cheney discussed ideals in his speech, some focusing on the role of Bush as president: "On the first hour of the first day, he will restore decency and integrity to the oval office." This utterance discussed ideals of what the office of president should represent and that Bush would restore these ideals if elected.

Leadership ability was discussed in 30 percent of character utterances found in featured Republican convention speeches. Cheney used some of his leadership utterances to acclaim the top of the ticket: "I have been in the company of leaders. I know what it takes, and I see in our nominee the qualities of mind and spirit our nation needs and our history demands." Cheney acclaimed Bush's leadership ability based on his past experience of serving in past Republican administrations. Powell discussed leadership ability less frequently. For example, when he discussed Bush's education record in Texas, Powell said "Governor Bush doesn't just talk about reform, he reforms." This utterance described Bush's leadership ability to accomplish needed changes in government policy.

Personal qualities accounted for 28 percent of all character utterances in the speeches given by Cheney and Powell. Cheney discussed personal qualities most often among his character utterances. An example is the way Cheney described how Bush would work with other government leaders: "You will never see him pointing a finger of blame for failure, only sharing credit for success." Cheney's utterance described Bush's humility as one of his assets. Powell spoke of Bush's desire to have the Republican party reach out beyond its traditional base of support:

"The party must follow the governor's lead in reaching out to minority communities and particularly the African-American community." Powell alluded to Bush's belief that Republicans should seek to be more inclusive.

No significant difference was found in discussion of the forms of character between the featured Democratic and Republican speeches ($\chi^2[df=2]=.6$, $ns$). Speakers from both parties in these featured speakers emphasized ideals in their addresses (47 percent Republican, 42 percent Democrat). We did find a significant difference between Republicans Cheney and Powell in the form of their character utterances ($\chi^2[df=2]=19$, $p < .001$). While Cheney discussed personal qualities with greater frequency in his speech, Powell discussed ideals with greater frequency in his address. Due to the small $N$, we could not test for a significant difference in the form of character utterances among the speeches given by Democrats Ford and Lieberman.

## Issues Addressed in Featured Convention Speeches

The economy was the top policy issue before the 2000 political convention in a survey of voters. Education was rated as the second most important, followed by health care, Social Security, taxes, gun control, abortion, national defense, Medicare, the environment, the budget surplus, jobs and foreign affairs. Our analysis of featured Democratic convention speeches found education was the policy topic discussed most frequently (24 percent). Both Ford (28 percent) and Lieberman (21 percent) discussed education more than any other issue cited in the pre-convention poll. Ford discussed the importance of good pay for educators: "Surely we can pay teachers what they are worth." Lieberman suggested that "schools need to be held to the highest standards of performance and accountability." Lieberman was using this utterance to show Democrats also favored the idea of making schools more accountable for student performance (see Table 8.4).

The environment (rated as the tenth most important issue in the pre-convention poll) was the second-most discussed issue by the Democratic candidates (18 percent). Ford discussed the environment in 24 percent of his policy utterances. In one part of his keynote address, Ford attacked the pro-business Republican environmental agenda by suggesting the GOP would take America "back to a past where polluters write our environmental laws." Fourteen percent of the policy utterances in Lieberman' speech: "I promise you that we will continue the work that he [Gore] and I have done together to keep our air, water, and land clean." This utterance reinforced the idea that Democrats had a long-term commitment to protect the environment.

The economy, designated as the most important issue by people questioned for the 2000 pre-convention poll, was discussed in 12 percent of the utterances coded in the featured Democratic convention speeches. Lieberman (14 percent) argued that Democrats could engineer greater economic growth: "We want to make the

Table 8.4. Issues in 2000 Democratic Featured Convention Speeches

|  | Poll | Ford* | Lieberman |
|---|---|---|---|
| Economy | 12 | 2 (4) | 6 (2) |
| Education | 12 | 7 (1) | 9 (1) |
| Health Care | 9 | 1 (6) | 6 (2) |
| Social Security | 8 | 1 (6) | 1 (8) |
| Taxes | 6 | 0 | 3 (6) |
| Gun Control | 6 | 0 | 0 |
| Abortion | 6 | 0 | 0 |
| National Defense | 5 | 1 (6) | 2 (7) |
| Medicare | 4 | 1 (6) | 1 (8) |
| Environment | 4 | 6 (2) | 6 (2) |
| Budget Surplus | 3 | 2 (4) | 4 (9) |
| Jobs | 3 | 1 (6) | 0 |
| Foreign Affairs | 2 | 0 | 0 |
| Other | – | 3 (3) | 5 (5) |
| Spearman ρ |  | .04, *ns* | .39, *ns* |

*Frequency (rank)    CNN/*USA Today* (2000)

investments that will keep our economy moving forward." Ford discussed the economy in only 8 percent of his policy utterances, warning that a return to Republican policies would "run the economy into the ground." Ford used this utterance as a way to attack the GOP on their ability to manage economic policy.

Issues other than the ones mentioned in the pre-convention poll were discussed in 12 percent of the policy utterances found in these Democratic speeches. Both Ford and Lieberman discussed other issues in 12 percent of their policy utterances. An example of one of these other issues was when Lieberman addressed affirmative action: "When it comes to affirmative action, mend it but please don't end it." Lieberman, in this instance, indicated Democratic support of a policy that has helped minorities.

Health care, which was listed as the third most important issue to voters surveyed in the pre-convention poll, was discussed in 10 percent of the policy utterances coded in the featured Democratic convention speeches. Lieberman (14 percent) discussed health care in addressing Bush's record in Texas: "And today, it ranks last for health insurance for both women and children." Lieberman used this reference to health care to criticize Bush's record as Texas governor. Ford addressed health care in only 4 percent of his policy utterances.

The budget surplus, rated as the eleventh most important issue in the pre-convention poll, was discussed in 9 percent of the policy utterances found in these featured Democratic speeches. Lieberman (10 percent) acclaimed it as "America's hard-earned surplus," while Ford (8 percent) predicted that Bush-Cheney would return the nation "back to a past where politicians run up enormous deficits." Ford used this utterance as an attack, warning about the potential of new federal deficits if Bush and Cheney are managing the budget. Taxes and national defense each accounted for 4 percent of the issues discussed in the featured Democratic convention speeches, Social Security and Medicare each accounted for 3 percent of the issues discussed, and jobs accounted for 1 percent. There was no discussion in either of the featured Democratic convention speeches regarding gun control, abortion, or foreign affairs.

Republicans, just as the Democrats, discussed education most frequently in their featured convention speeches (59 percent) (see Table 8.5). Education was also the top issue discussed by Powell in his convention address (72 percent): "These schools are failing our children, and they must be fixed, and they must be fixed now." Powell used this utterance to call attention to the need to reform the nation's education system. Cheney also made education his most frequently discussed issue among his policy utterances (42 percent). One way Cheney did this was in praising Bush's education record in Texas: "He said he would bring higher standards to public schools and he has." Cheney used this policy utterance to assure voters of Bush's ability to address education concerns.

Issues other than those listed in the pre-convention poll were discussed in 12 percent of the policy utterances found in the featured Republican convention speeches we coded. Powell discussed other issues in 16 percent of his policy utterances. One of these issues dealt with the question of caring for children: "With all we have to do on our national agenda, I am convinced that to deliver on that promise, we must begin with our children." In this utterance, Powell identified the care for children as a priority for the Republicans. Other issues accounted for only 8 percent of Cheney's policy topics.

National defense, which ranked as the eighth most important concern in the pre-convention poll, was discussed in 11 percent of policy utterances in featured Republican convention speeches. Cheney (12 percent) discussed providing additional help for the military: "I can promise them [the military] now, help is on the way." This utterance suggested that a Bush-Cheney administration would give greater attention to the military. Powell (9 percent) discussed military spending: Bush "will not repeat the mistakes of the past and let our insurance policy our armed forces, fall into disrepair." In this utterance, Powell attacked the Clinton-Gore administration for allowing our armed forces to deteriorate.

Table 8.5. Issues in 2000 Republican Featured Convention Speeches

| | Poll | Cheney* | Powell |
|---|---|---|---|
| Economy | 12 | 0 | 0 |
| Education | 12 | 10 (1) | 23 (1) |
| Health Care | 9 | 0 | 1 (4) |
| Social Security | 8 | 5 (2) | 0 |
| Taxes | 6 | 3 (3) | 0 |
| Gun Control | 6 | 0 | 0 |
| Abortion | 6 | 0 | 0 |
| National Defense | 5 | 3 (3) | 3 (3) |
| Medicare | 4 | 0 | 0 |
| Environment | 4 | 0 | 0 |
| Budget Surplus | 3 | 1 (6) | 0 |
| Jobs | 3 | 0 | 0 |
| Foreign Affairs | 2 | 0 | 0 |
| Other | – | 2 (5) | 5 (2) |
| Spearman $\rho$ | | .20, *ns* | .13, *ns* |

*Frequency (rank)    CNN/*USA Today* (2000)

We found that Social Security, ranked as the fourth most important issue in the pre-convention poll, was also the fourth most discussed issue in featured Republican convention speeches (9 percent). Social Security was discussed in 21 percent of Cheney's policy utterances. In discussing the need for reforming Social Security, Cheney promised there would be "no more delaying and excuse-making and shirking of our duties to the elderly." In this utterance, Cheney attacked the Clinton-Gore administration for failing to act to ensure Social Security would be available to future generations. We found no discussion of Social Security as an issue in Powell's convention speech.

Taxes, which ranked as the fifth most important issue in the pre-convention poll, was also the fifth most discussed issue in the featured Republican speeches we coded (5 percent). Cheney discussed taxes in 12 percent of his policy utterances, referring to Bush's record on tax cuts in Texas: "He did it [cut taxes] twice, with the biggest tax reduction in state history." This utterance was meant to show Bush had a proven track record on tax reductions. Powell did not discuss taxes in his convention speech.

The issues of health care and the budget surplus were each discussed in 2 percent of the policy utterances coded in the convention speeches given by Cheney and Powell. Neither Republican discussed several of the issues cited in the pre-convention poll, including the economy, which was designated as the top issue in the pre-convention poll. Cheney and Powell also failed to discuss gun control, abortion, Medicare, the environment, jobs, and foreign affairs.

We used Spearman's $\rho$ to determine the strength of the relationship between the number of utterances devoted to each policy topic and the importance to voters in the pre-convention poll. None of the featured speeches examined here had significant correlations with the issues most important to voters.

# Implications

Through our functional analyses of featured speeches from the 2000 Democratic and Republican conventions, we found the speakers made much greater use of acclaims (78 percent) than attacks (22 percent). As Edelman (1988) noted, political conventions can be construed as spectacles, in this case promoting the candidacies of the people who want to be president. As these spectacles cater more and more to television coverage, it can be argued that there is greater pressure for a positive image to emanate from the proceedings. As a result, these featured speeches, occurring during times of national network coverage, would naturally make use of more acclaims than attacks.

A significant difference was found among the Republican speakers in the functions of their speeches. While Powell used more acclaims (91 percent for Powell versus 64 percent for Cheney), Cheney utilized more attacks (36 percent for Cheney versus 9 percent for Powell). It should be noted that 78 percent of all utterances in the featured Republican speeches we coded were acclaims. The heavier emphasis in acclaims may result in part from the nature of the Bush campaign in 2000. Bush promoted the idea during the campaign that he was a "compassionate Conservative," and that his campaign was one of inclusion, reaching out to people. The prime-time television speeches given by Powell and Cheney could be expected to match the positive tone of Bush's campaign.

We found no significant difference among the featured Democratic speakers on the use of acclaims and attacks (77 percent versus 22 percent). Ford and Lieberman had about the same 4-to-1 ratio of acclaims to attacks in their addresses.

It should be noted that 2000 featured convention speeches went against historical trends found in past convention keynote addresses. Benoit, Blaney, and Pier (2000) had previously found that keynoters for the party out of office (in the case of 2000, the Republicans) attacked more than acclaimed in their speeches. In the speeches examined from the 2000 conventions, we found Republicans and

Democrats used virtually the same percentage of acclaims (78 percent Republicans and 77 percent Democrats). As suggested earlier, the two parties were concerned about the images presented to the nation from their conventions, which probably contributed to the heavy emphasis on acclaims by the Republican speakers.

Defenses were used in less than 1 percent of all utterances in the featured speeches we examined from the 2000 conventions. The use of defenses in convention addresses such as keynote speeches have been minimal in the past, as Benoit, Blaney, and Pier (2000) found defenses accounted for only 1 percent of all utterances. As convention speeches serve as vehicles for acclaiming the nominee of one's own party and attacking the opposing party's nominee, it would be expected that little time would be spent on addressing attacks brought up by their opponents.

When we examined topics of featured convention speeches, we found a greater emphasis on character than policy utterances (55 percent character versus 45 percent policy). A significant difference was found between topics discussed by Democrats and Republicans, as the featured speeches for the Democrats focused on policy (53 percent versus 47 percent character) while Republicans had more discussion about character (62 percent versus 38 percent policy). The circumstances surrounding the 2000 election probably played a role in the increased emphasis on character, particularly among Republicans. The GOP sought to make the personal conduct of Clinton and Gore while in office one of the issues of the 2000 campaign. By contrasting Bush (with platitudes about his personal qualities and values) with Clinton and Gore, the Republican speakers painted a contrast for voters to consider. This is particularly true when we look at Cheney's use of character utterances. While 58 percent of Cheney's character utterances were used to acclaim Bush or the Republican party, 42 percent were used to attack either Clinton-Gore or Gore as the Democratic candidate. Powell's speech, which focused on education, was less partisan and contained very few attack utterances (a total of seven). Democratic speakers, meanwhile, discussed policy and character in about the same ratio, as they sought to lay out Gore's agenda for the country, as well as acclaim his character.

When we examined forms of policy utterances in these featured 2000 convention speeches, general goals (53 percent) were discussed more than past deeds (44 percent) or future plans (3 percent). A significant difference was found between Democrats and Republicans in the forms of policy discussed in these speeches. While Democrats emphasized general goals (72 percent), Republicans focused more on past deeds (70 percent). The heavy use of past deed utterances by the Republican speakers had a twofold purpose: First, acclaiming the achievements of Bush as Texas governor, and second, attacking actions of the Clinton-Gore administration. The frequent discussion of general goals by the Democratic speakers may have been a deliberate effort to emphasize Gore's future agenda rather than discuss his past deeds working with Clinton.

In examining the use of character utterances, we found ideals were discussed in 44 percent of the time, compared with personal qualities (28 percent) and leadership ability (28 percent). We found no significant difference between the speakers from the two parties, as speakers from both parties emphasized ideals (47 percent Democrats, 42 percent Republicans). We did find a significant difference between Cheney and Powell in forms of character utterances, as Cheney discussed personal qualities most often (42 percent) while Powell emphasized ideals (64 percent). The nature of the two speeches may account for this difference. While Powell's speech was about a nonpartisan issue (improving education for children), and would be expected to contain a number of utterances concerning the ideal or value of having a good education, Cheney's speech was meant to make the case for electing Bush as president.

When we examined issues discussed in the featured convention speeches, we failed to find any significant correlations among either the Democratic or Republican addresses. While both parties chose to discuss education more than any other issue (59 percent Republican and 24 percent Democrats), there was little discussion of the economy, which was the top issue among voters. The featured Democratic we examined discussed the economy in only 10 percent of the policy utterances, while featured Republican speeches we examined had no discussion of the economy. It can be suggested that the overall strength of the economy at the time of the conventions played into the hands of the Democrats. It can be argued that Republicans decided to avoid discussion of the economy in favor of discussing other issues where they perceived public dissatisfaction (i.e., education). The failure of the featured Democratic speakers to discuss the economy at greater length may have been a strategy that was mistaken. As previously noted, it appeared the featured Democratic speakers used their speeches to offer a rationale for electing Gore as president, and focusing on the next four years. This may have been done at the expense of acclaiming the past deeds of the Clinton-Gore administrations, including a strong economy.

As Ford's speech was the only official keynote address given in the 2000 conventions, we can compare his address with past research by Benoit, Blaney, and Pier (2000). Ford's keynote address at the Democratic convention made far greater use of acclaims (77 percent) than all past keynoters dating back to 1960 (51 percent) and far fewer attacks (22 percent versus 48 percent for all keynote speeches). Ford's level of acclaim utterances even exceeded what had been found in previous Democratic keynote speeches in elections when they were the incumbent party (65 percent). The overwhelmingly positive tone of Ford's keynote address suggests that there was greater concern about the image the party was presenting to potential voters rather than attacking their opponents and drawing distinctions between the presidential tickets.

When examining the use of policy and character utterances, we found Ford made slightly more use of policy utterances (52 percent versus 48 percent character), similar to long-term trends in keynote speeches (56 percent policy versus 44 percent character). When we examined forms of policy used, Ford emphasized general goals (80 percent) far more than in past keynote addresses (5 percent) and made far less use of past deeds and future plans (16 percent; 4 percent) than past speakers (74 percent; 21 percent). Again, this suggests that Ford's speech was trying to give a rationale as to why Gore's administration would be different than the past two Clinton administrations.

Ford's use of more character utterances stating ideals (57 percent) than leadership ability (30 percent) or personal qualities (13 percent) is similar to the long-term trends found in keynote addresses (66 percent ideals, 17 percent personal qualities, 16 percent leadership ability). As Benoit et al. (2000) suggest, ideals about what the government should be like are an important selling point to voters.

# Chapter 9

# Acceptance Addresses

This generation was given the gift of the best education in American history, yet we do not share that gift with everyone. Seven of 10 fourth graders in our highest poverty schools cannot read a simple children's book. And still this administration continues on the same old path, the same old programs, while millions are trapped in schools where violence is common and learning is rare. This administration had its chance. They have not led. We will.

America has a strong economy and a surplus. We have the public resources and the public will, even the bipartisan opportunities to strengthen Social Security and repair Medicare. But this administration, during eight years of increasing need, did nothing. They had their moment. They have not led. We will . . . . And now they come asking for another chance, another shot. Our answer: Not this time, not this year. (Bush, Acceptance Address, 8/3/00)

Instead of the biggest deficits in history, we now have the biggest surpluses, the highest home ownership ever, the lowest inflation in a generation, and instead of losing jobs, we now have 22 million good new jobs, higher family incomes.

Together, let's make sure that our prosperity enriches not just the few, but all working families. Let's invest in health care, education, a secure retirement and middle-class tax cuts.

If you entrust me with the presidency, I know I won't always be the most exciting politician. But I pledge to you tonight, I will work for you every day, and I will never let you down. (Gore, Acceptance Address, 8/17/00)

The acceptance address allows the party to celebrate its new nominee. It also serves to mark the transition from primary to general campaign, and the nominees try out

145

the themes that (if things go as planned) will constitute the fall campaign (Trent & Friedenberg, 2000). We review the literature on this genre of campaign speeches, present the results of our analysis, and discuss the implications of our findings.

## Literature Review

Presidential nominating convention acceptance addresses, as a genre of rhetoric, gradually emerged in the early part of the nineteenth century (Trent & Friedenberg, 2000). In 1932, Franklin Roosevelt broke with tradition by attending the Democratic national convention in Chicago, the first presidential candidate to accept his nomination in person at the convention. Houck (1997) analyzed Franklin D. Roosevelt's airplane flight to the Democratic Nominating Convention and his acceptance address. Norvold (1970) analyzed Hubert H. Humphrey's Democratic acceptance address in 1968. Smith (1971, 1975) examined how Richard Nixon's 1968 Republican acceptance speech succeeded at persuading two audiences. Scheele (1984) examined the values presented in Ronald Reagan's 1980 acceptance address.

Other studies examined multiple presidential convention acceptance speeches. Wiethoff (1981) analyzed the 1980 acceptance speeches of Ronald Reagan and Jimmy Carter utilizing the notion of classical obscurantism. Gustainis and Benoit (1988) conducted an analogic analysis of the same two 1980 acceptance speeches. Valley (1974, 1988) investigated the genre of Democratic presidential nomination acceptance speeches. Ritter (1980, 1996) analyzed acceptance addressees from 1960 to 1976 by comparing them to Puritan jeremiad sermons. Benoit (2001b) analyzed the metaphors in Dole's and Clinton's 1996 acceptances, arguing that Clinton's "bridge to the future" metaphor framed how voters viewed himself as well as Gore.

Benoit, Blaney, and Pier (1998) examined the acceptances from the 1996 campaign. Acclaims predominated, but Clinton (90 percent) acclaimed even more than Dole (74 percent). Conversely, Dole (25 percent) attacked more than Clinton (10 percent). Only Dole used defenses (1 percent). Clinton devoted more comments to policy than character (73 percent to 27 percent), but Dole discussed character more than policy (58 percent to 42 percent).

Benoit, Wells, Pier, and Blaney (1999) analyzed every Republican and Democratic acceptance address from 1960 to 1996 using the functional approach. Acclaims (72 percent) were more common than attacks (27 percent) or defenses (1 percent). They found that, as a group, incumbent party candidates (77 percent) acclaimed more than challenger party candidates (67 percent). Challengers presented more attacks (32 percent) than incumbents (22 percent). Defenses were quite rare, but incumbents (who received the brunt of the attacks) also produced more defenses than challengers (sixteen to three). Recent acceptances are more likely to discuss than candidates as individuals (instead of the party) than previous ones; recent speeches (30 percent attacks from 1980 to 1996) are also more negative than earlier ones (22 percent attacks from 1960 to 1976).

They also found that these speeches focused more on policy (56 percent) than character (44 percent). Policy remarks were dominated by past deeds (46 percent) and general goals (41 percent), with some discussion of future plans (13 percent). Ideals dominated character comments (69 percent), not surprising given that these speeches are the climax of political party conventions. Personal qualities (23 percent) and leadership ability (9 percent) were also discussed in these addresses.

# Results

We analyzed Governor George W. Bush's August 3, 2000 acceptance address in Philadelphia and Vice President Al Gore's August 17, 2000 acceptance in Los Angeles. We discuss the functions, topics, forms of policy and character, and issues addressed.

## Functions of the 2000 Acceptance Addresses

In 2000, both candidates focused on acclaims, but Gore was even more positive than Bush (see Table 9.1). Ninety-five percent of Gore's utterances were acclaims, while 82 percent of Bush's statements were positive. For example, Gore declared that "Instead of the biggest deficits in history, we now have the biggest surpluses, the highest home ownership ever, the lowest inflation in a generation, and instead of losing jobs, we now have 22 million good new jobs, higher family incomes." Clearly, these accomplishments of the two terms of the Clinton/Gore administration are presented as reasons to elect Al Gore (and Joe Lieberman), as acclaims. Bush spoke of his aspirations in this passage: "And we will extend the promise of prosperity to every forgotten corner of this country: to every man and woman, a chance to succeed; to every child, a chance to learn; and to every family, a chance to live with dignity and hope." It is clear that Bush was telling his audience how our country would be better off if they chose him as the next president. The percentage of acclaims was a bit higher in 2000 than in 1996, when 90 percent of

Table 9.1. Functions of 2000 Acceptance Addresses

|       | Acclaim   | Attack    | Defense |
|-------|-----------|-----------|---------|
| Bush  | 125 (82%) | 27 (18%)  | 0       |
| Gore  | 160 (95%) | 9 (5%)    | 0       |
| Total | 285 (89%) | 36 (11%)  | 0       |

Clinton's, and 74 percent of Dole's, statements were acclaims (Benoit, Blaney, & Pier, 1998). However, statistical analysis reveals that this difference was not significant ($\chi^2[df=1]=3.7$, $ns$).

Bush employed attacks more frequently than Gore (18 percent to 5 percent). For example, Bush observed that Gore "leads the party of Franklin Delano Roosevelt, but the only thing he has to offer is fear itself. That outlook is typical of many in Washington, always seeing the tunnel at the end of the light." Here Bush was trying to stigmatize his opponent as a Washington insider, a beltway politician who preaches the politics of fear. Gore attacked the opposing party in this next passage. Ironically, he criticized the problems of the previous Republican administrations, Bush/Quayle and Reagan/Bush (of course, Bush was his opponent's father): "But your hard work then [before 1992], was undone by a government that didn't work, didn't put people first, and wasn't on your side" Attacks were less frequent in 2000 than they were in 1996: Clinton attacked in 10 percent of his utterances and Dole in 25 percent of his remarks (Benoit, Blaney, & Pier, 1998). Neither candidate employed defense in these speeches. In 1996, Dole, but not Clinton, used defense (and did so sparingly; Benoit, Blaney, & Pier, 1998).

## Topics of the 2000 Acceptance Addresses

Combined, these two nominees devoted slightly more of their utterances to policy (55 percent) than to character (45 percent). These data are displayed in Table 9.2. However, Bush focused on character (64 percent) whereas Gore emphasized policy (72 percent). For example, this passage from Gore combined attacks on the prior Republican (Bush/Quayle) administration with acclaims of the Clinton/Gore administration in discussion the economy: "Instead of the biggest deficits in history, we now have the biggest surpluses, the highest home ownership ever, the lowest inflation in a generation, and instead of losing jobs, we now have 22 million good new jobs, higher family incomes." Deficits and surpluses, home ownership, inflation, jobs, and family income are obviously policy topics. Bush, who couldn't deny that America's economy looked fairly rosy, chose another tack in discussing the administration's record: "America has a strong economy and a surplus. We have the public resources and the public will, even the bipartisan opportunities to strengthen Social Security and repair Medicare. But this administration, during eight years of increasing need, did nothing." Bush attempted to shift attention away from what the Clinton/Gore administration has accomplished to what it has not done.

Character was also a topic of these acceptance addresses. Bush used this passage to attack Gore's negativity:

A time of prosperity is a test of vision, and our nation today needs vision.

Table 9.2. Topics of 2000 Acceptance Addresses

|        | Policy     | Character  |
|--------|------------|------------|
| Bush   | 54 (36%)   | 98 (64%)   |
| Gore   | 122 (72%)  | 47 (28%)   |
| Total  | 176 (55%)  | 145 (45%)  |

> That's a fact. That's a fact. Or as my opponent might call it, a risky truth scheme. Every one of the proposals I've talked about tonight he's called a risky scheme over and over again. It is the sum of his message, the politics of the roadblock, the philosophy of the stop sign. If my opponent had been at the moon launch, it would have been a risky rocket scheme. If he had been there when Edison was testing the light bulb, it would have been a risky anti-candle scheme.

Clearly Bush was ridiculing Gore the man, rather than discussing policy differences between the two nominees. Although Gore did not spend as much time as Bush on character, he did visit this topic at times. For example, when discussing his running mate, Gore declared that Joe Lieberman is "a leader of character and courage." These utterances illustrate the candidates' use of character in their acceptance addresses.

In 1996, Clinton and Dole together discussed policy (61 percent) more than character (39 percent). However, Dole stressed character (58 percent) in his 1996 acceptance address, somewhat less than Bush did in 2000 (64 percent), while Clinton's 1996 acceptance devoted almost the same percentage of his utterances to policy (73 percent) as Gore's 2000 speech. There was no significant difference in topics between the 1996 and the 2000 acceptance addresses ($\chi^2[df=1]=2.6$, ns).

## Forms of Policy and of Character in the 2000 Acceptance Addresses

Jointly and individually, these candidates devoted most of their policy utterances to general goals (55 percent), followed by past deeds (23 percent) and then future plans (20 percent). Examination of Table 9.3 reveals that these two candidates allocated their remarks in roughly the same proportions across these three forms of character ($\chi^2[df=2]=0.9$, ns). For example, Bush attacked on past deeds when he declared that "Seven of 10 fourth graders in our highest poverty schools cannot read a simple children's book." Gore acclaimed the Clinton/Gore administration's past deeds while attacking the Reagan/Bush years: "Instead of the biggest deficits in history, we now have the biggest surpluses, the highest home ownership ever, the lowest inflation in a generation, and instead of losing jobs, we now have 22 million good new jobs, higher family incomes." Future plans are illustrated by this

Table 9.3. Forms of Policy and Character in 2000 Acceptance Addresses

|  | Policy | | | Character | | |
|  | Past Deeds* | Future Plans | General Goals | Personal Qualities | Leadership Ability | Ideals |
|---|---|---|---|---|---|---|
| Bush | 6    6 | 8    1 | 32    1 | 39    10 | 15    8 | 25    1 |
|  | 12 (22%) | 9 (17%) | 33 (61%) | 49 (50%) | 23 (23%) | 26 (27%) |
| Gore | 25    4 | 22    5 | 66    0 | 28    0 | 1    0 | 18    0 |
|  | 29 (24%) | 27 (22%) | 66 (54%) | 28 (60%) | 1 (2%) | 18 (38%) |
| Total | 31    10 | 30    6 | 98    1 | 67    10 | 16    8 | 43    1 |
|  | 41 (23%) | 36 (20%) | 99 (55%) | 77 (53%) | 24 (17%) | 44 (30%) |

*Acclaims/attacks.

passage from Gore: "Let's give middle-class families help in paying for college with tax-free college savings, and by making most college tuition tax deductible." Similarly, Bush declared that "Those with the greatest need should receive the greatest help, so we will lower the bottom [income tax] rate from 15 percent to 10 percent and double the child credit." Bush also offered more general goals which discussed ends more than means: "I will work to reduce nuclear weapons and nuclear tension in the world, to turn these years of influence into decades of peace," as did Gore: "We will move toward universal health coverage, step by step, starting with all children." These excerpts illustrate how the candidates used these forms of policy in their acceptance addresses.

Traditionally, past deeds are a larger component of policy utterances (42 percent). However, in 2000, Bush had little opportunity to attack the Clinton/Gore record because the economy was in relatively good shape (unlike, say, 1976, 1980, or 1992) and there was no huge foreign policy crisis (unlike Vietnam or the Iran hostage situation). Oddly enough, Gore chose not to emphasize the last eight years, probably because he desperately wanted to distance himself from Clinton's personal liabilities. In fact, in his acceptance address, Gore declared that: "I stand here tonight as my own man," clearly attempting to differentiate himself from President Clinton.

Together and separately, Bush and Gore allocated most of their character comments to personal qualities (52 percent), followed by ideals (30 percent) and then leadership ability (17 percent). For instance, Gore discussed personal qualities when he declared that Joe Lieberman is a man "of character and courage." Bush also praised his running mate's personal qualities: Dick Cheney "is a man of integrity." In this excerpt, Bush acclaimed his leadership while attacking the absence of leadership during the Clinton/Gore years: "This administration had its moment, they had their chance, they have not led. We will." Gore, of course, promised to lead if elected: "Now I want to lead America." He discussed ideals—"We will honor the ideal of equality"—as did Bush—"It is to put conservative values and conservative ideas into the thick of the fight for justice and opportunity." These passages show how the two nominees employed the three forms of character in their speeches.

There seemed to be more differences in allocation of character than policy remarks between the two nominees. A *chi-square* confirmed that these proportions were significantly different ($\chi^2[df=2]=10.7$, $p < .01$). Of the two candidates, Bush spent more time on character than Gore (60 percent to 50 percent). In contrast, Gore devoted more of the remaining character utterances to ideals (38 percent to Bush's 27 percent), barely mentioning leadership in his acceptance address (2 percent), while Bush discussed leadership almost as often as he addressed ideals (27 percent ideals, 23 percent leadership).

## Issues Addressed in the 2000 Acceptance Addresses

The policy utterances in these acceptances covered a wide array of topics (see Table 9.5). The most important issue to voters at the time of the nominating conventions was the economy. Gore acclaimed the record of the current administration on the economy: "Together, we changed things to help unleash your potential, and unleash innovation and investment in the private sector, the engine that drives our economic growth. And our progress on the economy is a good chapter in our history." Education was the second most important topic to voters. In this passage, Bush touted his positions on education:

One size does not fit all when it comes to educating our children, so local people should control local schools. And those who spend your tax dollars must be held accountable. When a school district receives federal funds to teach poor children, we expect them to learn. And if they don't, parents should get the money to make a different choice. Now is the time to make Head Start an early learning program to teach all our children to read and renew the promise of America's public schools.

The next issue after education is health care. Gore discussed this issue in his acceptance address: "It's just wrong to have life-and-death medical decisions made by bean-counters at HMOs, who don't have a license to practice medicine, and don't have a right to play God. It's time to take the medical decisions away from the HMOs and insurance companies and give them back to the doctors and the nurses and the health care professionals." The fourth most important issue was Social Security. For example, Bush took a strong stand on this topic: "Social Security has been called the third rail of American politics, the one you're not supposed to touch because it might shock you. But if you don't touch it, you cannot

Table 9.4. Issues Addressed in Acceptance Addresses

| Issue | Poll | Bush* | Gore |
|---|---|---|---|
| Economy | 12 | 1 (9) | 10 (3) |
| Education | 12 | 8 (2) | 18 (2) |
| Health Care | 9 | 4 (6) | 9 (4) |
| Social Security | 8 | 6 (4) | 9 (4) |
| Taxes | 6 | 6 (4) | 7 (7) |
| Guns | 6 | 1 (9) | 3 (9) |
| Abortion | 6 | 1 (9) | 2 (13) |
| National Defense | 5 | 8 (2) | 8 (6) |
| Medicare | 4 | 4 (6) | 3 (9) |
| Environment | 4 | 1 (9) | 6 (8) |
| Budget Surplus | 3 | 3 (8) | 3 (9) |
| Jobs | 3 | 0 | 3 (9) |
| Foreign Affairs | 2 | 0 | 1 (14) |
| Other | – | 11 (1) | 40 (1) |
| Spearman ρ | – | .18, ns | .43, ns |

*Frequency (rank). Gallup (2000)

fix it. And I intend to fix it. To the seniors in this country, you earned your benefits, you made your plans, and President George W. Bush will keep the promise of Social Security, no changes, no reductions, no way." Bush also illustrated how the candidates discussed the next issue, taxes. Here he called attention to his record in Texas: "we cut taxes, not only once, but twice." Gore talked about gun control in this passage: "But I want mandatory background checks to keep guns away from criminals and mandatory child-safety locks to protect our children." The seventh issue was abortion and the vice president declared that "And let there be no doubt. I will protect and defend a woman's right to choose. The last thing this country needs is a Supreme Court that overturns Roe v. Wade." Our national defense was addressed in Bush's speech: "And at the earliest possible date, my administration will deploy missile defenses to guard against attack and blackmail." These passages show how these issues appeared in these speeches.

Inspection of Table 9.4, however, suggests that Gore allocated more of his policy comments to topics that were more important to voters. In every case Gore devoted more remarks to the top six issues than Bush. Of course, Gore talked about policy more often than Bush. However, each candidate devoted more remarks to the "other" category than any other issue. A *Spearman* $\rho$ (including the "other" category) revealed that the correlation between Gore and the voters was 0.43, whereas the correlation between Bush and the voters (0.18). Neither correlation was significant. Neither candidate appears to be adapting to the interests of the voters in selection of topics to discuss in their acceptance addresses.

## Implications

The 2000 acceptance addresses were overwhelmingly positive at 89 percent acclaims. In previous acceptances (1960-1996), acclaims outnumbered attacks, but not by as great a margin (72 percent). Defenses, which are relatively rare in acceptances, were not used in 2000. Although it is difficult to know why he did so, Bush attacked at a noticeably higher percentage than Gore (18 percent to 5 percent). This could have been due in part to the fact that he represented the challenging party. The challenger attacked more (and acclaimed less) than the incumbent party candidate in previous acceptances (Benoit, Wells, Pier, & Blaney, 1999).

Together, these speeches emphasized policy a bit more than character (55 percent to 45 percent). However, Bush favored character (64 percent) while Gore concentrated on policy (72 percent). This is quite consistent with historical levels (56 percent policy, 44 percent character). Historically, Republicans discuss policy slightly more (57 percent) than Democrats (54 percent) (Benoit, Wells, Pier, & Blaney, 1999).

These speeches discussed goals more than past deeds, and past deeds more than specific plans. Traditionally (Benoit, Wells, Pier, & Blaney, 1999), these speeches focus more on past deeds (46 percent) than general goals (41 percent) or future plans (13 percent). As noted earlier, the status quo was in generally good shape after eight years of a Clinton/Gore administration. Bush had fewer problems to attack than did Clinton in 1992, or Reagan in 1980, or Carter in 1976, so it makes sense that he had less opportunity to attack on past deeds. Although presidential candidates who had been governors (e.g., Carter in 1976, Reagan in 1980; Dukakis in 1988; Clinton in 1992) did tout their accomplishments as governor, that is not as powerful as a record in the office of the presidency (for example, governors have no foreign policy to speak of). So, it is understandable that Bush would not have too many acclaims on past deeds either.

However, Gore could have spent more time on the accomplishments of the past eight years. He mentioned this idea but did not exploit it as much as he could have. For example, Clinton acclaimed past deeds in fifty-six themes in his 1996 acceptance (Benoit, Blaney, & Pier, 1998), whereas Gore did so only twenty-five times four years later. Two factors may have reduced Gore's use of past deeds in acclaims. First, he was vice president rather than president, and it should be clear that the president deserves a larger share of the credit. Still, he was part of the Clinton/Gore administration and could have done more here. Probably more important in Gore's reluctance to take greater advantage of the Clinton/Gore record was Gore's determination to distance himself from Clinton. Gore declared that "We're entering a new time. We're electing a new president. And I stand here tonight as my own man." Of course, a great many concerns had been raised about Clinton's character over the years and Bush's campaign attacked Gore's character in 2000. Still, Clinton's success made it clear that many Americans were willing to judge his actions as the chief executive (policy record) separately from his actions as a private citizen. We believe it was a mistake for Gore not to try to take greater advantage of the Clinton/Gore record by devoting more acclaims to past deeds.

When discussing character, these candidates stressed personal qualities (53 percent) more than ideals (30 percent) or leadership ability (17 percent). Historically (Benoit, Wells, Pier, & Blaney, 1999), ideals (69 percent) have accounted for the lion's share of acceptance addresses, with personal qualities comprising only about one-quarter of character utterances (23 percent). Leadership ability has been less common in the past (9 percent). The stress on personal quality may have been related to President Bill Clinton's character problems. Ironically, Gore (60 percent) discussed this more than Bush (50 percent), perhaps because the vice president desperately wanted to distance himself from his former running mate. Bush, whose executive branch experience was limited to being governor of Texas, stressed leadership ability over ten times more than the vice president.

When the candidates discussed policy, neither focused on the issues that were most important to voters. We would not expect to find a perfect correlation between the topics discussed by presidential candidates and voters' issue preferences—that would of necessity mean that the candidates correlated with one another, and it is important for candidates to distinguish themselves from opponents. However, we do think it advisable for candidates to do a better job of adapting their messages to audience interests.

# Chapter 10

# Spouses' Speeches

During this campaign you have graciously invited Al and me into your homes and communities, and you've talked to us about your lives and your dreams for the future. Now this evening, I want to share with you a little bit more about Al and the life of our family. Now, I'm going to do it in a way that I know best: though pictures that I've taken over the 30 years of our life together.

When I was 16, I met Al at a party after his graduation prom. Remember formal dresses and corsages? We had come with different dates but wound up hitting it off better with each other. I remember right from the start, he was a good listener, and he had the most intense and beautiful blue eyes. He called me the next day, and soon we began to fall in love.

A year and a half ago, Al lost his father. I wish his father could be here to see his son accept your nomination. I know how proud he'd be, not just of his son's sense of duty and love of country, but for his dedication as a husband, father and grandfather. You see to me, what is most important is that with all the past accomplishments and future promises, he's still the man I fell in love with in high school 30 years ago. (Tipper Gore's 8/17/00 Convention Address)

I'm so thrilled. And I'm honored to be here. And I have to say I'm just a little overwhelmed to help open the convention that will nominate my husband for president of the United States. You know I'm completely objective when I say you've made a great choice.

We wanted to teach our children what our parents had taught us, that reading is entertaining and interesting and important. And one of the major reasons George is running for president is to make sure that every child in America has that same opportunity.

I watched my husband make a difference as governor, not by giving one speech on reading, but by giving 100 speeches about reading, directing time, money and resources to our schools. And that's the kind of discipline and commitment George will bring to the presidency. He'll set great goals, and he'll work tirelessly to achieve them. (Laura Bush's 7/31/00 Convention Address)

The nominating conventions are an important phase in the political campaign process. During these events the parties stand united behind one candidate, political platforms are unveiled, and the presidential nominee is formally presented to the American electorate (Trent & Friedenberg, 2000). The pomp and circumstance of nominating conventions is created through a series of speakers whose job it is to create a feeling of unity and support for the party's chosen candidate.

Modern elections have seen increasing reliance upon family members as surrogate speakers for the party's chosen hopeful (Niedowske, 1996). Family members can serve as liaisons, or buffers, between the candidate and the electorate while still espousing the candidate's attitudes, values, and policy orientation. The 1996 nominating conventions marked a significant time in political history for candidates' spouses: Both spouses were first given prominent air time during the convention (Crawford, 1996).

Blankenship, Robson, and Williams (1997) argued that the speeches delivered by Hillary Rodham Clinton and Elizabeth Dole were the two most highly anticipated speeches of their respective nominating conventions. Furthermore, they noted that Elizabeth Dole's speech was designed to create an image of a compassionate and caring individual while Hillary Rodham Clinton focused primarily on the policy objectives her husband had outlined for his next term in office. Benoit, Blaney, and Pier (1998) also examined the spouses' convention addresses in 1996. They found that 95 percent of the spouses' utterances were praises, 5 percent attacks, and no defenses. In addition, overall the spouses tended to discuss character (67 percent) more than policy (33 percent). However, Elizabeth Dole focused mainly on character while Hillary Rodham Clinton primarily discussed policy implications of her husband's campaign.

The 2000 election also saw the inclusion of the spousal surrogate speeches during the nominating convention. Because the spouses were highlighted in the 2000 election, and because it seems as if the inclusion of spousal addresses is becoming a integral part of the nomination phase, the addresses delivered by these women deserve our attention.

# Results

We analyzed the addresses delivered by Tipper Gore and Laura Bush during the 2000 nominating conventions. The transcripts were obtained from CNN via Lexis-Nexis. First we will discuss the functions of these speeches, then the topics of the themes in the speeches, followed by forms of policy and character and, finally, the issues addressed in the spouses' speeches.

## Functions of Spouses' Speeches

Both Tipper Gore (twenty-three utterances) and Laura Bush (twenty-eight utterances) acclaimed their husbands but never engaged in either attacks or defenses. For example, Laura Bush praised her husband's leadership ability when she stated, "And that's the kind of discipline and commitment George will bring to the presidency." In this excerpt we see how Mrs. Bush acclaimed by identifying a specific characteristic that she felt exemplifies why her husband would be a good choice when casting a vote. In short, she attempted to create a positive image of her husband by extolling the virtues of his future executive leadership. Tipper Gore praised her husband as well when she declared:

> Family vacations were a very special time, and he enjoyed them as much as the kids did. Al always worked long hours, but as busy as he was, he put his family first. One year I remember Al going to Speaker Tip O'Neill and saying, "Sir, you scheduled votes on Halloween night." The speaker just looked back at him, and Al said, "Well there are a lot of us with kids who want to take them trick-or-treating." The speaker realized how important this was to Al and other young parents in Congress, and he changed the schedule.

In this passage Tipper Gore acclaimed her husband's character. Not only did she intimate that he is a hard worker, but that he is also a compassionate, caring, family man. See Table 10.1 for these data.

## Topics of Spouses' Speeches

Tipper Gore and Laura Bush discussed both policy (24 percent) and character (76 percent) in their convention speeches (Table 10.2). For example, Mrs. Bush stated, "But I know many teachers will agree that we need better training in what works to teach children to read. And as president, George will fund improved teacher training." It is clear that Mrs. Bush was acclaiming policy as she discussed

Table 10.1. Functions of 2000 Spouses' Speeches

|       | Acclaims    | Attacks | Defenses |
|-------|-------------|---------|----------|
| Bush  | 28 (100%)   | 0       | 0        |
| Gore  | 23 (100%)   | 0       | 0        |
| Total | 51 (100%)   | 0       | 0        |

Table 10.2. Topics of 2000 Spouses' Speeches

|       | Policy     | Character |
|-------|-----------|-----------|
| Bush  | 11 (39%)  | 17 (61%)  |
| Gore  | 1 (4%)    | 22 (96%)  |
| Total | 12 (24%)  | 39 (76%)  |

her husband's plans to support teacher training programs. Tipper Gore provided us with an example of character acclaims when she said, "He listened to his constituents' concerns. He took them back to Washington, and he made the system respond to them." In this passage Mrs. Gore attempted to show that her husband has certain leadership and personal characteristics that make him desirable as an elected official.

There were significant differences between Mrs. Bush and Mrs. Gore and the topics of their acclaims ($\chi^2[df=1]=17.56, p<.001$). While Tipper Gore (96 percent) and Laura Bush (61 percent) both discussed character more than policy, Mrs. Bush was much more likely (39 percent) to discuss policy than Mrs. Gore (4 percent). Of course, this meant that Mrs. Gore discussed policy even more than Mrs. Bush.

## Forms of Policy and Character in Spouses' Speeches

Mrs. Bush and Mrs. Gore discussed past deeds (58 percent) more than any other form of policy. An example of how Mrs. Bush acclaimed past deeds can be seen in the following statement: "George led a similar initiative as governor with fabulous results. The highly respected nonpartisan Rand study released just last week found that education reforms in Texas have resulted in some of the highest achievement gains in the country among all racial, socio-economic and family backgrounds." In this excerpt, Mrs. Bush acclaimed her husband's past accomplishments as governor in the state of Texas. Specifically, she talked about education reform he had implemented while governor of Texas. Mrs. Gore also

Table 10.3. Forms of Policy and Character in 2000 Spouses' Speeches

|       | Policy | | | Character | | |
|-------|----------------|-----------------|-------------------|-----------------------|------------|-----------|
|       | Past Deeds* | Future Plans | General Goals | Personal Qualities | Leadership | Ideals |
| Bush  | 6       | 2       | 3       | 6        | 5        | 6        |
| Gore  | 1       | 0       | 0       | 12       | 7        | 3        |
| Total | 7 (58%) | 2 (17%) | 3 (25%) | 18 (46%) | 12 (31%) | 9 (23%)  |

*all utterances were acclaims

acclaimed past deeds when she stated, "He took on powerful interests and held the first hearings on protecting families from toxic waste, the beginning of his commitment to the environment." In this excerpt Tipper Gore referred to past action taken by her husband on behalf of his constituency on the environment. By creating a positive image of his past accomplishments she gave the suggestion that future policy will also be beneficial to the electorate. It is important to note that Tipper Gore did not discuss any other form of policy in her convention address. These data are displayed in Table 10.3.

Governor Bush's general goals were also acclaimed by his wife, Laura, "And one of the major reasons George is running for president is to make sure that every child in America has that same opportunity." Immediately preceding this statement Mrs. Bush told the audience how she and her husband had enjoyed being read to as children and then as parents knew the value of reading to their own children. In turn Mrs. Bush argued that her husband will work to make sure that America's children will have the opportunity to read as well. There are no specific proposals here but rather a general promise of legislation to come.

Mrs. Bush also acclaimed her husband's future plans, "That's why he's proposed a $5 billion reading first initiative, with a great American purpose, to make sure every child in every neighborhood can read on grade level by the end of the third grade." In this excerpt Laura Bush outlined a specific policy initiative of her husband's political platform that she believed illustrated the type of positive legislation one can expect if they cast a vote for her husband. There were not enough instances of the three forms of policy to calculate a *chi-square*. These data are displayed in Table 10.3.

Laura Bush and Tipper Gore most frequently discussed the personal qualities (46 percent) of their husbands when presenting messages about character. Laura Bush provided an example of praising personal qualities when she said: "Finally, George has a strong sense of purpose. To quote the hymn that inspired his book, he believes that all of us have a charge to keep, a responsibility to use our different gifts to serve a cause greater than self." In this passage Mrs. Bush pointed out that her husband possesses a "strong sense of purpose." By acclaiming his personal characteristics she suggested that her husband has the personal fortitude it takes to serve the office of the presidency.

Mrs. Gore also focused on her husband's personal qualities in her convention address. In one such example Tipper told the audience of her husband's decision to enlist in the Army: "But soon Al faced the most important decision of his young life, Vietnam. We opposed the war, but for Al, as for many people, it was complicated. Al knew that if he didn't go, then someone else from Carthage could go in his place, so he did something I remain so proud of today. He decided to enlist in the Army." In this passage Mrs. Gore painted a patriotic picture of her husband that highlighted his personal qualities of courage and conviction. By praising Al Gore's personal qualities Mrs. Gore hoped to endear the audience to her husband.

Leadership ability (31 percent) was also a common character form for the two spouses to discuss. For example, Laura Bush praised her husband's leadership abilities when she declared, "And he worked with Republicans and Democrats to build consensus and to get things done. He shares credit and doesn't cast blame." Here Mrs. Bush made the audience aware that her husband has the leadership experience needed to work with a bipartisan legislature. Tipper Gore praised Al Gore's leadership abilities when she stated, "I believe Al's leadership style was formed early on in the hundreds of open meetings he held in Tennessee." In this statement Mrs. Gore directly addressed her husband's style of leadership. By declaring that his leadership style has worked in the past, Tipper implied that her husband's approach to leadership would also be successful in the White House.

Finally, ideals (23 percent) were discussed by both Laura Bush and Tipper Gore. An example can be seen when Laura Bush stated: "And as I thumbed through those old brochures what struck me is how the things George said then are the same things he believes now. That government should be limited. That local people make the best decisions for their schools and communities." In the preceding excerpt we see that Mrs. Bush attempted to strike a responsive chord with her audience by highlighting her husband's ideals of limited government and local control. Mrs. Gore offered her own example of praising ideals when she declared, "Many of you know that faith and family are at the center of Al's life." Clearly Tipper Gore indicated that her husband held values that parallel those commonly accepted by the American electorate thereby establishing a point of connection between the audience and her husband. There were no significant differences between Laura Bush and Tipper Gore and their use of forms of character ($\chi^2[df=2]=2.7$, $ns$).

## Issues Addressed in Spouses' Speeches

The breadth of issues covered by both Mrs. Bush and Mrs. Gore were very limited. Although Laura Bush discussed policy with some frequency (39 percent), her policy discussions were limited to education. For example, Mrs Bush stated: "George led a similar initiative as governor with fabulous results. The highly respected nonpartisan Rand study released just last week found that education reforms in Texas have resulted in some of the highest achievement gains in the country among all racial, socio-economic and family backgrounds." In this passage Laura Bush clearly commended her husband for a job well done with regard to education reforms in Texas. The implication is that if George Bush turned the Texas educational system around he could yield similar results at the national education level. No other policy issues were mentioned by Mrs. Bush. See Table 10.4.

Similarly, Tipper Gore restricted her policy discussion as well. Her one policy utterance dealt with the environment, "He took on powerful interests and held the

Table 10.4. Issues Addressed in 2000 Spouses' Speeches

|  | Poll | Bush* | Gore |
|---|---|---|---|
| Economy | 12 | 0 | 0 |
| Education | 12 | 11 (1) | 0 |
| Health Care | 9 | 0 | 0 |
| Social Security | 8 | 0 | 0 |
| Taxes | 6 | 0 | 0 |
| Guns | 6 | 0 | 0 |
| Abortion | 6 | 0 | 0 |
| National Defense | 5 | 0 | 0 |
| Medicare | 4 | 0 | 0 |
| Environment | 4 | 0 | 1 (1) |
| Budget Surplus | 3 | 0 | 0 |
| Jobs | 3 | 0 | 0 |
| Foreign Affairs | 2 | 0 | 0 |
| Other | – | 0 | 0 |
| Spearman's $\rho$ | – | .45, ns | -.14, ns |

*Frequency (rank) Gallup (2000).

first hearing on protecting families from toxic waste, the beginning of his commitment to the environment." In this excerpt Mrs. Gore praised her husband's past actions with regard to environmental policy. Specifically, she credits her husband with the initiating interest in environmental affairs. We used Spearman's $\rho$ to determine the strength of the relationship between the number of utterances devoted to each policy topic and the importance of that policy topic to the voters. Neither of these correlations reached significance.

## Implications

In 1996, the candidates' spouses focused mainly on acclaims (95 percent); in 2000 this tendency was taken to its logical conclusion, as the spouses offered no attacks or defenses. Thus, these data reinforce the idea that spouses have a strong tendency to acclaim their partners when serving as a surrogate (Benoit, Blaney, & Pier, 1998). In addition, previous research suggests that women are viewed as nurturing and are not expected to present attack messages (Trent & Freidenberg, 2000). Both Mrs. Bush and Mrs. Gore refrained from attacks thus making them seem accessible to the audience while still promoting their husbands' campaign.

As was the case in 1996, no defenses were given by either Mrs. Gore or Mrs. Bush on their husbands' behalf. Benoit, Blaney, and Pier (1998) suggested that defensives are very rare in convention situations so it is not surprising to see a dearth of defensives in the spouses' speeches. We argue that surrogate speeches serve to acclaim the candidate but not to engage in defenses.

Again, as in 1996, the focus of the spousal speeches centered around the character of the candidate rather than on policy. Tipper Gore mirrors Elizabeth Dole from the previous election in as much as she focused almost exclusively on character. However, when Mrs. Gore did discuss policy (rarely) she concentrated on past deeds. Although Laura Bush's policy statements centered around past deeds as well, she did discuss her husband's general goals and future plans. Both surrogate speakers were very selective in the policy issues they discussed. Laura Bush restricted her policy remarks to education, while Tipper Gore mentioned the environment. It is likely that these topics were chosen in an attempt to highlight either the candidate's area of expertise or to endear the candidate to specific groups of voters.

When discussing character, personal qualities were discussed most frequently. We argue that the surrogate speaker's focus on character, specifically the spouse of a candidate, is a function of the nominating convention. Because the spouse of the candidate has intimate knowledge of the candidate their testimonials may be seen as possessing a higher level of credibility than of other surrogates or testimonials (specifically with regard to personal characteristics). Further analysis of surrogate speakers is warranted to determine whether the spousal surrogate possess characteristics unique to political campaign communication.

# Chapter 11

# General Television Spots

I believe we need to encourage personal responsibility, so people are accountable for their actions. And I believe in government that is responsible to the people. There's a big difference in philosophy between my opponent and me. He trusts government; I trust you. I trust you to invest some of your own Social Security money for higher returns. I trust local people to run their own schools. I trust you with some of the budget surplus. We should help people live their lives, and not run them. I'm asking for your vote. (Bush, "Trust")

From high unemployment and record deficits, We now have record jobs and a record surplus. But George W. Bush has a tax plan that gives the fruits of that hard work to the richest 1%. Al Gore gives tax cuts directly to the middle class while strengthening Social Security . . . Medicare . . . improving education . . . paying down the nation's debt. Al Gore. Standing up for the people who turned the economy around. (Gore, "Word")

Why does Al Gore say one thing when the truth is another? His attacks on George Bush's record in Texas: Exaggerations. Newspapers say Al Gore has a problem telling the truth. Now Gore promises smaller government. But Gore is actually proposing three times the government spending President Clinton proposed, wiping out the entire surplus, and creating a deficit again. Why does Al Gore say one thing when the truth is another? (RNC, "Newspapers")

Before you look at George W. Bush's plans, look at his record. When the national minimum wage was raised to $5.15 an hour, Bush kept the Texas minimum wage at $3.35. When Congress passed a law to help states provide health insurance for kids, Bush opposed its expansion to 220,000 children in Texas. And a federal judge had to step in, ruling Texas fails to provide adequate health care for children. George Bush: His real plans hurt real people. (DNC, "National Minimum")

The general election contest between Vice President Gore and Governor Bush in campaign 2000 was played out, to a significant extent, on the nation's airwaves (although this campaign may be unprecedented in the extent to which the campaigns focused their resources on the "battleground" states). We review the literature on presidential television spots, present the findings of our content analysis, and then discuss the implications of our analysis.

## Literature Review

Political television spots are one of the most important components of contemporary presidential campaigns. West (1997) observes that "television ads are the single biggest expenditure in most major campaigns today" (p. 1). Jamieson explains that these dollars yield audience exposure:

> Political advertising is now the major means by which candidates for the presidency communicate their messages to voters. As a conduit of this advertising, television attracts both more candidate dollars and more audience attention than radio or print. Unsurprisingly, the spot ad is the most used and the most viewed of the available forms of advertising. (Jamieson, 1996, p. 517)

There can be no question that televised campaign commercials merit scholarly attention.

It should come as no surprise that researchers have lavished a great effort of attention on televised political advertising (see, e.g., Louden, 1989; Kaid, Nimmo, & Sanders, 1986). Some of the work that has been conducted on political spots is experimental, and that literature reveals that political spots are capable of influencing viewers (see, e.g., Basil, Schooler, & Reeves, 1991; Cundy, 1986; Garramone, 1985; Garramone, Atkin, Pinkleton, & Cole, 1990; Garramone & Smith, 1984; Hill, 1989; Just, Crigler, & Wallach, 1990; Kaid, 1991; Kaid, 1997; Kaid & Boydston, 1987; Kaid, Leland, & Whitney, 1992; Kaid & Sanders, 1978; Lang, 1991; Meadow & Sigelman, 1982; Newhagen & Reeves, 1991; and Thorson, Christ, & Caywood, 1991). In fact, research suggests that more voters learn about the candidates' issue position from these messages than from the news (Brians & Wattenberg, 1996; Kern, 1989; Patterson & McClure, 1976).

Research that investigates the nature of political television spots tends to employ two dimensions: positive versus negative ads (which correspond to our functions of acclaiming and attacking), and issue versus image (which correspond to our topics of policy and character). We will review this research before reporting the results of our investigation into the television spots of campaign 2000.

# Functions of General Television Spots

The literature on the nature of political advertising tends to divide political advertisements into those which are positive (acclaiming) and negative (attacking) commercials (see Johnson-Cartee & Copeland, 1991, 1997; Gronbeck, 1992). Kaid and Johnston (1991) found that 71 percent of the ads from 1960 to 1988 were positive and 29 percent negative. However, they reported that the number of negative ads has varied over time: negative spots spiked at 40 percent in 1964, dropped to 22-28 percent in the 1970s, and increased to 35-37 percent in the 1980s. Kaid and Johnston (1991) did not find that challengers used more negative ads than incumbents, or that Republicans used significantly more negative ads than Democrats. They updated their analysis (2001), reporting that 38 percent of television spots from 1952 through 1996 was negative, while 62 percent were positive. They again found no difference in the number of negative and positive ads by incumbency status. They did report that challengers are more likely than incumbents to use "issue concern" spots, which are similar to attacks on past deeds. This analysis reported that Democrats used more negative spots than Republicans.

West (1993) examined 150 "typical" political spots from 1952 to 1992, reporting that 43 percent were negative. He also reported that Republican ads were more negative than those from Democrats. West (1997) also conducted a study of "prominent" spots from 1952 to 1996, indicating that 54 percent of all ads and 53 percent of general election ads are negative. Again, he reported that Republican prominent ads were more negative (60 percent) than Democratic prominent ads (48 percent). Jamieson, Waldman, and Sherr (2000) analyzed television spots from 1952 to 1996 but they fail to report specific results for the functions of these television commercials.

Benoit (1999; see also Benoit, Pier, & Blaney, 1997) analyzed over 800 general television spots from every campaign to use this message form, 1952 to 1996. He found that 60 percent of themes were acclaims, 39 percent were attacks, and 1 percent were defenses. He indicated that these spots were becoming more negative over time. He also found that incumbent party candidates used more acclaims (66 percent) than challengers (54 percent), whereas challengers used more attacks (45 percent) than incumbents (33 percent).

We argue that an important limitation of past research (besides Benoit, 1999) is that it uses the entire spot as the coding unit, classifying each advertisement as *either* positive *or* negative. However, many political spots contain both positive and negative remarks (even adding a third category, comparative, only helps somewhat, because all comparative spots may not include equal amounts of positive and negative comments). The functional approach provides a more precise estimate by classifying each remark as acclaiming (positive), attacking (negative), or defending.

Johnson-Cartee and Copeland (1989) asked respondents to rate topics found in attacking ads as either fair or unfair. The topics congregated into two groups, "Political Issues" (political record, stands on issues, criminal record, and voting record) and "Personal Characteristics" (personal life, marriage, family, religion, medical history, and sex life). At least 83 percent rated each political issue as a fair topic for an attack; however, at least 64 percent rated all of the personal characteristics as an unfair topic for political attack. This study suggests that voters do not condemn political attacks wholesale, but believed that attacks on some topics (policy) are more appropriate than attacks on other topics (candidate character).

## Topics of General Television Spots

Previous investigation of presidential television spots has also probed the relative emphasis of these messages on issues (policy) and image (character). Patterson and McClure (1976), studying the 1972 campaign, indicated that 42 percent of the television advertisements focused on issues, and another 28 percent included issue information. Hofstetter and Zukin (1979) found that 85 percent of the commercials for Nixon and McGovern in 1972 addressed issues. Joslyn (1980) found that while 77 percent of the ads discussed issues, only 47 percent focused on images. Kern's study of the 1984 advertising campaign concluded that "issues were mentioned in 84 percent of such [30-second] spots" (1989, p. 51).

Kaid and Johnston (1991), who studied 830 television spots from 1960 to 1988, found that 67 percent of the positive ads and 79 percent of the negative ads provided issue information, and that 65 percent of the positive spots and 64 percent of the negative spots included image information. Their more recent analysis (2001) reported that 66 percent of spots from 1952 to 1996 were issue spots and 34 percent were image spots. Challengers and Democrats devoted a higher percentage of their television spots to issues than did Incumbents and Republicans.

West (1993) found that 65 percent of the 150 "typical" ads from 1952 to 1992 that he analyzed concerned issues, while 23 percent addressed character (the remainder discussed the campaign or party). His study of "prominent" spots (1997) revealed that 59 percent addressed issues and 39 percent personal qualities.

Jamieson, Waldman, and Sherr (2000) again do not report the percentages for policy versus character. They do conclude, however, that "This analysis demonstrates that the majority of verbal content in political advertisements is not discussion of policy" (p. 60). This conclusion, however, is inconsistent with the rest of the literature. Their research is also suspect because of poor inter-coder reliability (see, e.g., Benoit, 2001b).

Benoit (1999; see also Benoit, Pier, & Blaney, 1997) found that 60 percent of these in presidential television spots from 1952 to 1996 concerned policy and 40 percent addressed character. He also found that, beginning in 1980, there has been a clear trend toward more focus on policy and less on character. Thus, previous research has found that political spots address both issues (policy) and image (character), and that policy tends to be more prominent than character.

Two studies provide more details on the use of issues and image in political advertising. Joslyn's (1986) analysis of 506 political ads from 1960 to 1984 reported that 37 percent of the ads revealed future policy plans, 60 percent evaluate past governmental policy, and 57 percent mention candidate qualities (compassion, empathy, integrity, strength, activity, and knowledge). Shyles (1986), who studied 140 ads from 1980, found mentions of these topics: Carter's record, domestic, economy, energy, federalism, foreign policy, government management, national security, and national well-being (issue); altruism, competence, expertise, honesty, leadership, personal, strength, and other qualities (image). It is clear that political advertising addresses both issues and images.

Again, one limitation of past research is that many studies do not use themes as the coding unit, reporting only that an ad contained (or "mentioned") some issue information. Because political spots vary in how much time they devote to policy, this is a crude index. The functional approach analyzes each utterance in a commercial to provide a more precise indication of the extent to which policy and character are addressed in a political advertisement.

## 2000 General Election TV Spots

We obtained nineteen TV spots from Bush, twenty-three from the Republican National Committee, twenty-one from Gore, and twenty-six from the Democratic National Committee, for a total of eighty-nine general election television spots (see Table 11.1). Some of these spots were videotaped from local television (luckily, Missouri was a "battleground" state in 2000); some were downloaded from the Bush and Gore campaigns' web pages; and some were downloaded from other websites (www.NationalJournal.com).

We report multiple findings from our analysis of these 2000 general election

Table 11.1. Distribution of Spots in the Sample

|  | Spots |
| --- | --- |
| Gore | 21 |
| DNC | 26 |
| Democratic | 47 |
| Bush | 19 |
| RNC | 23 |
| Republican | 42 |
| Total | 89 |

Table 11.2. Functions of 2000 General Television Spots

|  | Acclaims | Attacks | Defenses |
|---|---|---|---|
| Bush | 101 (79%) | 26 (20%) | 1 (0.8%) |
| RNC | 53 (46%) | 59 (52%) | 2 (2%) |
| Republican | 154 (64%) | 85 (35%) | 3 (1%) |
| Gore | 120 (69%) | 53 (30%) | 1 (0.6%) |
| DNC | 54 (36%) | 98 (64%) | 0 |
| Democratic | 174 (53%) | 151 (46%) | 1 (0.3%) |
| Total | 328 (58%) | 236 (42%) | 4 (0.7%) |

presidential television spots. Our results are discussed under four headings: functions, topics, forms of policy and character, and issues addressed.

## Functions of 2000 General Television Spots

These television spots featured numerous acclaims (58 percent; see Table 11.2). For example, the spot "Bean Counter" by Gore declared that "we need a patients' bill of rights to take the medical decisions away from the HMOs and insurance companies and give them back to the doctors and nurses." This utterance acclaimed a proposal (future plan) to enhance the treatment of patients by protecting them from (allegedly) greedy HMOs and insurance companies. This idea would surely appeal to many voters. Similarly, Bush asserted that "We will strengthen Social Security and Medicare for the greatest generation and for generations to come" ("No Changes, No Reductions"). While a more general campaign promise, this is a goal that many voters would embrace. These excerpts show how acclaims were used in these campaign messages.

However, these advertisements also frequently attacked the opposition (42 percent). For example, the DNC argued that "In Texas he [Bush] appointed a chemical company lobbyist to enforce environmental laws. He made key air pollution rules voluntary—even for plants near schools. Schools now use smog meters to see if it's safe to play outside. Texas now ranks last among all states in air quality" ("Smog"). The premise of this message was that we can learn about how Bush might perform as president by looking at his record in Texas, and that record reveals serious problems. Bush's record on the environment is clearly a policy topic. Similarly, the RNC discussed policy in the area of education when it ran an ad which stated "America's having a recession—an education recession that's hurting our children. Out students rank last in the world in math and physics and most fourth graders in our cities can't read. The Clinton-Gore education recession: It's failing our kids" ("Education Recession"). Here, the current administration (of which Gore is a part) was blamed for problems in our educational system. The clear implication is that we do not want to continue the Clinton-Gore policies by electing Gore to be the next president. Thus, attacks were common in these television spots.

Defense was quite rare in these commercials: Gore used defense once, Bush once, and the RNC twice. All four were instances of simple denial. For example, the Democrats charged that Bush threatened Social Security, promising the same money to young workers and retirees. However, in this RNC spot ("Solvent") we are told that Gore's "attacks on George Bush's Social Security plan" are "exaggerations. The truth: Non-partisan analysis confirms George Bush's plan sets aside $2.4 trillion to strengthen Social Security." This ad functions to deny the Democratic attacks on Bush's Social Security proposal. Defense was used in the general television spots of 2000, but it was uncommon.

We contrasted the ads sponsored by the candidates and those produced on their behalf by their respective parties (a few spots late in the campaign said they were sponsored by both the candidate and the party; we counted these as candidate ads). Bush and the Republicans used acclaims more frequently than Gore and the Democrats (64 percent; 53 percent). On the other hand, the Democrats attacked more than the Republicans (46 percent; 35 percent). A *chi-square* calculated on the Republicans' (Bush + RNC) versus the Democrats' (Gore + DNC) use of acclaims and attacks was significant ($\chi^2[df=1]=6.7, p < .01$; defenses were omitted because there were only four instances of this function). However, in this campaign the Democrats were the incumbent party and the Republicans were the challenger party. We cannot tell whether these differences were a result of influences from the political parties, from incumbency status, or whether these differences stem from the two candidates' preferred campaign styles. See Table 11.3.

Table 11.3. Topics of 2000 General Television Spots

|  | Policy | Character |
|---|---|---|
| Bush | 87 (69%) | 40 (31%) |
| RNC | 73 (65%) | 39 (35%) |
| Republican | 160 (67%) | 79 (33%) |
| Gore | 125 (72%) | 48 (28%) |
| DNC | 111 (73%) | 41 (27%) |
| Democratic | 236 (73%) | 89 (27%) |
| Total | 396 (70%) | 168 (30%) |

We wondered whether there was a difference between spots sponsored by the candidates and spots sponsored by the party. A *chi-square* calculated on candidates (Bush + Gore) versus parties (DNC + RNC) for acclaims and attacks was also significant ($\chi^2[df=1]= 63.4, p < .001$). Inspection of the means reveals that the television commercials from the parties were more than twice as negative as the ads from the two candidates (attacks were 59 percent of themes in party ads; 26 percent in candidate spots).

We also compared the general television spots from 1996 and 2000. There was a significant shift from attacks to acclaims: Attacks dropped from 53 percent in 1996 to 42 percent in 2000; acclaims increased from 47 percent in 1996 to 58 percent in 2000 ($\chi^2[df=1]=14.9, p < .001$). Clearly, the 2000 television spot campaign was more positive than the previous cycle.

## Topics of 2000 General Television Spots

These presidential spots from the 2000 campaign focused much more on policy than on character: Over twice as many themes addressed policy (70 percent) as character (30 percent). See Table 11.3. For instance, Bush ("Expect More") discussed the issue of education: "We need to raise standards in our schools. We need more accountability and more discipline." Many voters could see these as positive reforms, and they were obviously concerned with policy. Gore ("Ball") used a retired Social Security commissioner to attack Bush's Social Security plan: "I've looked at Governor Bush's plan. He takes one trillion dollars out of Social Security for savings accounts. But Social Security is counting on that money to pay benefits. His plan simply doesn't add up and would undermine Social Security." Many voters would react negatively to a threat to Social Security, and a discussion of Social Security reforms concerned policy rather than character. Thus, these passages show how the candidates discussed policy in their general television spots.

Character themes also occurred in these messages (39 percent). Many Republican ads questioned Gore's credibility. For example, two RNC ads ("Newspapers," "Solvent") began by asking, "Why does Al Gore say one thing when the truth is another?" Clearly this question was intended to impugn his honesty. This DNC ad ("Penny") discusses Bush's Social Security proposal. However, it begins and ends by questioning his character:

> George W. Bush is back in New Hampshire. Will he come clean on Social Security? In this year's election John McCain said Bush's plan has not one penny for Social Security. Now Bush is promising young workers one trillion dollars from Social Security for them to invest. Yet the same money is needed to pay current benefits. If Bush gives it away, it could cut benefits for Seniors. Think about it. Bush is promising younger workers and Seniors the same money. That's anything but straight talk.

First, it was alleged that Bush needs to "come clean." Then, the ad used John McCain and his slogan ("The Straight Talk Express") to attack fellow-Republican Bush (in the analysis, this ad was coded as containing both with policy and character themes). These excerpts illustrate how these spots discussed character. The second spot also shows how a campaign message can slide from policy (Social Security) to character (honesty).

Every one of the four groups of television ads stressed policy, with percentages ranging from 65 percent to 73 percent (Gore: 72 percent, DNC: 73 percent, Bush: 69 percent, and RNC: 65 percent). A *chi-square* calculated on Republican ads (Bush + RNC) versus Democratic ads (Gore + DNC) for topic was not significant ($\chi^2[df=1]=2.1$, *ns*). Nor was there a difference in topic from candidate- versus party-sponsored spots ($\chi^2[df=1]=0.1$, *ns*). Thus, the discussion of topics (policy versus character) was not influenced by source of ads. In 1996, Clinton and Dole both devoted 71 percent of their comments to policy (Benoit, 1999). There was no difference between the 1996 and 2000 campaigns in discussion of policy and character ($\chi^2[df=1]=0.1$, *ns*).

## Forms of Policy and of Character in 2000 General Television Spots

Overall, the policy remarks tended to be distributed among the three forms of policy in roughly equal amounts: past deeds 28 percent, future plans 39 percent, and general goals 33 percent. See Table 11.4. For instance, in the Bush ad, "Challenge the Status Quo," voters were asked: "Is the status quo in America's schools good enough? Under Al Gore and Bill Clinton, national reading scores stagnated. America's high school students place almost dead last in international math tests. The achievement gap between poor and non-poor students remains wide. Gore and Clinton had eight years, but they've failed." This spot attacks Gore on past deeds (failures) in education over the eight years he was vice president. Gore also focused on the last eight years in this advertisement, but he acclaimed economic accomplishments: "You know, for the last eight years, we've had the strongest economy in all of American history" ("Prosperity"). Past deeds were used both to acclaim and attack in these spots.

Some policy comments concern campaign promises in the form of future plans. For example, a DNC advertisement ("Promise") criticized Bush for his Social Security proposal:

> He's promising to take a trillion dollars out of Social Security so younger workers can invest in private accounts. Sounds good. The problem is: Bush has promised the same money to pay seniors their current benefits. The Wall Street Journal shows he can't keep both promises. Which promise is he going to break? George W. Bush: his promises threaten Social Security.

This message argued that Bush's proposal, to allow younger workers to invest part

Table 11.4. Forms of Policy and Character in General Television Spots

| | Policy | | | | | Character | | | | | |
| | Past Deeds* | | Future Plans | | General Goals | | Personal Qualities | | Leader-ship | | Ideals | |
|---|---|---|---|---|---|---|---|---|---|---|---|---|
| Bush | 3 | 9 | 21 | 7 | 47 | 0 | 10 | 8 | 4 | 0 | 16 | 2 |
| RNC | 8 | 8 | 26 | 15 | 9 | 7 | 20 | 12 | 0 | 1 | 4 | 2 |
| | 11 | 17 | 47 | 22 | 56 | 7 | 30 | 20 | 4 | 1 | 20 | 4 |
| Repub | 28 (18%) | | 69 (43%) | | 63 (39%) | | 50 (63%) | | 5 (6%) | | 24 (30%) | |
| Gore | 15 | 19 | 23 | 21 | 47 | 0 | 21 | 11 | 8 | 2 | 6 | 0 |
| DNC | 2 | 48 | 20 | 21 | 20 | 0 | 7 | 29 | 0 | 0 | 5 | 0 |
| | 17 | 67 | 43 | 42 | 67 | 0 | 28 | 40 | 8 | 2 | 11 | 0 |
| Dem | 84 (36%) | | 85 (36%) | | 67 (28%) | | 68 (76%) | | 10 (11%) | | 11 (12%) | |
| Total | 28 | 84 | 90 | 64 | 123 | 7 | 58 | 61 | 12 | 3 | 31 | 4 |
| | 112 (28%) | | 154 (39%) | | 130 (33%) | | 119 (70%) | | 15 (9%) | | 35 (21%) | |

*Acclaims/attacks

of their Social Security funds in the stock market, would put Social Security at risk. This excerpt from an RNC advertisement acclaimed Bush's tax cut proposal: "Under Bush, every taxpayer gets a tax cut and no family pays more than a third of income to Washington." Thus, when candidates discuss policy, one option is to talk about their policy proposals or future plans.

The third policy choice is to discuss ends rather than means, or general goals. For instance, Gore discussed health care in this commercial ("Prosperity II"): "In a time when our health is everything, we've got to have more access to affordable health care." No reference was made to a particular proposal for achieving this goal, so this illustrates a general goal. In the spot, "Save Michigan Jobs," Lee Iacocca argued that "Al Gore's extreme ideas about cars could cost a lot of Michigan families their jobs. Mr. Gore writes: 'We need to raise gas taxes, and the gasoline engine is a threat to our future and we should scrap it.'" This attacked Gore's general goal of eliminating gasoline powered cars. Thus, candidates dispute over policy ends as well as means in their advertisements.

Closer examination of the data reveals that there was more variation in the Republican (Bush + RNC) policy remarks (past deeds 18 percent, future plans 43 percent, general goals 39 percent) than in the Democratic (Gore +DNC) policy utterances (past deeds 36 percent, future plans 36 percent, general goals 28 percent). A *chi-square* reveals a significant difference in the distribution of policy utterances ($\chi^2[df=2]=15.8$, $p < .001$). Inspection of the means reveals that the Republican ads relied less on past deeds, and more on future plans, than the Democratic spots. It also appears that the Republicans had a tendency to attack on past deeds and acclaim on future plans (although the Democrats also tended to attack on past deeds).

When these spots from the 2000 general campaign discussed character, they focused much more heavily on personal qualities (70 percent) than on leadership ability (9 percent) or ideals (21 percent). The RNC ad "Agenda" complained that Gore had allowed zinc mining on his land. However, the conclusion drawn was one of character: "Even on the environment, Al Gore says one thing but does another." This statement clearly questions Gore's integrity. In this ad for Gore, he told voters something about his character: "And I believe the next president has to have a passion in his heart to fight for the people who most need a champion" ("Keep the Faith"). Thus, these ads used character for acclaims and attacks.

A second form of character utterance discussed a candidate's leadership ability or experience in office. Phyllis Hunter explained that "we have George leading the way. People ask me why have I followed him so intently in education and reading. I followed him because he's been a leader" ("Hunter"). An advertisement for Gore began with policy, arguing that Governor Bush gave a tax break to "Big Oil," opposed health care for children, failed to raise the minimum wage, allowed polluters to regulate themselves, and is now promising the same trillion dollars to younger workers and retirees. The spot concluded by asking, "Is he ready to lead America?" ("Ready to Lead"). The implication, of course, was that Bush was not ready to lead our country. These excerpts illustrate how leadership ability can be used to acclaim and attack.

The third form of character utterance, ideals, discusses the values or principles held by the candidates. The DNC spot "Protect" discussed the need for protection for crime victims. It articulated the principle that "The people who are hurt by crime need to be heard." Bush's commercial explained his philosophy of educational control: "I trust local people to run their own schools" ("Trust"). These passages show how ideals were used in these television spots.

As with policy, a *chi-square* found a difference in forms of character ($\chi^2[df=2]=8.7$, $p < .025$). It appears that Bush and the RNC focused more on ideals (30 percent) than did Gore and the DNC (12 percent). See, for example, the Bush ad "Trust" at the beginning of this chapter: "He trusts government; I trust you." Gore devoted more utterances to leadership ability than Bush (11 percent, 5 percent) and more on personal qualities (76 percent, 65 percent). This is somewhat surprising given the Republican's attempt to make Gore's character (exaggerations or lies) an issue, as in the RNC ad "Newspapers" at the beginning of this chapter.

## Issues Addressed in 2000 General Television Spots

The issue that was most important to voters, the economy, ranked seventh in number of themes in these spots (see Table 11.5). However, in all but one instance, the Democrats were the ones who were discussing the economy. For example, in "Word" Gore explained that "From high unemployment and record deficits, we now have record jobs and a record surplus." He attacked the previous Republican administrations for a poor economic record and then acclaimed the Democratic economic turnaround. Education and health care were tied for second most important issue in this poll. Education, of course, is traditionally a Democratic issue. However, this issue ranked first in the spots and the Republicans devoted almost twice as many themes to education as the Democrats (77 to 41). In this ad, Bush attacked the Clinton/Gore record and then acclaimed his ideas for improving education:

> Is the status quo in America's schools good enough? Under Al Gore and Bill Clinton, national reading scores stagnated. America's high school students place almost dead last in international math tests. The achievement gap between poor and non-poor students remains wide. Gore and Clinton had eight years, but they've failed. As President, George W. Bush will challenge the status quo with a crusade to improve education. He'll fight for reforms hailed as the most fundamental in a generation: demand high standards and accountability for students and teachers, restore local control of schools, increase funding but change the system so successful schools are rewarded and failing ones must improve. He'll turn Head Start into a reading program and close the

Table 11.5. Issues Addressed in 2000 General Television Spots

|  | Poll | Bush* | Gore |
|---|---|---|---|
| Economy | 18 | 1 (8) | 11 (7) |
| Education | 16 | 77 (1) | 41 (3) |
| Health Care | 16 | 24 (2) | 75 (1) |
| Social Security | 11 | 15 (4) | 21 (4) |
| Taxes | 8 | 9 (5) | 20 (5) |
| National Defense | 8 | 5 (7) | 2 (8) |
| Environment | 3 | 6 (6) | 18 (6) |
| Other | – | 23 (3) | 46 (2) |
| Spearman $\rho$ |  | -.30, *ns* | -.19, *ns* |

*Frequency (rank)   NBC News/*Wall Street Journal* (2000)

achievement gap that hurts those on the edges of poverty. His goal? Teach every child to read because there are no second rate children, no second rate dreams. Governor George W. Bush: A Fresh Start for Education. ("Challenge the Status Quo")

Health care ranked second in these spots and the Democrats allocated over three times as many comments to health as the Republicans (seventy-five to twenty-four). The DNC weighed in on the issue of health, acclaiming Gore's stands while attacking Bush:

> The issue: health care. Al Gore is for a real patients' bill of rights and a prescription drug benefit under Medicare. George W. Bush says no. He sides with the big drug companies, the HMOs and the insurance industry. In Texas, Bush even opposed health coverage for 200,000 more children. Texas now ranks second to last in America for children with health insurance and last for people with health coverage. George Bush—his plan protects special interests instead of working families. ("Health Comparative")

The category with the third most themes was "Other." Social Security (fourth in the poll) was also fourth in spots, with the Democrats edging out the Republicans (twenty-one to fifteen). For example, this DNC ad attacked Bush's proposals for Social Security:

> What would George W. Bush's plan do to Social Security? He's promising to take a trillion dollars out of Social Security so younger workers can invest in private accounts. Sounds good. The problem is: Bush has promised the same money to pay seniors their current benefits. The *Wall Street Journal* shows he can't keep both promises. Which promise is he going to break? George W. Bush: his promises threaten Social Security. ("Promise")

Taxes ranked fifth in the poll and was also the fifth most common policy topic in the ads. Despite the fact that taxes is usually considered a Republican issue, in 2000 the Democrats devoted about twice as many comments to taxes as the Republicans (twenty to nine). For example, this Gore spot contrasted Bush's across-the-board tax cut proposal with his own targeted tax reductions:

> The facts on George W. Bush's $1.6 trillion tax cut promise: Almost half goes to the richest 1 percent. What trickles down? An average of 62 cents a day for most taxpayers. Bush gives almost half to the richest 1 percent, leaving 62 cents to trickle down to us. Al Gore builds on a foundation of fiscal discipline. Pay down the nation's debt. Protect Social Security and Medicare. A $10,000 a year tax deduction for college tuition. Because the middle class has earned more than trickle down. ("Down")

National defense was virtually ignored (seven total comments in the ads). For instance, the RNC criticized Gore because "Al Gore says he wants a test for the Joint Chiefs of Staff. A litmus test—not about readiness, but about politics. General Colin Powell couldn't pass Al Gore's litmus test. Neither could Norman Schwartzkopf. Schwartzkopf and Powell—the heroes of Desert Storm." ("Litmus"). The environment, ranked seventh for voters, was sixth in the commercials, and the Democrats addressed this topic three times as often as the Republicans (eighteen to six). In the ad "Prosperity II," Gore revealed his feelings about the environment: "You look at young children and think about how important it is for them to breathe clean air." These excerpts illustrate how the candidates addressed these issues.

Thus, in general, the rank order of the frequency of the policy topics in these spots tended to parallel the rank order of importance in public opinion polls. However, the surprises were the lack of attention to the top issue, the economy (especially Gore's neglect), the fact that Republicans coopted education, and the fact that the Democrats discussed taxation more than the Republicans. We calculated Spearman $\rho$ on the rank order of issues to the public and rank order of frequency of mention in these television spots. Neither correlation was significant.

## Implications

In these 2000 general television spots, acclaims were more common than attacks, while defenses were relatively uncommon. This pattern is consistent with previous research (Benoit, 1999). However, a general trend toward a larger proportion of attacks in these messages through 1996 was reversed in 2000: a drop to 42 percent attacks in 2000 from 53 percent in 1996. It was unusual (albeit not unprecedented) that the incumbent party candidate, Gore (and the DNC), attacked more (46 percent) than the challenger, Bush (and the RNC, 35 percent). This could be attributable to the fact that Bush led through much of the campaign. Benoit (1999) found that between 1952 and 1996, the candidate who trailed throughout the campaign attacked more than front-runners or those in close elections.

In these commercials, Gore (and the DNC) employed attacks more frequently than Bush (and the RNC). This seems to fly in the face of tradition, because the incumbent party candidate—Gore in 2000—tends to use acclaims more than the challenger party candidate (who in contrast exhibits a greater tendency to attack). If we look only at those candidates who most closely resemble Gore—a sitting vice president running for the presidency—we find that not one of them (Nixon in 1960, Humphrey in 1968, Bush in 1988) attacked more than their challenger party opponent (Benoit, 1999).

We also found that party-sponsored (DNC, RNC) spots used attacks significantly more than the candidate-sponsored ads. We suspect this may be an attempt to shield the candidates from the possibility of backlash from voters who profess to dislike mudslinging (Merritt, 1984; Stewart, 1975). However, we doubt that voters distinguish between commercials sponsored by the candidates (Bush-Cheney or Gore-Lieberman) and spots run by the parties (DNC or RNC).

The advertisements in 2000 focused more on policy than character, as has been the case in general television spots since 1980 (Benoit, 1999). We found that there was no significant difference in topic from 1996 to 2000. Research has shown that, in the aggregate, winners devote a larger percentage of their television spot utterance to policy than losers (Benoit, 2000). Using the outcome of the popular vote, which Gore won, this finding was replicated in 2000 (Democratic spots: 73 percent policy; Republican spots: 67 percent policy). Two important caveats here, however, are that the Electoral College was won by Bush and that the difference between Republicans and Democrats on topics of policy and character in 2000 was not statistically significant.

There were significant shifts in the allocation of policy and character remarks in 2000. Fewer policy utterances were devoted to past deeds in 2000 than in years past (58 percent, 28 percent). Most of the slack was taken up by a significant increase in discussion of future plans in 2000 (39 percent; 16 percent). A slight increase in general goals also occurred in 2000 (33 percent; 27 percent). There were shifts in character as well. Personal qualities increased from 49 percent historically to 72 percent in 2000 (Benoit, 1999). Discussion of leadership ability dropped from 38 percent (1952-1996) to only 8 percent in 2000. Ideals were roughly the same, increasing slightly from 17 percent historically to 21 percent in 2000. We believe that Gore erred by not acclaiming the Clinton/Gore record more often than he did, which would have increased the number of utterances addressing past deeds.

Both parties (but especially the Republicans) tended to ignore the issue that was most important to voters: the economy. Given the relatively healthy economy enjoyed by America, it was hardly surprising to see the Republicans avoid the economy. However, it seems very odd that the Democrats did not devote more time to an issue that clearly favored the incumbent party. Education, traditionally a Democratic issue, was discussed far more by the Republicans in 2000. The Democrats spent more time on health care, Social Security, and taxes. Thus, with the one glaring exception of the economy, the frequency of discussion of the policy themes in the general television spots tended to parallel importance to voters. The Democrats may have had a slight edge in distribution of policy topics.

Much can be explained by looking at Gore's campaign. We believe that the vice president wanted to distance himself from Bill Clinton because of questions about the president's character. However, in our opinion, this concern also seems to have manifested itself in a neglect of the Clinton/Gore record (past deeds) generally and of the economy specifically. The Republicans were probably delighted at the lack of a concerted effort to exploit the generally strong economy and avoided this topic as well. This choice manifests itself in several places in the data. First, the Democrats devoted far more utterances to criticizing Governor Bush's record in Texas (sixty-seven attacks on past deeds) than to acclaiming

Gore's successes (seventeen acclaims on past deeds). As suggested above, one would expect an incumbent party candidate to rely heavily on acclaims of past deeds and attacks on (the challenger's) future plans and the challenger to devote a substantial portion of utterances to attacks on past deeds and acclaims on future plans (acclaims of future plans are, of course, a reason to evict the incumbent from office). Indeed, in 1996 Clinton devoted 64 percent of his policy remarks to past deeds (Benoit, 1999). In 2000 Bush attacked on past deeds more than he acclaimed them (seventeen; eleven) and he acclaimed future plans far more than he attacked them (forty-seven; twenty-two) which is appropriate for a challenger. However, Gore also looked like a challenger, attacking more on past deeds than acclaiming accomplishments (sixty-seven; seventeen). His future plan utterances were devoted almost equally to acclaims (forty-three) and attacks (forty-two), rather than emphasizing attacks on Bush's proposals.

Second, despite the fact that the economy was ranked as the single most important issue to voters, Gore and the DNC devoted only eleven themes to the economy, leaving it ranked seventh out of nine issues (including "other"). Gore seemed desperate to win the campaign without Clinton or the Clinton/Gore record (reminding us of a child who insists that he or she will "do it *myself*!"). Ironically, an argument can be made that Clinton's lies concerned his private sexual behavior (and many Americans accepted his attempt at transcendence, arguing that this was none of their business). However, Gore's exaggerations (or lies) concerned use of prescription drugs and his trips to disaster areas as the vice president. Gore's credibility problems concerned public life, not private life. It is, therefore, a questionable choice to devote twenty-eight acclaims to personal qualities and only seventeen to past accomplishments.

We believe that the discourse produced by Gore in his television advertisements failed to effectively exploit the situation. He should have spent much more time acclaiming the economy (past deeds) and arguing that we need to continue the policies (of the Clinton/Gore administration) which created our current prosperity. He should not have allowed the Republicans to coopt education. This is not to say that Bush ran a perfect campaign, but Gore seemed to make more questionable decisions than Bush.

# Chapter 12

# General Debates

The Boston Massachusetts Debate: October 3, 2000

Bush: [My opinion] is that I want to empower people in their own lives. I also want to go to Washington to get some positive things done. It's going to require a new spirit, a spirit of cooperation. It's going to require the ability of a Republican president to reach out across the partisan divide and to say to Democrats, "Let's come together to do what's right for America." It's been my record as governor of Texas. It'll be how I conduct myself if I'm fortunate enough to earn your vote as president of the United States.

I want to finally get something done on Medicare. I want to make sure prescription drugs are available for all seniors. And I want seniors to have additional choices when it comes to choosing their health care plans. I want to finally get something done on Social Security. I want to make sure the seniors have the promise made will be a promise kept. But I want younger workers to be able to manage some of their own money, some of their own payroll taxes in the private sector under certain guidelines to get a better rate of return on your own money.

I also want to make sure the education system fulfills its hope and promise. I've had a strong record of working with Democrats and Republicans in Texas to make sure no child is left behind. I understand the limited role of the federal government, but it can be a constructive role when it comes to reform, by insisting that there be strong accountability systems.

And my intentions are to earn your vote and earn your confidence. I'm asking for your vote. I want you to be on my team. And for those of you working, thanks. Thanks from the bottom of my heart. And for those of you making up your mind, I'd be honored to have your support.

Gore: I want to thank everybody who watched and listened tonight because this is, indeed, a crucial time in American history. We're at a fork in the road. We have this incredible prosperity, but a lot of people have been left behind. And we have a very important decision to make: Will we use the prosperity to enrich all of our families and not just the few? One important way of looking at this is to ask, "Who are you going to fight for?"

Throughout my career in public service, I have fought for working men and women of this country, middle class families. Why? Because you are the ones who have the hardest time paying taxes, the hardest time making ends meet. You are the ones who are making car payments and mortgage payments and doing right by your kids. And a lot of times, there are powerful forces arrayed against you. And make no mistake about it, they do have undue influence in Washington, D.C., and it makes a difference if you have a president who will fight for you.

There's a woman named Winifred Skinner here tonight from Iowa. I mentioned her earlier. She's 79 years old, she has Social Security. I'm not going to cut her benefits or support any proposal that would. She gets a small pension. But in order to pay for her prescription drug benefits, she has to go out seven days a week, several hours a day, picking up cans. She came all the way from Iowa in a Winnebago with her poodle in order to attend here tonight. And I want to tell her, I am going to fight for a prescription drug benefit for all seniors. And I am going to fight for the people of this country for a prosperity that benefits all.

The 2000 general election campaign saw three formal debates between Governor Bush and Vice President Gore. Each debate employed a different format ranging from a rebuttal style to a town hall atmosphere. Because the general debates have become an increasingly important means of disseminating information to the voting public, it is vital that we continue to make them an important unit of analysis when discussing the election as a whole. This chapter will review the literature on presidential general election debates, present the results of our analysis of the 2000 general election debates, and discuss the implications of those findings

## Literature Review

Presidential debates have become an integral part of the electoral process in the United States. Since 1976 there has been expectation, and anticipation, of the two individuals who have gained their party's nomination to square off in the public arena (Denton & Woodward, 1990; Freidenberg, 1994; Swerdlow, 1987). The debates have become an invaluable tool for voters because the extended format of a debate can provide the electorate with more in-depth attention to the platforms advocated by the candidates (Carlin, 1994; Jamieson, 1987; Hellweg, Pfau & Brydon, 1992; Lamoureaux, Entrekin, & McKinney, 1994; Swerdlow, 1984). It has also been argued that because the general election debates attract a large number of viewers they serve as a main source of information for many constituents (Jamieson & Birdsell, 1988; Wayne, 1992).

There has also been a substantial amount of research done on the effects of presidential debates on voters (Becker, Sobowale, Cobbey, & Eyal, 1978; Desmond

& Donohue, 1981; Hagner & Rieselbach, 1978; Lang & Lang, 1978; Lanoue & Schrott, 1989; McLeod, Bybee, & Durall, 1979; Nimmo, Mansfield, & Curry, 1978). Many scholars have found that when voters watch the debates it increases their general knowledge of the candidates and their stance on the issues, which could in turn influence voting behavior (Benoit, McKinney, & Holbert, 2001; Bishop, Oldendick, & Tuchfarber, 1978; Drew & Weaver, 1991; Graber & Kim, 1978; Jamieson & Birdsell, 1988; Hellweg, Pfau, & Brydon, 1992; Jacoby, Troutman, & Whittler, 1986; Lemert, 1993; McLeod, Durall, Ziemke, & Bybee, 1979; Swerdlow, 1984). Some scholars assert that debates have limited effects on voter behavior (Abramowitz, 1978; Lang & Lang, 1977; Lanoue, 1991; Lubell, 1977; Miller & MacKuen, 1979) while other scholars argue that the debates can be a mitigating factor of voter choice (Davis, 1982; Geer, 1988; Kelly, 1983; Middleton, 1962; Roper, 1960; Wayne, 1992). In short, there has been extensive research on the importance and impact of presidential debates.

Finally, there is a body of work that addresses the nature of presidential debates. Benoit and Wells (1996) analyzed the 1992 debates for instances of attack and defense. Although they did not analyze for acclaims, later analysis (as reported in Benoit, Blaney, & Pier, 1998) indicated that acclaims were the most frequent (56 percent) followed by attacks (30 percent) and then defenses (14 percent) (see also Brydon, 1985; Ellsworth, 1965; Tiemens, Hellweg, Kipper, & Phillips, 1985). Benoit, Blaney, and Pier (1998) found that in the 1996 debates acclaims were most frequent (59 percent) followed by attacks (33 percent) and then defenses (7 percent). In addition, they found that both candidates focused on policy more than character. They also found that the challenger was more likely to attack than the incumbent and the incumbent was more likely to focus on policy. In their analysis of the 1960 debates Benoit and Harthcock (1999) also found that acclaims were more frequently used than attacks or defenses, policy was more common than character, challengers were more likely to attack, and the incumbent focused more on policy. Similar results were reported by Wells (1999) in his analysis of the 1976, 1980, and 1984 presidential debates and by Benoit and Brazeal (2002) in their analysis of the 1988 debates.

We analyzed all three debates from the 2000 presidential general election which included: the October 3, 2000, debate held in Boston, Massachusetts, the October 11, 2000, debate which took place in Winston-Salem, North Carolina, and the October 17, 2000, debate in St. Louis, Missouri. The transcripts were obtained from CNN via Lexis-Nexis. First we will discuss the functions of these primary debates, then discuss the targets of attacks, followed by topics (policy and character), forms of policy and character, and finally we will discuss the issues addressed in these debates.

# Results

In this section we will take up several topics as we report the results of our analyses. First, we discuss the functions of these debates. Then we address the topics of these messages. This will be followed by a breakdown of the forms of policy and character. Finally, we present results of our analysis of the issue topics the candidates addressed in these campaign messages.

## Functions of 2000 General Debates

Both candidates acclaimed (74 percent) more than they attacked (24 percent) or engaged in defense (3 percent) (see Table 12.1). Gore provides us with an example on an acclaim when he stated: "We need to call upon Syria to release the three Israeli soldiers who have been captured. We need to insist that Arafat send out instructions to halt some of the provocative acts of violence that have been going on" (October 11, North Carolina). In this passage, Gore outlined his future foreign policy plans for the audience. Because this excerpt is a direct response to a question posed, we can assume that this statement serves as positive reinforcement of Gore's ability to create sound foreign policy. Bush acclaimed as well when he stated, "I want everybody to know should I be the president, Israel's going to be our friend" (October 11, North Carolina). This statement clearly articulates Bush's general attitude toward Israel and how ties to that nation will be viewed.

Attack messages (24 percent) also occurred frequently in these presidential debates. For example, Bush attacked Gore when he said, "I remember what the administration tried to do in 1993. They tried to have a national health care plan" (October 17, St. Louis). In this statement Governor Bush attacked Gore's past policy initiatives in which nationalization of health care was attempted. Gore also engaged in attack when he stated, "Now look, if you want someone who will spend a lot of words describing a whole convoluted process and then end up supporting legislation that is supported by the big drug companies, this is your man" (October 17, St. Louis). In this passage Gore attacked Bush by implying that his legislation looks out for the best interest of big business rather than the voter when it comes to healthcare legislation.

Although it was used infrequently, defenses (3 percent) did occur in the 2000 presidential debates. In response to a question from the moderator Gore declared,

Table 12.1. Functions of 2000 General Debates

|       | Acclaims   | Attacks    | Defenses |
|-------|------------|------------|----------|
| Bush  | 469 (73%)  | 162 (25%)  | 11 (2%)  |
| Gore  | 391 (75%)  | 119 (23%)  | 13 (2%)  |
| Total | 860 (74%)  | 281 (24%)  | 24 (3%)  |

"I have actually not questioned Governor Bush's experience; I have questioned his proposals" (October 3, Massachusetts). Here, Gore defended himself against the assertion that he has unfairly questioned his opponent's experience or qualifications. Instead, he argues that his statements have been misunderstood. Bush also engaged in defense, for example: "No. Wait a minute, all seniors are covered under prescription drugs in my plan" (October 3, Massachusetts). This defense was an attempt to deny the allegations set forth by Gore that Bush's comprehensive health plan denies prescription drug benefits to seniors. There were no significant differences between Bush and Gore and their use of attacks, acclaims, and defenses ($\chi^2[df=2]=1.6$, *ns*).

## Topics of 2000 General Debates

The majority of the messages in the presidential debates focused on policy (76 percent). For example, in the October 11, 2000, debate in North Carolina Gore stated: "It means addressing the problems of injustice and inequity, along the lines of race and ethnicity here at home, because in all these other places around the world where they're having these terrible problems, when they feel hope, it is often because they see in us a reflection of their potential." Here Gore made reference to policy that addresses issues of racial inequity. Another example of policy discourse is presented by Bush: "And so we ought to do everything we can to end racial profiling. One of my concerns, though is I don't want to federalize the local police forces" (October 11, North Carolina). This statement clearly identifies Bush's stance on racial profiling policies practiced by law enforcement in the United States.

Character (24 percent) was also a subject of the messages in the 2000 presidential debates. Bush offered an example of a message focusing on character in the October 3, 2000, debate: "This man's been disparaging my plan with all this Washington-fuzzy math." In the middle of a discussion of the tax code Bush clearly attacks Gore for being less than honest when criticizing Bush's plans. Specifically, Bush accused Gore of misrepresenting the statistical implications of his tax code. If Bush convinced the electorate that Gore was willing to misrepresent information to voters during the election phase he could cast doubt on whether voters wish to elect such an individual into office. Gore questioned Bush's character as well

Table 12.2. Topics of 2000 General Debates

|       | Policy     | Character  |
|-------|------------|------------|
| Bush  | 448 (71%)  | 183 (29%)  |
| Gore  | 417 (81%)  | 93 (19%)   |
| Total | 865 (76%)  | 276 (24%)  |

during a discussion of tax cuts when he stated, "It's a question of values and priorities" (October 3, Massachusetts). This statement was used to emphasis Gore's disapproval of Bush's tax cuts to the wealthy thereby intimating that Bush's morals and values should be called into question.

There were significant differences between Bush and Gore and their discussion of policy and character in the presidential debates ($\chi^2[df=1]=17.8$, $p < .001$). Although both candidates discussed policy more than character, Gore discussed policy more than Bush (81 percent to 71 percent) which meant that Bush addressed character more than Gore (29 percent to 29 percent).

## Forms of Policy and Character in 2000 General Debates

When the candidates discussed policy, general goals (57 percent) were discussed most frequently, followed by future plans (24 percent) and then by past deeds (19 percent) (see Table 12.3). Gore provided us with an example of past deeds in the October 11, 2000, debate in North Carolina, "When I was in the Senate before I became Vice President I was pushing for stronger action against Milosevic." In this excerpt it is clear that Gore was recalling past actions that he has taken in foreign policy matters. By drawing attention to past actions in foreign policy he presumably hoped to convince the electorate that he had the capability to create future foreign policy. In the same debate Bush praised his past deeds when he stated, "As a matter of fact, I brought Republicans and Democrats together to do just that in the State of Texas to get a patient's bill of rights through." Like Gore, by bringing attention to his past legislative victories Bush can foster the image of a strong and effective leader in the voter's mind.

General goals were also used frequently; for example, Bush praised his general goals for foreign policy, "If I think it's in our nation's strategic interest I'll commit troops" (October 11, North Carolina). Here Bush discussed his approach to foreign policy but he did so in very broad terms (discussing ends rather than means). Gore

Table 12.3. Forms of Policy and Character in 2000 General Debates

|  | Policy | | | | | | Character | | | | | |
|  | Past Deeds | | General Goals | | Future Plans | | Personal Qualities | | Leadership Ability | | Ideals | |
| Bush | 46 | 34 | 246 | 39 | 61 | 22 | 26 | 43 | 60 | 20 | 30 | 4 |
| Gore | 61 | 21 | 178 | 36 | 74 | 47 | 24 | 9 | 28 | 0 | 26 | 6 |
| Total | 107 | 55 | 424 | 75 | 135 | 69 | 50 | 52 | 88 | 20 | 56 | 10 |
|  | 162 (19%) | | 499 (57%) | | 204 (24%) | | 102 (37%) | | 108 (39%) | | 66 (24%) | |

offered praises of his general goals when he said, "I think we should move step-by-step toward universal health coverage" (October 13, St. Louis). In this excerpt Gore claims that universal health coverage is the desired outcome, and he even says we should move step-by-step, but he never articulates what those steps are. Therefore, he discusses the topic generally rather than specifically.

Future plans were also discussed in the debates. For example Bush declared, "I want to take one-half of the surplus and dedicate it to Social Security" (October 3, Massachusetts). Here Bush specifically states what he will do with the budget surplus if elected president. Another example of future plans can be found in the October 17, 2000, debate in St. Louis when Gore stated, "I want to give small business employers a tax credit, 25 percent, to encourage the providing of health insurance for the employees in small businesses." In this excerpt Gore outlined the exact steps he will take in his approach to increasing health coverage for Americans.

Comparing the two candidates' use of the three forms of policy we find a significant difference in emphasis ($\chi^2[df=2]=16.1, p < .001$). Bush stressed general goals (64 percent) more than Gore (51 percent), whereas Gore used future plans (29 percent) more than Bush (18 percent).

Bush and Gore also discussed the topic of character in the debates. They discussed leadership ability (39 percent) and personal qualities (37 percent) about equally, with somewhat less emphasis on ideals (24 percent). An example of acclaiming leadership abilities can be found in the October 3 debate, when Bush declares that "I've been a governor. Governor is the chief executive officer and learns how to set agendas." Clearly Bush was trying to equate his experience as governor of Texas with the type of leadership that is required to run the White House. Gore also discussed leadership abilities when he stated, "Now I could probably give you some other examples of decisions over the last 24 years. I have been in public service for 24 years, Jim" (October 3, Massachusetts). It is clear in this passage that Gore is trying to relate to his audience that he is a seasoned leader with the kind of experience it takes to run the country.

In the same debate Bush provided us with an example of an attack against personal qualities when he said, "He talks about numbers. I'm beginning to think, not only did he invent the Internet, but he invented the calculator." In this passage Bush insinuated that Gore had a tendency to misrepresent not only facts and figures, but also personal accomplishments. By calling Gore's ethical principals into question Bush tried to create doubt about Gore's personal character in the mind of the voter. Gore gave also us an example of an attack of personal qualities when he stated, "That was in an ad, Jim, that was knocked down by the journalists who analyzed the ad and said it was misleading" (October 17, St. Louis). In this passage Gore attacked Bush for running commercials that stated Gore's federal budget proposal increased spending to three times the current budget. It is important for Gore to let the voters know that, not only is the information incorrect, but the opposition deliberately presented misinformation.

Although not as frequent as leadership abilities and personal qualities, ideals were discussed in the 2000 presidential debates. For example, Al Gore stated, "Once you have that understanding and mutual respect, then we can transcend the differences and embrace the highest common denominator of the American spirit" (October 17, St. Louis). In this excerpt Gore told the audience that he values those who are different and believes in an ideal of a common American society. Bush also discussed ideals when he said, "I think what the next president ought to do is to—is to promote a culture of life in America" (October 3, Massachusetts). In this excerpt Bush clearly introduces his ideals and values when he indicates he is a pro-life supporter. There were significant differences between Bush and Gore and forms of character mentioned in the presidential debates ($\chi^2[df=2]=9.5$, $p <.01$). While Gore discussed all three forms of character about equally, Bush focused more on leadership ability.

## Issues Addressed in 2000 General Debates

Both Bush and Gore (setting aside the comments on "other" topics) focused primarily on national defense (see Table 12.4). For example Gore stated: "Now, I think we should be reluctant to get involved in someplace, in a foreign country. But if our national security is at stake, if we have allies, if we've tried every other course, if we're sure military action will succeed, and if the costs are proportionate to the benefits, we should get involved" (October 3, Massachusetts). Here Gore articulates a general disposition in his approach to engaging in military action. Bush's second most frequently discussed issue was taxes followed by education. An example of Bush's discussion of taxes can be seen in the October 17 debate in St. Louis when he said, "Let me talk about tax relief. If you pay taxes you ought to get tax relief." In this statement Bush reveals his general outlook on tax policies. In contrast, Gore's second most frequently discussed issue was education. In the same debate Gore offers an example of a discussion of educational policies when he stated, "My proposal gives $10,000 hiring bonuses for those teachers who are —who get certified to teach in the areas where they're most needed." In this excerpt Gore provides specific details of his future plans for educational reform. The economy was also an important issue for both candidates as Bush ranked fourth and Gore third. For example, in the October 3, 2000, debate in Boston Gore highlighted his past economic triumphs when he said, "Look, we have gone from the biggest deficits to the biggest surpluses." In this statement it is clear that Gore takes responsibility for past economic success, indicating a repeat performance if elected. Both candidates ranked the same on the issue of health care, while Bush ranked sixth with Social Security issues (Gore seventh) and seventh in his discussion of the environment (Gore sixth). Statistical analysis reveals that neither candidates' issue emphasis in the debates correlated with the issues most important to the public.

Table 12.4. Issues Addressed in 2000 General Debates

|  | Poll | Bush* | Gore |
|---|---|---|---|
| Economy | 18 | 44 (4) | 57 (3) |
| Education | 16 | 49 (3) | 62 (2) |
| Health Care | 16 | 43 (5) | 34 (5) |
| Social Security | 11 | 24 (6) | 25 (7) |
| Taxes | 8 | 55 (2) | 51 (4) |
| National Defense | 8 | 82 (1) | 76 (1) |
| Environment | 3 | 22 (7) | 32 (6) |
| Other | – | 129 | 80 |
| Spearman's ρ |  | -.301 *ns* | -.193 *ns* |

*Frequency (rank)   NBC News/*Wall Street Journal* (2000)

# Implications

The results of the analysis of the 2000 presidential debates are similar to those found by Benoit and Harthcock (1999b) in the 1960 debates, Wells (1999) in the 1976, 1980, and 1984 debates, Benoit and Brazeal (2002) in the 1988 debates, and Benoit, Blaney, and Pier (1998) in the 1996 election (see also Benoit & Wells, 1996, on the 1992 debates). Acclaims (74 percent) were the most common functions in the debates, less frequent were attacks (24 percent), and defenses (3 percent) were somewhat rare. There is one striking difference between the results of previous debates and the 2000 debates. In previous debates, the incumbent was more likely to acclaim than the challenger. In this election cycle there were no significant differences between the candidates' use of acclaiming, attacking, or defending. It is possible that, while Al Gore was the incumbent party candidate, Gore may have been seen as "less" of an incumbent (as vice president) than President Bill Clinton in 1996 or President George Bush in 1992.

As with earlier debates the candidates discussed policy (76 percent) more than character (24 percent). In 2000, Gore discussed policy more often than the challenger. This may have occurred because Gore has a longer record of public service than Bush. Although Bush did hold an executive state office (governor of Texas), we know that governors obtain little experience in foreign policy.

Although the focus on policy considerations in earlier debates tended to center around past deeds, in 2000 both candidates discussed general goals (57 percent) most often. However, Gore was more likely than Bush to address future plans.

Ordinarily, one would expect a challenger to discuss future plans more than the incumbent—operating from the assumption that every proposal is an implicit attack on the incumbent. However, as noted earlier, Gore was not a sitting president. We also believe that Gore worked to distance himself from Clinton; proposing changes to the status quo (over which Clinton presided for eight years) may have helped show his independence (we feel this was a mistake and that Gore would have been better advised to run vigorously on the Clinton/Gore record, and particularly the economy).

In earlier debates personal qualities and ideals were most commonly discussed forms of character. In 2000, leadership ability (39 percent) was the most commonly discussed character consideration. Gore discussed all three forms of character somewhat equally. However, George Bush focused his discussion of character on leadership ability. Because Bush did not hold a national office prior to the 2000 election cycle, and because he could be labeled the "challenger," he may have felt that it was important to highlight the leadership qualities that make him fit for the job.

Neither candidate's debate utterances correlated significantly with the issues that were most important to the public. However, this may be more a reflection on the questions asked of the two candidates than an indication that the candidates were out of touch with voters (see Benoit & Hansen, 2001).

# Chapter 13

# General Web Pages

Most Americans are better off today than they were eight years ago. America owes its current prosperity to the hard work of its people, but also to the winning policy formula of the Clinton-Gore Administration, combining fiscal responsibility with investments in our people. Al Gore wants to keep the prosperity going and expand it to those who have not yet enjoyed its benefits. His economic plan includes balancing the budget and paying down the national debt—to keep interest rates low and economic growth high; saving Social Security and Medicare; cutting taxes to help families and small businesses afford key investments in their future; investing in new technologies; and opening up foreign markets. (Gore, 2000 Internet site)

Governor Bush will reform the nation's public schools as he has in Texas, which is one of two states that have made the greatest recent progress in education. He will close the achievement gap, set high standards, promote character education, and ensure school safety. States will be offered freedom from federal regulation, but will be held accountable for results. Performance will be measured annually, and parents will be empowered with information and choices. (Bush, 2000 Internet site)

## Literature Review

The Internet was first used in a presidential campaign in 1992 by Bill Clinton and

Al Gore (Davis, 1999; Whillock, 1997). Since 1992, the Internet has became a common campaign tool (Hall, 1997) that candidates cannot afford to ignore (Casey, 2001). However, not surprising is the fact that the higher the office being sought the more likely it is that the candidate will utilize an Internet site (D'Alessio, 1997). Stromer-Galley, Foot, Schneider, and Larsen (2001) confirmed D'Alessio's finding for the 2000 election. They indicated that all major presidential candidates maintained an Internet site during the general election, that 77 percent of the candidates in Senate races had Internet sites, and for House races, that this number dropped to 54 percent. So presidential candidates, as well as other elected officials, utilized the Internet in the 2000 election.

Several studies suggest that a number of people used the presidential candidates' Internet sites in the 2000 election. During August of 2000 467,000 unique people visited Bush's Internet site and 350,000 unique people visited Gore's Internet site (Media Metrix, 2000). Media Metrix (2000) also reported that 60,000 different people visited both sites during the month of August 2000 (8 percent of combined audience). D'Alessio (1997) reported that the number of viewers increased at political Internet sites after the Labor Day weekend which suggests that the quantity of viewers could have also increased for Bush and Gore as the campaign progressed. Sedberry (2001) indicated that during a two-week period in October the Bush Internet site provided information to five million unique visitors. Finally, the Pew Research Center (2000) reported that 6 percent of online users visited Gore's Internet site and 7 percent visited Bush's site.[1] Pew also found that these numbers increased to 21 percent for Gore and 24 percent for Bush among Internet users who were considered "election news consumers."[2] Thus, there is evidence indicating that the candidate's Internet sites were utilized by the public during the general campaign of the 2000 election.

A number of scholars have examined the resources available to voters on candidate Internet sites. Selnow (1998) had this assessment of content of candidate Internet sites: "The philosophy was simple: dump the information on the Web because someone, somewhere might want it. And if they don't, so what?" (p. 139). Others indicted that candidates were more methodical in the information that they disseminated on their Internet site. For example, Davis (1999) indicated that the content of candidate Internet sites has several functions: "information dissemination, opinion gauge, reinforcement of vote choice and GOTV (Get Out To Vote), volunteer ID and fund raising, and interactivity" (p. 97). Tedesco, Miller, and Spiker (1999) reported that candidate sites in the 1996 election provided issue and campaign information that could work to benefit the electorate. Benoit (2000b) reported that in the 1998 midterm elections web pages were more positive than other media (e.g., television spots, newspaper ads, and direct mail), contained no defenses, and favored character topics over policy topics. Stromer-Galley (2000) reported that the content of candidate Internet sites did not rise to the level of human interaction but remained at the level of media interaction given candidates' concerns for the potential loss of control and ambiguity of communication. Finally, Klotz and Broome (1998) indicated that candidate Internet sites addressed issues important to women in greater detail than traditional media.

Several authors have specifically addressed the content of the 2000 presidential Internet sites. Stromer-Galley, Foot, Schneider, and Larsen (2001) reported that for the 2000 election candidates provided photographs, biographical information, issue statements, volunteer sign-up, online donations, links to other political Internet sites, and opportunities to receive an e-mail newsletter. Lewicki and Ziaukas (2001) found that Bush's and Gore's sites contained the following common areas: issue section, biography, speeches, press releases, contributions, volunteer information, contact information (e-mail), e-mail lists, Spanish language version, kids page, audio and video of candidate, and merchandise for sale. As indicated by this research, candidate Internet sites address numerous topics that could potentially be appealing to a variety of voters.

Based on the research reported above it is clear that the scholars are beginning to understand the role of the candidate Internet sites in presidential elections but so far there has been no Functional Study of presidential Internet sites. The results of this chapter will be an important addition in this area. This research will be important because it will allow scholars to systematically compare the discourse of candidate Internet sites with other media formats (e.g., TV spots, debates) and allow for the analysis of campaign Internet sites longitudinally.

# Results

In this section, first, we provide information about the Internet sites we analyzed. Secondly, we discuss the functions of general election web pages and the topics addressed. Next, the forms of policy and character and issues addressed will be presented. Finally, some implications for the findings will be offered in the final section of the paper.

We analyzed George W. Bush's and Al Gore's Internet sites based on the November 1, 2000, content. November 1 was chosen because both candidates had significant time to update and fine-tune their Internet sites. We analyzed the same sections in the general election as we did in the primary: the candidates "home page," biography section, and issue section. The candidates did provide audio and video in these sections but we only analyzed the text portion of their Internet site. As indicated in the primary web page chapter, the "homepage" was analyzed because it is the page most visitors to the site will view and also the most often updated page on the Internet site (Hansen, 2000a). The biography and issue section of the candidates' Internet sites were analyzed because these are two areas where the candidates provide important information about themselves, their candidacy, and their position on various issues.

## Function of General Campaign Web Pages

For the 2000 general campaign, the Internet sites were predominately composed of

Table 13.1. Functions of 2000 General Campaign Web Pages

|        | Acclaims     | Attacks   | Defenses |
|--------|--------------|-----------|----------|
| Bush   | 1162 (95%)   | 64 (5%)   | 0        |
| Gore   | 3290 (99%)   | 22 (1%)   | 0        |
| Total  | 4452 (98%)   | 86 (2%)   | 0        |

helping the country's economic growth in this quote: "Al Gore fought hard to help bring about the longest economic expansion in U.S. history." Likewise, Bush acclaimed his record on crime as governor in this utterance: "As a result of Governor Bush's appointments, Texas has the toughest parole board in history, compiling the lowest parole approval rate in history." In this utterance, Bush touted his role in toughening the Texas parole record. Both of these excepts suggest how acclaims were used on the candidates' Internet sites in the 2000 election.

Only 2 percent of the utterances were attacks. For example, Gore contrasted his health care plan with Bush's in this statement: "The Bush-Cheney plan, which diverts billions in Medicare surpluses to pay for their tax cut; relies on state grants instead of real prescription drug benefit—leaving 95 percent of seniors who now lack coverage; and forces seniors into health maintenance organizations (HMOs) for their coverage." In this quote, Gore obviously criticized Bush's health care proposal. Bush advanced this attack against the Clinton-Gore record on health care: "There are 43 million uninsured Americans—4 million more then when the current Administration took office." Thus, even though attacks were rare on the candidate Internet sites they did exist.

There were no defenses used by either Gore or Bush on their Internet sites. For acclaims and attacks a chi-square comparison of Gore and Bush suggests a significant difference existed ($\chi^2[df=1]=99.9$, $p < .001$). On their Internet sites, Gore (99 percent) acclaimed more than Bush (95 percent) and conversely Bush (5 percent) attacked more than Gore (1 percent).

## Topics of General Campaign Web Pages

The topics of candidates' Internet sites focused much more on policy (90 percent) than character (10 percent). See Table 13.2. In this example, Gore discussed the Clinton/Gore administration's policy efforts in the area of welfare reform: "Under this administration, more recipients have made the transition from welfare to work. Since 1992, the welfare rolls have been cut in half to their lowest level since 1968." Bush said this about welfare reform: "As President, Governor George W. Bush will commit himself and the nation to mobilizing the armies of compassion—charities and churches, communities and corporations, ministers and mentors—to save and change lives, as he has done in Texas. This is the next bold step of welfare reform." This quotation from Bush outlined his policy for "welfare reform." These excerpts illustrate how the candidates utilized their Internet sites to discuss policy positions.

Table 13.2. Topics of 2000 General Campaign Web Pages

|       | Policy      | Character   |
| ----- | ----------- | ----------- |
| Bush  | 982 (80%)   | 244 (20%)   |
| Gore  | 3112 (94%)  | 200 (6%)    |
| Total | 4094 (90%)  | 444 (10%)   |

As indicated, character themes comprised 10 percent of the topics discussed. Gore, for example, provided this statement regarding his "understanding" of veterans (understanding for others is a personal quality and therefore concerns character): "As a veteran himself, Al Gore understands the commitment that veterans made to this country." This example was from Bush's Internet site: "He is committed to ensuring that society respects American's seniors, and helps them lead lives of security and dignity." This quotation is a character utterance that is reflective of Bush's character (respect for others). As indicated in these two quotes the candidates devote a portion of their Internet site to discussing character.

We also wanted to know whether Bush and Gore differed significantly in the topics that they addressed in their webpages. A *chi-square* indicated that there is a significant difference in topics addressed ($\chi^2[df=1]=194.8, p < .001$). Gore (94 percent) focused more on policy when compared to Bush (80 percent) which meant that Bush's Internet site (20 percent) focused more on character than Gore's (6 percent).

## Forms of Policy and Character in General Campaign Web Pages

Overall, policy statements were skewed towards past deeds (64 percent) rather than future plans (19 percent) or general goals (17 percent). See Table 13.3. For instance, Gore discussed defense spending on his Internet site: "The Administration has already achieved significant savings by streamlining the defense infrastructure." This excerpt acclaimed Clinton-Gore's past deeds, on defense spending. Bush attacked the Clinton-Gore administration's past record on education in this quotation: "The Clinton-Gore Administration has failed to narrow the achievement gap between the disadvantaged students and their peers." These statements from Gore and Bush help voters to understand how the candidates used past deeds to both acclaim and attack.

As indicated, future plans (means to an end) were used less often than past deeds (19 percent to 64 percent). This Gore statement is an example of a future plan: "Making high-quality voluntary preschool available to every child and increase investment in Head Start and Early Head Start." This statement is an example of a future plan that suggests how a Gore administration would improve education. Similarly, this utterance illustrates the use of future plan by Bush: "Offer enhanced Pell grants (an additional $1,000) to low-income students who

Table 13.3. Forms of Policy and Character in 2000 General Campaign Web Pages

| | Policy | | | Character | | |
|---|---|---|---|---|---|---|
| | Past Deeds* | Future Plans | General Goals | Personal Qualities | Leader-ship | Ideals |
| Bush | 321  56 | 233  0 | 370  2 | 24  1 | 11  1 | 203  4 |
| | 377 (38%) | 233 (24%) | 372 (38%) | 25 (10%) | 12 (5%) | 207 (85%) |
| Gore | 2242  18 | 552  0 | 297  3 | 82  0 | 38  1 | 79  0 |
| | 2260 (73%) | 552 (18%) | 300 (10%) | 82 (41%) | 39 (20%) | 79 (40%) |
| Total | 2563  74 | 785  0 | 672  5 | 106  1 | 49  2 | 282  4 |
| | 2637 (64%) | 785 (19%) | 677 (17%) | 107 (24%) | 51 (11%) | 286 (64%) |

*acclaims/attacks

take rigorous math and science courses in high school." In this statement, Bush acclaimed his proposal to make additional resources available for collage students.

The third policy choice, general goals (17 percent), was used less often than past deeds (64 percent) and about the same as future plans (19 percent). For example, Gore discussed two general goals (quality education and job training) in this quotation: "And Gore will make sure every American can get the quality education and job training they need to succeed in the New Economy." Similarly, Bush presented a general goal in this utterance: "Therefore, as President, Governor Bush will set high environmental standards, and work to build conservation partnerships between the federal government and state governments, local communities and private landowners to meet—and exceed—those standards." Bush acclaimed his vision for the environment in this statement. Neither candidate indicated a means to be used, so these utterances are examples of general goals. Thus, candidates discussed both policy means (future plans) and policy ends (goals) on their Internet sites.

Assessment of policy types by candidate indicates that Gore used more past deeds (73 percent) and less future plans (18 percent) and general goals (10 percent). Bush, on the other hand, utilized a more equal distribution between past deeds (38 percent), future plans (24 percent), and general goals (38 percent). The *chi-square* indicated that there was a significant difference in their use of the forms of policy ($\chi2[df=1]=512.5, p < .001$).

For character utterances, the candidate's Internet sites utilized ideals (64 percent) the most followed by personal qualities (24 percent) and leadership (11 percent). In this statement Gore acclaimed his values concerning racial and religious diversity: "I believe that God has given the people of our nation not only a chance, but a mission to prove to men and women throughout this world that people of different racial and ethnic backgrounds, of all faiths and creeds, can not only work together, but can enrich and ennoble both themselves and our common purpose." Bush touted his energy policy: "Governor Bush believes that markets—and not the government—should set prices and should determine which energy sources prevail." This excerpt from Bush concerned his principle for governing energy policy. These excerpts document how the candidates used their Internet sites to communicate their ideals.

Personal qualities were also discussed on the candidates' Internet sites. For example, in this statement Gore acclaimed his willingness to "fight" for children and families: "Al Gore has fought to improve the lives of children and families across America." Being willing to fight for these groups is considered a positive personal quality. Bush discussed his respect for Hispanics in this utterance: "He makes an effort to speak the Spanish language and respects Hispanic culture and tradition." The idea of respecting the Hispanic culture is a personal quality that Bush espoused in this statement.

Candidates also presented information concerning their leadership abilities. Gore's webpage said this about his leadership: "He has been a leader in this Administration's efforts to strengthen family farms." Bush's Internet site made this statement concerning his ability to lead: "Governor Bush has a strong record of bipartisan leadership, uniting people behind common goals." Thus, candidates also used their Internet sites to discuss leadership.

As is the case with policy, a *chi-square* indicated the candidates utilized types of character in significantly different ways ($\chi^2[df=1]=99.4, p<.001$). Bush devoted a majority of his character utterances to ideals (85 percent) and therefore fewer to personal qualities (10 percent) and leadership (5 percent). Gore, on the other hand, focused equally on personal qualities (41 percent) and ideals (40 percent) and less on leadership (39 percent).

## Issues Addressed in General Campaign Web Pages

We also compared the issues that the candidates discussed on their Internet sites with the issues that were most important to the public (see Table 13.4). According to public opinion poll data, the issue most important to the electorate was the economy. The economy was addressed fourth most by Gore but was ignored by Bush. The Democratic candidate's webpage included this comment regarding the economy on his general campaign Internet site: "Gore and the administration have overseen the longest economic expansion in U.S. history." The issue addressed most by Gore was national defense. For example, Gore said this about national defense: "Al Gore understands clearly the classic security agenda of 'war and peace' as well as the new security agenda our military faces in the 21$^{st}$ century: America must maintain its nuclear strength, with adequate offensive forces to ensure deterrence and be ready to participate in peacekeeping, humanitarian, and other efforts." This issue, national defense, was the fourth most important issue on the public agenda. Likewise, the issue Bush addressed most was education, which

Table 13.4. Issues Addressed in 2000 General Campaign Web Pages

| Issue | Poll | Bush* | Gore |
|---|---|---|---|
| Economy | 18 | 0 (8) | 197 (4) |
| Education | 16 | 129 (2) | 243 (3) |
| Health Care | 16 | 66 (3) | 185 (5) |
| Social Security | 11 | 25 (7) | 74 (8) |
| Taxes | 8 | 44 (5) | 88 (7) |
| National Defense | 8 | 50 (4) | 821 (2) |
| Environment | 3 | 35 (6) | 118 (6) |
| Others | – | 633 (1) | 1386 (2) |
| Spearman ρ | | -.34, ns | -.16, ns |

*Frequency (rank)   NBC News/*Wall Street Journal* (2000)

was the second most important issue on the public agenda. Bush made this comment on his web site regarding education: "Governor Bush will reform the nation's public schools, as he has in Texas, which is one of two states that have made the greatest recent progress in education." The Spearman's ρ correlating the candidates' ranking for issues addressed with the public's ranking did not reach significance for either Bush or Gore.

## Implications

Both Gore and Bush's general election Internet sites resemble other campaign message forms (e.g., TV spots, radio spots, and debates) in that acclaims are more common than attacks, and attacks more frequent than defenses. This distribution of acclaims, attacks, and defenses seems sensible given that voters say they do not like negative campaigning. When candidates contemplate use of defenses, there are several drawbacks. When defending against an attack the candidate is taken off message and forced to address a topic that may be more favorable to the opponent. In addition, candidates could be perceived as reactive versus proactive when defending. Finally, because the candidate must identify the attack in order to defend against it voters may learn about a candidate's alleged weakness.

As indicated acclaims should outnumber attacks, which in turn should be greater than defenses, but we would argue that Gore and Bush went too far in their high percentage of acclaims (98 percent) and low percentage of attacks (2 percent). We suggest, as we did in the primary web page chapter, that Gore and Bush could have used a more effective strategy. With proper web page design, Gore and Bush could have pleased both those who dislike attacking (mudslinging) and those who like comparative information about opposing candidates (attacks). Gore and Bush could have made comparative information available with hyperlinks. This would allow those who want comparative information access to this type of information. It would also allow those who do not want comparative information to easily ignore and read only what they are interested in reading. If candidates had designed their Internet sites in this way it would be more appealing to those who are interested in comparing candidates and their policy positions.

In addition, Bush (5 percent) attacked more on his Internet site than Gore (1 percent) and therefore Gore (99 percent) acclaimed more than Bush (95 percent). This finding is consistent with research on TV spots in that the challenger attacks more than the incumbent candidate does (Benoit, 1999). From this perspective, these candidates' Internet sites function similar to other media formats.

The largest difference between Gore and Bush for forms of policy was for past deeds. Gore devoted 73 percent of his policy utterances to past deeds whereas Bush only devoted 38 percent. This seems plausible if the political careers of both candidates are examined. Gore had been an elected official since 1976 (House of Representatives: eight years, Senate: eight years, and vice president: eight years) whereas Bush had only held elected office since 1995 (Texas governor: six years). Given Gore's eighteen additional years of political experience it seems plausible that Gore would have more past deeds to discuss than Bush. In addition, it seems like experience as the vice president is more relevant than experience as governor particularly in the area of foreign policy. This could be another reason why Gore devoted more policy utterances to past deeds than did Bush.

One final implication concerns the issues addressed in the general election web pages. As indicated previously, Hansen and Benoit (2001) argued that if certain policy issues are important to the American public then candidates should address these issues most often. They argued that this holds true for TV spots, radio spots, and debates because the candidates are limited by the amount of material they can make available. However, this is not the case for candidate websites because candidates can place nearly unlimited amounts of material on their Internet site. Given this, the finding that there were no significant relationships between the public agenda and the candidates' Internet sites is not troubling.

In conclusion, this chapter has added significant new information in the area of presidential general election Internet sites and the functions utilized. Given the ever-changing use of Internet technology in presidential political campaigns, this chapter should serve as a useful reference for future presidential elections.

## Notes

1. According to NUA Internet Surveys (2001) 153.84 million Americans had Internet access in November 2000. This would equate to 9.2 million viewers of Gore's Internet site and 10.8 million viewers for Bush's Internet site.

2. The Pew Research Center (2000) indicated that 25.6 percent of Internet users were considered "election news consumers."

# Chapter 14

# General Radio Spots

> Vermeil: Hello, this is Dick Vermeil. You know, I've coached football a long time, including my wonderful years with the Super Bowl champion St. Louis Rams. Now I'm not a politician, but when it comes to issues that matter most to me, I agree with Governor George W. Bush's blueprint for America. Social Security is important to all of us. George Bush's plan protects Social Security benefits for all seniors. No changes. No cuts. No reductions: period.

> Male Voice: Running the country isn't like keepin' a car runnin': no owner's manual. Is George Bush prepared? Well, it's not like we're one big Texas. It's a complicated world and we're leading it. A lot could go wrong. Bush might not realize the consequences of his actions.

Radio was one of the various media used to persuade voters during the 2000 presidential general election campaign. Some of the spots in our sample were created by the candidates themselves, whereas others were developed in support of or in opposition to a particular candidate. While we acknowledge that our total sample of general election radio spots is relatively low, we believe a functional analyses of these spots from the 2000 campaign can enhance our understanding of how candidates employ radio advertising in a contemporary presidential general election.

# Literature Review

The medium of radio offers advantages to candidates during a presidential election (see chapter 6 for a discussion of this issue). One of the ways in which the impact of radio spots in general elections has been examined is its use with other forms of media. Weaver-Lariscy and Tinkham (1987) compared the use of radio spots by congressional candidates in 1982 general elections to television, newspapers, and outdoor advertising. Candidates for open congressional seats used radio ads more frequently than incumbents or challengers. The authors suggest the use of radio and other media is dependent on the goals of the candidate and dynamics of the campaign.

Atkin and Heald (1976) also examined how exposure to radio and television advertising during a congressional campaign impacted voters. The researchers concluded that radio and television advertising contributes to a voter's cognitive and affective orientation toward candidates. The level of attention paid to television ads by subjects was found to have the strongest correlation with the variables being examined (e.g., knowledge about a candidate, interest in the campaign).

Thorson and Coyle (1994) examined the impact of radio and other media in a general election for a community's board of education. The majority of respondents in the study cited television and newspapers as their primary source of information about the elections, while only a small percentage cited radio as their primary source. This research suggests that use of radio spots is a secondary way of communicating with voters.

Other studies have examined the content of political messages. Rudd (1989) constructed two radio spots for each of the Democratic and Republican candidates in a hypothetical race for Congress. One set of messages offered specific proposals from the candidates while the other set stated ambiguous goals. Candidate spots offering specific proposals elicited a more favorable reaction than the spots stating ambiguous goals. Rudd, however, noted that the use of a radio-style spot was a limitation on his study, as voters would be exposed to campaign messages from multiple media sources, as opposed to just radio. Another limitation which can be noted is that the spots were created by the researcher as opposed to actual political messages. Shapiro and Rieger (1992) also created their own political radio spots for a fictitious local election in Lawrence, Kansas, classifying the message content as either positive or negative. They reported that negative radio spots can benefit the sponsoring candidate if they are perceived as fair. They also suggest that subjects have better recall of ads considered to be negative versus those that are positive. Again, the fictitious content of these radio spots created is an obvious limitation of the study.

Blaney (2001) has perhaps done the most extensive research on content of radio spots actually used in general presidential elections. He conducted a functional analysis on available general radio spots dating back to the McGovern-Nixon campaign of 1972 through the Bush-Gore election of 2000 (he was unable to locate any radio ads from 1996). Blaney found that candidates had used their radio messages to attack slightly more than to acclaim (52 percent versus 48 percent) and to address policy slightly more than character (54 percent versus 46 percent). Blaney also found that no use of defenses were made in any of the general radio spots he examined. When examining forms of policy utterances, Blaney found past deeds (56 percent) were discussed more often than future plans (31 percent) and general goals (13 percent). Leadership ability (55 percent) was discussed more than ideals (27 percent) and personal qualities (18 percent).

Blaney found Democratic spots made greater use of attack utterances (57 percent, versus 43 percent acclaims) while Republican spots focused more on acclaims (55 percent, versus 45 percent attacks). While Republicans focused more on policy discussion in these general radio spots (59 percent, versus 41 percent character), Democrats balanced discussion of policy and character in this type of campaign message (51 percent character, 49 percent policy). Blaney also found that while challengers in presidential general elections were likely to use more acclaims in their messages (59 percent, versus 41 percent attacks), incumbents employed more attacks (60 percent, versus 40 percent acclaims). Incumbents were also more likely to employ discussion of policy in their general radio spots (59 percent, versus 41 percent character), whereas challengers balanced their discussion of policy and character (52 percent character versus 48 percent policy).

This literature review suggests that while radio is not the primary medium for the delivery of messages in a general election, it can still play a role. And as noted in the chapter on radio spots in the presidential primary season, radio can be an effective medium when targeted to specific audiences (Hutchens, 1999). This review also suggests emerging patterns in the content of past general radio spots. Blaney (2001) identified through a functional analysis that presidential campaigns used general radio spots to both acclaim and attack, but not defend, as well to discuss both policy and character.

## Campaign 2000 Radio Spots

A total of fifteen radio spots were examined from the 2000 general election campaign of the spots for the Gore-Lieberman campaign, the Bush-Cheney ticket, and organizations either supporting the Bush-Cheney ticket or opposing the Gore Lieberman ticket (the National Rifle Association, the United Senior Association, the Missouri State Republican Committee, and the Log Cabin Republicans). Although two of the spots (those produced by the United Senior Association) do not mention the Bush-Cheney ticket, we classified these spots as pro-Bush because they attempt to sway voters away from his main rival, Gore. All of the spots were sixty seconds in length. The spots were obtained via the Internet as well as over-the-air radio stations.

# Results

We will begin with an analysis of the functions of these spots. Then we will present the results of our analysis of topic of utterance, forms of policy and character, and the issues addressed in these radio spots. Finally, we will discuss the implications of our analysis.

## Functions of General Election Radio Spots

The radio spots we examined from the general election campaign emphasized attacks (78 percent) on the opposing presidential ticket (see Table 14.1). Gore's utterances relied overwhelmingly on attacks (97 percent): "The Bush tax plan is a giveaway to those making over $300,000 a year" ("Bush-Texas Record 2"). This was an attack by Gore on Bush for gearing his tax cut plan to help the wealthy. Attacks accounted for 47 percent of all utterances found in Bush and pro-Bush general election radio spots. In "Education Recession," an announcer said, "parents are still denied the right to choose the best schools for their children." Bush criticized the Clinton-Gore administration for failing to support school choice for parents.

Acclaims in general radio spots account for 22 percent of all utterances. Bush used slightly more of his utterances to make acclaims (53 percent) than attacks. In one spot produced by the Log Cabin Republicans political organization, Bush's effort to reach out to diverse social groups was praised: "He says he's an inclusive new Republican. He proved it, with prominent Black, Latino, and gay speakers at his convention" ("Thelma and Louise"). This spot highlights Bush's stated effort to expand the base of the Republican party. Acclaims in Gore's general election radio spots accounted for only 3 percent of all utterances examined. We also found no defenses in these general election radio spots.

A *chi-square* revealed a significant difference in functions between the Gore radio spots and the Bush and pro-Bush radio spots ($\chi^2[df=1]=53.2, p < .001$). While Gore's radio spots consisted almost entirely of attack utterances (97 percent to 3 percent acclaims), radio spots supporting Bush favored acclaims slightly more than attacks (53 percent versus 47 percent).

Table 14.1. Functions of 2000 General Radio Spots

|        | Acclaims  | Attacks   | Defenses |
|--------|-----------|-----------|----------|
| Bush   | 31 (53%)  | 27 (47%)  | 0        |
| Gore   | 3 (3%)    | 94 (97%)  | 0        |
| Total  | 34 (22%)  | 121 (78%) | 0        |

## Topics of General Election Radio Spots

The general radio spots revealed a clear emphasis on policy (74 percent). Gore discussed policy in 77 percent of all utterances in the general election radio spots (see Table 14.2). In "Children," Gore targeted Bush's policies in Texas that affected families:

> Hadn't thought much about the election until I read a report in *Working Woman Magazine* on child care. It shows that under Governor Bush, Texas has the lowest adult-to-child ration of any state. That worried me a lot. So I looked into George Bush's record. Found out he vetoed a bill to help families afford child care. And Texas ranks second to last in the U.S. for children with health care coverage.

Gore's spot (read by a female announcer) appeared to be aimed at women, attacking Governor Bush's policies in Texas for hurting families. Policy was discussed in 69 percent of all utterances found Bush and pro-Bush general radio spots. In "Insurance," the narrator, Art Linkletter, said: "Al Gore's prescription drug plan is wrong for senior citizens." This is an attack targeted at Gore's approach to addressing the high costs of prescription drugs.

Character was discussed in only 26 percent of all utterances in the general radio spots we examined. Bush and pro-Bush spots discussed character in 31 percent of all utterances. In "Thelma and Louise, the actors emphasized character differences between Bush and Gore:

> Thelma: So what do you think of the presidential candidates?
> Louise: I don't know. Do you think there's any difference
> Thelma: You bet there is. Al Gore will say anything to get elected President.

The spot raised doubts about Gore's veracity during the course of the 2000 campaign. Character was discussed in only 23 percent of Gore's utterances. In "Children," a Gore spot, an announcer remarked that it "seems Bush doesn't think things through." This utterance attacked Bush's ability to lead.

When comparing topics of 2000 general radio spots, no significant difference was found ($\chi^2[df=1]=1.2, ns$). Both campaigns put a greater emphasis on discussing policy than character.

Table 14.2. Topics of 2000 General Radio Spots

|  | Policy | Character |
| --- | --- | --- |
| Bush | 41 (71%) | 17 (29%) |
| Gore | 78 (80%) | 19 (20%) |
| Total | 119 (77%) | 36 (23%) |

## Forms of Policy and Character in General Election Radio Spots

Past deeds (44 percent) were the most common form of policy utterance found in 2000 general radio spots (see Table 14.3). Gore made past deeds the most common form of policy utterance (54 percent). In "Texas Record-2," Gore cast Bush's environmental policies as Texas governor in a negative light: "Bush appointed a chemical lobbyist to enforce environmental laws. He let polluters police themselves. And today, Texas ranks last in the nation in air quality." Gore's spot cited past deeds by the governor of Texas to raise questions about Bush's ability to deal with the environment. Almost all past deed utterances found in Gore's general radio spots (95 percent) were attacks on Bush's past deeds whereas only 5 percent discussed Gore's past deeds as part of the Clinton administration. Bush noted past deeds in only 25 percent of his policy utterances: "His plan for education follows his success in Texas, where test scores are up in every grade for every year Bush has been Governor" ("Education Recession"). Here Bush cited rising test scores to praise his work in Texas. Although the Bush and the pro-Bush spots had few utterances involving past deeds (ten in all), the majority were used as attacks on Gore (80 percent attacks versus 20 percent acclaims).

General goals accounted for 32 percent of all policy utterances in general radio spots. Bush discussed goals in 55 percent of his policy utterances. In "Education Recession," an announcer emphasized Bush's goal to improve education: "Schools will receive freedom, flexibility, and resources in exchange for results." This Bush spot stated the candidate's goal of improving education by providing assistance to successful schools. Gore used 20 percent of his policy utterances to discuss general goals: "Bush said higher education isn't a priority" ("Children"). This Gore spot attacked Bush for neglecting an important part of the educational system.

Future plans were discussed in 24 percent of all policy utterances. Gore discussed future plans in 26 percent of his policy utterances: "Will George W. Bush be good for your bottom line? His tax plan takes half the budget we helped create and gives it to the richest one percent" ("Bush-Texas"). Gore attempted to show that Bush wants to use the federal budget to benefit the wealthiest people in the country. Bush and pro-Bush spots discussed future plans in 20 percent of policy utterances. In "Social Security," the narrator attacked Gore's future plan for prescription drugs: "Now take Al Gore. Al said he'd give senior citizens a $5000

Table 14.3. Forms of Policy and Character in 2000 General Radio Spots

|  | Policy | | | | Character | | |
|  | Past Deeds* | Future Plans | General Goals | Personal Qualities | Leader-ship | | Ideals |
|---|---|---|---|---|---|---|---|---|
| Bush | 2 | 8 | 0 | 2 | 17 | 12 | 6 | 11 | 6 | 0 | 0 | 1 |
| Gore | 2 | 39 | 0 | 0 | 1 | 36 | 0 | 7 | 0 | 9 | 0 | 5 |
|  | 4 | 47 | 0 | 2 | 18 | 48 | 6 | 11 | 6 | 9 | 0 | 6 |
| Total | 51 | | 2 | | 66 | | 17 | | 15 | | 8 | |
|  | (43%) | | (2%) | | (55%) | | (42%) | | (38%) | | (20%) | |

benefit to help pay for prescription drugs. Sounds good, but what Mr. Gore isn't telling us is that the money would be phased in over eight years!" This utterance is a future plan, as it criticized what Gore would do about prescription drug costs.

Due to the small $n$, we were unable to use *chi-square* to determine if there was a significant difference in the forms of policy utterances among Gore and Bush in the 2000 general radio spots we examined.

When examining character utterances in the 2000 general radio spots, we found leadership ability (43 percent) discussed most frequently. Gore discussed leadership ability in half (50 percent) of all his character utterances. In Gore's "Texas Record-1," the end of the spot presented a blunt question: "Is George W. Bush ready to lead America?" Leadership ability in the Bush and pro-Bush spots was discussed in 33 percent of his character utterances. In the pro-Bush spot "Thelma and Louise," phrases like "Leadership is important" and "Leadership does matter" were used, and the spot urged listeners to support "the kind of leadership we want" with Bush. These utterances focused attention on Bush's competence to lead the nation.

Personal qualities of the candidates accounted for 40 percent of character utterances in general radio spots. In the Bush and pro-Bush spots examined, personal qualities were cited in 56 percent of all character utterances. A well-known professional football coach, Dick Vermeil, was used as a surrogate for the Texas governor: "I know George Bush. When he gives you his word, you can take it to the bank" ("Vermeil Testimonial"). Vermeil, in this instance, boasted that Bush is trustworthy. A pro-Bush spot used personal qualities as a way of attacking Gore in "Thelma and Louise," when one actor stated "And I don't care what they say say—honesty and integrity still matter." These spots highlighted the perception that Bush was free of the personal scandals that plagued both Clinton-Gore administrations. Gore discussed personal qualities in 29 percent of his character utterances. In "Bush-Texas Record," Gore attacked Bush's relationship with big oil companies in light of the state's pollution problems: "Bush pocketed $7 million from oil and gas interest for his campaigns. 7 million!" This was an attack on personal qualities because Gore implied that Bush personally benefitted from an industry he was charged with regulating as Texas governor.

Ideals represented only 17 percent of character utterances used in general radio spots. Ideals constituted 21 percent of the character utterances used by Gore. In a Gore spot called "Taxes," Bush was attacked for what is considered to be his anti-union views: "It's an attitude that doesn't value factory workers. That doesn't appreciate manufacturing jobs. Do we need a President that thinks that way?" This spot tried to highlight perceptions that Bush was opposed to the ideal of workers having the right to unionize. In the Bush and pro-Bush spots we examined, ideals were discussed in only 11 percent of all character utterances: "To vote freedom first . . . means a vote for George W. Bush" ("Heston Testimonial"). This spot, sponsored by the National Rifle Association, discussed Bush's feelings about the right of Americans to bear arms.

Due to our overall small *n*, we were unable to use *chi-square* to determine whether there was a significant difference in the form of character utterances among Gore and Bush in the 2000 general radio spots we examined.

## Issues Addressed in General Election Radio Spots

A poll prior to the 2000 general election suggested the economy was the top concern among likely voters (18 percent), followed by education (16 percent) and health care (16 percent). Social Security was ranked fourth in the election survey, followed by taxes, national defense, and the environment (see Table 14.4). We found, however, that other issues were brought up most often in general radio spots we examined (28 percent). This was particularly true in Gore's radio spots, where issues other than ones cited in the national poll were cited in 34 percent of his policy utterances. Other issues were discussed in only 18 percent of the Bush and pro-Bush policy utterances.

We found that Gore discussed Social Security most frequently (16 percent). Although Social Security ranked only fourth in the survey of likely general election voters, Gore frequently discussed the issue in his spots: "Bush has promised to take money out of Social Security and give it to younger workers to invest in private accounts. But Bush has also promised seniors that the same money will be there to pay for their Social Security benefits" ("Social Security 2"). The economy, the top concern among voters surveyed in the poll prior to the general election, was discussed in 12 percent of Gore's policy utterances: "We need more jobs, better

Table 14.4. Issues Addressed in 2000 General Radio Spots

| Issue | Poll | Bush* | Gore |
|---|---|---|---|
| Economy | 18 | 0 | 9 (3) |
| Education | 16 | 13 (2) | 3 (6) |
| Health Care | 16 | 14 (1) | 9 (3) |
| Social Security | 11 | 6 (4) | 12 (2) |
| Taxes | 8 | 0 | 9 (3) |
| National Defense | 8 | 0 | 0 |
| Environment | 3 | 0 | 7 (5) |
| Other | – | 7 (3) | 25 (1) |
| Spearman ρ | | .23, *ns* | -0.3, *ns* |

*Frequency (rank) NBC News/*Wall Street Journal* (2000)

jobs, more secure jobs" ("Taxes"). Two other issues, health care and taxes, were each discussed in 12 percent of the policy utterances we analyzed in Gore's general election radio spots, with the environment discussed in 10 percent of the policy utterances and education in 4 percent. We found no discussion of national defense in any of Gore's policy utterances in these spots.

In the Bush and pro-Bush general radio spots examined, health care was the policy issue discussed most often (35 percent). In "Insurance," narrator Art Linkletter said Gore's prescription drug plan would create more federal red tape: "Gore's plan would put bureaucrats in charge of deciding which new drugs would be covered by Medicare. And worse, in order to receive any prescription drugs, drugs that fight cancer under Medicare, senior citizens would have to drop their own insurance and join the government's plan." We again note that neither of the spots released by United Seniors Association made any reference to Bush or any of his plans concerning prescription drugs. Thirty-three percent of the policy utterances in the Bush and pro-Bush radio spots concerned education. In "Thelma and Louise," one of the actors noted a contradiction in Gore's stand on education reform: "Well, he tells parents he'll reform education, then he tells the unions he won't change a thing." Later the spot said, "George Bush promised education reform, and he's offered a detailed plan that will require accountability for students and teachers." These statements were intended to show voters worried about the quality of education that Bush is the candidate who stands for change. Social Security is discussed in 15 percent of the policy utterances found in general election radio spots: "George Bush's plan protects Social Security for all seniors. No changes. No cuts. No reductions—period" (Vermeil Testimonial"). Our analysis of the Bush and pro-Bush general election radio spots showed no mention of the economy (the number one issue in the poll), taxes, national defense, or the environment.

We used Spearman's $\rho$ to determine the strength of the relationship between the number of utterances devoted to each policy topic and the importance to general election voters. We found that both Bush and Gore had a negative, yet non-significant, relationship between the issues discussed in their general radio spots and those listed in the national poll (-.3 for Bush, -.45 for Gore). Gore was emphasizing Social Security over other issues that voters felt were more important (e.g., the economy, education). Bush, while concentrating on education and health care (the second and third-highest rated issues in the poll), made no mention of the top rated issue, the economy.

## Implications

We acknowledge that these results should be considered tentative because of the small sample of general radio spots we located. We particularly lament the absence of Bush spots. This also prevented us from running some statistical analysis. Yet we can use this functional analysis to suggest implications about the use of radio spots by candidates in the 2000 general election. In addition, we can compare the use of radio spots in 2000 with research done by Blaney (2001) on general radio spots dating back to 1972. We can also contrast results of our functional analyses of general radio spots with the analyses of general television spots in this campaign (see chapter 11 for more discussion of general television spots).

In examining functions of 2000 general radio spots, we found attacks were used over three times as often as acclaims (78 percent to 22 percent). We also found no use made of defenses in any of the general radio spots examined. We found a significant difference between the use of acclaims and attacks in the Gore and Bush/pro-Bush radio spots. While 97 percent of the utterances in the Gore radio spots were attacks, the Bush and pro-Bush radio spots we examined classified only 47 percent attacks. Thus, Gore used radio for attacking his opponent in the 2000 general election. Past research by Benoit (1999) shows the candidate trailing in the general election is more inclined to use attacks. As Gore trailed Bush in national polls as the 2000 general election day approached, it is evident Gore's radio spots were meant to raise doubts about Bush and diminish his standing among voters.

When we examined the topics of 2000 general radio spots, we found candidates emphasized policy over character (74 percent versus 26 percent). Gore discussed policy slightly more often in the radio spots we analyzed when compared with Bush and pro-Bush spots (77 percent versus 69 percent). We also found that the Bush and pro-Bush spots discussed character (31 percent) slightly more than Gore (23 percent). We can attribute part of Bush's emphasis on policy to some of the single-issue spots run by groups we classify as pro-Bush. Spots such as those sponsored by United Senior Association focus on specific policy concerns (e.g., health care, prescription drug policies) for that organization.

No significant difference was found between the Gore and Bush/pro-Bush spots concerning topics of general radio spots. The emphasis on policy utterances found in general radio spots is in line with past research (Benoit, 1999) on television spots showing policy is stressed more by candidates in general elections than character, as voters focus more on what the candidate is proposing to do if elected.

When we examined forms of policy in 2000 general radio spots, past deeds were discussed most often (44 percent), followed by general goals (32 percent) and future plans (24 percent). Gore discussed past deeds (54 percent) most often in his radio spots when compared with future plans (26 percent) and goals (20 percent). The Bush and pro-Bush spots discussed goals most often (55 percent) compared with past deeds (25 percent) and future plans (20 percent). Although the small sample size prevented a comparison of forms of policy utterances used by the candidates, one implication we can suggest from our research concerns the use of past deed utterances as attacks. When we examined Gore's general radio spots, we found past deeds were used as attacks 95 percent of the time, focusing on Bush's record as governor of Texas. Past deeds cited in the Bush and pro-Bush spots were used as attacks 80 percent of the time. Most of the past deeds cited by Bush and pro-Bush spots discussed Gore's role in the two Clinton administrations. We see this strategy as a mistake on the part of the candidates, as both Gore and Bush could have touted their past government experience as a rationale for why they should be president. Instead, the candidates dwelled on the past record of their opponent.

When examining character utterances in 2000 general radio spots, we found a slightly higher emphasis on leadership ability (43 percent) then personal qualities (40 percent) while ideals were discussed infrequently (17 percent). Gore emphasized leadership (50 percent) in his general radio spots, followed by personal qualities (29 percent) and ideals (21 percent). When we examined Bush's radio spots, we found the emphasis on personal qualities (56 percent compared to 33 percent leadership and 11 percent ideals). While our sample size was too small to make a comparison of forms of character utterances, we note that Gore and Bush employed character utterances in different ways. Benoit (1999) found personal qualities have been discussed most frequently in presidential general election television spots. While Bush followed this trend in his 2000 general radio spots, we found Gore emphasized leadership ability more often. This resulted from Gore's effort to raise questions about Bush's past leadership in Texas, and thus, his future ability to lead the nation. Benoit has also found that in the discussion of character, presidential candidates have used these types of utterances as acclaims more often than attacks. While Bush and pro-Bush spots generally used character utterances as acclaims, Gore used 100 percent of his character utterances at attacks on Bush. This supports our contention that Gore viewed radio as a means for attacking his opponent in the 2000 general election.

When we examined issues discussed in general election radio commercials, we failed to find any significant, positive correlation between what the candidates were discussing and the issues reported as being important to voters nationwide. The economy, which was listed as the top issue by survey participants, was never discussed in Bush's radio or television spots. Gore also limited discussion regarding the economy. The issue was the third-most discussed issue in Gore's radio spots. Education, rated as the second-most important issue, was also the second-most issue discussed in Bush's radio spots. Health care, rated third on the national survey, was the issue Bush/pro-Bush radio spots discussed most frequently while it was among the second most-discussed issues in general radio spots for Gore. Issues other than those listed in the poll were those discussed most frequently in Gore's radio spots, followed by Social Security, which rated as the fourth-most important issue among voters surveyed. It can be suggested that Bush fared slightly better than Gore in addressing major issues of concern to voters (education, health care), but that both candidates were mistaken in their failure to address the economy, the primary concern of voters surveyed.

Blaney (2001) examined general radio spots aired from 1972 through the 2000

Table 14.5. Functions of General Radio Spots, 1972-1992 and 2000

|           | Acclaims | Attacks | Defenses |
|-----------|----------|---------|----------|
| 1972-1992 | 52%      | 48%     | 0        |
| 2000      | 22%      | 78%     | 0        |

general election, but for the purpose of analyzing the 2000 campaign, we will use figures he compiled from the 1972 through 1992 elections (no general spots from the 1996 campaign were available for analysis). Blaney's research on functions of general spots found that, historically, acclaims (52 percent) were used more than attacks (48 percent) (see Table 14.5). 2000 general radio spots showed a significant change from this trend, as attacks (78 percent) were used far more frequently than acclaims (22 percent). A *chi-square* revealed a significant difference in the functions of 2000 general radio spots compared to those in previous campaigns ($\chi^2[df=1]=46.8$, $p < .001$). Gore's emphasis on attacks in his radio spots (97 percent) is a major reason for the significant difference found in functions between 2000 general radio spots and those of past campaigns. As previously mentioned in Benoit (1999), candidates who are trailing will choose to attack more often, as Gore did in his 2000 general radio spots.

A similarity found between Blaney's research and our analysis concerned the lack of defense utterances. None of the radio spots examined by Blaney from 1972 to 1992 employed any form of a defense utterance. The same outcome concerning the lack of defense utterances was found in our analysis of 2000 general radio spots. Thus, a second implication from our research suggests that candidates do not use general radio spots to defend themselves from attacks by opponents.

When comparing topics of general election radio spots, Blaney found policy and character were discussed almost equally (each at 50 percent) by past candidates (see Table 14.6). 2000 general election spots broke with this pattern, with Gore and Bush placing a greater emphasis on policy (74 percent versus 26 percent character). A significant difference was found between topics in 2000 general election radio spots and those of past general elections ($\chi^2[df=1]=30.8$, $p < .001$), as policy was discussed with greater frequency than character in 2000. Part of this difference results from Gore's extensive use of policy utterances in his 2000 general radio spots. As Blaney (2001) has found, incumbents (in this case, Gore) discuss policy more than character in general radio spots. It is interesting to note that the lone general radio spot which we coded that was directly from the Bush campaign also showed policy emphasized much more than character (91 percent policy, 9 percent character). Outside spots coded as pro-Bush either emphasized policy (such as those produced by the United Senior Association and the Missouri Republican

Table 14.6. Topics of General Radio Spots, 1972-1992 and 2000

|           | Policy | Character |
|-----------|--------|-----------|
| 1972-1992 | 50%    | 50%       |
| 2000      | 74%    | 26%       |

Table 14.7. Forms of Policy and Character in General Radio Spots, 1972-1992 and 2000

| | Policy | | | Character | | |
|---|---|---|---|---|---|---|
| | Past Deeds | Future Plans | General Goals | Personal Qualities | Leadership | Ideals |
| 1972-1992 | 59% | 28% | 13% | 26% | 18% | 56% |
| 2000 | 44% | 24% | 32% | 40% | 43% | 17% |

Party) or a balance of policy and character (such as the spots run by the Log Cabin Republicans or the National Rifle Association).

When comparing forms of policy, we found candidates in the 2000 general election, as in past elections studied, stressed past deeds most often among policy utterances. In past elections studied, past deeds were discussed in 59 percent of all policy utterances (see Table 14.7). In the 2000 general radio spots examined, past deeds were discussed in 44 percent of all policy utterances. While past general radio spots discussed future plans (28 percent) more often then general goals (13 percent), we found the opposite to be true in 2000, as general goals (32 percent) were stressed more than future plans (24 percent). There was a significant difference in the forms of policy used in past general radio spots and those employed in 2000 ($\chi^2[df=2]=22$, $p < .001$). Fewer past deeds and more general goals were discussed in 2000 general radio spots compared to past general elections. There was roughly the same number of future plans cited by the 2000 candidates as compared to those in past races. The relatively large number of past deed utterances found in 2000 general radio spots was strongly influenced by Gore's effort to cite Governor Bush's past deeds in Texas in order to attack the Republican's ability to serve as president.

A further examination of the use of past deeds by candidates in recent elections also reinforces our contention that this form of policy utterance is used primarily for attacking an opponent. In 2000, we found that 92 percent of all past deed utterances were used as attacks. Blaney found 78 percent of all past deed utterances in 1992 general radio spots were used as attacks, while that figure was 74 percent in 1988 general radio spots. This trend supports the notion that radio spots in a general election are frequently used as a means for attacking one's opponent on their past record.

When we examined forms of character in general radio spots, past elections found that ideals (56 percent) were stressed more than personal qualities (26 percent) or leadership ability (18 percent). The 2000 general radio spots we examined, however, found a greater emphasis on leadership ability (43 percent) than personal qualities (40 percent) or ideals (17 percent). We found a significant difference between forms of character in past general radio spots and those used in 2000 ($\chi^2[df=2]=26.1$, $p < .001$). Leadership ability and personal qualities were discussed more often in 2000 general radio spots than those from past presidential campaigns. At the same time, the discussion of ideals was down significantly in 2000 general radio spots compared to past general radio spots. We again focus on

Gore's radio spots as to why this difference occurred. In attacking Bush's record in Texas, the Gore radio spots were not only raising questions about Bush's performance in Texas, but also to create doubt about Bush's ability to lead the country. It was this emphasis on leadership ability in the Gore spots that contributed to this difference with past elections.

In comparing the functions of general radio and television spots in the 2000 campaign, Gore was found to use radio primarily for attacks (97 percent, versus 47 percent television). Gore's general television spots (those run by his campaign as well those paid for by the Democratic National Committee) emphasized acclaims (53 percent, versus 3 percent radio). Bush had about the same amount of acclaims and attacks in his general television spots (those run by his campaign as well as those sponsored by the Republican National Committee). In his television spots, acclaims accounted for 58 percent of all utterances, compared to 42 percent attacks. In the Bush/pro-Bush radio spots acclaims made up 53 percent of all utterances, versus 47 percent attacks.

A *chi-square* revealed a significant difference in the functions of general radio and television spots in the 2000 campaign ($\chi^2[df=1]=63$, $p < .001$). Thus, a third implication from our analysis suggests attacks were used more frequently in general radio spots then general television spots. In the 2000 election, the Gore campaign in particular used the medium of radio for attacking Bush. One reason why radio may have been used this way is discussed by Hutchens (1999), who says campaigns can buy advertising time on radio stations that reach specific groups of voters. While Gore's television spots, reaching a general audience, stressed acclaims more than attacks, radio spots could be targeted to specific stations (and the demographic groups they attract) to attack Bush.

When comparing topics of 2000 general radio spots with television, we found both candidates chose to emphasize policy utterance, regardless of the medium. Policy was discussed in 74 percent of all general radio utterances, compared with 70 percent for general television. Gore discussed policy virtually the same amount in the radio spots we analyzed when compared with his television spots (77 percent versus 73 percent). Bush and pro-Bush spots were also virtually the same (69 percent radio versus 67 percent television).

Character was discussed in 30 percent of all general television spots versus 26 percent in general radio spots. Gore discussed character slightly more in his television spots compared to radio (27 percent versus 23 percent). Bush also relied on more character utterances in his general television spots (33 percent versus 31 percent for radio). A *chi-square* found no significant difference in topics found in general radio spots versus television ($\chi^2[df=1]=.8$, *ns*). As noted earlier, policy utterances are found to be more common than character utterances in studies of past general election spots. The 2000 general election was no different.

In comparing forms of policy in general radio and television spots, we found past deeds discussed most frequently (44 percent) in radio spots (compared with 32 percent goals and 24 percent plans). General television spots emphasized future plans most frequently (39 percent) compared with general goals (33 percent) and past deeds (28 percent). Gore's general radio spots discussed past deeds (54 percent) most often while general goals and future plans were discussed equally (36 percent each) in his general television spots. The Bush and pro-Bush spots discussed general goals most often in radio spots (55 percent) while the emphasis was on future plans (43 percent) in general television spots. A *chi-square* revealed a significant difference in the forms of policy in 2000 general radio spots when compared with general television spots ($\chi^2[df=2]=12.5, p < .01$). While past deeds were emphasized more frequently in the general radio spots, future plans were emphasized more often in general television spots. General goals were discussed in about equal measure in the general radio and television spots. These results again suggest that radio and television spots served different purposes in 2000, particularly for the Gore campaign. The radio spots we examined emphasized past deeds to attack Bush's record as governor of Texas. When we examined Gore's television spots, we found that all of the general goal utterances were used as acclaims (there was a balance between acclaims and attacks in Gore's discussion of future plans in his television spots). It is again difficult to make judgments regarding the Bush general television spots versus the Bush and pro-Bush radio spots, as most of the general radio spots we coded were sponsored by outside groups.

As with general radio spots, we note both candidates used past deed utterances for attacks more often than acclaims in their television spots. We found that in Gore's television spots, 80 percent of all past deed utterances were used as attacks (95 percent on radio) and Bush general television spots used past deeds as attacks 61 percent of the time (80 percent in the Bush and pro-Bush radio spots).

When comparing character utterances found in 2000 general radio and television spots, we found a slightly higher emphasis on leadership ability in the radio spots (43 percent) over personal qualities (40 percent) and ideals (17 percent). This is in contrast with the general television spots we analyzed, which found personal qualities (72 percent) stressed far more often than ideals (21 percent) or leadership (8 percent). Gore's radio spots differed from his television spots when examining the forms of character utterances. On radio, Gore emphasized leadership (50 percent), followed by personal qualities (29 percent) and ideals (21 percent). In Gore's television spots, personal qualities (76 percent) were discussed far more often than ideals (12 percent) or leadership (11 percent). When we examined Bush's radio spots, we found an emphasis on personal qualities (56 percent, compared with 33 percent leadership and 11 percent ideals). In the television spots we examined, we found an even greater emphasis on personal qualities for Bush (65 percent) than for ideals (30 percent) or leadership (5 percent). A *chi-square* revealed a significant difference in the forms of character in 2000 general radio spots when compared with general television ($\chi^2[df=2]=32.3, p < .001$). While Bush chose to emphasize personal qualities in his general radio and television spots (to a greater extent on television), Gore emphasized personal qualities in the television spots and leadership ability in the radio spots examined. Utterances about leadership ability accounted for 50 percent of all character utterances used by Gore in his radio spots. As noted earlier, Gore tied his attacks on Bush's past deeds as Texas governor to Bush's ability to lead the country. This appears to be another aspect of Gore's strategy concerning the use of radio and television spots in the 2000 campaign. Gore seemed to use one type of message about character (acclaiming Gore's personal qualities) for television and the general audiences it reached and another (attacking Bush's leadership ability) for radio and more targeted audiences.

# Chapter 15

# General Television Talk Show Appearances

> Number 10: Vote for me or I'll come to your home and explain my 191 page economic plan to you in excruciating detail. (Gore, *Late Night with David Letterman*)

> It really touches me that each in their own way, each child, has been very, very helpful and supportive, and it's a family decision. Has to be. You know, you can't do anything important in life without—without doing it in the context of family. (Gore, *The Oprah Winfrey Show*)

> I'm a person who recognizes the fallacy of humans. I think all of us need forgiveness. I think ours is a society—I mean, ours is a life that is—should be based upon forgiveness and tolerance. (Bush, *Oprah*)

> Number 2: [I promise to] give the oval office one heck of a scrubbing. (Bush, *Late Night with David Letterman*)

As the two major party candidates scrambled to get time on non-news talk shows in the 2000 general presidential campaign, the importance of the political role of these programs increased. Politicians have occasionally appeared on talk shows in the past. John F. Kennedy appeared on Jack Parr's *The Tonight Show*. Clinton appeared on a number of talk shows in his 1992 campaign, including appearances in which he played the saxophone with program house bands. Clinton was also adept at using a talk show format on MTV in 1992. While there were a few appearances in 1996 (Dole appeared on *Live with Regis and Kathy Lee*), we have witnessed a tremendous explosion of such appearances in the 2000 campaign. Talk shows were a frequented venue for the presidential candidates in the 2000 campaign. At one point, Jay Leno commented:

> What a week we have! This is unbelievable. We have George W. Bush on tonight. [Cheers] We have Al Gore on tomorrow night. [Cheers] You know what's even more amazing? We had Ralph Nader the other day. You know what's even more . . . You know who was on *Meet The Press* this week? Richard Simmons and Carrot Top. [Laughter] What's going on? The whole world is backwards. (Leno, *The Tonight Show*)

Gore and Bush appeared on numerous talk shows in the 2000 general election campaign. It was an innovation for the candidates to appear on daytime talk shows, including the *Oprah Winfrey Show*, *Live with Regis*, and *The View*. Gore also appeared on the *Rosie* talk show program. Likewise, the two major party candidates frequented the late night talk show circuit, an increasingly important venue for presidential candidates. Both major party candidates appeared on *The Late Show with David Letterman* and *The Tonight Show with Jay Leno*. Vice presidential candidate Joe Lieberman appeared on *Conan O'Brien*, and Dick Cheney also appeared on talk shows. Green Party candidate Ralph Nader circulated on television talk shows. Less innovative were the appearances by the two candidates on news talk show programs such as *Larry King Live*. Candidates and campaigns increasingly regard the television talk shows as a valuable campaign venue.

There are several reasons that candidate appearances on these programs merit study. The first reason appearances on talk shows are important is their ability to reach a large audience: Millions of voters watch these programs. For instance, Oprah regularly has over seven million viewers, Letterman has about four million viewers, and Larry King has over one million viewers (Fineman, 2000). Thus, these programs reach a significant number of viewers. Second, talk show programs are a source of news for many people. As noted in chapter 7, according to the Pew Research Center for the People and the Press, 10 percent of those polled reported that they gained news information from talk shows (Marks, 2000). Pfau, Cho, and Chong (2001) reported that nontraditional campaign discourse forms, including television entertainment talk shows and television talk shows, exerted much influence on perceptions of the candidates. Thus, candidates have the opportunity to provide voters with information about themselves and their candidacy. Third, these programs reach audiences that do not rely extensively on evening news programs. Mark Fabiani, a Gore spokesperson, has commented that these appearances reflect "a recognition that in this day and age, working mothers and fathers don't get their news from the evening news programs solely" (Moore, 2000). Candidates are using talk shows in addition to traditional news outlets to provide information that would make these mothers and fathers more likely to choose them. In fact, those who gather information from talk shows may not even watch nightly news programs, especially those who have left the traditional political process. As Brent Bozell from the Media Research Center commented, "If you want to find them [the politically uninvolved], you're not going to find them on *Meet The Press*. You're going to find them on *Oprah*" (Moore, 2000). Fourth, appearances on talk shows provide the candidates an opportunity to deliver their messages unfiltered by news media. On television talk shows, the candidates can put out their own spin. Fifth, the different genres of talk shows have appeal to unique audiences. The talk shows are tailored for specific target audiences. Ari Fleischer, a Bush aide, said of programs like *Oprah*, "there are millions of Americans who watch them, including millions of women, and that's a very important group in this election" (Moore, 2000). Candidates must connect with as many audiences as possible as they desire the most possible votes. Finally, candidates are well advised to cover the same bases as their opponents. If one major candidate appears on talk shows, their competition should appear on those talk shows as well in order to counteract any advantage. Thus, talk shows have become an important venue in the race for the presidency.

Thus, it is justified to study this important political arena. Initially, studying talk show appearances increases our understanding of the full range of communicative media (and audiences) available to those seeking the presidential office. The list of appropriate television media that can be used by candidates is widening. This knowledge is valuable for understanding how talk shows function in presidential campaigns. In this chapter, we examine the use of talk show appearances by presidential candidates in the general campaign in an effort to better understand this type of discourse.

## Literature Review

Many aspects of television talk shows have been explored in previous scholarship on the program form. These include general study of television talk show programs, study of specific programs, use of talk shows by European politicians, and the impact of candidate discourse of television talk show programs. However, little academic attention has been expended on critical content analysis of the functions of presidential campaign rhetoric on television talk shows.

Several studies have focused on general aspects of television talk show programs. For instance, the appeal of talk show television programs has been explored. McKenzie (2000) contended that television talk shows performed an epideictic function that leads audience members to perceive that the ceremonial aspects of the programs enabled viewers to deem the programs important on a number of levels. McKenzie further suggested that as some audience members view television talk shows, they have a heightened sense of civic involvement, a feeling that the viewer was a part of a larger community. These aspects of television talk show programs, concluded McKenzie, contribute to the large audience for these programs. The uses of television talk shows by audience members have also been explored (Surlin, 1986). Armstrong and Rubin (1989) studied talk show viewing as interpersonal communication. Radio talk shows have also been the focus of previous research (Andreasen, 1985; Benoit, Blaney, & Pier, 1998; Bierig & Dimmick, 1979; Tramer & Jeffres, 1983; Turow, 1974).

Specific television talk shows have been the subject of critical analyses. However, these critical pieces have not focused on the appearances of political candidates on television talk shows. Schaefer and Avery (1993) studied audience interpretation of *Late Night with David Letterman* and found that many viewers saw the program as a satire of the talk show genre. However, they did not explore the political value of this television program. Oprah Winfrey has also been the topic of communication scholarship. Cloud (1996) looked at biographical representations of Oprah Winfrey's personal story and argued that some of the myths that arise from such minority public personalities such as Oprah can function as a rhetorical mechanism for the legitimation of liberal hegemony. Cloud's work, while intriguing, was of little relevance to our study except to establish that Oprah is an important figure for a large population of Americans. Haag (1992/1993) explored the rhetorical strategies used by Oprah on her show to establish an intimate relationship with her viewers. Haag recognizes that Oprah focuses on personal issues and mannerisms in a public sphere. A particularly important contribution of both of these studies is the discussion of the pseudo-relationships developed with the host of the viewers' favorite talk show programs. Many nonpolitical aspects of talk shows have been examined in previous literature. Tolson (2001) edited a tome that contained a number of critical pieces on American, British, and Israeli television talk shows, although the work did not highlight the role of television talk show programs in political campaigns. Hammerback (1974) studied William F. Buckley's *Firing Line* and concluded that the talk show format promotes certain types of rhetoric. Borgers (1962) critically evaluated the *Paul Coates Show*, arguing that nonentertainment interview programs emphasizing dramatic elements could increase appeal to viewers.

The appearance of politicians on European television talk shows has been the focus of some research. Lang and Lang (1961, 1968, 1984) suggested that politicians tend to focus more on personality than on issues, although they relied upon European studies for their evidence. The prevalence of image (character) topics by politicians in talk shows has been noted in studies of European television talk shows (Bock, 1982; Fibiger, 1981; Hoffmann, 1982; Weiss, 1976). European studies of European talk show appearances have also suggested these appearances have a more personal nature than other venues used by elected officials (Hoffman, 1982; Holly et al., 1986). Schutz (1995) studied German talk shows and found that politicians offered less information about their personal lives than entertainer talk show guests, but less factual information than experts. However, this previous research has not systematically studied this phenomenon in the American context, during a presidential campaign, or systematically examined the composition of personality discussion.

Several scholars have studied the influence of presidential candidate appearances on television talk shows. Just, Crigler, and Buhr (1999) studied the tone and emphasis of the appearances of the presidential candidates on television talks shows in the 1992 presidential race. The results, according to the authors, indicated that these programs contained more information about the policy positions and character of the candidates than other forms of mass communicated candidate messages. The authors also found that talk show programs offer more opportunity for the candidates to speak for themselves than television news programs. The authors concluded that television talk shows offered much substance, the voice of the candidates, and low cynicism. Chaffee, Zhao, & Leshner (1994) studied the effects of various media forms on political learning during the 1992 presidential campaign and found that television talk shows contributed to viewers learning about particular candidates. Pfau and Eveland (1996) studied the influence on voting intentions of the presidential candidates' television talk show appearances during the 1996 election. Path analysis revealed that candidate appearances on these programs have an indirect influence on voter intentions. Pfau and Eveland revealed that nontraditional news media (television talk shows) were more influential in the early stages of the general race than in the latter, and that their influence may be less than that of tradition television news programs. They found that the influence of these nontraditional news sources were stronger for Clinton than for Bush or Perot. Nevertheless, this research does suggest that television talk shows can influence voters. When an election is close, the authors contended, nontraditional television news media could influence the outcome of an election. As noted earlier, Pfau, Cho, and Chong (2001) concluded that television entertainment talk shows and television talk shows influenced perceptions of the candidates. However, the authors found that these nontraditional communication modalities have no significant effect on perceptions of the democratic process. The authors also emphasized the importance of comparatively evaluating the effects of various forms of candidate communication instead of studying the isolated effects of any single form of mass communicated campaign discourse.

While scholars have studied general aspects of television talk show programs, study of specific programs, use of talk shows by European politicians, and the impact of candidate discourse of television talk show programs, the existing literature does not analyze the functions of the rhetoric of U.S. presidential nominees on talk shows. This chapter is an initial step towards understanding the characteristics of presidential campaign rhetoric in the television talk show genre. Analysis of data will reveal the functional features of this increasingly important mass media modality in the electoral decisions rendered by U.S. voters.

# Results

We obtained six episodes of talk shows during the general campaign on which Gore and Bush appeared (Appendix 15.1). The appearances of both candidates on *The Oprah Winfrey Show* represented the daytime talk show genre. Gore appeared on *Oprah* on September 11, 2000, and Bush appeared on the program on September 19. The two episodes on which the candidates appeared on the *Larry King Live* program were also chosen as examples of the news talk show format. Gore's appearance was on September 28 and the Bush appearance we used was on September 26. Finally, the appearances of the two candidates on *The Late Show with David Letterman* were chosen as an example of the late night genre. Gore appeared on the program on September 14 and Bush appeared on October 19. These programs provide a varied sample with subgenera symmetry.

## Functions of 2000 General Talk Show Appearances

The two major party presidential candidates acclaimed (91 percent) much more than they attacked (5 percent) or defended (4 percent), as displayed in Table 15.1. For example, on *Oprah*, Gore acclaimed his personal qualities: "I've never been hesitant to stand up to—to powerful interests that didn't necessarily have the American people's best interests at heart." In this statement, Gore suggested that he is the kind of person who works for the people. Bush also acclaimed in many instances, such as a comment he offered to Oprah: "I mean, I'm well educated. But I'm certainly not the kind of person that talks down to people because of my education." In this instance, Bush acclaimed his formal education and his humility. On the other hand, Bush implicitly attacked the Clinton Administration for a moral decline in Washington when, on *Larry King Live*, he said, "I think there's a lot of kids who are disillusioned right now. I frankly think that what's taken place in Washington the last couple of years has tended to disillusion children, young voters." Gore also attacked Bush: On *Larry King Live*, Gore criticized Bush's position on abortion choice: Bush "said he will do everything he can to overturn Roe v. Wade. I think that's a mistake, Larry." Here Gore attacked Bush's expressed standard for nominees to federal court positions. Defenses were also enacted. For instance, Gore denied that he kissed Tipper on the Democratic convention stage just to send a message about his strong family values: "And when I went into the

Table 15.1. Functions of 2000 General Talk Show Appearances

|       | Acclaims   | Attacks  | Defenses |
|-------|------------|----------|----------|
| Bush  | 375 (90%)  | 22 (5%)  | 21 (5%)  |
| Gore  | 260 (91%)  | 15 (5%)  | 10 (4%)  |
| Total | 635 (91%)  | 37 (5%)  | 31 (4%)  |

hall there were all these thousands of people and I got up there and it was a moment that she and I had worked for together, and I don't think it's particularly unusual to want to share it with her." Here Gore suggested that he was simply overtaken with emotion, thus denying the charge that he was being manipulative. Bush likewise defended himself. On *Oprah*, Bush defended himself against the accusation that he was running to get revenge for his father's defeat in 1996 when he said, "I mean, basically, what you are saying is, 'Are you running because of revenge?' Revenge is such a negative thought. I'm running for positive reasons." Bush here offered his positive attitude as proof that he was not running for president out of a desire for revenge. While the candidates defended themselves, as noted, acclaims were by far more frequent than attacks or defenses.

A *chi square* analysis revealed that the distribution of acclaims, attacks, and defenses of the two candidates was not significantly different ($\chi^2[df=2]=.925$, *ns*). Gore acclaimed 260 times, which accounted for 91 percent of his utterances. Bush acclaimed in 90 percent of his utterances. Gore devoted 5 percent of his utterances to attacks, while Bush attacked in 5 percent of his utterances. Gore defended in 4 percent of his discourse, while Bush devoted 5 percent to defending. Neither candidate defended often. When defenses occurred, the accusations had been stated by the talk show host. For instance, on *The Late Show with David Letterman*, Gore defended himself against the accusation that his extended kiss with Tipper at the Democratic convention was political theater. David Letterman referred to the suspicion that Gore was manipulatively theatrical when he kissed his wife at the convention: "But you know I mean the guy is right and even I said it—sending that message where it is something you thought about her something you didn't think about, undeniably, symbolically it says, 'you can count on me. I've got a wife that I am still crazy about. I'm not going to be chasing interns.' I mean that's really . . . that's really what it said." Gore responded: "Come on. Come on. Give me a break. I was off-stage watching her do a slide show. Right beforehand she presented all these pictures that she had taken of our life together and our kids." This was a simple denial of an attack on Gore's personal qualities.

## Topics of 2000 General Talk Show Appearances

Gore and Bush discussed policy in 33 percent of their comments on the talk shows. Gore advocated change in health policy when, on *Oprah*, he contended, "We need a prescription drug benefit under Medicare for all seniors." On *The Late Show with David Letterman*, Bush stated his policy toward terrorism: "We need to send a message to terrorists that there's gonna be a price to pay. You mess with the United States and kill our citizens, there will be a serious price to pay." Character utterances (67 percent) were more frequent than policy statements. For example, Bush proclaimed his character on *Oprah* when he said, "I want people to know I care a lot about our fellow citizens. I love my country. I love the people that live

Table 15.2. Topics of 2000 General Talk Show Appearances

|  | Policy | Character |
|---|---|---|
| Bush | 121 (30%) | 276 (70%) |
| Gore | 98 (36%) | 177 (64%) |
| Total | 219 (33%) | 453 (67%) |

in America." One of the unique features of television talk show appearances is that it provides an opportunity for the candidates to express a sense of humor. Much of the top ten lists were implicitly self-critical: The candidate reading the list was roasting himself. The candidates displayed their sense of humor, a personal quality.

There was no significant difference in the distribution of policy and character utterances of the two candidates ($\chi^2[df=1] = 1.97$, *ns*). Policy accounted for 30 percent of Bush's utterances and 36 percent of Gore's utterances. Character accounted for 70 percent of Bush's remarks and 64 percent of Gore's themes. Thus, the candidates adopted similar strategies for their discourse on television talk shows: Both of the candidates devoted most of their discourse to the topic of character.

## Forms of Policy and Character in 2000 General Talk Show Appearances

The proportion of comments in talk shows devoted to the three forms of policy were: past deeds, 17 percent; future plans, 18 percent; and general goals, 65 percent. Bush provided an example of acclaim for his past deeds on *Larry King Live* when he contended, "One of my proudest accomplishments is I worked with Republicans and Democrats to close that achievement gap in Texas. Our test scores for minority students are some of the best in the nation." Gore praised his past deeds to David Letterman when he commented, "I was able to go to international negotiation on global warming and help to get a treaty called the Kyoto Treaty, it sounds a little arcane but actually it's a very serious environmental problem that we have to take the leading role in addressing." Here Gore acclaimed his own contribution to environmental protection. Gore advertised his future taxation proposals on *Oprah* when Oprah asked, "Are you going to give a tax cut to the person who's staying at home?" Gore answered, "Yep. Yep." This statement concerns future plans rather than general goals because Gore provided a specific aspect of his tax plan. Bush also discussed his future plans when he explained his campaign finance reform proposal to Larry King: "I think we ought to ban corporate soft money and labor union soft money, so long as there is dues checkoff. I know we need to have instant disclosure." Bush here asserts that banning soft money would be his plan for the future of political contribution law. General goals

Table 15.3. Forms of Policy and Character in 2000 General Talk Show Appearances

| | Policy | | | Character | | |
| | Past Deeds* | | Future Plans | | General Goals | | Personal Qualities | | Leader-ship | | Ideals | |
|---|---|---|---|---|---|---|---|---|---|---|---|---|
| Bush | 15 | 8 | 12 | 0 | 83 | 3 | 194 | 10 | 17 | 0 | 54 | 1 |
| Gore | 11 | 3 | 18 | 10 | 56 | 0 | 112 | 2 | 11 | 0 | 52 | 0 |
| Total | 26 | 11 | 30 | 10 | 139 | 3 | 306 | 12 | 28 | 0 | 106 | 1 |
| | 37 (17%) | | 40 (18%) | | 142 (64%) | | 318 (70%) | | 28 (6%) | | 107 (24%) | |

*Acclaims/attacks.

accounted for most of the policy statements. For instance, on *Larry King Live*, Bush identified his general goals on public safety issues such as the distribution of faulty Firestone tires on Ford SUVs: "We expect [the tires] to be good, you expect the people to make up on their warranty, but if there is information showing that there may be some—a batch of tires that are being manufactured that are going to create hazards for the American people, yes, the federal government ought to be warning people." This example discusses a general goal because Bush proposed future policy in general terms rather than specific plans. Likewise, Gore addressed general goals in utterance such as one he enacted with David Letterman: "Nuclear secrets have to be protected." This statement is a general goal because Gore offered no specific course of action. General goals were the most frequent form of policy statements. See Table 15.3.

Character remarks focused more on personal qualities (70 percent) than leadership ability (6 percent) or ideals (24 percent). Both candidates often emphasized personal qualities on television talk shows. For example, on *Oprah*, Gore portrayed himself as an ordinary family guy: "Going to the lake near our home in Tennessee on a houseboat and just water-skiing with the kids, and floating and swimming—that's probably my favorite thing." Bush praised his own personal quality when he explained to David Letterman that he was working hard; "I'm working hard, as I say, to rally the troops and do my best to get the people to show up" to vote. Bush acclaimed his leadership abilities on *Oprah*: "Well, a leader's somebody who's not afraid to take positions. A leader is somebody who's willing to bring people together to get things done." Likewise, Gore praised his leadership ability to Larry King when he explained. "I want [voters] to support me on the basis of the good things we can make happen together in the future." Finally, ideals accounted for almost a quarter of all character utterances. On *The Late Show with David Letterman*, Bush acclaimed his ideals concerning the importance of the legal system: "And our society is a society that is a society of law." In this utterance, Bush extolled his high regard for the normative legitimacy of the U.S. legal system.

Gore also extolled his ideals: On *Oprah*, Gore contended, "I want to keep our prosperity going, but to make sure that it enriches not just a few but all of our families." Here Gore acclaimed his belief in the ideal of increased economic equity. Overall, however, personal qualities were the most frequently mentioned character subject in these appearances.

## Issues Addressed in 2000 General Talk Show Appearances

Both Gore and Bush devoted most policy utterances to the education issue (see Table 15.4). However, their discussion of environmental issues (for Bush, environment ranked third; for Gore, environment ranked second) did not appear to be on the minds of voters as much as it was on the minds of the candidates, according to poll information (mentioned as the most important issue by only 3 percent of the respondents: it ranked seventh). Voters cited health care as the third most important issue (for Bush, health care ranked fifth; for Gore, health care ranked third). Social Security was the fourth most important issue to voters, while for Bush and Gore, Social Security ranked seventh. Taxes were reportedly the fifth most salient issue in the minds of poll respondents and ranked third in the discourse of both candidates. National defense, ranked sixth by voters, ranked second in Bush's television talk show discourse but sixth in Gore's.

The candidates discussed a wide variety of issues on their talk show appearances. We utilized Spearman's ρ to determine the strength of the relationship between the number of utterances devoted to each policy topic and the importance

Table 15.4. Issues Addressed in 2000 General Talk Show Appearances

|  | Poll | Bush | Gore |
|---|---|---|---|
| Economy | 18 | 8 | 12 |
| Education | 16 | 30 | 16 |
| Health Care | 16 | 9 | 13 |
| Social Security | 11 | 0 | 1 |
| Taxes | 8 | 11 | 13 |
| National Defense | 8 | 22 | 4 |
| Environment | 3 | 11 | 15 |
| Other | – | 30 | 24 |
| Spearman ρ |  | -.48, *ns* | -.38, *ns* |

NBC News/*Wall Street Journal* (2000)

of that policy topic to voters. Neither ρ was significant.

# Implications

The application of the functional theory of campaign discourse reveals that the discourse of the candidates on talk shows has distinct features. The candidates devoted most of their utterances to acclaiming (91 percent). When presidential candidates appear on television talk shows, there is also much discussion of character, particularly personal qualities. There are several reasons why presidential campaign discourse on talk shows features these characteristics.

The candidates were very positive (acclaims were 91 percent of the discourse) in their talk show appearances during the 2000 race. One reason is that talk shows are a primarily positive venue, and the candidates likely viewed excessively attacking the other candidate as inappropriate.

There were few attacks enacted on television talk shows by the candidates in the 2000 presidential race. In other media forms (Benoit, 1999), persons other than the candidate, such as anonymous announcers or ordinary people, more often voice attacks than candidates themselves. For instance, Benoit et al. (1998) argued that keynote speeches are more negative than other campaign messages because surrogates rather than the candidate deliver them. There are no surrogates or anonymous narrators available to enact attacks on the opposition for the candidates, as is the case in advertisements or keynote speeches. Attacking other candidates is risky because most of the voting public dislikes attacks (Merritt, 1984; Stewart, 1975). Thus, attacks would be less appropriate in this discourse form than others, as indicated in chapter 7.

There were few defenses enacted on television talk shows as well. This was because the talk show hosts spent little time repeating attacks launched previously against the candidates. If the host did not bring up the attack, candidates would have to reiterate the attacks enacted by opponents to defend against attacks on television talk shows. As in other discourse forms, candidates are likely reluctant to restate attacks when discussing their character with David Letterman or Oprah.

The candidates discussed character in most (67 percent) of their television talk show discourse. This may suggest that the hosts of the programs handled the candidates in similar ways. The type of questions asked of the candidates surely affects the content of their answers. All three of the talk show hosts in this study encouraged the candidates to discuss their devotion to family by asking questions about the candidates' families. For instance, Oprah asked both candidates about their relationships with their children. In one example, Oprah asked Bush, "Were you an active participant in their [his childrens'] life?" The general topics of the two candidates' talk were similar. For example, Oprah asked both of the candidates about the demands of heavy campaigning. Bush and Gore both responded with acclaims about their character. In response to Oprah's questions about how he could campaign six days a week: "It's a lot of work . . . . And—but you know something? I love it. I love the people of the country. I love what America stands for." In this excerpt, Bush acclaimed his personal quality of being a hard worker and his ideals. Similarly, Oprah asked Gore, "I know on Labor Day you campaigned for 27 hours straight. I mean, how do you do that and remain sane?" Gore also responded by acclaiming his character: "Well, there's one secret to that. If you believe in what you're doing then you get more energy." In this instance, Gore acclaimed his sincerity, a personal quality. These answers to a similar question from Oprah suggest that Bush and Gore were similar in their emphasis on character.

The prominence of character talk is consistent with the particular features of the talk show genre. Talk shows are a personal medium. As identified in previous studies (Haag, 1992/1993), audiences often develop pseudo-personal relationships with a talk show host. This personal ambiance likely influences the discourse of the candidates. The candidates' target audiences when they appear on these talk shows are likely less concerned with the policies of the candidates than with their personalities. Accordingly, the candidates would want to emphasize their character to these audiences: The candidates seek to portray an impression of high character value. This is consistent with research on television talk show appearances by political candidates in Europe (Bock, 1982; Hoffmann, 1982; Holly, Kuhn, & Puschel, 1986; Lang & Lang, 1968, 1984; Weiss, 1976). The candidates' primary goal in this venue is not to inform the audience on policy questions, when they did turn to questions of policy.

General goals (64 percent) were the most often used form of policy utterances, followed by future plans (18 percent) and past deeds (17 percent). Talk show programs are not the most appropriate venue for intricate details of specific policy proposals, so an emphasis on general goals is very appropriate. Candidates also focused more discussion on personal qualities (70 percent) than ideals (24 percent) or leadership ability (6 percent). The candidates used these appearances to portray themselves as personally agreeable rather than as policy wonks. In fact, when Gore appeared on *The Late Show with David Letterman*, Gore accused Letterman of being a "policy wonk" on the global warming issue. Gore, as well as Bush, on this program and other talk show programs, avoided intellectually challenging policy discussion and engaged in pleasant, friendly, and humorous personal conversation.

The issues addressed by the candidates did not appear to mirror the issues of most importance to voters. However, the issue most discussed by the two candidates, education, was the second most salient issue in the minds of those polled. We were surprised that there was not more consistency between the issues that were important to voters and the issues discussed by the candidates on television talk show programs. It is also possible that the issues important to the segment of voters who watched the programs were different from the sample used in the poll we selected. This is a possible line of future research: Do the candidates discuss the issues that are important to Oprah's viewers more when they appear on that program than when they appear on talk shows broadcast in other time slots? Future research could investigate such questions in an effort to better understand candidate discourse in this genre.

The results from this study suggest that the nature of candidate discourse on television talk shows possesses several characteristics, including a high number of acclaims and much discussion of character. The results of this study suggest that these candidates adapted to the talk show format rather than simply imposing their stock statements into the media form. As the discourse of these candidates was primarily positive and focused on character, voters may see aspects of the candidates in this format that are emphasized less in other media genres.

There are some limitations to this study of talk shows. First, we lack longitudinal data on candidate appearances on television talk shows. However, our analysis is a valuable attempt to begin to gather the data necessary for longitudinal analysis. Secondly, our functional approach favors words over images. For instance wardrobe decisions may impact audience evaluation of candidates. However, with the high dollar handlers on both sides, it is safe to assume that this type of appearance issue would be handled in similar ways. Also, nonverbal gestures, such as Bush's kissing Oprah on her program, could impact voter evaluation of candidate character. However, as evident in the Oprah example, if such nonverbal activity is notable, it is likely to be referred to in subsequent discourse. Despite these minor limitations, this study substantially increases our knowledge about presidential candidate discourse on television talk shows. Future research on other talk show appearances should include analysis using the functional theory of campaign discourse. We are establishing a "base-line" for a message form, television talk show discourse, that appears to be growing in importance in presidential campaigns.

## Appendix 15.1: Talk Show Appearances Studied

### Bush

*The Oprah Winfrey Show*, 9/19
*Larry King Live*, 9/26
*The Late Show with David Letterman*, 10/19

### Gore

*The Oprah Winfrey Show*, 9/11
*Larry King Live*, 9/28
*The Late Show with David Letterman*, 9/14

# Chapter 16

# Implications

This chapter will take up two topics. First, what was the outcome of the 2000 presidential primary and general campaigns? Second, what have we learned from our study of the messages in this election?

## Who Won (and by How Much)?

We will first discuss the outcome of the Republican and Democratic primary campaigns. Then we will discuss the contest between Bush and Gore in the conventions and general election campaign.

### 2000 Primary

The Republican primary was far more interesting and eventful than the Democratic primary. Senator John McCain was Governor George W. Bush's chief competitor. Husbanding his resources, McCain chose not to contest Iowa. Bush won with 41 percent of the Republican vote in the Iowa caucuses; Forbes came in second with 30.5 percent (Leip, 2001). However, McCain did contest New Hampshire, winning this primary handily (48.5 percent to 30.3 percent for Bush). Bush won Delaware and South Carolina (the latter challenged by McCain). McCain, in turn, won Michigan (49.1 percent to 41.5 percent) and Arizona (60.0 percent to 35.7 percent;

McCain also won Connecticut, Massachusetts, Rhode Island, and Vermont). From this point, however, the campaign turned in Bush's favor. He clinched the nomination with the Super Tuesday southern state elections (Kennedy, 2000). In the end, Bush prevailed with 60.2 percent of the Republican primary votes to McCain's 17.6 percent, and 84.8 percent of the delegates to McCain's 13.4 percent (Leip, 2001).

Senator Bill Bradley challenged Vice President Al Gore for the Democratic nomination. However, Gore clinched this nomination at the same time as Bush, during the southern Super Tuesday primaries (Kennedy, 2000). Gore received 75.9 percent of the Democratic primary votes and 90.6 percent of the delegates. Bradley obtained 20 percent of the votes and 9.4 percent of the delegates (Leip, 2001).

## Nominating Conventions and General Campaign

The campaign between Bush and Gore proved to be more interesting than even the Republican primaries had been. Bush began the race with a clear and consistent lead in the polls. Newport (2000a) wrote that "Bush has been ahead of Gore in every poll conducted by Gallup over the last two years" (p. 22). Bush padded his lead during the Republican Nominating Convention with the typical "convention bounce": The governor's lead increased by four percentage points (Saad, 2000). Bush had the early lead.

However, the situation did not remain static for long. The Democrats followed the Republican Convention with their own celebration. Saad reported that Gore gained ground against Bush:

> Gore's recent eight-point increase from 39 percent to 47 percent compares with a four-point bounce for Bush following the GOP convention earlier this month. Gore's increase in support also compares favorably with candidate post-convention bounces historically . . . . The average bounce across most of the Republican and Democratic conventions held since 1964 is roughly six percentage points. (p. 46)

Thus, both candidates improved their standing after their own party's convention, but Gore gained more than did Bush. Gore was beginning to assume the lead in the campaign for the presidency.

After the conventions, Gore slowly added to his advantage. Immediately following the Democratic convention, Gore had a one point lead, 47 percent to 46 percent (Saad, 2000), which was within the margin of error. Newport (2000c) explained that during September, Gore led by an average margin of 47 percent to 44 percent. On September 20, Gore led by a 51 percent to 41 percent margin (Newport, 2000b). Now it appeared as if Gore was in command.

But then came the presidential debates and the vice president was unable to maintain his advantage through this phase of the campaign. By the first two weeks of October, Bush managed to reverse their standing, with an average of 47 percent to 43 percent. Once again, the lead had shifted in this hotly contested race.

## The Outcome

On election eve, the networks first called Florida for Bush, then for Gore, and then decided not to call the Florida election for anyone. This state proved to be pivotal, because neither Bush nor Gore had 270 electoral votes without it. The election was hotly contested, both in the precincts where vote recounts occurred and in the courts where the legality of recounts was questioned. Key players included Kathleen Harris, Florida secretary of state, whose responsibility is to certify the election outcome. However, controversy arose because Harris was a Bush campaign official who refused to recuse herself from this task (George W. Bush's brother Jeb, governor of Florida, did recuse himself). The Florida Supreme Court was entirely Democratic (although they were not Gore campaign officials). Eventually, the Supreme Court of the United States stopped the recount process. We find it ironic that a Republican who advocates state power over federal power (Bush) would ask the (federal) Supreme Court to intervene in a state election recount.

Ultimately, Gore won the popular vote by 533,002 votes (National Archives, 2001) while Bush won the Electoral College by 271 to 266. While Gore persuaded more citizens to vote for him, constitutionally, the winner of the Electoral College vote is the candidate who becomes president.

# Implications

This chapter will discuss the findings of our investigation into the discourse of the presidential campaign 2000. First, we examine separately the phases of this campaign. Then, we compare primary discourse with general campaign messages (television spots, debates, web pages, radio spots, and talk show appearances). Third, we will compare the discourse from 2000 with the campaign messages from 1996. Finally, we will discuss the contributions of this study to our understanding of presidential campaign discourse.

## Primary Campaign Discourse

The primary phase of Campaign 2000 was particularly interesting because, unlike the case in 1996, both parties featured contested nominations. This is an important difference, because in 1996 Bill Clinton could use primary messages to attack his likely opponent, Bob Dole, instead of trying to deal with challengers from within his own party. In 2000, George W. Bush quickly emerged as the Republican favorite, with the most money and endorsements. Nevertheless, the Texas governor faced a serious challenge from Senator John McCain, particularly in New Hampshire, South Carolina, and Michigan. Other Republicans, including Gary Bauer, Pat Buchanan, Elizabeth Dole, Steve Forbes, Orrin Hatch, Alan Keyes, and Dan Quayle, also vied for the 2000 GOP nomination. On the Democratic side, former Senator Bill Bradley was Vice President Al Gore's only challenger for the nomination. We investigated campaign 2000 Republican and Democratic primary campaign messages in five media: television spots, debates, web pages, radio spots, and television talk show appearances.

Inspection of Table 16.1 reveals that acclaims were the most common function of 2000 primary discourse. This was true across all five message forms (a mean of 80 percent acclaims) and in each message form (72 percent-95 percent acclaims). Web pages were clearly the most positive message form (95 percent acclaims) in this campaign. However, television spots were also extremely positive (86 percent). The other message forms were clustered together: Radio spots remarks were 75 percent positive, debate utterances were 73 percent positive, and television talk shows comments were 72 percent positive.

Attacks in primary messages were less common than acclaims, but still occurred with some frequency. Negative remarks constituted 17 percent of all primary themes and ranged from 5 percent to 25 percent in specific message forms, so attacks were much less common than acclaims but more frequent than defenses. Attacks were most frequent in radio spots (25 percent) and debates (24 percent). Talk shows (17 percent) and television spots (13 percent) had noticeably fewer attacks. Web pages had the fewest attacks of any primary medium we investigated in 2000 (5 percent).

Defenses were uncommon in the 2000 primary campaign: In the aggregate, defenses were the least frequent function at 3 percent. They varied from none to 12 percent in the primary message forms. Defenses were most common in television talk shows (12 percent), less so in debates (3 percent) and television spots (0.7 percent), virtually nonexistent in web pages (0.1 percent). Although defenses were not very frequent, only one message form—radio spots—included no defenses whatsoever.

This distribution of campaign discourse functions is readily explicable. Acclaims (if accepted by the audience) can increase a candidate's perceived preferability without any disadvantages. Attacks may increase a candidate's *net* preferability by diminishing the apparent favorability of an opponent. However, voters routinely report that they do not like mudslinging (Merritt, 1984; Stewart, 1975) which means it is possible that there could be some backlash from an attack. This is not to say attacks should never be employed; voters need to know both the pros and cons of a candidate. No wise candidate will dwell on his or her weaknesses, so voters must turn to opponents to learn of a candidate's disadvantages (or to the news, which is less effective in conveying candidates' drawbacks because

Table 16.1. Functions of 2000 Campaign Messages

|  | Acclaims | Attacks | Defenses |
|---|---|---|---|
| Primary | | | |
| TV Spots | 86% | 13% | 1% |
| Debates | 73% | 24% | 3% |
| Web Pages | 95% | 5% | 0.1% |
| Radio Spots | 75% | 25% | 0.2% |
| Talk Shows | 72% | 17% | 12% |
| Primary | 80% | 17% | 3% |
| Conventions | | | |
| Featured | 78% | 22% | 0.1% |
| Acceptances | 89% | 11% | 0 |
| Spouses | 100% | 0 | 0 |
| Conventions | 89% | 11% | 0.3% |
| General | | | |
| TV Spots | 58% | 42% | 1% |
| Debates | 74% | 24% | 2% |
| Web Pages | 98% | 2% | 0 |
| Radio Spots | 22% | 78% | 0 |
| Talk Shows | 91% | 5% | 4% |
| General | 69% | 30% | 1% |
| Total | 79% | 19% | 1% |

of its heavy emphasis on horse race coverage). Thus, we should expect attacks to occur but be less common than acclaims. This was true in the aggregate and in every primary message form.

Defenses, in contrast, possess several important liabilities. First, it is impossible to counter an accusation with certainty without identifying the criticism being refuted. However, the act of identifying an attack, in order to refute it, could inform (or remind) voters of an attack that they had not heard (or that they had forgotten). Second, the very act of defending is reactive rather than proactive and candidates may not wish to appear "on the defensive." Third, attacks, by their very nature, usually occur on topics that do not favor the target of the attack. In other words, responding to an attack probably takes a candidate "off message," spending time on topics favorable to the defending candidate's opponent. Of course, attacks can be damaging, reducing the target's apparent preferability, and so defense is at times appropriate. Nevertheless, there are three clear drawbacks to defenses, so it is no surprise that defenses were the least common function in the primary campaign of 2000. In fact, both in the aggregate and in every primary message form, defenses were the least common function of Campaign 2000.

These data mirror historic trends. Benoit, Pier, Brazeal, McHale, Klyukovski, and Airne (2002) found that in primary debates from 1948 to 2000, acclaims were most common (63 percent), attacks occurred at moderate levels (32 percent), and defenses were the least frequent function (4 percent). Similarly, Benoit's (1999) analysis of primary television spots from 1952 to 1996 found that acclaims (68 percent) outnumbered attacks (31 percent) which in turn outnumbered defenses (1 percent).

Overall, more attacks (42 percent) were directed toward other members of one's own party in the Campaign 2000 primary messages we analyzed. The preferred target of attack in three primary message forms (debates, radio spots, and talk shows) was other members of the attacker's own political party. The status quo was the recipient of most attacks in two message forms (television spots and web pages). No message form in the 2000 primaries directed most attacks to the opposing party. These data are displayed in Table 16.2.

Analysis of presidential primary debates from 1948 to 2000 (Benoit, Pier, Brazeal, McHale, Klyukovski, & Airne, 2002) found that those candidates attacked their own party (47 percent) more than candidates from the other party (30 percent) or the status quo (24 percent). Although there is scant research on target of campaign attacks, this finding in Campaign 2000 primary message forms is consistent with previous research.

Table 16.2. Target of Attack in 2000 Primary Campaign Messages

|  | Own Party | Other Party | SQ |
|---|---|---|---|
| TV Spots | 33% | 14% | 53% |
| Debates | 57% | 25% | 18% |
| Web Pages | 6% | 37% | 57% |
| Radio Spots | 62% | 15% | 23% |
| Talk Shows | 68% | 20% | 12% |
| Total | 45% | 22% | 33% |

It is reasonable for candidates to attack members of their own party most frequently. For example, in 2000, John McCain (or Forbes, Hatch, Bauer, Keyes) had to get past the front-runner, George Bush, before he earned the "right" to face Clinton. An attack by McCain on Gore, for example, might not narrow the gap between Bush and McCain as much as an attack on Bush. The other members of one's own party are one's immediate opponents in the primary candidate, and, in the aggregate, that is where most attacks are directed.

Two message forms (television spots, web pages) attacked the status quo most frequently. This may be in part due to the dynamics of Campaign 2000. Virtually every candidate ran as a "Washington outsider." Bush was a state governor. Forbes, Keyes, and Bauer had never held elective office in Washington. Bradley had been a senator but was not currently in office. McCain was a senator, but he was positioned as a maverick senator, often opposed to the establishment line. Even Vice President Al Gore was reluctant to fully exploit his incumbency status, choosing to distance himself not just personally from Clinton but to a large extent downplaying Clinton/Gore policy accomplishments (unwisely in our opinion). Thus, in Campaign 2000 many candidates attacked the status quo, positioning themselves as "Washington Outsiders," and this emphasis emerged particularly in television spots and web pages.

We also examined the topics of these messages, which are summarized in Table 16.3. Overall, 56 percent of primary message functions addressed policy, whereas 44 percent concerned character. However, these messages were not as consistent in distribution of topics as they were in functions. Policy dominated web pages (79 percent), debates (68 percent), and television spots (56 percent). However, character prevailed in television talk show appearances (65 percent) and radio spots (58 percent).

An emphasis on policy, observed in three of the message forms in our sample, may stem from voter preferences. A poll taken in at the beginning of the primary season in October of 1999 revealed that 90 percent of voters indicated that policy was the most important determinant of their presidential vote; only 8 percent cited character (Princeton, 1999). Thus, an emphasis on policy in campaign messages may be a shrewd response to voter interests.

Web pages devoted almost four out of every five comments to policy. This is, we believe, due to the fact that web designers have (virtually) unlimited space, compared with the limited amounts of time in television or radio spots or talk show appearances. Policy, particularly at the presidential level, is arguably more complex than character. That is, a candidate can say more about foreign policy (e.g., trade, immigration, global warming, national defense) and domestic policy (e.g., taxes, education, employment, health care, poverty, transportation, labor) than about character. Not only is it possible that there are more policy than character topics, but it may also be the case that there is often more to say about a given topic (national defense could include discussion of troop size and pay, of weapons systems and procurement, of particular global "hot-spots" and troop deployment,

Table 16.3. Topics of 2000 Campaign Messages

|  | Policy | Character |
|---|---|---|
| Primary | | |
| TV Spots | 56% | 44% |
| Debates | 68% | 32% |
| Web Pages | 79% | 21% |
| Radio Spots | 42% | 58% |
| Talk Shows | 35% | 65% |
| Primary | 56% | 44% |
| Conventions | | |
| Featured | 45% | 55% |
| Acceptances | 55% | 45% |
| Spouses | 24% | 76% |
| Conventions | 41% | 59% |
| General | | |
| TV Spots | 70% | 30% |
| Debates | 76% | 24% |
| Web Pages | 90% | 10% |
| Radio Spots | 74% | 26% |
| Talk Shows | 33% | 67% |
| General | 69% | 31% |
| Total | 55% | 45% |

of the number and location of military bases, and so forth; it might be challenging to find as many subtopics when discussing, say, courage or compassion). In designing a web page, a candidate need not make choices about allocating scarce resources. If there is a policy topic of interest to some voters, the candidate can take a position on it in a web page at (comparatively) little cost. Thus, we should expect that, given the peculiar nature of this campaign medium, presidential campaign web pages should devote more space to policy than character.

Television talk shows, one of the two message forms which discussed character more than policy, would be expected to focus on character, given that many such programs are driven by personalities. The audiences such shows attract are probably not populated mainly by those obsessed with the details of policy, which encourages hosts to ask about the candidates as individuals and candidates to emphasize introducing themselves to the audience.

The other message form with more discussion of character than policy was radio spots. Chapter 6 reveals that our sample of primary radio spots consisted of over twice as many Republican as Democratic spots. The Democrats discussed policy more than character in their primary radio spots. However, Republicans (who had more spots in our sample than Democrats) emphasized character more than policy. Thus, the tendency of radio spots to emphasize character over policy can be attributed to Republican candidates. Ever since Bush faced Clinton in the 1992 general election, Republicans have worked to make character an issue in presidential campaigns. It seems that this effort continued in the 2000 primary campaign.

A tendency to address policy more often than character is also consistent with historic trends. Data from presidential primary debates from 1948 to 2000 (Benoit, Pier, Brazeal, McHale, Klyukovski, & Airne, 2002) indicate that policy was discussed more than character (63 percent to 37 percent). Benoit (1999) found a slight preference for policy in television spots from 1952 to 1996 (52 percent to 48 percent).

Next, we considered the forms of policy and character deployed in these primary messages. Overall, general goals (58 percent) were the most common form of policy, whereas personal qualities dominated the character discussion (52 percent). These two kinds of utterances predominated in four messages forms: television spots, debates, radio spots, and talk shows. See Table 16.4.

There are reasons to expect an emphasis on general goals in campaign discourse. As indicated before, in the 2000 primary campaign many candidates had not held office (Bauer, Forbes, and Keyes). Bradley had left the Senate; Bush was a state governor. Only McCain currently held federal office (Senate). Even Gore was reluctant to run on the Clinton-Gore record. This meant that opportunities for acclaiming or attack past deeds were relatively scarce. Furthermore, general goals are much easier to proclaim than (specific) future plans. Hence, especially in a field of candidates who could not or would not stress past deeds, general goals are a plausible policy utterance.

However, this emphasis on general goals is not a consistent feature of presidential primary rhetoric. In presidential primary debates, past deeds are the most common form of policy remark (Benoit, Pier, Brazeal, McHale, Klyukovski, & Airne, 2002) at 43 percent. Similarly, primary television spots from 1952 to 1996 (Benoit, 1999) tend to stress general goals. These results suggest that Campaign 2000 may have differed from previous campaigns in use of the forms of policy.

Table 16.4. Forms of Policy and Character in 2000 Primary Campaign Messages

| | Policy | | | Character | | |
|---|---|---|---|---|---|---|
| | Past Deeds* | Future Plans | General Goals | Personal Qualities | Leader-ship | Ideals |
| TV Spots | 66    44 | 74    16 | 309    19 | 214    44 | 60    2 | 90    6 |
| | 110 (21%) | 90 (17%) | 328 (62%) | 258 (63%) | 62 (15%) | 96 (23%) |
| Debate | 481    501 | 542    227 | 1741    136 | 386    407 | 273    22 | 598    25 |
| | 982 (27%) | 769 (21%) | 1877 (52%) | 793 (46%) | 295 (17%) | 623 (36%) |
| Web Pages | 705    102 | 1143    3 | 949    25 | 151    5 | 70    2 | 510    34 |
| | 807 (28%) | 1146 (39%) | 974 (33%) | 156 (20%) | 72 (9%) | 544 (70%) |
| Radio Spots | 44    37 | 24    11 | 184    47 | 192    68 | 48    6 | 137    37 |
| | 81 (23%) | 35 (11%) | 231 (67%) | 260 (53%) | 54 (11%) | 174 (36%) |
| Talk Shows | 30    29 | 36    4 | 249    41 | 427    118 | 45    3 | 119    26 |
| | 59 (15%) | 40 (10%) | 290 (75%) | 545 (75%) | 48 (7%) | 135 (19%) |
| Total | 23% | 20% | 58% | 51% | 12% | 37% |

*acclaims/attacks. Note: because of the wide variance in frequency of utterances, the figures for totals are means of means (rather than means of total utterances).

The distribution of character comments in 2000 stressed personal qualities. Primary television spots (Benoit, 1999) also stressed personal qualities, but primary debates (Benoit, Pier, Brazeal, McHale, Klyukovski, & Airne, 2002) emphasized ideals. This could mean that no single form of character utterance stands out in presidential primary messages. It is possible that the emphasis on personal qualities in 2000 is a result of an intensification of the Republican attack on Bill Clinton's personal qualities. Gore, too, discussed his personal qualities in this campaign. Although it was not a primary message, his nomination acceptance address stressed that "We're entering a new time. We're electing a new president. And I stand here tonight as my own man. And I want you to know me for who I truly am." Thus, the stress on personal qualities in Campaign 2000 may in part be due to a reaction—even on the part of Democrats—to President Clinton's personal foibles.

The anomalous message form in the distribution of forms of policy and character was web pages. Web pages stressed future plans (41 percent) more than general goals (31 percent; or than past deeds, 29 percent). However, this is likely an understandable result for this medium. One of the problems with discussing future plans is that it is much quicker to posit a goal (reduce poverty) than to provide specific plans for implementing that goal. However, unlike other message forms, web pages have (virtually) unlimited space at a very low cost. Therefore, it makes good sense that the message form with the most discussion of future plans would be web pages.

It is unclear why web pages would be so enamored with ideals; 70 percent of all of the character comments on Internet sites dealt with ideals. It is possible that this is a reaction to the likely audiences. Although anyone (with web access)—friend, foe, or undecided voter—can log onto a candidate's web page and browse, we suspect that the most common web visitor would be the candidate's partisan supporters. This could lead candidates to stress their ideals and lofty principles (ideals).

## Convention Discourse

The convention speeches we examined focused on acclaims in the aggregate (89 percent) and individually (79-100 percent). Attacks were the second most common function collectively (11 percent) and individually (0-21 percent). Finally, defenses were quite rare in convention speeches (0.3 percent). These data are included in Table 16.1. As indicated above, it is reasonable to find that acclaims are more frequent than attacks, which in turn should outnumber defenses.

Acceptance addresses were more positive (89 percent) than featured speeches (79 percent). This is consistent with previous research on acceptances (Benoit, Wells, Pier, & Blaney, 1999) and keynotes (Benoit, Blaney, & Pier, 2000). Surrogates are likely to attack more than the candidates themselves. Benoit (1999) also found that presidential television spots were more negative when someone other than the candidate (an anonymous announcer, an ordinary citizen; in short, a surrogate) was speaking. Presumably the belief is that when a surrogate attacks, any backlash from voter dislike of mudslinging will hurt the surrogate more than the candidate. But when a candidate attacks, such backlash must strike the candidate. So, surrogates are used more frequently to deliver attacks than the candidates themselves.

Convention speeches as a group tended to focus on character (61 percent) more than policy (39 percent). This was particularly pronounced in speeches from the spouses (76 percent), who might be expected to focus on their husbands' character. The candidates' acceptance addresses were the only convention form studied that emphasized policy (55 percent) more than character (45 percent). Given the fact that recent conventions celebrate the parties' nominees rather than select them, it seems reasonable for convention speeches to focus on character. However, because the nominee will oversee the federal government if elected, it makes sense for candidates to address policy more in their acceptance speeches than the other convention speakers. These data can also be found in Table 16.3.

Acceptance addresses from 1960 to 1996 discussed policy in 56 percent of utterances and character in 44 percent of their remarks (Benoit, Wells, Pier, & Blaney, 1999). Thus, the acceptances in 2000 were quite consistent with historic trends. Keynote speeches from 1960 to 1996 (Benoit, Blaney, & Pier, 2000) also revealed an advantage for policy (56 percent) over character (44 percent). Featured speeches in 2000 discussed character more than keynotes in the past (again, the Republicans did not designate a keynote in 2000, which makes comparisons more difficult).

Turning to forms of policy and character, we find an emphasis on general goals (46 percent overall; over 50 percent in acceptances and featured speeches; there were only twelve policy comments in spouses' speeches so it makes little sense to dwell on forms of policy in those messages). This result is, again, probably due to an effort to portray the Republican nominee as a Washington outsider—and an effort by the Democratic nominee to distance himself from President Clinton. We also find that (except for featured speakers, who might be expect to embrace lofty goals) that convention speeches stressed personal qualities (44 percent). These data are displayed in Table 16.5.

General goals were the most common form of utterance in keynotes (Benoit, Blaney, & Pier, 2000);  Acceptances from 1960 to 1996  stressed past deeds (74 percent; Benoit, Wells, Pier, & Blaney, 1999). While Bush was a governor, and did discuss past deeds, arguably a record in that office is not as powerful as evidence

Table 16.5. Forms of Policy and Character in 2000 Convention Speeches

|  | Policy | | | Character | | |
|---|---|---|---|---|---|---|
|  | Past Deeds* | Future Plans | General Goals | Personal Qualities | Leadership | Ideals |
| Accept | 31    10 | 30    6 | 98    1 | 67    10 | 16    8 | 43    1 |
|  | 41 (23%) | 36 (20%) | 99 (55%) | 77 (53%) | 24 (17%) | 44 (30%) |
| Spouse | 7    0 | 2    0 | 3    0 | 18    0 | 12    0 | 9    0 |
|  | 7 (58%) | 2 (17%) | 3 (25%) | 18 (46%) | 12 (31%) | 9 (23%) |
| Featured | 36    18 | 3    1 | 51    14 | 37    7 | 34    10 | 58    12 |
|  | 54 (44%) | 4 (3%) | 65 (53%) | 42 (28%) | 44 (28%) | 70 (44%) |
| Total | 42% | 13% | 44% | 42% | 25% | 32% |

*Acclaims/attacks.  Note: because of the wide variance in frequency of utterances, the figures for totals are means of means (rather than means of total utterances).

from the record of a sitting president (like Clinton in 1996 or Bush in 1992). Gore occasionally touted his past deeds (and attacked Bush's record in Texas), but he failed to adequately exploit the Clinton/Gore record. Both keynotes (66 percent) and acceptances (69 percent) from 1960 to 1996 emphasized ideals. Again, the emphasis on personal qualities in 2000 may have been a backlash against President Clinton.

## General Campaign Discourse

Acclaims also were the predominant discourse function in the general campaign (see Table 16.1). Overall, 69 percent of the utterances in these messages were acclaims. Virtually all of the utterances on candidate web pages were positive (98 percent). Television talk show appearances were heavily skewed to acclaims (91 percent). Three-quarters of the utterances in the debates were positive. Television spots employed 58 percent acclaims. Only general radio spots devoted fewer than half of their remarks to acclaims (22 percent). Thus, overall (and with only one exception, radio spots) general campaign messages employed acclaims most frequently.

Again with only a single exception, attacks were the second most common function in these messages. Television spots employed numerous attacks (42 percent). Negative statements accounted for a quarter of the candidates' debate utterances. Attacks were quite rare in television talk shows (5 percent) and web pages (2 percent). In contrast, attacks were the most common utterance function in radio spots (78 percent). Thus, again except for radio ads, general campaign discourse used attacks as the second most common function.

Defenses were the least common function in the 2000 presidential campaign (1 percent). Defenses were most frequent in TV talk shows (4 percent), less so in debates (2 percent) and in television spots (1 percent). Web pages and radio spots in our sample of messages contained no defenses. As discussed earlier, there is good reason to expect acclaims to outnumber attacks and for defenses to be the least frequent function.

This distribution of functions mirrors past presidential campaign discourse. Television spots from 1952 to 1996 employed 60 percent acclaims, 39 percent attacks, and 1 percent defenses (Benoit, 1999). It is also consistent with past research on presidential debates (Benoit & Brazeal, in press; Benoit & Harthcock, 1999b; Benoit, Blaney, & Pier, 1998; Benoit & Wells, 1996; Wells, 1999). As explained earlier, this distribution of message functions is readily understandable.

General radio spots in 2000 bucked this trend in allocation of functions. There are two possible explanations. First, we were not completely satisfied with the composition of our sample of general radio spots, as discussed in chapter 14. It is possible that our sample was skewed toward negative radio spots. Second, radio advertisements tend to "fly underneath the radar." Ad watches and stories frequently discuss television spots (e.g., consider the furor over the apparent use of subliminal use of "RATS" in a Republican television spot), but we are not aware of any ad watches focusing on radio spots. The campaigns may feel more free to attack the opposition in this particular campaign medium.

General campaign messages tended to emphasize policy (69 percent) over character (31 percent). These data are also included in Table 16.2. In fact, with one exception (television talk shows), every message form devoted at least 70 percent of utterances to policy. The content of candidate web pages were 90 percent policy. This means that, again with a single exception, no more than 30 percent of any of the general campaign message forms we analyzed concerned character. Only television talk shows focused more on character (67 percent) than policy (33 percent). As noted earlier, voters have expressed a decided preference for policy over character in their presidential votes. Furthermore, as noted above, there is less reason for character to be prominent in the general than the primary campaign. Thus, it makes sense for these messages to emphasize policy over character. This emphasis on topic is also consistent with findings for television spots (Benoit, 1999) and debates (Benoit & Brazeal, in press; Benoit & Harthcock, 1999b; Benoit, Blaney, & Pier, 1998; Benoit & Wells, 1996; Wells, 1999).

The lone exception to this emphasis of general campaign messages on policy, as just noted, was television talk shows. As discussed earlier, talk shows are more about meeting than candidates (about character) than delving into the nuances of policy. These are personal encounters, in which the host or hostess interacts with candidates one-on-one. Some television talk shows (daytime and late night) are designed more for entertainment and personalities than for serious policy discussion. Only news-oriented talk shows, like *Larry King Live*, might be expected to have much emphasis on policy.

Once again we see that Campaign 2000 messages emphasized general goals (46 percent of policy utterances in the general campaign) and personal qualities (49 percent of character utterances in the general campaign). While both candidates had past accomplishments they could acclaim (or their opponent could attack), neither candidate was a sitting president. George Bush's experience as Texas governor was a source for both acclaims (by Bush) and attacks (by Gore), and it was used occasionally by both candidates. However, those accomplishments were not stressed as much as they could have been. This may be because having been a governor is seen as a form of governmental (executive) experience, but it is not the same as being president (in particular, governors have no foreign policy experience). Similarly, while Gore could (and did, occasionally) acclaim the Clinton/Gore record, just as Bush could (and did) attack it, experience as vice president is seen to be as valuable as being president (e.g., Clinton running for re-election in 1996 or Bush in 1992). Furthermore, as mentioned earlier, Gore appeared to be exerting considerable effort to distance himself from Clinton (and Clinton/Gore accomplishments). Thus, these candidates tended to stress their goals more than their accomplishments. See Table 16.6.

This is not what one would expect from previous research. Television spots emphasize past deeds (58 percent) most frequently (Benoit, 1999), as do debates (Benoit & Brazeal, in press; Benoit & Harthcock, 1999b; Benoit, Blaney, & Pier, 1998; Benoit & Wells, 1996; Wells, 1999). As suggested above, neither Bush nor Gore were "true" incumbents, which might account for less frequent use of past deeds.

Web pages are one exception; possibly the almost unlimited space allows ample opportunity to recount the minutia of governmental experience for visitors inclined to "dig" through the web page. It was surprising that television spots (often rather vague) had so many future plans (39 percent). Perhaps these candidates were reacting to the idea that TV spots were fluff by stressing their policy proposals in them. Of course, thirty seconds is not enough time to discuss policy in any depth, but the candidates could, and did, appraise voters of the existence of their plans (e.g., for prescription drug coverage).

As in the primary, general candidate web pages stressed ideals (64 percent) more than the norm, presumably for much the same reasons (difficulty of targeting the audience for web pages may lead candidates to stress their values and lofty

Table 16.6. Forms of Policy and Character in 2000 General Campaign Messages

| | Policy | | | | | Character | | | | | |
| --- | --- | --- | --- | --- | --- | --- | --- | --- | --- | --- | --- | --- |
| | Past Deeds* | | Future Plans | | General Goals | | Personal Qualities | | Leader-ship | | Ideals | |
| TV Spots | 28 | 84 | 90 | 64 | 123 | 7 | 58 | 61 | 12 | 3 | 31 | 4 |
| | 112 (28%) | | 154 (39%) | | 130 (33%) | | 119 (70%) | | 15 (9%) | | 35 (21%) | |
| Debates | 107 | 55 | 135 | 69 | 424 | 75 | 50 | 52 | 88 | 20 | 56 | 10 |
| | 162 (19%) | | 204 (24%) | | 499 (57%) | | 102 (37%) | | 108 (39%) | | 66 (24%) | |
| Web Pages | 2563 | 74 | 785 | 0 | 672 | 5 | 106 | 1 | 49 | 2 | 282 | 4 |
| | 2637 (64%) | | 785 (19%) | | 677 (17%) | | 107 (24%) | | 51 (11%) | | 286 (64%) | |
| Radio Spots | 4 | 46 | 0 | 27 | 17 | 20 | 6 | 11 | 6 | 12 | 1 | 6 |
| | 50 (44%) | | 27 (24%) | | 37 (32%) | | 17 (40%) | | 18 (43%) | | 7 (17%) | |
| Talk Shows | 26 | 11 | 30 | 10 | 139 | 3 | 306 | 12 | 28 | 0 | 106 | 1 |
| | 37 (17%) | | 40 (18%) | | 142 (65%) | | 318 (70%) | | 28 (6%) | | 107 (24%) | |
| Total | 34% | | 25% | | 41% | | 49% | | 21% | | 30% | |

*Acclaims/attacks. Note: because of the wide variance in frequency of utterances, the figures for totals are means of means (rather than means of total utterances).

principles). The other exception to the emphasis of general campaign messages on personal qualities were the debates. However, personal qualities were a close second (37 percent personal qualities; 39 percent leadership ability). The fact that debates discussed policy almost twice as much as other general message forms (the mean was 20 percent) may have more to do with the questions posed to the candidates in the debates than with their preferred emphasis.

Historically, personal qualities (49 percent) are the most common form of utterance in general television spots (Benoit, 1999). General debates, on the other hand, used ideals (40 percent) somewhat more than personal qualities (35 percent; Benoit & Brazeal, in press; Benoit & Harthcock, 1999b; Benoit, Blaney, & Pier, 1998; Benoit & Wells, 1996; Wells, 1999). These two forms of character are typically the most common form of character utterance.

As with other campaign phases, we find important similarities and differences across these message forms. Both similarities and differences occur within the 2000 campaign message forms and in comparison with findings on earlier campaign messages. The similarities—like the fact that acclaims tend to be more frequent than attacks, which in turn are more common than defenses—are evidence that the situation (presidential campaign) exerts an important influence on the discourse produced by these candidates. However, the fact that some message forms deviate from the norm (e.g., television talk shows or spousal speeches emphasize character or personality more than other messages forms) reveals that the situation does not necessarily determine the nature of discourse and that message form (medium) influences discourse production.

## Primary Versus General Campaign Discourse

We next compare the discourse produced in the primary and the general phases of campaign 2000. In our study, we investigated five message forms in both of these campaign phases: television spots, debates, web pages, radio spots, and television talk show appearances. We will discuss functions and topics of these messages forms in primary and general campaign phases.

No clear picture emerges from our analysis of the functions of primary and general messages (see Table 16.7). In the aggregate, primary messages employed more acclaims (80 percent to 69 percent) and defenses (3 percent to 1 percent) than general messages, whereas general messages used more attacks than primary messages (30 percent to 17 percent). Television spots are more positive in the primary (86 percent) than the general campaign (58 percent), and this difference is significant ($\chi^2[df=1]=159.1$, $p < .001$; defenses were excluded because they were infrequent). Radio spots were also significantly more positive in the primary (78 percent) than the general (22 percent) campaign ($\chi^2[df=1]=165.3$, $p < .001$; defenses were excluded because they were infrequent). However, web pages were extremely positive in both phases of the campaign (95 percent acclaims in the primary; 98 percent acclaims in the

Table 16.7. Functions of 2000 Campaign Messages by Campaign Phase

| | Acclaims | | Attacks | | Defenses | | $\chi^2$ |
|---|---|---|---|---|---|---|---|
| | Pri. | Gen. | Pri. | Gen. | Pri. | Gen. | |
| TV Spots | 828 | 328 | 129 | 236 | 7 | 4 | 164.4 |
| | (86%) | (58%) | (13%) | (42%) | (7%) | (7%) | $p < .001$ |
| Debates | 4021 | 860 | 1318 | 281 | 159 | 24 | 2.5 |
| | (73%) | (74%) | (24%) | (24%) | (3%) | (2%) | ns |
| Web Pages | 3593 | 4452 | 200 | 86 | 4 | 0 | 3.7 |
| | (95%) | (98%) | (5%) | (2%) | (1%) | | ns* |
| Radio | 630 | 34 | 211 | 121 | 0 | 0 | 165.3 |
| Spots | (76%) | (22%) | (24%) | (78%) | | | $p < .001$ |
| Talk | 896 | 635 | 211 | 37 | 144 | 31 | 67.9 |
| Shows | (72%) | (91%) | (17%) | (5%) | (11%) | (4%) | $p < .001$ |
| Total | 80% | 69% | 17% | 30% | 3% | 1% | |

*Defenses excluded because of infrequency. Note: because of the wide variance in frequency of utterances, the figures for totals are means of means (rather than means of total utterances).

general campaign) and there was no significant difference in web page function by campaign phase. About three-quarters of debate utterances were acclaims in both phases (once again, the difference was not significant).

In contrast, discourse from television talk show appearances was significantly ($\chi^2[df=2]=93.2, p < .001$) more negative in the primary (17 percent) than in the general (5 percent) campaign. Attacks were the mirror image of acclaims (fewer attacks in the primary stage in radio and television spots; no difference by stage in debates and web pages; more attacks in the primary for television talk show appearances).

Previous research (Benoit, 1999) has found that primary television spots (1952-1996) employed more acclaims and fewer attacks than general television spots, so the finding that 2000 primary spots are more positive than general spots is consistent with previous research. However, research on primary debates found that they too tend to have more acclaims than general debates (Benoit, Pier, Brazeal, McHale, Klyukovski, & Airne, 2002). In 2000, there were no significant differences in the functions of debate utterances between the two campaign phases. It may be that, particularly in the Republican primary debates, the campaign became more heated and more attacks were used (Republicans did attack significantly more often than Democrats in 2000).

Why would talk shows be more positive in the general campaign? In our sample, television talk shows were the only message form to have significantly more attacks in the primary than the general campaign. This is probably due to the nature of our sample of talk show discourse. The primary talk shows tended to be news-oriented (*Meet the Press*, *Face the Nation*, *Larry King Live*) while the general talk shows were more entertainment focused (*The Oprah Winfrey Show, Late Night with David Letterman*, and, once again, *Larry King Live*). It seems likely that candidates moderated their attacks on the more entertainment-oriented shows of our general campaign sample. Thus, it may be that there are what might be termed "subgenres" of television talk shows, with some being more news-oriented and others more entertainment-oriented. It appears that in campaign 2000, candidates tended to appear more frequently on news-oriented talk shows in the primary and entertainment-oriented talk shows in the general campaign. This could account for the fact that (in our sample) television talk show discourse was more negative in the primary than the general campaign.

Primary messages (except television talk shows) focused less on policy, and more on character, than general messages. Primary television spots focused significantly less ($\chi^2[df=1]=3.0$, $p < .001$) on policy (56 percent) than general spots (70 percent). Similarly, primary debates discussed policy (68 percent) less frequently than general debates (76 percent) ($\chi^2[df=1]=27.4$, $p < .001$). Primary web pages devoted significantly fewer ($\chi^2[df=1]=211.2$, $p < .001$) comments to policy (79 percent) than primary web pages (90 percent). Primary radio spots had significantly fewer ($\chi^2[df=1]=64.5$, $p < .001$) policy remarks (42 percent) than general ads (77 percent). There was no difference ($\chi^2[df=1]=1.0$, *ns*) in the number of policy utterances in primary (35 percent) and general (33 percent) TV talk show appearances. See Table 16.8.

There are several reasons to expect primary messages to discuss character more, and policy less, than general messages. First, candidates are less well known in the

Table 16.8. Topics of 2000 Campaign Messages by Campaign Phase

| | Policy | | Character | | $\chi^2$ |
|---|---|---|---|---|---|
| | Primary | General | Primary | General | |
| TV Spots | 533 | 396 | 414 | 168 | 9.6 |
| | (56%) | (70%) | (44%) | (30%) | $p < .01$ |
| Debates | 3626 | 865 | 1711 | 276 | 27.4 |
| | (68%) | (76%) | (32%) | (24%) | $p < .001$ |
| Web Pages | 2992 | 4094 | 805 | 444 | 2.6 |
| | (79%) | (90%) | (21%) | (10%) | *ns* |
| Radio Spots | 351 | 119 | 490 | 36 | 1.9 |
| | (42%) | (77%) | (58%) | (23%) | *ns* |
| TV Talk | 390 | 219 | 727 | 453 | 10.5 |
| | (35%) | (33%) | (65%) | (67%) | $p < .01$ |
| Total | 56% | 69% | 44% | 31% | |

Note: because of the wide variance in frequency of utterances, the figures for totals are means of means (rather than means of total utterances).

primary phase. First, the primary features such candidates as Gary Bauer and Orrin Hatch. Neither is as well known as Bush or Gore (the principal general campaign contestants). Furthermore, even Bush and Gore were surely better known in the general campaign than they were in the primary. Thus, primary messages have a greater need to introduce the candidates and this should encourage them to discuss character. Second, primary contests are contests between the politicians from the same political party, vying for the nomination. While there are differences between Republicans (or between Democrats), ordinarily there should be more policy differences between a Republican and a Democrat (in the general campaign) than between Republicans or between Democrats. In other words, there is a greater opportunity to discuss policy in the general phase.

## Campaign 1996 Versus Campaign 2000

We would also like to contrast our results from this investigation of campaign 2000 with the results of an earlier functional study of the 1996 presidential campaign (Benoit, Blaney, & Pier, 1998). Six message forms were studied in both campaigns: primary television spots, primary debates, acceptance addresses, spouses' convention presentations, general television spots, and general debates.

There was a tendency for the 2000 campaign to be less negative than the 1996 campaign. Every message form had more acclaims, and fewer attacks, in 2000 than in 1996. Significant differences in functions occurred in primary television spots ($\chi^2[df=2]=164.4$, $p < .001$), primary debates ($\chi^2[df=2]=142.1$, $p < .001$), and general debates ($\chi^2[df=2]=67.9$, $p < .001$). There was no significant difference in acclaims and attacks between the 1996 and 2000 acceptance addresses ($\chi^2[df=]=3.7$, $ns$; defenses were excluded because of their infrequency), spouses (there were no defenses and too few attacks to calculate $\chi^2$), or general television spots ($\chi^2[df=1]=2.4$, $ns$; defenses were excluded because of their infrequency). See Table 16.9.

There was some tendency towards a greater emphasis on policy topics from 1996 to 2000 campaign messages. Primary television spots discussed policy significantly more in 2000 (56 percent) than in 1996 (48 percent; $\chi^2[df=1]=9.6$, $p < .01$). This was true of primary debates as well, which increased discussion of policy from 58 percent to 68 percent ($\chi^2[df=1]=142.8$, $p < .001$). The general debates also stressed policy more in 2000 (76 percent) than in 1996 (72 percent; $\chi^2[df=1]=10.5$, $p < .01$). However, there was no difference in topic emphasis between the two most recent campaigns in acceptance addresses ($\chi^2[df=1]=2.6$, $ns$), spouses' speeches ($\chi^2[df=1]=1.3$, $ns$), or general television spots ($\chi^2[df=1]=1.9$, $ns$). See Table 16.10 for these data.

Benoit (1999) observed that discussion of policy in television spots had increased (while discussion of character diminished) since 1980. Although that shift was not evident in 2000 general television spots, he argued that campaign messages may be focusing more on policy as a response to voter demands. In 1996, 65 percent of voters reported that policy was the most important determinant of their presidential vote,

Table 16.9. Functions of 1996 and 2000 Campaign Messages

| | Acclaims | | Attacks | | Defenses | | $\chi^2$ |
|---|---|---|---|---|---|---|---|
| | 1996 | 2000 | 1996 | 2000 | 1996 | 2000 | |
| Pri. Spots | 366 (58%) | 828 (86%) | 257 (40%) | 129 (13%) | 12 (2%) | 7 (7%) | 164.4 $p < .001$ |
| Pri. Debates | 584 (54%) | 4021 (73%) | 389 (38%) | 1318 (24%) | 76 (9%) | 159 (3%) | 142.8 $p < .001$ |
| Acceptances | 320 (83%) | 285 (89%) | 62 (16%) | 36 (11%) | 2 (5%) | 0 | 3.7 $ns$* |
| Spouses | 58 (95%) | 51 (100%) | 3 (5%) | 0 | 0 | 0 | ** |
| Gen. Spots | 378 (54%) | 328 (58%) | 325 (46%) | 236 (42%) | 3 (5%) | 4 (7%) | 2.4 $ns$* |
| Gen. Debates | 621 (59%) | 860 (74%) | 347 (33%) | 281 (24%) | 78 (7%) | 24 (2%) | 67.9 $p < .001$ |
| Total | 67% | 90% | 30% | 19% | 3% | 1% | |

*Defenses were excluded due to low frequency. **Could not calculate $\chi^2$ due to small cell sizes. Note: because of the wide variance in frequency of utterances, the figures for totals are means of means (rather than means of total utterances).

compared with 27 percent who cited character (NBC/*Wall Street Journal*, 1996). In late 1999, 90 percent of respondents indicated that policy was the most important determinant of their vote for president, compared with 8 percent who selected character (Princeton, 1999). It is possible that, in some of the messages forms in 2000, candidates were responding to a change in voter preferences.

## Overall Implications

First, this investigation has provided insights into the nature of the campaign discourse in the 2000 campaign. We examined messages in all three phases of the campaign: primary, convention, and general. We examined both traditional (debates, television spots) and less well-studied message forms (web pages, radio spots, television talk show appearances). We offered tentative explanations for the outcome of the 2000 presidential campaign. While the Functional Theory of Political Campaign Discourse does not answer every question or explore every nuance of campaign messages, it provided a variety of useful insights into these campaign messages.

We have demonstrated some fairly consistent features of presidential campaign

Table 16.10. Topics of 1996 and 2000 Campaign Messages

| | Policy | | Character | | $\chi^2$ |
|---|---|---|---|---|---|
| | 1996 | 2000 | 1996 | 2000 | |
| Primary Spots | 301 | 533 | 322 | 414 | 9.6 |
| | (48%) | (56%) | (52%) | (44%) | $p < .01$ |
| Primary Debates | 578 | 3628 | 414 | 1711 | 35.2 |
| | (58%) | (68%) | (42%) | (32%) | $p < .001$ |
| Acceptances | 227 | 176 | 146 | 145 | 2.6 |
| | (61%) | (55%) | (39%) | (45%) | ns |
| Spouses | 21 | 12 | 42 | 39 | 1.3 |
| | (33%) | (24%) | (67%) | (76%) | ns |
| General Spots | 518 | 396 | 185 | 168 | 1.9 |
| | (74%) | (70%) | (26%) | (30%) | ns |
| General Debates | 621 | 865 | 274 | 276 | 10.8 |
| | (72%) | (76%) | (28%) | (24%) | $p < .01$ |
| Total | 58% | 58% | 42% | 42% | |

Note: Because of the wide variance in frequency of utterances, the figures for totals are means of means (rather than means of total utterances).

discourse. Acclaims outnumbered attacks in twelve message forms; only in general radio spots were attacks the most frequent function. In no message form were defenses more frequent than attacks or acclaims. The remarkable consistency in allocation of functions (acclaims > attacks > defenses) in campaign 2000, as well as in earlier campaigns and in campaigns for other offices (Benoit, 2000b) strongly suggests that the situation of campaigning for office is a significant constraint on the functions of campaign discourse. The Functional Theory accounts for this allocation of message functions as explained above.

Second, it appears that the target of attack varies by campaign phase. Republicans do not always focus most of their attacks on Democrats, and vice versa. In three primary message forms (debates, radio spots, and talk shows), the most attacks were directed toward members of one's own party, the immediate opponent. This is reasonable, because, in order to win the nomination, a candidate must be perceived as preferable to the other candidates for the party nomination. In television spots and web pages, the establishment received the brunt of attacks. This may be the result of a deliberate attempt to portray oneself as rejecting "politics as usual."

There does not appear to be as strong a situational constraint on the topic of political campaign discourse. The general campaign phase, and to a somewhat lesser extent, the primary campaign phase, emphasizes policy over character. This is consistent with voter preferences. However, convention discourse exhibits a clear proclivity for character discussion. This is probably due to the fact that, in essence, the entire convention is about the nominee, the person who will personify the party in the general campaign. Note that the tendency to stress character is strongest in speeches by spouses and featured speakers. The candidates' acceptance addresses are the only convention speech studied that stresses policy over character. This is reasonable, because, if elected, the nominee is the one who will head the Executive Branch of government, creating and implementing governmental policy.

We also found a surprising lack of relationship between the topics which were most important to voters and the topics actually addressed by the presidential candidates. Of course, a successful candidates must demonstrate some distinctiveness, or there would be no reason for any voter to prefer him or her over an opponent. Furthermore, when one candidate takes up an issue it may be a mistake for opponents to ignore that issue (even if that topic seemed somewhat less important to voters). This would mean that there is some motivation for opposing candidates to discuss the same issues. Thus, we did not expect a one-to-one relationship between voter issue concerns and the issues addressed in presidential campaign discourse. Nevertheless, it seems surprising to us that none of the correlations were significant.

Given the unexpected nature of this result, we decided to conduct further analyses to attempt to determine what relationships were present in the data on issues addressed. We will look to see if there are significant correlations between opponents (were opponents discussing the same issues?) and between the various messages from a particular candidate (were the candidates staying "on message"?). It should be noted that because these additional analyses were not planned, they should not be considered strong tests. In particular, we omitted the category of "other" because there is no way to know what topics are included in any "other" utterances. This decision may have the effect of attenuating relationships (e.g., some candidates may have discussed the same topic, such as gun control, which would be counted in the "other" category). However, to run correlations when candidates all have large frequencies in the category of "other" would overstate the relationships.

The results of these analyses indicate that candidates did not all discuss the same topics, although there were incidents of overlaps. For example, Bradley's and Gore's messages were significantly correlated in three of the five message forms: television spots ($\rho$=.775, $p < .05$), debates ($\rho$=.929, $p < .01$), and radio spots ($\rho$=.832, $p < .05$). Several Republican candidates' messages were significantly correlated. In television spots, Bush-Forbes ($\rho$=.810, $p < .05$) and Bush-Keyes ($\rho$=.810, $p < .05$) were significantly related (two out of ten comparisons). There were ten significant correlations (out of fifteen possible comparisons) in Republican primary debates: Bauer-Forbes (.929, $p < .01$), Bauer-Keyes (.955, $p < .01$), Bauer-McCain (.786, $p < .05$), Bush-Forbes (.893, $p < .01$), Bush-Keyes (.811, $p < .05$), Bush-McCain (.964, $p < .01$), Forbes-Hatch (.786, $p < .05$), Forbes-Keyes (.955, $p < .01$), Forbes-McCain (.929, $p < .01$), and Keyes-McCain (.883, $p < .01$). Republican web pages had two significant correlations (out of fifteen possibilities): Bush-Keyes (.899, $p < .01$) and

Keyes-McCain (.863, $p < .05$). Four comparisons (out of ten) were significant in radio spots: Bush-Forbes (.769, $p < .05$), Bush-Keyes (.832, $p < .05$), Bush-McCain (.874, $p < .05$), and Forbes-McCain (.874, $p < .05$). Finally, on television talk show appearances, only Bauer-Bush (.867, $p < .05$) out of the fifteen possibilities (the number of comparisons varied because the number of candidates in each message form varied) was significant.

What does this mean? First, it means that the issue topics in some messages from different candidates (in the same medium) were related (nineteen significant correlations), but not for most (sixty-five possible comparisons). If we consider which candidate had the most in common with other candidates, then Bradley and Gore were correlated in three of five message forms. For Republicans, Bush correlated ten times, Forbes and Keyes eight times, McCain seven times, and Bauer four times, with opponents. This may suggest that there is a tendency to discuss topics addressed by the front-runner, Bush. Forbes, Keyes, and McCain also overlapped to a fair amount. It also suggests that Bauer's messages did not overlap (issue topics) with other candidates very much. The fact that the largest number of correlations occurred in debates is surely a function of the format (the questions have a strong influence on topic of discussion).

We also address the question of the extent to which candidates stayed "on message," or provided a consistent message across message forms. Table 16.11 reveals that some variance in the extent to which a given candidate discusses issue topics in the same proportion across message forms. Bradley, Gore, and Keyes each had significant correlations in three of five possibilities. Bush and McCain had significant correlations in two sets of possibilities. Bauer and Forbes's messages had significant correlations in issue topics in one pair of primary messages. Turning to the general campaign, Bush and Gore each had one significant correlation between two message forms. This means that only seventeen of ninety possible combinations were statistically significant. The number of significant correlations varies by candidate.

These results (like those on correlations with opponents) must be considered highly tentative. First, as noted above, these calculations omitted the category of "other" remarks. This could have reduced the amount of overlap in these messages. Second, there could be consistency on character issues (e.g., Bush stressing that he was compassionate—or harping on Gore's alleged dishonesty). Still, these analyses suggest several conclusions. The public's issue agenda does not appear to be a significant factor in the candidates' choice of issue topics. This may be a weakness in their messages. However, there is some tendency to discuss what one's opponents are saying (and it seems plausible that, say, if Gore talks about the environment Bradley might want to let voters know his position as well). Finally, candidates appear to vary in the extent to which they stay "on message," at least insofar as issue topics are concerned. Future research could provide stronger tests of these tentative claims by (1) resolving "other" remarks into their specific topics and (2) expanding the scope beyond issues to include character.

Table 16.11. Candidate Consistency

| Candidate | Significant Correlations | Between Message Forms |
|---|---|---|
| Primary Campaign | | |
| Bradley | 3 | debate-web, debate-radio, web-radio |
| Gore | 3 | TV spot-debate, TV spot-radio spot, debate-radio spot |
| Bauer | 1 | TV spot-debate |
| Bush | 2 | TV spot-debate, TV spot-radio spot |
| Forbes | 1 | TV spot-radio spot |
| Keyes | 3 | TV spot-radio spot, debate-web, web-radio spot |
| McCain | 2 | TV spot-web, debate-web |
| General Campaign | | |
| Bush | 1 | TV spot-radio spot |
| Gore | 1 | debate-web |
| Total | 17 (of 90) | |

# Conclusion

This investigating has extended our knowledge of presidential campaign discourse. First, it analyzes campaign messages from the most recent presidential campaign. This campaign was particularly interesting, not only because of the delayed resolution (due to chads in Florida) but also because it featured contested primaries in both major political parties. Second, it includes messages which are not commonly studied, like television talk shows, radio spots, and Internet sites. We have investigated all three phases of the campaign: primary, convention, and general. We have investigated both functions and topics of these messages, extending the reach of the Functional Theory of Political Campaign Discourse. We offer numerous specific findings (e.g., that the target of attacks in the primary are often members of one's own political party; that candidates do not have as much consistency in the topics of their campaign messages as we might have guessed). Of course, much work remains to be accomplished. We purposely limited our analysis to the two major political parties, even though Ralph Nader and Pat Buchanan deserve consideration. We examined a wide range of message forms (rather than limiting ourselves to the two media most typically studied, television spots and debates). However, unexamined are such other message forms as recorded telephone messages, direct mail brochures, or stump speeches. Presidential campaigns (and political campaigns more generally) are rich and diverse, but we are beginning to understand some of the key features.

# References

Abramowitz, A. (1978). The impact of a presidential debate on voter rationality. *American Journal of Political Science, 22*, 680-690.

Ahem, R. K., Stromer-Galley, J., & Neuman, R. W. (2000). *When voters can interact and compare candidates online: Experimentally investigating political web effects.* Paper presented at the International Communication Association, Acapulco, Mexico.

Andreasen, M. V. (1985). Listener recall for call-in versus structured interview radio formats. *Journal of Broadcasting and Electronic Media, 29*, 421-430.

Ansolabehere, S., & Iyengar, S. (1995). *Going negative: How attack ads shrink and polarize the electorate.* New York: Free Press.

Armstrong, C. B., & Rubin, A. M. (1989). Talk radio as interpersonal communication. *Journal of Communication, 39*, 84-94.

Atkin, C., & Heald, G. (1976). Effects of political advertising. *Public Opinion Quarterly, 40*, 216-228.

Basil, M., Schooler, C., & Reeves, B. (1991). Positive and negative political advertising: Effectiveness of ads and perceptions of candidates. In F. Biocca (Ed.), *Television and political advertising* (vol. 1, pp. 245-262). Hillsdale, NJ: Erlbaum.

Becker, L. B., Sobowale, I. A., Cobbey, R. E., & Eyal, C. H. (1978). Debates' effects on voters' understanding of candidates and issues. In G. F. Bishop, R. G. Meadow, & M. Jackson-Beeck (Eds.), *The presidential debates: Media, electoral, and policy perspectives* (pp. 126-139). New York: Praeger.

Benoit, W. L. (1982). Richard M. Nixon's rhetorical strategies in his public statements on Watergate. *Southern Speech Communication Journal, 47*, 192-211.

Benoit, W. L. (1995a). *Accounts, excuses, and apologies: A theory of image restoration strategies.* Albany: State University of New York Press.

Benoit, W. L. (1995b). Sears' repair of its auto service image: Image restoration discourse in the corporate sector. *Communication Studies, 46*, 89-105.

Benoit, W. L. (1997). Image restoration discourse and crisis communication. *Public*

*Relations Review, 23*, 177-186.

Benoit, W. L. (1998). Merchants of death: Persuasive defenses by the tobacco industry. In J. Klumpp (Ed.), *Argument in a time of change: Definition, frameworks, and critiques* (pp. 220-225). Annandale, VA: National Communication Association.

Benoit, W. L. (1999). *Seeing spots: A functional analysis of presidential television advertisements from 1952-1996*. New York: Praeger.

Benoit, W. L. (2000a). Comparing the Clinton and Dole advertising campaigns: Identification and division in 1996 presidential television spots. *Communication Research Reports, 17*, 39-48.

Benoit, W. L. (2000b). A functional analysis of political advertising across media, 1998. *Communication Studies, 51*, 274-295.

Benoit, W. L. (2001a). Framing through temporal metaphor: The "Bridges" of Bob Dole and Bill Clinton in their 1996 Acceptance Addresses. *Communication Studies, 52*, 70-84.

Benoit, W. L. (2001b). The functional approach to presidential television spots: Acclaiming, attacking, defending 1952-2000. *Communication Studies, 52*, 109-126.

Benoit, W. L., & Anderson, K. K. (1996). Blending politics and entertainment: Dan Quayle versus Murphy Brown. *Southern Communication Journal, 62*, 73-85.

Benoit, W. L., & Benoit, P. J. (2000). *The virtual campaign: Presidential primary websites in campaign 2000*. Available: http://www.roguecom.com/roguescholar/benoit.html.

Benoit, W. L., Blaney, J. R., & Pier, P. M. (1998). *Campaign '96: A functional analysis of acclaiming, attacking, and defending*. New York: Praeger.

Benoit, W. L., Gullifor, P., & Panici, D. A. (1991). President Reagan's defensive discourse on the Iran-Contra affair. *Communication Studies, 42*, 272-294.

Benoit, W. L., Pier, P. M., & Blaney, J. R. (1997). A functional approach to televised political spots: Acclaiming, attacking, and defending. *Communication Quarterly, 45*, 1-20.

Benoit, W. L., Blaney, J. R., & Pier, P. M. (2000). Acclaiming, attacking, and defending: A functional analysis of nominating convention keynote speeches, 1960-1996. *Political Communication, 17*, 61-84.

Benoit, W. L., & Brazeal, L. M. (2002). A functional analysis of the 1988 Bush-Dukakis presidential debates. *Argumentation and Advocacy, 38*, 219-233.

Benoit, W. L., & Brinson, S. L. (1999). Queen Elizabeth's image repair discourse: Insensitive royal or compassionate queen? *Public Relations Review, 25*, 145-156.

Benoit, W. L., & Brinson, S. (1994). AT&T: Apologies are not enough. *Communication Quarterly, 42*, 75-88.

Benoit, W. L., & Czerwinski, A. (1997). A critical analysis of USAir's image repair discourse. *Business Communication Quarterly, 60*, 38-57.

Benoit, W. L., & Dorries, B. (1996). Dateline NBC's persuasive attack on Wal-Mart. *Communication Quarterly, 44*, 464-477.

Benoit, W. L., & Gustainis, J. J. (1986). An analogic analysis of the keynote addresses at the 1980 presidential nominating conventions. *Speaker and Gavel, 24*, 95-108.

Benoit, W. L., & Hanczor, R. S. (1994). The Tonya Harding controversy: An analysis of image repair strategies. *Communication Quarterly, 42*, 416-433.

Benoit, W. L., & Hansen, G. J. (2001). Presidential debate questions and the public agenda. *Communication Quarterly, 49*, 130-141.

Benoit, W. L., & Harthcock, A. (1999a). Attacking the tobacco industry: A rhetorical analysis of advertisements by The Campaign for Tobacco-Free Kids. *Southern Communication Journal, 65*, 66-81.

Benoit, W. L., & Harthcock, A. (1999b). Functions of the Great Debates: Acclaims, attacks, and defense in the 1960 presidential debates. *Communication Monographs, 66*, 341-357.

Benoit, W. L., & McHale, J. P. (1999). Kenneth Starr's image repair discourse viewed in 20/20. *Communication Quarterly, 47*, 265-280.

Benoit, W. L., & Nill, D. M. (1998a). A critical analysis of Judge Clarence Thomas's statement before the Senate Judiciary Committee. *Communication Studies, 49*, 179-195.

Benoit, W. L., & Nill, D. M. (1998b). Oliver Stone's defense of JFK. *Communication Quarterly, 46*, 127-143.

Benoit, W. L., Pier, P. M., Brazeal, L., McHale, J. P., Klyukovski, A., & Airne, D. (2002). *The primary decision: A functional analysis of debates in presidential primaries.* Westport, CT: Praeger.

Benoit, W. L., Blaney, J. R., & Pier, P. M. (2000). Acclaiming, attacking, and defending: A functional analysis of nominating convention keynote speeches, 1960-1996. *Political Communication, 17*, 61-84.

Benoit, W. L., McKinney, M. S., & Holbert, R. L. (2001). Beyond learning and persona: Extending the scope of presidential debate effects. *Communication Monographs, 68*, 259-273.

Benoit, W. L., McKinney, M. S., & Stephenson, M. T. (2002). Effects of watching campaign 2000 presidential primary debates. *Journal of Communication, 52*, 316-332.

Benoit, W. L., & Stephenson, M. T. (2003). *Effects of watching a presidential primary debate.* Unpublished manuscript.

Benoit, W. L., & Wells, W. T. (1996). *Candidates in conflict: Persuasive attack and defense in the 1992 presidential debates.* Tuscaloosa: University of Alabama Press.

Benoit, W. L., Wells, W. T., Pier, P. M., & Blaney, J. R. (1999). Acclaiming, attacking, and defending in nomination convention acceptance addresses, 1960-1996. *Quarterly Journal of Speech, 85*, 247-267.

Berelson, B. (1952). *Content analysis for the social sciences and humanities.* Reading, MA: Addison-Wesley.

Berquist, G. F. (1960). The Kennedy-Humphrey debate. *Today's Speech, 8*, 2-3, 31.

Best, S. J., & Hubbard, C. (2000). The role of televised debates in the presidential nominating process. In W. G. Mayer (Ed.), *In pursuit of the White House 2000: How we choose our presidential nominees* (pp. 255-284). NY: Chatham House.

Bierig, J., & Dimmick, J. (1979). The late night talk show as interpersonal communication. *Journalism Quarterly, 56*, 92-96.

Bishop, G. F., Oldendick, R. W., & Tuchfarber, A. J. (1978). The presidential debates as a device for increasing the "rationality" of electoral behavior. In G. F. Bishop, R. G. Meadow, & M. Jackson-Beeck (Eds.), *The presidential debates: Media, electoral, and policy perspectives* (pp. 179-196). New York: Praeger.

Blaney, J. R. (2001). *Radio and the functional theory of political communication.* Paper presented at the Central States Communication Association, Cincinnati, OH.

Blaney, J. R., & Benoit, W. L. (1997). The persuasive defense of Jesus in the Gospel according to John. *Journal of Communication and Religion, 20*, 25-30.

Blaney, J. R., & Benoit, W. L. (2001). *The Clinton scandals and the politics of image restoration.* Westport, CT: Praeger.

Blaney, J. R., Benoit, W. L., & Brazeal, L. M. (2002). Blowout! Firestone's image restoration campaign. *Public Relations Research, 28*, 379-392.

Blankenship, J., Fine, M. G., & Davis, L. K. (1983). The 1980 Republican primary debates: The transformation of actor to scene. *Quarterly Journal of Speech, 64*, 25-36.

Blankenship, J., Robson, D. C., & Williams, M. S. (1997). Conventionalizing gender: Talk by and about women at the 1996 national political conventions. *American Behavioral Scientist, 40*, 1020-1047.

Blumenthal, S. (1980). *The permanent campaign: Inside the world of elite political operatives.* Boston: Beacon Press.

Bock, J. (1982). *Zur Inhalts-und Funktionsanalyse der Politikerrede. Ein Beitrag zur Verbesserung der Kommunikation zwischen Staatsburger und Politiker* [*Analysis of content and function in politician's speeches. Toward a better understanding between citizens and politicians*]. Frankfurt, Germany: Haag und Herrchen.

Borgers, E. W. (1962). Structural analysis of an interview series. *Journal of Broadcasting, 6*, 239-242.

Breglio, V. (1987). Polling in campaigns. In L. P. Devlin (Ed.), *Political persuasion in presidential campaigns* (pp. 24-34). New Brunswick, NJ: Transaction Books.

Brians, C. L., & Wattenberg, M. P. (1996). Campaign issue knowledge and salience: Comparing reception from TV commercials, TV news, and newspapers. *American Journal of Political Science, 40*, 172-193.

Brinson, S., & Benoit, W. L. (1996). Dow Corning's image repair strategies in the breast implant crisis. *Communication Quarterly, 44*, 29-41.

Brinson, S. L., & Benoit, W. L. (1999). The tarnished star: Restoring Texaco's damaged public image. *Management Communication Quarterly, 12*, 483-510.

Brydon, S. R. (1985). *Reagan versus Reagan: The incumbency factor in the 1984 presidential debates.* Paper presented at the Speech Communication Association Convention, Denver, CO.

Bucholz, L. M., & Smith, R. E. (1991). The role of consumer involvement in determining cognitive response to broadcast advertising. *Journal of Advertising, 20*, 4-17.

Carlin, D. B. (1994). A rationale for a focus group study. In D. B. Carlin & M. S. McKinney (Eds.), *The 1992 presidential debates in focus* (pp. 3-19). Westport, CT: Praeger.

Casey, C. (2001). Net campaign 2000. In S. Coleman (Ed.), *Elections in the age of the Internet: Lessons from the United States* (pp. 9-16). London: Hansard Society.

Chaffee, S. H., Zhao, X., & Leshner, G. (1994). Political knowledge and the campaign media of 1992. *Communication Research, 21*, 305-324.

Chester, E. W. (1969). *Radio, television, and American politics.* New York: Sheed and Ward.

Cloud, D. L. (1996). Hegemony or concordance? The rhetoric of tokenism in "Oprah" Winfrey's rags-to-riches biography. *Critical Studies in Mass Communication, 13*, 115-137.

Cohen, A. A. (1978). Radio vs. TV: The effect of the medium. *Journal of Communication, 26(2)*, 29-35.

Crawford, D. (1966, August 28). Wives enjoy new roles in presidential politics: When Hillary Clinton and Elizabeth Dole speak, the voters listen and like what they hear. *The Orlando Sentinel*, p. A1.

Crotty, W., & Jackson, J. S. (1985). *Presidential primaries and nominations.* Washington, DC: Congressional Quarterly Press.

Cundy, D. T. (1986). Political commercials and candidate image: The effect can be substantial. In L. L. Kaid, D. Nimmo, & K. R. Sanders (Eds.), *New perspectives on political advertising* (pp. 210-234). Carbondale: Southern Illinois Press.

D'Alessio, D. D. (1997). Use of the World Wide Web in the 1996 US election. *Electoral Studies, 16*, 489-500.

Davis, J. W. (1997). *U.S. presidential primaries and the caucus-convention system: A sourcebook*. Westport, CT: Greenwood Press.

Davis, M. H. (1982). Voting intentions and the 1980 Carter-Reagan debate. *Journal of Applied Social Psychology, 12*, 481-492.

Davis, R. (1999). *The web of politics: The Internet's impact on the American political system*. New York: Oxford University Press.

Denton, R. E., & Woodward, G. C. (1990). *Political communication in America* (2nd ed.). New York: Praeger.

DeRosa, K. L., & Bystrom, D. G. (1999). The voice of and for women in the 1996 presidential campaign: Style and substance of convention speeches. In L. L. Kaid & D. G. Bystrom (Eds.), *The electronic election: Perspectives on the 1996 campaign communication* (pp. 97-111). Mahwah, NJ: Lawrence Erlbaum.

Desmond, R. J., & Donohue, T. R. (1981). The role of the 1976 televised presidential debates in the political socialization of adolescents. *Communication Quarterly, 29*, 302-308.

Devlin, L. P. (1986). An analysis of presidential television commercials, 1952-1984. In L. L. Kaid, D. Nimmo, & K. R. Sanders (Eds.), *New perspectives on political advertising* (pp. 21-54). Carbondale: Southern Illinois Press.

Devlin, L. P. (1987). Campaign commercials. In L. P. Devlin (Ed.), *Political persuasion in presidential campaigns* (pp. 208-216). New Brunswick, NJ: Transaction Books.

Devlin, L. P. (1989). Contrasts in presidential campaign commercials of 1988. *American Behavioral Scientist, 32*, 389-414.

Devlin, L. P. (1993). Contrasts in presidential campaign commercials of 1992. *American Behavioral Scientist, 37*, 272-290.

Devlin, L. P. (1995). Political commercials in American presidential elections. In L. L. Kaid & C. Holtz-Bacha (Eds.), *Political advertising in western democracies: Parties & candidates on television* (pp. 186-205). Thousand Oaks, CA: Sage.

Downs, A. (1957). *An economic theory of democracy*. New York: Harper and Row.

Drew, D., & Weaver, D. (1991). Voter learning in the 1988 presidential election: Did the debates and the media matter? *Journalism Quarterly, 68*, 27-37.

Dulio, D. A., Goff, D. L., & Thurber, J. A. (1999). Untangled web: Internet use during the 1998 election. *PS: Political Science and Politics, 32*, 53-58.

Edelman, M. (1988). *Constructing the political spectacle*. Chicago: University of Chicago Press.

Ellsworth, J. W. (1965). Rationality and campaigning: A content analysis of the 1960 presidential campaign debates. *Western Political Quarterly, 18*, 794-802.

Enslow, R. (1999). *Los Angles Times* Poll Alert [Internet]. Available: http://www.latimes.com/news/timespoll/pdf/432pa1da.pdf.

Felknor, B. L. (1992). *Political mischief: Smear, sabotage, and reform in U.S. elections*. New York: Praeger.

Fibiger, B. (1981). Danish elections campaigns in the seventies. In Karl E. Rosengren (Ed.), *Advances in content analysis* (pp. 159-177). Beverly Hills, CA: Sage.

Fineman, H. (2000, October 2). The talk-show primary. *Newsweek*, 26-27.

Finkel, S. E., & Geer, J. G. (1998). A spot check: Casting doubt on the demobilizing effect of attack advertising. *American Journal of Political Science, 42*, 573-595.

Fisher, W. R. (1970). A motive view of communication. *Quarterly Journal of Speech, 56*, 131-139.

Fletcher, B. (1999). Radio ads. In D. Perlmutter (Ed.), *The Manship School guide to political communication* (pp.164-170). Baton Rouge, LA: LSU Press.

Friedenberg, R. V. (1994). Patterns and trends in national political debates, 1960-1992 (pp.

235-259). In R. V. Friedenberg (Ed.), *Rhetorical studies of national political debates, 1960-1992* (2nd ed.). New York: Praeger.

Frye, J. K., & Krohn, F. B. (1977). An analysis of Barbara Jordan's 1976 keynote address. *Journal of Applied Communications Research, 5,* 73-82.

Gallup Poll. (1999, April 9). *Independents rank as largest U.S. political group.* Accessed 6/20/2001: http://www.gallup.com/poll/releases/pr990409c.asp.

Gallup Poll. (2000, July 25-26). *CNN/USA Today* (obtained via Lexis-Nexis).

Garramone, G. M. (1985). Effects of negative political advertising: The roles of sponsor and rebuttal. *Journal of Broadcasting and Electronic Media, 29,* 147-159.

Garramone, G. M., Atkin, C. K., Pinkleton, B. E., & Cole, R. T. (1990). Effects of negative political advertising on the political process. *Journal of Broadcasting and Electronic Media, 34,* 299-311.

Garramone, G. M., & Smith, S. J. (1984). Reactions to political advertising: Clarifying sponsor effects. *Journalism Quarterly, 51,* 771-775.

Geer, J. G. (1988). The effects on presidential debates on the electorate's preference on candidates. *American Politics Quarterly, 16,* 486-501.

Gold, E. R. (1978). Political apologia: The ritual of self-defense. *Communication Monographs, 46,* 306-316.

Graber, D. A., & Kim, Y. Y. (1978). Why John Q. Voter did not learn much from the 1976 presidential debates. In B. Rubin (Ed.), *Communication yearbook 2* (pp. 407-421). New Brunswick, NJ: Transaction.

Gronbeck, B. E. (1978). The functions of presidential campaigning. *Communication Monographs, 45,* 268-280.

Gronbeck, B. E. (1992). Negative narrative in 1988 presidential campaign ads. *Quarterly Journal of Speech, 78,* 333-346.

Gustainis, J. J., & Benoit, W. L. (1988). Analogic analysis of the presidential candidates' acceptance speeches at the 1980 national nominating conventions. *Speaker and Gavel, 25,* 14-23.

Haag, L. (1992/93). Oprah Winfrey: The construction of intimacy in the talk show setting. *Journal of Popular Culture, 26,* 115-121.

Hacker, K. L., Zahaki, W. R., Giles, M. J., & McQuitty, S. (2000). Components of candidate images: Statistical analysis of the issue-persona dichotomy in the presidential campaign of 1996. *Communication Monographs, 67,* 227-238.

Hagner, P. R., & Rieselbach, L. N. (1978). The impact of the 1976 presidential debates: Conversion or reinforcement? In G. F. Bishop, R. G. Meadow, & M. Jackson-Beeck (Eds.), *The presidential debates: Media, electoral, and policy perspectives* (pp. 157-178). New York: Praeger.

Hall, M. (1997). One-to-one politics in cyberspace. *Media Studies Journal, 2,* 97-103.

Hallin, D. (1992). Sound bite news: Television coverage of elections, 1968-1988. *Journal of Communication, 42(2),* 5-24.

Hammerback, J. C. (1974). William F. Buckley, Jr., on *Firing Line*: A case study in confrontational dialogue. *Today's Speech, 22,* 23-30.

Hansen, G. J. (2000a). *Characteristics of updates made to presidential candidates Internet sites.* Paper presented at the Workshop on Website Analysis, Philadelphia, PA, Annenberg Public Policy Center.

Hansen, G. J. (2000b). *Internet presidential campaigning: The influences of candidate Internet sites on the 2000 election.* Paper presented at the National Communication Association, Seattle, WA.

Hansen, G. J., & Benoit, W. L. (2001). The role of significant policy issues in the 2000 presidential primaries. *American Behavioral Scientist, 44*, 2082-2100.

Hellweg, S. A., Pfau, M., & Brydon, S. R. (1992). *Televised presidential debates: Advocacy in contemporary America*. New York: Praeger.

Hellweg, S. A., & Phillips, S. L. (1981). A verbal and visual analysis of the 1980 Houston Republican primary debate. *Southern Speech Communication Journal, 47*, 23-38.

Hill, R. P. (1989). An exploration of voter responses to political advertisements. *Journal of Advertising, 18*, 14-22.

Hinck, E. A. (1993). *Enacting the presidency: political argument, presidential debates, and presidential character*. Westport, CT: Praeger.

Hoffmann, R. (1982). Politische Fernsehinterviews [Televised political interviews]. *Reihe Medien in Forschung und Unterricht, 9*, 37-58.

Hofstetter, C. R., & Zukin, C. (1979). TV network news and advertising in the Nixon and McGovern campaigns. *Journalism Quarterly, 56*, 106-115, 152.

Holly, W., Kuhn, P., & Puschel, U. (1986). *Politische Fernsehdiskussionen [Political debates on television]*. Tubingen, Germany: Niemeyer.

Holsti, O. (1969). *Content analysis for the social sciences and humanities*. Reading, MA: Addison-Wesley.

Houck, D. W. (1997). Reading the body in the text: FDR's 1932 speech to the Democratic National Convention. *Southern Communication Journal, 62*, 20-36.

Hutchens, J. M. (1999). Political media buying. In D. Perlmutter (Ed.), *The Manship School guide to political communication* (pp. 122-130). Baton Rouge, LA: LSU Press.

Iyengar, S., & Kinder, D. R. (1987). *News that matters: Television and American opinion*. Chicago: University of Chicago Press.

Jacoby, J., Troutman, T. R., & Whittler, T. E. (1986). Viewer miscomprehension of the 1980 presidential debate: A research note. *Political Psychology, 7*, 297-308.

Jamieson, K. H. (1987). Television, presidential campaigns, and debates. In J. L. Swerdlow (Ed.), *Presidential debates 1988 and beyond* (pp. 27-33). Washington, DC: Congressional Quarterly Inc.

Jamieson, J. H. (1992). *Packaging the presidency: A history and criticism of presidential campaign advertising* (2nd ed.). New York: Oxford University Press.

Jamieson, J. H. (1996). *Packaging the presidency: A history and criticism of presidential campaign advertising* (3rd ed.). New York: Oxford University Press.

Jamieson, K. H., & Birdsell, D. S. (1988). *Presidential debates: The challenge of creating an informed electorate*. New York: Oxford University Press.

Jamieson, K. H., Waldman, P., & Sherr, S. (2000). Eliminate the negative? Categories of analysis for political advertisements. In J. A. Thurber, C. J. Nelson, & D. A. Dulio (Eds.), *Crowded airwaves: Campaign advertising in elections* (pp. 44-64). Washington, DC: Brookings Institution.

Johnson, L. B. (1964). *Storm* (television spot).

Johnson-Cartee, K. S., & Copeland, G. (1989). Southern voters' reactions to negative political ads in the 1986 election. *Journalism Quarterly, 66*, 888-893, 986.

Johnson-Cartee, K. S., & Copeland, G. (1991). *Negative political advertising: Coming of age*. Hillsdale, NJ: Erlbaum.

Johnson-Cartee, K. S., & Copeland, G. (1997). *Manipulation of the American voter: Political campaign commercials*. Westport, CT: Praeger.

Joslyn, R. A. (1980). The content of political spot ads. *Journalism Quarterly, 57*, 92-98.

Joslyn, R. A. (1981). The impact of campaign spot advertising on voting defections. *Human Communication Research, 7*, 347-360.

Joslyn, R. (1986). Political advertising and the meaning of elections. In L. L. Kaid, D.

Nimmo, & K. R. Sanders (Eds.), *New perspectives on political advertising* (pp. 139-183). Carbondale: Southern Illinois Press.

Just, M., Crigler, A., & Buhr, T. (1999). Voice, substance, and cynicism in presidential campaign media. *Political Communication, 16,* 25-44.

Just, M., Crigler, A., & Wallach, L. (1990). Thirty seconds or thirty minutes: What viewers learn from spot advertisements and candidate debates. *Journal of Communication, 40,* 120-132.

Kaid, L. L. (1991). The effects of television broadcasts on perceptions of presidential candidates in the United States and France. In L. L. Kaid, J. Gerstle, & K. R. Sanders (Eds.), *Mediated politics in two cultures: Presidential campaigning in the United States and France* (pp. 247-260). New York: Praeger.

Kaid, L. L. (1994). Political advertising in the 1992 campaign. In R. E. Denton (Ed.), *The 1992 presidential campaign: A communication perspective* (pp. 111-127). Westport, CT: Praeger.

Kaid, L. L. (1997). Effects of the television spots on images of Dole and Clinton. *American Behavioral Scientist, 40,* 1085-1094.

Kaid, L. L. (1998). Videostyle and the effects of the 1996 presidential campaign advertising. In R. E. Denton (Ed.), *The 1996 presidential campaign: A communication perspective* (pp. 143-159). Westport, CT: Praeger.

Kaid, L. L., & Ballotti, J. (1991). *Television advertising in presidential primaries and caucuses.* Paper presented at the Speech Communication Association, Atlanta, GA.

Kaid, L. L., & Boydson, J. (1987). An experimental study of the effectiveness of negative political advertisements. *Communication Quarterly, 35,* 193-201.

Kaid, L. L., & Davidson, D. K. (1986). Elements of videostyle: Candidate presentation through television advertising. In L. L. Kaid, D. Nimmo, & K. R. Sanders (Eds.), *New perspectives on political advertising* (pp. 184-209). Carbondale: Southern Illinois Press.

Kaid, L. L., & Johnston, A. (1991). Negative versus positive television advertising in U.S. presidential campaigns, 1960-1988. *Journal of Communication, 41,* 53-64.

Kaid, L. L., & Johnston, A. (2001). *Videostyle in presidential campaigns Style and content of televised political advertising.* Westport, CT: Praeger.

Kaid, L. L., Leland, C. M., & Whitney, S. (1992). The impact of televised political ads: Evoking viewer responses in the 1988 presidential campaign. *Southern Communication Journal, 57,* 285-295.

Kaid, L. L., Nimmo, D., & Sanders, K. R. (1986). (Eds.), *New perspectives on political advertising.* Carbondale: Southern Illinois Press.

Kaid, L. L., & Sanders, K. R. (1978). Political television commercials: An experimental study of type and length. *Communication Research, 5,* 57-70.

Kaid, L. L., & Tedesco, J. C. (1999). Presidential candidate presentation: Videostyle in the 1996 presidential spots. In L. L. Kaid & D. G. Bystrom (Eds.), *The electronic election: Perspectives on the 1996 campaign communication* (pp. 209-221). Mahwah, NJ: Erlbaum.

Kane, T. (1987). The Dewey-Stassen primary debate of 1948: An examination of format for presidential debates. In J. Wenzel (Ed.), *Argument and critical practices* (pp. 249-253). Annandale, VA: Speech Communication Association.

Kelley, S. (1983). *Interpreting elections.* Princeton, NJ: Princeton University Press.

Kendall, K. A. (1997). The 1996 Clinton-Dole presidential debates: Through media eyes. In R. V. Friedenberg (Ed.), *Rhetorical studies of national political debates—1996* (pp. 1-29). Westport, CT: Praeger.

Kendall, K. E. (2000). *Communication in the presidential primaries: Candidates and the media, 1912-2000*. Westport, CT: Praeger.

Kennedy, H. (2000, March 15). Vice Prez and Bush win south, lock up nomination. *Daily News [New York]*, p. 8.

Kennedy, K. A., & Benoit, W. L. (1997). Newt Gingrich's book deal: A case study in self-defense rhetoric. *Southern Communication Journal, 63*, 197-216.

Kern, M. (1989). *30 second politics: Political advertising in the eighties*. New York: Praeger.

Klein, G. (1981). Relative advertising channel effectiveness: A test of learning vs. involvement orientations. In J. H. Leigh & C. R. Martin, Jr. (Eds.), *Current issues and research in advertising, 1981* (pp. 71-84). Ann Arbor, MI: University of Michigan.

Klinenberg, E., & Perrin, A. (2000). Symbolic politics in the information age: The 1996 Republican presidential campaigns in cyberspace. *Information, Communication, and Society, 3*, 17-38.

Klotz, R. (1997). Positive spin: Senate campaigning on the web. *PS: Political Science & Politics, 30*, 482-486.

Klotz, R. (1998). Virtual criticism: Negative advertising on the Internet in the 1996 Senate races. *Political Communication, 15*, 347-365.

Klotz, R., & Broome, A. (1998). Discussion of women's issues in the 1996 Internet campaign. *Women and Politics, 19(4)*, 67-86.

Kraus, S. (1996). Winners of the first 1960 televised presidential debate between Kennedy and Nixon. *Journal of Communication, 46(4)*, 78-96.

Lamoureaux, E. R., Entrekin, H. S., & McKinney, M. S. (1994). Debating the debates. In D. B. Carlin & M. S. McKinney (Eds.), *The 1992 presidential debates in focus* (pp. 55-67). Westport, CT: Praeger.

Landis, J. R., & Koch, G. G. (1977). The measurement of observer agreement for categorical data. *Biometrica, 33*, 159-174.

Lang, A. (1991). Emotion, formal features, and memory for televised political advertisements. In F. Biocca (Eds.), *Television and political advertising* (vol. 1, pp. 221-243). Hillsdale, NJ: Erlbaum.

Lang, K., & Lang, G. E. (1961). Zuchauerreaktionen bei den Kennedy-Nixon Debatten [Viewers reactions after the Kennedy-Nixon debates]. *Rundfunk und Fernsehen, 9*, 162-287.

Lang, K., & Lang, G. E. (1968). *Politics and television*. Chicago: Quadrangle.

Lang, K., & Lang, G. E. (1977). Reactions of viewers. In S. Kraus (Ed.), *The great debates: Carter versus Ford, 1976* (pp. 313-330). Bloomington: Indiana University Press.

Lang, G. E., & Lang, K. (1978). The formation of public opinion: direct and mediated effects of the first debate. In G. F. Bishop, R. G. Meadow, & M. Jackson-Beeck (Eds.), *The presidential debates: Media, electoral, and policy perspectives* (pp. 61-80). New York: Praeger.

Lang, K., & Lang, G. E. (1984). *Politics and television re-viewed*. Beverly Hills: Sage.

Lanoue, D. J. (1991). The "turning point": Viewers' reactions to the second 1988 presidential debate. *American Politics Quarterly, 19*, 80-95.

Lanoue, D. J., & Schrott, P. R. (1989). Voter's reactions to televised presidential debates: Measurement of the source and magnitude of opinion change. *Political Psychology, 10*, 275-285.

Lau, R. R., Sigelman, L., Heldman, C., & Babbitt, P. R. (1999). The effectiveness of negative political advertising: A meta-analytic assessment. *American Political Science Review, 93*, 851-876.

Leip, D. (2001). *Dave Leip's Atlas of U.S. Presidential Elections.* Available on-line: http://www.uselectionatlas.org/.

Leff, M. C., & Mohrmann, G. P. (1974). Lincoln at Cooper-Union: A rhetorical analysis of the text. *Quarterly Journal of Speech, 60*, 346-358.

Lemert, J. B. (1993). Do televised presidential debates help inform voters? *Journal of Broadcasting and Electronic Media, 37*, 83-94.

Levine, M. A. (1995). *Presidential campaigns and elections: Issues and images in the media age.* Itasea, IL: Peacock Publishers.

Lewicki, D., & Ziaukas, T. (2001). *The digital tea leaves of election 2000: The Internet and the future of presidential politics.* Available: http://www.firstmonday.dk/issues/-issue5_12/lewicki/.

Lichter, S. R., & Noyes, R. E. (1995). *Good intentions make bad news: Why Americans hate campaign journalism.* Lanham, MD: Rowman & Littlefield.

Lichter, S. R., Noyes, R. E., & Kaid, L. L. (1999). No news or negative news: How the networks nixed the '96 campaign. In L. L. Kaid & D. G. Bystrom (Eds.), *The electronic election: Perspectives on the 1996 campaign communication* (pp. 3-13). Mahwah, NJ: Erlbaum.

Lichtman, A. J. (1996). *The keys to the White House, 1996: A surefire guide to predicting the next president.* Lanham, MD: Madison.

Louden, A. D. (1989). Political advertising bibliography. *Political Communication Review, 14*, 19-46.

Lubell, S. (1977). Personalities versus issues. In S. Kraus (Ed.), *The great debates: Carter versus Ford, 1976* (pp. 151-162). Bloomington: Indiana University Press.

Margolis, M., Resnick, D., & Tu, C. (1997). Campaigning on the Internet: Parties and candidates on the World Wide Web in the 1996 primary season. *Press/Politics, 2(1)*, 59-78.

Marks, P. (2000, July 21). Candidates invited to a late-night debate. *New York Times*, p. A15.

Martel, M. (1983). Political campaign debates: Images, strategies, and tactics. New York: Longman.

McClure, R. D., & Patterson, T. E. (1974). Television news and political advertising: The impact of exposure on voter beliefs. *Communication Research, 1*, 3-21.

McKenzie, R. (2000). Audience involvement in the epideictic discourse of television talk shows. *Communication Quarterly, 48*, 190-203.

McLeod, J. M., Bybee, C. R., & Durall, J. A. (1979). Equivalence of informed political participation: The 1976 presidential debates as a source of influence. *Communication Research, 6*, 463-487.

McLeod, J., Durall, J., Ziemke, D., & Bybee, C. (1979). Reactions of young and older voters: Expanding the context of effects. In S. Kraus (Ed.), *The great debates: Carter versus Ford 1976* (pp. 348-367). Bloomington: Indiana University Press.

Meadow, R. G., & Sigelman, L. (1982). Some effects and non-effects of campaign commercials: An experimental study. *Political Behavior, 4*, 163-175.

Media Metrix. (2000). Campaign 2000: *Party politics on the World Wide Web.* Available: http://www.mediametrix.com/data/campaign2000.pdf.

Merritt, S. (1984). Negative political advertising: Some empirical findings. *Journal of Advertising, 13*, 27-38.

Middleton, R. (1962). National TV debates and presidential voting decisions. *Public Opinion Quarterly, 26*, 426-429.

Miles, E. A. (1960). The keynote speech at national nominating conventions. *Quarterly*

*Journal of Speech, 46,* 26-31.

Miller, A. H., & MacKuen, M. (1979). Learning about the candidates: The 1976 presidential debates. *Public Opinion Quarterly, 43,* 326-346.

Moore, M. T. (2000, September 21). Talk shows become a campaign staple. *USA Today,* p. A8.

Murphy, J. M. (1992). Presidential debates and campaign rhetoric: Text within context. *Southern Communication Journal, 57,* 219-228.

Mulder, R. (1979). The effects of televised political ads in the 1975 Chicago mayoral election. *Journalism Quarterly, 56,* 335-341.

NBC News/*Wall Street Journal.* (2000, September 7-10). *Poll.* (obtained via Lexis-Nexis).

Newhagen, J. E., & Reeves, B. (1991). Emotion and memory responses for negative political advertising: A study of television commercials used in the 1988 presidential election. In F. Biocca (Ed.), *Television and political advertising* (vol. 1, pp. 197-220). Hillsdale, NJ: Erlbaum.

Newport, F. (2000a). Bush increases lead over Gore after GOP convention: Public overwhelmingly thinks Bush will win in November. *Gallup Poll Monthly, 419,* 22-25.

Newport, F. (2000b). Bush pulls even with Gore once again: Presidential race now back where it started after Labor Day. *Gallup Poll Monthly, 420,* 12-14.

Newport, F. (2000c). Debates net positive for Bush: Gore led Bush by an average of 47% to 44% in the 30 days leading up to October 3, while Bush has lead Gore 47% to 43% in the 15 days since. *Gallup Poll Monthly, 421,* 4-6.

Nie, N. H., Verba, S., & Petrocik, J. R. (1999). *The changing American voter* (enlarged ed.). San Jose: toExcel in arrangement with Harvard University Press.

Niedowski, E. (1996, October 16). It's a family affair: Spouses, kids prove invaluable campaign resources in '96 races. *The Hill,* p. 12.

Nimmo, D., Mansfield, M., & Curry, J. (1978). Persistence and change in candidate images. In G. Bishop, R. Meadow, & M. Jackson-Beech (Eds.), *The presidential debates: Media, electoral, and policy perspectives* (pp. 140-156). New York: Praeger.

Norvold, R. O. (1970). Rhetoric as ritual: Hubert H. Humphrey's acceptance address at the 1968 Democratic National Convention. *Today's Speech, 18,* 34-38.

NUA Internet Surveys. (2001). *How many online?* Available: http://www.nua.net/surveys/how_many-_online/in_america.html.

Orren, G. R. (1985). The nomination process: Vicissitudes of candidate selection. In M. Nelson (Ed.), *The elections of 1984* (pp. 27-82). Washington, D.C.: Congressional Quarterly, Inc.

Palda, K. S. (1973). Does advertising influence votes? An analysis of the 1966 and 1970 Quebec elections. *Canadian Journal of Political Science, 6,* 638-655.

Patterson, T. E. (1980). *The mass media election: How Americans choose their president.* New York: Praeger.

Patterson, T. E. (1994). *Out of order.* New York: Random House, Vintage Books.

Patterson, T. E., & McClure, R. D. (1973). Political advertising on television: Spot commercials in the 1972 presidential election. *Maxwell Review,* 57-69.

Patterson, T. E., & McClure, R. D. (1976). *The unseeing eye: The myth of television power in national politics.* New York: Putnam.

Payne, J. G., Marlier, J., & Barkus, R. A. (1989). Polispots in the 1988 presidential primaries. *American Behavioral Scientist, 32,* 365-381.

Peck, J. (1995). TV talk shows as therapeutic discourse: The ideological labor of the televised talking cure. *Communication Theory, 5,* 58-81.

Pew Research Center. (2000). *Youth vote influenced by online information: Internet election news audience seeks convenience, familiar names.* Available: http://www.people-press.org/online-00que.htm.

Pfau, M. (1984). A comparative assessment of intra-party political debate formats. *Political Communication Review, 8,* 1-23.

Pfau, M. (1987). The influence of intraparty debates on candidate preference. *Communication Research, 14,* 687-697.

Pfau, M. (1988). Intra-party political debates and issue learning. *Journal of Applied Communication Research, 16,* 99-112.

Pfau, M., Cho, J., & Chong, K. (2001). Communication forms in U.S. presidential campaigns: Influences on candidate perceptions and the democratic process. *The Harvard International Journal of Press/Politics, 5(4),* 88-105.

Pfau, M., & Eveland, Jr., W. P. (1996). Influence of traditional and non-traditional news media in the 1992 election campaign. *Western Journal of Communication, 60,* 214-232.

Pfau, M., & Kenski, H. C. (1990). Attack politics: Strategy and defense. New York: Praeger.

Pomper, G. M. (1975). *Voters' choice: Varieties of American electoral behavior.* New York: Dodd, Mead, & Company.

Pool, I. D. (1959). TV: A new dimension in politics. In E. Burdick and J. Broadbeck (Eds.), *American voting behavior* (pp. 236-261). New York: Free Press.

Popkin, S. L. (1994). *The reasoning voter: Communication and persuasion in presidential campaigns.* Chicago: University of Chicago Press.

Popkin, S. L., Gorman, J., Smith, J., & Phillips, C. (1976). Comment: toward an investment theory of voting behavior: What have you done for me lately? *American Political Science Review, 70,* 779-805.

Princeton Survey Research Associates. (1999, October 7-11). *Poll.* Obtained on-line via Lexis-Nexis Academic Universe.

Ray, R. F. (1961). Thomas E. Dewey: The great Oregon debate of 1948. In R. Reid (Ed.), *American public address: Studies in honor of Albert Craig Baird* (pp. 245-270). Columbia: University of Missouri Press.

Ritter, K. W. (1980). American political rhetoric and the jeremiad tradition: Presidential nomination acceptance addresses, 1960-1976. *Central States Speech Journal, 31,* 153-171.

Ritter, K. (1996). The presidential nomination acceptance speech since 1980: An evolving American jeremiad. In D. D. Cali (Ed.), *Generic criticism of American public address* (pp. 201-210). Dubuque, IA: Kendall/Hunt.

Robinson, M. J., & Sheehan, M. A. (1983). *Over the wire and on tv: CBS and UPI in campaign '80.* New York: Russell Sage.

Roper, E. (1960, November). Polling post-mortem. *Saturday Review,* 10-13.

Rosenthal, P. I. (1966). The concept of ethos and the structure of persuasion. *Speech Monographs, 33,* 11-26.

Rubin, B. (1967). *Political television.* Belmont, CA: Wadsworth.

Rudd, R. (1986). Issues as image in political campaign commercials. *Western Journal of Speech Communication, 50,* 102-118.

Rudd, R. (1989). Effects of issue specificity, ambiguity on evaluations of candidate image. *Journalism Quarterly, 66,* 675-682, 691.

Ryan, H. R. (1982). *Kategoria* and *apologia:* On their rhetorical criticism as a speech set. *Quarterly Journal of Speech, 68,* 256-261.

Ryan, H. R. (1988). (Ed.). *Oratorical encounters: Selected studies and sources of twentieth-century political accusations and apologies.* Westport, CT: Greenwood.

Saad, L. (2000). Gore gains in race for president as a result of Democratic convention.

*Gallup Poll Monthly, 419,* 46-52.

Sabato, L. (1981). *The rise of political consultants.* New York: Basic Books.

Sadow, J. D., & James, K. (1999). *Virtual billboards? Candidate web sites and campaigning in 1998.* Paper presented at the American Political Science Association, Atlanta, GA.

Schaefer, R. J., & Avery, R. K. (1993). Audience conceptualizations of Late Night With David Letterman. *Journal of Broadcasting and Electronic Media, 37,* 253-273.

Schlenker, B. R. (1980). *Impression management: The self-concept, social identity, and interpersonal relations.* Monterey, CA: Brooks/Cole.

Schneider, S. M. (2000). *The 2000 presidential primary candidates: The view from the web.* Paper presented at the International Communication Association, Acapulco, Mexico.

Schutz, A. (1995). Entertainers, experts, or public servants? Politicians' self-presentation on television talk shows. *Political Communication, 12,* 211-221.

Selnow, G. (1998). *Electronic whistle stops: The impact of the Internet on American politics.* Westport, CT: Praeger.

Shapiro, M. A., & Rieger, R. H. (1992). Comparing positive and negative political advertising on radio. *Journalism Quarterly, 69,* 135-145.

Shyles, L. (1986). The televised political spot advertisement: Its structure, content, and role in the political system. In L. L. Kaid, D. Nimmo, & K. R. Sanders (Eds.), *New perspectives on political advertising* (pp. 107-138). Carbondale: Southern Illinois Press.

Smith, C. A. (1990). *Political communication.* San Diego, CA: Harcourt Brace Jovanovich.

Smith, C. R. (1971). Richard Nixon's 1968 acceptance speech as a model of dual audience adaption. *Today's Speech, 19,* 15-22.

Smith, C. R. (1975). The Republican keynote address of 1968: Adaptive rhetoric for the multiple audience. *Western Speech, 39,* 32-39.

Steele, C. A., & Barnhurst, K. G. (1996). The journalism of opinion: Network news coverage of U.S. presidential campaigns, 1968-1988. *Critical Studies in Mass Communication, 13,* 187-209.

Stelzner, H. G. (1971). Humphrey and Kennedy court West Virginia, May 3, 1960. *Southern Speech Communication Journal, 37,* 21-33.

Stewart, C. J. (1975). Voter perception of mud-slinging in political communication. *Central States Speech Journal, 26,* 279-286.

Stromer-Galley, J. (2000). On-line interaction and why candidates avoid it. *Journal of Communication, 50,* 111-132.

Stromer-Galley, J., Foot, K. A., Schneider, S. M., & Larsen, E. (2001). What citizens want, where they went, and what they got online in the U.S. election 2000. In S. Coleman (Ed.), *Elections in the age of the Internet: Lessons from the United States* (pp. 26-36). London: Hansard Society.

Stuckey, M. E., & Antczak, F. J. (1995). The battle of issues and images: Establishing interpretive dominance. In K. E. Kendell (Ed.), *Presidential campaign discourse: Strategic communication problems* (pp. 117-134). Albany: State University of New York Press.

Surlin, S. H. (1986). Uses of Jamaican talk radio. *Journal of Broadcasting and Electronic Media, 30,* 459-466.

Swerdlow, J. L. (1984). *Beyond debate: A paper on televised presidential debates.* New York: Twentieth Century Fund.

Swerdlow, J. L. (1987). The strange—and sometimes surprising—history of presidential debates in America. In J. L. Swerdlow (Ed.), *Presidential debates 1988 and beyond* (pp. 3-16). Washington, DC: Congressional Quarterly Inc.

Tedesco, J. C., Miller, J. L., & Spiker, J. A. (1999). Presidential campaigning on the information superhighway: An exploration of content and form. In L. L. Kaid & D. G. Bystrom (Eds.), *The electronic election: Perspectives on the 1996 campaign communication* (pp. 51-63). Mahwah, NJ: Lawrence Erlbaum.

Thorson, E., Christ, W. G., & Caywood, C. (1991). Effects of issue-image strategies, attack and support appeals, music, and visual content in political commercials. *Journal of Broadcasting and Electronic Media, 35*, 465-486.

Thorson, E., & Coyle, J (1994). *A comparison of the impact of political ads appearing in radio, newspaper, and television.* Paper presented to the annual meeting of the International Communication Association, Sydney, Australia.

Tiemens, R. K., Hellweg, S. A., Kipper, P., & Phillips, S. L. (1985). An integrative verbal and visual analysis of the Carter-Reagan debate. *Communication Quarterly, 33*, 34-42.

Tolsen, A. (2001). TV talk shows. Mahwah, NJ: Erlbaum.

Toner, R. (1996, March 17). In this race, it's the center against the middle. *New York Times*, p. 4.3.

Tramer, H., & Jeffres, L. W. (1983). Talk radio-forum and companion. *Journal of Broadcasting, 27*, 297-300.

Trent, J. D., & Trent, J. S. (1974). The rhetoric of the challenger: George Stanley McGovern. *Central States Speech Journal, 25*, 11-18.

Trent, J. D., & Trent, J. S. (1995). The incumbent and his challengers: The problem of adapting to prevailing conditions. In K. E. Kendall (Ed.), *Presidential campaign discourse: Strategic communication problems* (pp. 69-92). Albany: State University of New York Press.

Trent, J. S., & Friedenberg, R. V. (1995). *Political campaign communication: Principles and practices* (3rd ed.). Westport, CT: Praeger.

Trent, J. S., & Friedenberg, R. V. (2000). *Political campaign communication: Principles and practices* (4th ed.). Westport, CT: Praeger.

Turow, J. (1974). Talk show radio as interpersonal communication. *Journal of Broadcasting, 18*, 171-179.

Valley, D. B. (1974). Significant characteristics of Democratic presidential nomination acceptance speeches. *Central States Speech Journal, 25*, 56-62.

Valley, D. B. (1988). *A history and analysis of Democratic presidential nomination acceptance speeches to 1968.* Lanham, MD: University Press of America.

Vancil, D. L, & Pendell, S. D. (1987). The myth of viewer-listener disagreement in the first Kennedy-Nixon debate. *Central States Speech Journal, 38*, 16-27.

Vivian, J. (1999). *The media of mass communication.* Boston: Allyn and Bacon.

Wanat, J. (1974). Political broadcast advertising and primary election voting. *Journal of Broadcasting, 18*, 413-422.

Wayne, S. J. (1992). *The road to the White House 1992: The politics of presidential elections.* New York: St. Martin's Press.

Weaver-Lariscy, R. A., & Tinkham, S. E. (1987). The influence of media expenditures and allocating strategies in congressional advertising campaigns. *Journal of Advertising, 16(3)*, 13-21.

Weiss, H. J. (1976). *Wahlkampf im Fernsehen [Election campaigns on television].* Berlin: Spiess.

Weisberg, H. F., & Kimball, D. C. (1993). *The 1992 presidential election: Party identification and beyond.* Paper presented at the American Political Science Association, Washington, DC (quoted in M. A. Levine, (1995). *Presidential campaigns and elections: Issues and images in the media age.* Itasea, IL: Peacock Publishers.)

Weithoff, W. E. (1981). "I accept your nomination": Carter, Reagan, and classical obscurantism. *Indiana Speech Journal, 16,* 33-40.

Wells, W. T. (1999). *An analysis of attacking, acclaiming, and defending strategies in the 1976-1984 presidential debates.* Ph.D. Dissertation University of Missouri, Columbia.

West, D. M. (1993). *Air wars: Television advertising in election campaigns 1952-1992.* Washington, DC: Congressional Quarterly.

West. D. M. (1997). *Air wars: Television advertising in election campaigns 1952-1996* (2nd ed.). Washington, DC: Congressional Quarterly.

Whillock, R. K. (1991). *Political empiricism: Communication strategies in state and regional elections.* New York: Praeger.

Whillock, R. K. (1997). Cyber-politics: The online strategies of '96. *American Behavioral Scientist, 40,* 1208-1225.

Yawn, M., Ellsworth, K., Beatty, B., & Kahn, K. F. (1998). How a presidential primary debate changed attitudes of audience members. *Political Behavior, 20,* 155-181.

# Topic Index

# Author Index

# About the Authors

William L. Benoit (Ph.D., Wayne State University, 1979) is a Professor of Communication at the University of Missouri, Columbia. He has published 8 books and over 120 journal articles and book chapters, including *Seeing Spots: A Functional Analysis of Presidential Television Advertisements from 1952-1996, Candidates in Conflict: Persuasive Attack and Defense in the 1992 Presidential Debates, The Primary Decision: A Functional Analysis of Debates in Presidential Primaries*, and *Campaign '96: A Functional Analysis of Acclaiming, Attacking, and Defending* He has served as the Chair of the Political Communication Division of NCA and is currently editor of the *Journal of Communication*.

John P. McHale (Ph.D., University of Missouri) is an Assistant Professor of Communication at Illinois State University. He has published a book and several articles and presented several convention papers. He also wrote, directed, and produced an award-winning documentary about Joe Amrine and the death penalty.

Glenn J. Hansen (M.A., Bethel College, 1999) is a doctoral student and the University of Missouri, Columbia. He has published several journal articles and presented numerous conference papers in the area of political communication and mass media. He serves as the Editorial Assistant for the *Journal of Communication*.

Penni M. Pier (Ph.D., University of Missouri-Columbia, 2002) is a lecturer of Communication Arts at Wartburg College in Waverly, IA. She has coauthored two other texts and 5 journal articles and has presented original research at numerous conventions. She has served as a reviewer for the National Communication

Association Convention and currently serves on the National Faculty Advisory Board for Lambda Pi Eta.

John P. McGuire (M.A., Northwest Missouri State, 1999) is a doctoral candidate at the University of Missouri, Columbia and works as an Assistant Professor in the School of Journalism and Broadcasting at Oklahoma State University, Stillwater. His background is in broadcast news, including twelve years as News Director at KXCV-FM in Maryville, Missouri. McGuire has received several reporting awards from professional news and broadcast organizations, including the Associated Press, the Missouri Broadcasters Association, and Public Radio News Directors Incorporated. McGuire has also had research published in the *Journal of Radio Studies*.

Printed in Great Britain
by Amazon